Dormitory Old Ohio
Sturgis,

PLATE II

Frances Knight Wells

F. Wells

Valley Baptist College
Kentucky

Sturgis, Kentucky
The First 100 Years

IT ISN'T YOUR TOWN, IT'S YOU

If you want to live in the kind of town
    Like the kind of town you like,
You needn't slip your clothes in a grip
    And start on a long, long hike.
You'll only find what you've left behind,
    For there's nothing that's really new;
It isn't a knock at yourself when
      you knock your town—
    For it isn't the town, it's you!

Real towns are not made by men afraid
    Lest somebody else gets ahead.
When everyone works and nobody shirks
    You can raise a town from the dead.
And, if, while you make your personal stake,
    Your neighbors can make one, too.
Your town will be what you want to see—
    It isn't the town, it's you.

Sturgis, Kentucky
The First 100 Years

Turner Publishing Company

Copyright © Sturgis Centennial History Book
Committee, Sturgis, KY 42459

Designed by David Hurst, Publishing Consultant

Library of Congress Catalog Card No. 89-051690
ISBN: 978-1-68162-558-4

Limited edition of 1,000 copies

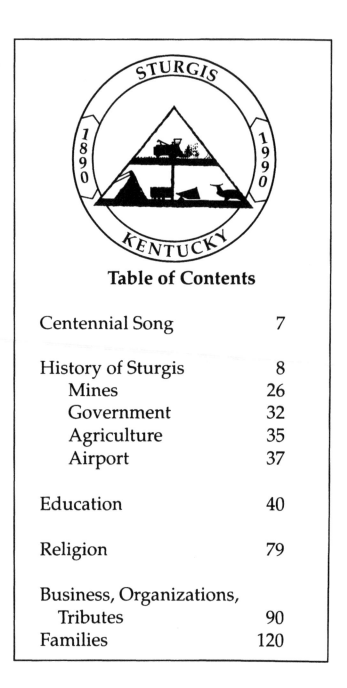

Table of Contents

Centennial Song	7
History of Sturgis	8
Mines	26
Government	32
Agriculture	35
Airport	37
Education	40
Religion	79
Business, Organizations, Tributes	90
Families	120

Commonwealth of Kentucky
Department of State

Office of Secretary of State

THELMA L. STOVALL
SECRETARY
FRANKFORT, KENTUCKY

CERTIFICATE

I, THELMA L. STOVALL, Secretary of State for the Commonwealth of Kentucky,

do certify that the foregoing writing has been carefully compared by me with the original

record thereof, now in my official custody as Secretary of State and remaining on file in my

office, and found to be a true and correct copy of

Chapter 1210, Acts of the General Assembly of the Commonwealth of Kentucky,
1889-90, Vol. 2, Approved May 3, 1890, An Act to incorporate the town
of Sturgis, in Union County.

IN WITNESS WHEREOF, I have hereunto
set my hand and affixed my official seal.

Done at Frankfort this......28th......day of

......December......, 19..56..

Thelma L. Stovall
Secretary of State, Commonwealth of Kentucky

By *Frances L. Thurkell*
Assistant Secretary of State

ACKNOWLEDGMENTS

The Sturgis Centennial History Book Committee is indebted to many Sturgis residents, businesses, churches, and organizations for making this publication possible. This book was a project undertaken by the "Sturgis Sittin' Pretty Community Group." The Committee spent a year planning and putting the book together. This book is dedicated to all the people of Sturgis—past and present. The better we understand and appreciate our heritage, the better we can understand ourselves. In our individual lives, what happens to us today is related to what happens tomorrow. The past gives meaning and direction to the present. We cannot change the past, but we can still act in a positive manner on the future.

The Centennial Book Committee:

Chairmen	Nadine Baldwin
	Sharry West
History Chairmen	Rebecca Kearney
	Virgil Kearney
Marketing Chairman	Marty Shaffer
Promotional Chairman	Heidi Thayer
Treasurer	Garland Certain

Special acknowledgements must go to **The Sturgis News**, radio station WMSK in Morganfield, and the Union County Fair Board for their help in promoting this book. We are especially indebted to Farmers State Bank in Sturgis for the use of their conference rooms for our many meetings throughout the year. There are a number of individuals who deserve special mention for the many hours of work, talent, and support they have offered: Clara Ann Ames, Sandy Arnold, Kelly Beaver, Elizabeth Benge, Janice Blackburn, Gene Bondurant, Vinnu Deshetty, Dee Dee Edmondson, Doug Hooper, Helen McKeaig, Patsy Ruth Steelman, Clarisa Wallace, Zela Wallace, Frances Wells, Ashley Woodring, Janie Young, Co-Ed Y sponsors Bonnie Edmondson and Julie Oaks, and Co-Ed Y members: Mary Ruth Clements, Sandy Davis, Brady Gibson, Ann Lamb, Katherine Lamer, Stephanie Shouse and Keith Stevenson.

SPECIAL TRIBUTE

THE BUDDY R. MORRIS FAMILY

Through the generous donation of the Buddie R. Morris family, Sturgis will have a beautiful Gazebo, landscaped and ready for use during the 1990 Centennial festivities. The twenty-two foot gazebo will be located on the corner of Washington and Sixth Streets. This Gazebo will be the center for many future community activities which will benefit and be enjoyed by all the people of Sturgis.

Mr. Buddie R. Morris has lived in Sturgis for seventeen (17) years and has been associated with the coal mining industry for forty (40) years. In 1975 Mr. Morris formed Morris & Sons and its subsidiaries. Mr. Morris has retained the position of President and all of his family hold positions in these companies: Buddie R. Morris II, Vice President; Thomas A. Morris, Vice President; Veatrice Fern Morris, Vice President; and Ella Renee' Norman, Lisa Eubanks, and Kena L. Morris hold positions of Secretary-Treasurer. Mr. Morris employees five hundred people to work in his various holdings which include: Midwest Energy and Development (Marion, Illinois); Midwest Coal Handling (Madisonville, Kentucky) the railroad operates in Western Kentucky area, Midwest Hauling, (Marion, Illinois) the railroad operates in Southern Illinois, and Kenellis Energies (Marion, Illinois) operating company from Brushy Creek Underground Mines in Southern Illinois.

When asked what qualities a person should possess to achieve success, Mr. Morris replies with these four words, "Honesty, Integrity, Ambition, and Spiritual Values." These are also qualities that helped to make our country great, and are still found in small towns throughout our country.

Sturgis is indebted to the Morris family for their generous donation and is proud to claim the Buddie R. Morris family as their own.

5

SPECIAL THANKS

FRANCES KNIGHT WELLS is a professional artist with a studio located in her home at 909 Main Street, Sturgis. She is also an art teacher at Union County High School, having taught for 25 years. A graduate of Murray State University with a B. S. in Fine Arts, she has painted many art works, some of which have been reproduced as limited edition art prints.

Many homes and businesses in the Tri-State area have art work by Frances Wells on display. Corporate collections include Colonel Sanders Technical Center, Louisville, Kentucky; Radisson Hotel, Evansville, Indiana; Ohio Valley National Bank, Henderson, Kentucky; and Liberty National Bank, Louisville, Kentucky.

Art work displayed in this book include:
Inside Cover (front) - "Dormitory Old Ohio Baptist College, Sturgis, Kentucky"
Inside Cover (back) - "Sturgis High School" 1937-1964
Section - "Sturgis History" - "Where There's Smoke"
Section - "Schools" - "Old Sturgis Elementary School" Sturgis, Kentucky
Section - "Family History" - "Old Family Quilt"

HELEN MCKEAIG, a life-long resident of Sturgis, designed (incorporating the Centennial logo) and made the Sturgis Centennial flag shown at right. Helen considers sewing her avocation, and she is known throughout Union County for her sewing skills. At an early age she learned the basics of sewing from her mother. For approximately 30 years Helen has made costumes for plays, pageants, and numerous community and school projects. Over the years her sewing entries at the Union County Fair have netted her many winning ribbons. She was awarded the First Place Trophy, Clothing Division, at the 1989 Union County Fair.

JEFF BENSON, a life-long resident of Sturgis, designed the Sturgis Centennial logo shown on the cover of this book. Jeff earned his B. S. Degree in Industrial Technology at Western Kentucky University, Bowling Green, Kentucky where he was a member and president of Pi Kappa Alpha social fraternity for one term.

Jeff has been employed for three years at Saturn Machine and Welding Company in Sturgis as a Draftsman and Computer Operator (Computer Aided Design). In his hobby of Air Brush work, he employs his skills on tee shirts and in technical illustrations.

In 1985 Jeff won the First Place Award at the Kentucky Industrial Education Conference in Louisville Kentucky, for his drafting exhibit.

KELLY B. BEAVER composed the music and wrote the lyrics for "Sturgis, Our Home Town" above. Kelly, a creative and multi-talented person, resides on Washington Street in Sturgis, Kentucky. He has held the position of Minister of Music and Youth at First Baptist Church, Sturgis, Kentucky, since April 1981. Kelly holds a Bachelor of fine Arts Degree from Piedmont College, Demorest, Georgia, where he graduated "Summa Cum Laude." He also holds a Master of Arts in Education Degree from Eastern Kentucky University, Richmond, Kentucky, and Master of Church Music Degree from The Southern Baptist Theological Seminary, Louisville, Kentucky. Throughout the years, Kelly's talents and skills for floral design, arts & crafts, gardening, and interior decorating have enhanced the beauty of many church and community endeavors in Sturgis. Kelly has composed several cantatas, anthems, and songs, all of which are unpublished at the present time.

Sturgis, Our Home Town
Commissioned for the Centennial of Sturgis, Kentucky (1890-1990)

1. From the coal down un-der-ground, to the farm-land all a-round, to the sky where planes can get a birds eye view, From the out-skirts to down town, in and out and up and down, Stur-gis, there's no place on earth that's quite like you.

Chorus

You are our home town, our old Ken-tuck-y home town, and Stur-gis, may you nev-er cease to be. Day by day and year by year in our hearts you grow more dear; Stur-gis, you're the place for home town folk like me.

Words and Music by
KELLY B. BEAVER

2. Thru the days of boon and bust,
You've survived and so you must
To preserve the heritage of our city, fair
Thru the plagues of fire and flood,
From the ashes and the mud,
You've rebuilt with pride, integrity and care.

3. At the time of intergration,
You made news across the nation
When the school house was patrolled by national guard
We are grateful now to see
All can live in harmony,
Where no child from school in our town is now barred.

4. From the days of rivalry—
With school spirit high and free,
When the Bears and the Gorillas played the game,
To the very present time
With our forces all aligned,
And Union County Braves is now our name.

5. From those eighteen-ninety days,
To more new and modern ways,
From the horse and buggy to the Aeroplane;
Thru the days of toil and ease,
Time has flown by like a breeze,
And you've linked each generation like a chain.

"Where Th

's Smoke"

Sturgis, Kentucky—The First 100 Years

HISTORY OF STURGIS AS OUTLINED ON OCCASION OF ITS 50TH BIRTHDAY

Brief Outline Of City's History Since 1881; Named After Samuel Sturgis; Incorporated May 2, 1890.

Wilson Lamb Town's First Mayor. Steve Hammack Its First Postmaster;

Town Laid By Col. Jordan Giles.

(Brief sketch of the history of the community, as it was compiled and written by the late Miss Carrie Eble for The News' 50th Anniversary Edition of the City of Sturgis, May 2, 1940.)

When a visitor enters the front portals of the Library of Congress, Washington, D. C., his attention is caught by a picture on the opposite wall, some distance away. This, a framed figure of a woman, a Mosaic of rich, ruby, blass, with so much color and flame, that the figure seems alive. The effect is both beautiful and startling.

This brief history of Sturgis is also a Mosaic. Its fitted bits of informational color and flame have been gleaned from a few newspapers and pamphlets now extant, and from the memories of men and women. Neither of these sources is wholly infallible; but, accepted tradi-tions, the printed page, and memory have established in the early history of Sturgis certain historical facts which justify their relation. It has been suggested that this history shall not be biographical in character, but in summarizing the high points in the growth and development of the city, biography must necessarily have a place; since behind each event there is a cause, and the result is nearly always determined by the action of its citizens, either individual or cooperative. Furthermore, such a brief sketch must omit detailed narration.

Grateful acknowledgement is made to Messrs. Sam Sizemore, William Bradburn, A. L. Hoerth, B. W. Dyer, Ruby Holt, J. I. McGraw, A. S. Winston, Sr., and A. S. Winston, Jr., and other for firsthand information concerning the early history of Sturgis.

Excerpts will be frequently quoted from printed matter available, particularly from a 22-page pamphlet published in 1900, as a supplement to the Herald, the local newspaper. Its title is "Sturgis of Today. Special Industrial Edition of The Sturgis Herald, June, 1900." This interesting and valuable pamphlet is the possession of Mr. A. L. Hoerth.

The forward is signed by Mr. Jesse L. Edmondson, publisher, and reads as follows: "Sturgis presents one of the most interesting examples of Twentieth Century Progress in Western Kentucky. Situated in one of the best counties in the state, surrounded by natural and material resources, it is no wonder it is prospering. Its attractions and advantages are set forth here. Sturgis is now in the hey day of its prosperity, and it is the sincere wish of the Herald that it may continue to grow and that is estimable citizens may live long and prosper."

Following is Mr. Edmondson's concept of Sturgis in 1900: "On the banks of the Tradewater River, about five miles from the Ohio River, and on the Ohio Valley Branch of the Illinois Central R.R. is situated the beautiful little city of Sturgis. The annals of its history tell of no bloody deeds, and, being of post bellum origin, it bears no witness of great battles. It lays no claim to being the hub of the universe, nor even the center of our own solar system. It cannot point a visitor to any ancient ruins. It has never been the home of the poet, painter, or president; nor has it ever basked in the regal gaze of any foreign potentate. Beautifully situated, with neat residences and flowery lawns, surrounded on the sides of

The town of Sturgis grew in the midst of fertile farmland into a vital coal town.

The Goad home, built in 1903, is still in the family.

billowy seas of its wheat and corn and pointing down to the great laughing throats of its coal mines, It stands like the Queen City that it is, and looks out invitingly upon the modern world of progress."

In 1881 the idea of building the Ohio Valley R. R. was conceived, to open up facilities for the transportation of coal. River transportation only was available. This was seriously handicapped by low water in summer and ice in winter, and the only market, except for the local one, was by river. Mr. S. S. Brown of Pittsburgh, and other Eastern capitalists, organized the Ohio Valley R. R. and Mining Company with

Brown as President. Its object was to provide an outlet by rail for the coal supply of Union County.

Actual constructions of this R. R. between Henderson and Corydon was begun in 1883. This road connected Henderson and Princeton, Kentucky. In 1886 the mining interests were organized under a separate company; viz, the Ohio Valley Coal and Mining Company, of which Mr. Samuel P. Sturgis was secretary and manager.

The history of the Cumberland Iron and Land Company is virtually the history of early Sturgis. This company was organized in 1886, at the time the Ohio Valley Railroad was being built.

At the present site of Sturgis was farm land, part of which was owned by Mr. Peter Casey. His original farm home, then occupied by Mr. A. J. Berry, is now occupied by his son, Jones Berry.

About his time, Mr. Samuel P. Sturgis, an officer of the Ohio Valley R. R., purchased an option in his name, on occupied by Mr. A. J. Berry, is now occupied by his son, Jones Berry.

About this time, Mr. Samuel P. Sturgis, an officer of the Ohio Valley R. R. right-of-way. After considerable negotiations, the Cumberland Iron and Land Company secured these options from Mr. Samuel P. Sturgis, through its Secretary and Treasurer, Colonel Jordan Giles, resident manager. There was laid off and platted in its present shape the city that bears the name, STURGIS, from the above mentioned Samuel P. Sturgis.

The Streets of Sturgis were laid off and graded under the direction of Colonel Jordan Giles who built and occupied the home where Mr. O. C. Quirey now lives.

In May, 1890, the City was incorporated. By this time the hotel and bank building, a number of residences and some business houses had been erected. The first brick building was the Palace Hotel on Main and Fourth. In a few years two brick buildings were erected on Adams Street, one where Holt's Dry Goods Store now stands and one across the street now occupied by the Westco Furniture Mart. Gradually, the busi-

Historical marker at Fifth and Main Streets

ness section was transferred from Main to Adams Street.

The Post Office was founded in 1888, Mr. Steve Hammack was appointed first Postmaster. Mr. Wilson Lamb was elected first mayor in 1890. He transferred his newspaper, the Enterprise, from Caseyville to Sturgis in 1885 thus becoming the editor of Sturgis' first paper. In 1893 the Legislature passed a law classifying all cities of the Commonweath, thus making Sturgis governed by a Board of Trustees, whose chairman occupies the position as was formally occupied by the mayor. Mr. A. J. Berry and Mr. W. J. Bishop served successive terms as Police Judge from 1891 to 1899. The city officers were, J. J. Bradburn, chairman; L. L. Hill, clerk; J. S. Wilson, treasurer; Wood Omer, marshal. The Board of Trustees was composed of George B. Simpson, Jr., Hampton Granger, Porter Graham and Sherman Davis. Mr. J. Mack Thompson was Judge of City Police Court. Bert F. Wallace was City Attorney.

The Bank of Sturgis was founded in 1886 by Messrs. T. N. Givens and W. W. Pierson, as a branch of their private bank at Caseyville. In 1983 the Caseyville Bank was mover to Sturgis and the Bank of Sturgis was incorporated with Mr. W. W. Pierson as its President. Mrs. C. T. Wallace, nee Miss

Pattie Person, was made Cashier, the only lady holding that position in the State of Kentucky at that time.

In 1898 the firm of Alloway, dealers in lumber and building materials, moved to Sturgis and established their business on the site on which it is still located.

By 1900 the business section consisted of a variety store—drygoods, furniture, hardware, implement and carriage business, hotel, bank, millinery, groceries, undertaker, blacksmith and machinist shops, drugs, barber shops, restaurants, livery stables, physicians and dentist offices, produce house, brick and tile plant, jewelry and optician establishment, and the Sturgis Milling Company.

To give in detail the history of a gigantic corp. like the West Kentucky Coal Company and to recount its expansion and progress over a period of thirty five years is a task requiring more time and space than is allotted here. It would embrace the biography of many, many people, each in his own particular niche in its immense number of employees. We will recall the original company when in August, 1905, the West Kentucky Coal Company was organized and its only property was composed of the Sturgis Electric Light Company and Mine No. 1 and No. 2.

The output at that time was about 90,000 tons per year. The river equipment was almost nil, but soon after its start the Company began to broaden. Briefly, the expansion of this great company meant additional mines, towns, departments, real estate, stores, farms, railroad and its equipment, river transportation equipment, retail offices and yards. It became an asset as a taxpayer, an institution to utilize labor and last but not least a dispenser of payrolls without which the present standard of its communities could not survive. Mr. C. F. Richardson came with the company in 1911 from a large railroad company and was president until his death on July 17, 1939. His untiring efforts and his ability to install loyalty, and industry in the very souls of his employees made him loved and admired executive.

Mr. W. H. LeGate, Vice-President, was connected with the Wheatcroft Coal Company previous to its purchase by the West Kentucky Coal Company in 1904. Mr. LeGate, in addition to his many other duties, is interested in the operations of the stores and for their operation are of material benefit to the managers.

The following is an excerpt from the Sturgis News, August 29, 1935: that being its 50th anniversary edition: "Speaking of the West Kentucky Coal Company, the service that it has been

Knights of Pythians, circa 1900. Frank Cissell standing left, Carl Buchanan, seated. Other unknown.

responsible for, the improvements, the civic pride that it has demonstrated, the enviable record that it holds, make it one of the outstanding corporations in the entire county. Its untiring efforts to promote harmony and good-fellowship, its constant care in attempting to make its communities better places in which to live, causes a feeling of goodwill toward it, such as few large corporations are able to enjoy."

Just as coal is its chief product, so the children of Sturgis constitute its chief wealth. The old Cypress school, located where the Sizemore Station now stands, was here before Sturgis was platted. There was one or more subscription schools taught in Sturgis. very early in its history, Mr. W. J. Bishop laid off the first public school district of the town, and through his influence, a free public school was established. He was the sole trustee for several years.

The Corner Stone of the Ohio Valley College, or Sturgis Academy, was laid in the presence of several thousand people on June 11, 1895. This school was opened that same autumn. This beautiful building was located in a campus of 12 acres green with grass, and shaded with native trees. Besides sciences and classics, the college had a regular organized department for the special preparation of teachers, a business and a music department. The influence of this school is yet felt in the community. It was succeeded by the public school system which we enjoy today. This has grown from one building to three which occupy two city blocks. A paved street extends around the entire campus. Enrollment has increased in the elementary school of 1906 250 to 533 in 1940. High school enrollment during the same time was from 50 to 400. Each building is larger, finer and more commodious than the preceding one. All have modern conveniences. The faculty has increased from 10 to 28. The curriculum has been

Bettie Davis and Lizzie Welch, 1910

broadened and enriched by the addition of vocational departments. Agriculture, home economics, and commercial courses. Varied extra-curricula activities provide recreation and test for both mental and physical skill. Six motor buses and one wagon bus transport 375 pupils to this school each day. The daily mileage is 300 miles.

Verge and Elmo Lindle, 1925

13

Memories of Yester-Years

Adams Street, Sturgis, Kentucky in the early 1900s. This was the first picture postcard advertising "A Live Town in the Richest County In the Best State In The Greatest Country On Earth." It also stated, this was "The Land of Corn, Wheat and Coal."

Left to right: Albert Gibbs, George B. Simpson, Sr., William (Billy) Wilson, Sr., Dan Hammock, George Wa;lace Sr. John Burr Humphrey, ?, ?, Dennie O'Nan. Mrs. McGill in rear.

Street Scene, 1910. First National Bank, (building with balconey) New First Christian Church with old frame building in background.

Adams Street after 1913 fire. *Above, looking north; below, looking south*

Virginia and E. H. Long with son, Randolph at the wheel of a 1909 Chalmers car in front of Rake's Theatre

1917-1918 Red Cross Girls. Left, Miss Critchfield; right Miss Carrie Eble

Above: J. R. "Buck" McGee shoveling coal into the E. H. Long Brick furnace around 1900. At left, standing, Catlett and Phillip Otto; sitting "Wick" and George

Adams Street, winter of 1917-1918. *Above, Sturgis residents crawling through a tunnel to the cafe. Below, looking north.*

STURGIS IMPLEMENT COMPANY

AGRICULTURAL
IMPLEMENTS,
WAGONS,
WIRE FENCE,
SINGER SEWING
MACHINES,
FIELD SEED,
Cream Separators
Etc.

The Most Popular Tractor of The Day.   Come and let us show you the I. H. C. MULE.

PHONE 11   STURGIS, KENTUCKY

Above and left—These advertisements from the 1920 Sturgis Annual show the latest technology was available in the town at that time.

Fatty Barker, Lena Jo Calvert, Mrs. Ward Carr and Brown Shackleford in 1930

NUNN & SISCO

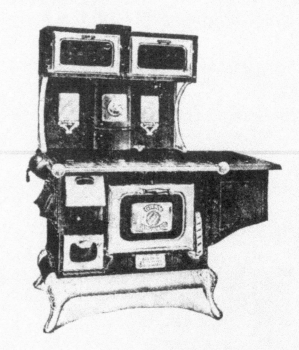

Dealers in

Furniture. Hardware, Pianos,
Graphophones, Stoves, Ranges and
MOLINE TRACTORS.

ADAMS STREET   STURGIS, KENTUCKY

The Sturgis Concert Band was just one of many that furnished music and entertainment throughout the county in the early years of this century. The group pictured above are shown as they appeared in Morganfield on July 18, 1922. They are, left to right, Front—Kilburn Wallace, Joe Stone, ?, and Jones Berry; Second row—Lawrence Holt, Oscar Reynolds, Earl Holt, Herbert Chancellor, Bill McKeaig, Fred Edwards and the leader, Lewis Talbott with Bob Holt on the sidelines. Back Row—Cantrell Nunn, Howard McKeaig, H. D. Holt, Sr, Edward Wallace, Brown Simpson and Jay Markham. All are deceased except Lawrence Holt.

The chairwarmers of Sturgis, 1922. Left to right, Tom Williams, Wood Omer, George Tate, Journey Winston, Bill Wynn, Sr., Edgar "Sonny" Wynn, Al Shipley and Mack Thomson.

View from '25

Quite an interesting book was furnished us by A. L. Heorth of the company store, which tells the story of Sturgis prior to 1900. This book was an industrial edition of the Sturgis Herald of June 22, 1900, and for the information of those who are interested we will give a review of the events mentioned in it.

In 1886 Sam P. Sturgis, representing the Ohio Valley Railroad Company, purchased a tract of 600 acres, on which Sturgis now stands and later conveyed this tract of the Cumberland Iron and Land Company, whose officers were the promoters of the railroad and the planning of the city began immediately. In May, 1900 the county was incorporated, at which time a hotel had been built known as the Palace Hotel which was located at 4th and Main, the Sturgis Bank building had been erected and also quite a number of business houses. The post office was founded in April, 1888 and Steve Hammack was the first postmaster.

The first mayor was elected in 1890, Mr. Wilson Lamb, but in 1893 the Legislature passed a law classifying all cities and Sturgis was governed by a board of trustees, the chairman of which occupied the same position of mayor.

The officers of the town in 1900 were, J. J. Bradburn, chairman; L. L. Hill, clerk; J. S. Wilson, treasurer; Wood Omer, marshall; and Messrs. Geo. B. Simpson, Hampton Grainger, Porter Graham and Sherman Davis, members of the Board of Trustees.

J. Mack Thompson, a young attorney, was police judge and Bert F. Wallace was city attorney.

Much is said about the natural advantages of Sturgis as well as the farming conditions, and for mining the following is copied:

"Sturgis is in the midst of a mining district wonderfully productive of coal. Union County ranks among the very first of all counties in Kentucky in the production of coal and using the words of old coal men, "Kentucky could furnish the world with coal for a century." Union County is underlaid with about

Lindle Brothers Grocery, 1925

twelve veins of coal of an average thickness of three feet. This coal is easy of access and of the very best quality mined anywhere. It is unsurpassed for both steam and domestic purposes, burns quickly and brightly and leaves no clinkers. Besides several small operated by individual capital there are in the vicinity of Sturgis three large mines operated by corporations, which, with their railroads, boats and barges, are gigantic enterprises, and besides supplying coal to home trades, ship largely to all towns and cities along the Ohio and Mississippi Rivers from Evansville to New Orleans."

Much comment is given about the Sturgis Academy or Ohio Valley College which was organized in 1890 and 1898 it enjoyed an enrollment of 100 pupils.

One of the prominent industries was

at that time the Sturgis Milling Company whose product was the famous Jeannette and Twin Brothers Flour. This firm was made up of R. F. Bishop, J. R. Mitchell, S. E. Bennett, A. S. Winston and W. C. Quirey.

The Bank of Sturgis was a very promising institution at that time and had the distinction of having the only lady cashier in the State of Kentucky, Miss Pattie Pierson being the cashier.

In the photographs that appear in the booklet the first thing that attracts our attention is the old fashioned stepping stones on Adams Street together with some of the old wooden shacks that made up the business sections, and we cannot help but enjoy a feeling of pride over the progress that Sturgis has made in the past and what an inspiration it is for the future advancement of the good town.

Fires and Floods

FIRE AND FLOODS HAVE FAILED TO HALT CITY'S PROGRESS

"A disastrous fire Sunday night at Sturgis, Kentucky, resulted in the damaged of between $200,000 and $250,000 the most severe fire in the history of the town. The fire started about 8 o'clock in the evening at Segraves drug store which was destroyed along with Perkins' restaurant, Dodd and O'Mann Furniture store, Sales and Higgins rest., Welch jewelry store, Mrs. Katie Wilcox's millinery shop, two banks, Y.M.C.A. building, Bradburn Shipley's and Simpson's furniture store, Stevens and Thompson's tinware store, Nugent drug store, Truitt grocery, Stone hardware and Rake's theatorium. People rushed from the churches to help fight the fire. Several residences were damaged. John Berry, agent for the Illinois Central, lost his home. The West Kentucky Coal Company suffered extensive losses.

"With the business section of Sturgis destroyed by fire, it was necessary

Adams Street, Christine Rehm house in background. Dick Vincent house upper left. Fred Alloway Sr. standing in motor boat pulling barge.

to bring in supplies of food and temporary business houses are being established in tents."

Many local citizens will recall the evening of the disastrous fire here on Sunday, July 12, 1913. And the days that followed, when a tent city composed the business section of the town. And how the Bank of Sturgis became

famous for opening on time the next day, in the little Bank on Wheels.

And though business men were never able to accurately estimate their heavy losses, due to the excitement and unsettled condition following the fire, it has been agreed the 1913 fire was after all the best thing that could have happened to the town.

Unsightly and antiquated business houses were leveled to the ground and a new city grew out of the ruins, giving to the community the ever progressive little city of the present day.

The flood of 1937 has done practically for the residential section what the fire did to the business district, with renovating and improving of the city's homes, a modern and well kept city is the result.

Historical facts pertaining to Sturgis would be incomplete, if one did not chronicle the most harrowing experience in the history of its citizens in January, 1937, when "Old Man River" went on a spree and reduced Sturgis to an island and did damage in excess of a million dollars.

Flood waters went 7.26 feet past the previous crest of 1913, with the result that families had to evacuated, while the entire colored population of

Boxtown became wards of the city and the local Red Cross officials, Churches and homes out of the high water region became a refuge for the less fortunate. Furniture was scaffolded in practically all homes on the north end of Main, Adams, Washington and Kelsey Streets. Men from fifteen to forty-five in number kept a constant vigil to succor those in need for twenty-four hours each day, and to transport people and is some instances part of their belongings to dry territory.

In but a few days, Sturgis, an inland city, ten miles as the crew flies from the Ohio River, became an island cut off by from thirty to fifty feet of water. Over 400 homes were flooded and 184 blocks of normally dry street was inundated with the exception of eighteen blocks. Local suffering was minimized by concerted efforts on the part of its citizens, property damage was tremen-

dous, but no lives were lost. Residences of Boxtown and that section south of the Illinois Central tracks lost practically their entire belongings. 748 families became charges of the city and the Red Cross headed by E. C. "Bud" Calman, cared for upwards of three thousand persons with the aid of private donations.

Despite this situation Sturgis met its own problems of housing, feeding and caring for its citizens, as well as succoring the influx of neighbors, driven from their homes by the flood.

Quick action on the part of businessmen, led by Mayor Wilcox, provided safeguards and speeded up the evacuation facilities. With publicly donated funds a ferry was built that ran on regular schedule over highway sixty and was large enough to carry one hundred people. Obtaining funds to make this possible and the construc-

tion work was all completed within a 24-hour period and the liberality of by labor and money freely donated.

Red Cross food stations under the direction of local ladies cared for hundreds. The list of donators to make all these efforts possible, sounds like the roster of the citizens of Sturgis. Improvised dams saved the mines from inundation protecting the communities' source of livelihood when normally returned. This effort required a 24-hour vigilance and hard work during the entire flood period.

Then came the period of rehabilitation. The cleaning up of sewerage and filth when the waters receded. Guarding against cave-ins, health measures to prevent influx of contagious diseases and with the help of a special health committee appointed for this occasion, and the combined help of the Red Cross officials and Federal agencies, plus local

WPA workers, this was accomplished in a creditable manner.

Not only destitute families were cared for by Red Cross but practically everyone whose burden was too great to carry was added and assisted. Relief was based upon need and not upon loss. Financial aid was liberally accorded.

Sturgis citizens have just cause to be proud of their achievements in this trying ordeal notwithstanding an unprecedented situation in an inland city not prepared for such an emergency, not a single life was lost, suffering minimized, rehabilitation was swiftly carried to conclusion within a very short period rehabilitation was an established fact and citizens of Sturgis resumed a normal life, jittery from its experiences, but rebuilt in a manner that will remain a lasting credit to its citizens.

1908 Rev. W. W. Wynn's Reunion

Those in the picture are, back row L to R, Addie Watson, Gertrude Wynn, Lula Kuykendall, Nannie Wallace Curry, Bula Kuykendall, Brooks Hughes and baby Hazel, Robert Steelman, Bill Kuykendall and Harvie Steele; second row, Mabel White, Roberta Wynn Wesley, Retta Kuykendall, Lucy White and baby Helen, Sallie Kuykendall, Ama Wynn and baby R. E.; third row, Pierce Curry, Nellie Kuykendall, Grandma Pet Kuykendall, Grandma Nack Wynn, Grandma Jennie Withers, Nettie Kuykendall, Amos Kuykendall and Grandpa Sam Withers; fourth row, Irma Ray Carter, Annie B. Kuykendall, Jim Hughes and son Harold, Bill Wynn and baby Elaine, William Berrry and John Wynn in lap, R. E. Wynn and baby Bill White; standing Nina S. Wynn, Juanita Wynn and John White, sitting out front. This photograph was taken in 1908 at the Rev. W. W. Wynn's in Pond Fork section of Union County. Rev. W. W. Wynn was a Cumberland Presbyterian preacher. His children were: R. E. Wynn, Salley Wynn Kuykendall, William Wynn, Steve Wynn, Dr. John Wynn and Gertrude Wynn Watkins. Rev. W. W. Wynn died in 1900. Photo furnished by George B. Simpson.

West Kentucky Coal Company

Incorporated

General Offices: Sturgis, Kentucky
General Sales Offices: Paducah, Kentucky

BRANCH OFFICES
Memphis, Tenn., Donaldson, La., Evansville, Ind.

TWENTY-TWO MODERN MINES
Daily Capacity 25,000 Tons

Tradewater and Caney Fork Gas Coal. The Mines are located on the Illinois
Central and L. & N. Railroads. River Loading Station at
Caseyville, Ky. Barges, flat, and also Steamboats.

COAL ANY PLACE ON THE OHIO AND MISSISSIPPI RIVERS
MODERN UP-TO-DATE CAMPS
The Company with the Coal Service

TWELVE MODERN STORES—Carrying complete line of
Dry Goods, Furniture, Fresh Meats and Groceries

The West Kentucky Coal Company was established in 1905 with four mines, two at Sturgis and two at Wheatcroft, but it stayed in this infant state only a short time for its growth started immediately and we find it today operating the following mines:

Mine No. 1, at Sturgis, No. 9 vein, C. W. Edwards, Mine Foreman, giving employment to 130 men.

Mine No. 2, at Sturgis, No. 9 vein, A. J. Edwards, Mine Foreman, giving employment to 220 men.

Mine No. 3, at Wheatcroft, No. 11 vein, C. O. Shade, Mine Foreman, giving employment to 125 men.

Mine No. 6, at Wheatcroft, No. 9 vein, O. H. O'Bryant, Mine Foreman, giving employment to 150 men.

Mine No. 7, at Clay, No. 12 vein, W. J. Edwards, Mine Foreman, giving employment to 310 men.

Mine No. 8, at Sturgis, No. 9 vein, W. J. Edwards, Mine Foreman, giving employment to 185 men.

Mine No. 9, at Sturgis, No. 9 vein, Neal McCann, Mine Foreman, giving employment to 210 men.

Mine No. 10, at Wheatcroft, No. 9 vein, Dick Gregory, Mine Foreman, giving employment to 200 men.

Shamrock Mine at Providence, No. 11 vein, W. H. Harris, Mine Foreman, giving employment to 375 men.

Mine No. 2 of Madisonville, No. 11 vein, Snowden Davis, Mine Foreman, giving employment to 180 men.

Fox Run Mine of St. Charles, No. 9 vein, Aut Robinson, Mine Foreman, giving employment to 250 men.

No. 11 Mine of Earlington, No. 11 vein, A. R. O'Bannon, Mine Foreman, giving employment to 280 men.

No. 9 Mine of Earlington, No. 9 vein, Jim Cloern, Mine Foreman, giving employment to 175 men.

North Diamond of Earlington, No. 9 vein, Roy Cobb, Mine Foreman, giving employment to 285 men.

In addition to the mines there is the Store Department employing 65 men.

The Sales Department with 50 men.

The different agencies with 125 men; the Railroad with 10 men; the River Transportation Department with 200 men; the Office force and Mine Clerk of 150; the Engineering Department with 20; the Farms with 40; the Property Department with 5; the Construction Department with 40; and probably a few others who escaped our minds right at this time.

We are a big company, prepared to do some real service, and the service that we do give is the determining factor as to the degree of success that we will attain.

Office and store building of West Kentucky Coal Company

Volney Wright   *Chas. Jenkins*

Warren Ray   *W. C. Davis*

O. H. Wilcox   *Margaret King*

Rex Hamby   *Margaret Durham*

Sturgis Office department—Back row, L to R, Byers Winston, Eng. Dept; C. W. McKenzie and Gervis Herron, Pay Roll; H. M. Thomspson, Voucher; Mrs. Judith Lindle, Pay Roll; Miss L. Tate, Telephone Operator; T. E. Jenkins, Vice-President; W. S. Williams, Purchasing Agent, Charles Pritchett, Pay Roll and David Read, Chief Engineer Second row: W. H. LeGate, Comptroller; H. W. Haapenanen, Eng. Dept.; Ralph Dudley, Asst. Treasurer.; S. G. Collins, Chief Clerk; Miss Gwendolyn McGregor, Pay Roll; Miss Bella Thompson, Purchasing Dept. Miss Ruth Stevenson, Stenographer; Miss Elizabeth Chancellor, Audting Dept. Front row: James Omer, Pay Roll; Miss Myrtle McGee, Voucher; Miss Myra Brooks, Purchasing Dept.: Wilbur Shields, Voucher; Cecil Holeman, Office boy; Orville Hagan, Shipping Dept.; Mrs. Margaret Holt, Auditing dept.; Miss Edyth Hagan, Pay Roll; Mrs. Dedman, Stenographer; M. P. Brooks and Mrs. Edwards, Auditing Dept.

"Force at Store No. 2—Store No. 2 is a real store and for service and real merchandise can not be beat.
In the picture are shown, reading left to right: H. O. Barkley, manager Grocery Department; Oswyen Daniels, Miss B. Richey, Tom Cullen, Miss Lucy Dyer. J. F. Dodge, manager Dry Goods Department; Mrs. Payne, A. L. Hoerth and Marshal Jones."

Clockwise from top right: 1) General Office—Ladies: Mrs. Quirey, Pay Roll; Miss McGee, Voucher; Mrs. Lindle, Pay Roll; Miss Tate, Telephone; Mrs. Wright and Miss Hagan, Pay Roll; Miss Thompson, Purchasing; Mrs. Holt, Accounting; Mrs. Dedman, Stenographerr. Men C. A. Bishop, Chief of Pay Roll, Robt. Sauers, Eng.; W. S. Williams, Purchasing; S. G. Collins, Voucher; Lester Via, Accounting; C. W. McKinzie, Pay Roll; H. M. Thompson, Voucher;; T. E. Jenkins, VP; Robt. Dixon, Accounting; James Omer, Shipping; Logan Fisher, Office boy; H. W. Haapenan, Eng.; Ralphy Dudley, Accounting; Gervis Herron, Pay Roll; D. B. Luttrell, Chief Clerk and W. H. LeGate, Asst. Treas. 2)Force at Store No. 2. Miss Lucy Dyer, Miss Gwendolyn McGregor, Miss Clella Carr, Miss Beatrice Richey. Oswny Daniels, Clarence McGee, Metcalf Talbott, Milburn Keykundall, Tom Cullen, A. L. Hoerth and J. F. Dodge 3) Grocery Store clerks at Store No. 2— Manager Harry Barkley with glasses in center, salesmen Jimmie Coleman and Albert "Fatty "Barker. 4) Twins Dorothy and Charles Christian with their guardian Jim. 5) The Four Horsemen—O. C. Quirey, William Davis, Oakley Hall and Claud Wright. 6) Store No. 1 —I. O. Chandler, Hazel Wright, Miss McGee and manager H. T. Reynolds.

DISTRICT NO. 2

Disatrict No. 2 covers Mine No. 2 only which holds its meetings on the second and fourth Wednesday nights of each month. A live organization is in control this year and deserves the backing of every member.

Mine No. 2 located at Sturgis is the second oldest of the orginal group of West kentucky Mines. It can well be called the headquarters mine since here is located the central power station that not only furnishes power to all the Sturgis mines but also for Sturgis and vicinity. It is also the home of the supply house which is under management of O. C. Quirey, the machine shop which has as its foreman, Willis reynolds, the Casey Jones of the 20th century; the car building shops headed by "Preach" Bush, the railraod department deaded by H. D. Holt and the R. R. section crew who has for its foreman Doss Quirey.

The foreman at Mine No. 2 is A. J. Edwards, who has been with the company since the fall of 1905. He was mine foreman at No. 2 until the tipple was destroyed by fire on March 31, 1907, at

which time he was made mine foreman at No. 1 for a term of six years, was transferred back to No. 2 in 1913 and is still on the job and very active. Mr. Edwards believes in his ability to get along with men and cites as one proof the fact that he has two drivers with him now who have followedhim as he transferred for the past 24 years and have worked for him continually during that time. These men are Sam Shead and Marshall Early.

Cecil McCann, the assistant mine foreman started to work for this com-

pany in March 1917 as hostler at No. 7 and was there at the time of the explosion. After returning from the hospital he was contractor at No. 7. In 1921 he moved to Sturgis and after a year of efficient service he became foreman and then assistant mine foreman.

The part that should interest us most in the service records of our foremen is the fact that the men who really perform are the ones who are sure to be promoted. The official position are almost invariably filled from the organization and not from outsiders.

MINE NO. 1

Mine No. 1 at Sturgis is the oldest mine of the orginal group of mines and has been in operation continually for many years. Its tonnage has never been of any extraordinary amount per day but its quality has been such that the coal from this mine is very much in demand. It has been handicapped materially from the fact that no screens are in their tipple so that only mine run coal can be produced.

DISTRICT NO. 9

District No. 9 is the district under which Mine No. 9 functions. No. 9 is no doubt the deepest shaft in the state, being over fourhundred feet deep but is one of the large producers of the West Kentucky Coal Company. The equipment at No. 9 is of the late type and not only can a large tonnage be produced, but it can also be well prepared, so as to satisfy the most particular customer.

MINE NO. 8

Mine No. 8 is not as old as some of the other mines but its experience has been much and varied. Many tons of coal have been produced and many workmen have been furnished with employement. No. 8 coal of the best quality is its product which is famous now but would be much more so if a little more effort were put forth at the face to reduce the amount of impurities. The loaders are fast coming into their own and the coal which comes from this mine from now on will be as good in every instance and much better in many instances than has ever been known before.

Mine foreman Walter Edwards who does not have such a long service record but a record which shows good service is always on the job and does much to make No. 8 the ideal place for men to work.

The river tipple at Caseyville

Office force and machine shop crew—mine no. 2, L to R, back row, Charles Christian, George Roberts and Eli Brantley. Front, H. D. Holt, Lonnie Duckworth, Oscar Reynolds, Willis Reynolds, O. C. Quirey, J. O. Hall.

Machine Shop crew—mine no. 2, Back row, Eli Brantley, Chas. Christian, Buel Sholders, Harley McCarnahan, Bennie Small. Front, Lonnie Duckworth, Willie Brantley, Hubert Austin, Chas Sholders and Geo. Roberts.

"The construction crew at the Sturgis mines is ever equal to their task. The foreman, Luke Sholders, "knows his stuff," and his fellow workmen are the kind that can carry out instructions."

Union County Construction Crew—L to R, Clyde Omer, W. A. Hinton, Leslie Bright, George Sholders, W. J. Omer and Luke Shoulders, foreman.

Car Shop Crew—"The car shop is the scene of much labor, and the boys shown above are always equal to their task. Frank Bush, third from the left, is foreman.

The "Fixem Boys"
"Standing is Oscar Reynolds, seated on left is J. P. Sheridan, and on the right, Sutch Deshon. Electrically speaking, they are continually in search of more worlds to conquer."

The No. 7 Buffalo Chasers
"The above picture is of the No. 7 Buffalo Chasers will show the prize winners of the mine. Colon Trice, first on the left is the only one in captivity to ever catch the buffalo during a chase, but Al Bernard and Wallace, the next two in order are due some of the credit since they helped surround it."

31

Sturgis City Government

Old City Hall, clerk's office, fire station and jail. Site of present KU building.

Present day municipal building.

Administrative Staff—*L to R, Joan Omer, City Clerk; Lisa Jones, City Clerk/Treasurer; Earl Daniel Quirey, Mayor; Paula K. Pierson, Sec'y/Receptionist; Vicki D. Sheffer, Utility/Cashier/Clerk; not pictured, Pamela Collins.*

Police Department—*L to R, Lucy Crittenden, Lt. Michael DeMoss, David Grounds, Charles Collins, Chief Wesley Bradburn, Capt. Maurice Smith Jr., Jerry Cullen, Michael McCaw, Peggy Pease, Gary Dean. Thomas Stevenson, not pictured.*

Fire Department—*L to R, Chief Norris L. Sheely, Capt. Jessie E. Young, Peggy Pease, Thomas Powell. Not pictured, Capt. Phillip Edmonson*

Maintenance Department—*L to R, Front row, Ronald Burkins, Sylvester Barnhill and Michael Harris, sanitation department. Second row, Freddie R. Cullen, Terry George, Donald K. Jones, gas superintendent, Marshall Hughes, James Shockley, Timothy Pierson, Charles Fredrick Williamson, superintendent of public works, Leslie E. Barnhill, Anthony L. Collins and William D. Grounds.*

Sturgis Community Rest Home

The Sturgis Rest Home had its beginning as a hospital. For many years the hospital was in the beautiful old home on the corner of 7th and Main under the direction of Dr. G. B. Carr. For many years Dr. Carr carried patients up the steps to the second floor according to local lore.

Around 1954 or 1955 Dr. Carr donated the land for a newer, modern hospital. Shares were bought by the people of Sturgis and the surrounding communities. A small brick hospital was built on the lot Dr. Carr had operated as Sturgis Hospital for many years. The hospital officially opened the fall of 1956 as Sturgis Community Hospital and served the community as such until 1970, when Hospital Corporation of America opened Union County Hospital.

The Board of Directors, wanting the building to be utlilized, began thinking of possible ways to use the building. With much planning the hospital was turned into an eighteen bed personal care facility. The Sturgis Community Rest Home opened in 1971 with three patients, an administrator, three nurses aides and a part time bookkeeper. There were 18 beds, an office and a small sitting room. The filing of old Medicare forms provided money for operation and a start on a building fund.

In a short time the rest home was fully occupied and more space was needed. The Certificate of Need and Licensure Board granted a building permit for eight additional beds. Because of the interest and tireless efforts of Albert Thornsberry and Ralph Alexander two four bed rooms were built, giving the home a 27 bed capacity. The multi purpose room was used as a dining room, television room and recreation room.

A couple of years later another addition was completed. This included two shower rooms, a beauty shop, storage room and a large dining room. Through the years a sprinkler system, modern fire alarm system and several employees have been added. State regulations change annually.

The staff now includes, in addition to an administrator, a consulting nurse, consulting dietition, activity director, several nursing aides and maintains a superior rating.

Truly, the Sturgis Community Rest Home is a monument to the cooperative spirit of the people of Sturgis. Because of the continuous efforts of individuals and groups we have a living, working service building in our community.

1989 Union County

FAIR

July 8 - 15, 1989

UNION COUNTY AGRICULTURAL FAIR

40

"40 Years Of Serving Union County As An Agricultural Fair"

SEE YOU AT THE —

Fairgrounds

STURGIS AIRPORT - STURGIS, KY
Fair Office: (502) 333-4107 or (502) 333-4108

Agriculture

1935—Hulling Clover Seed, Barbee White, Will Markham, Glen Dorrah, Steve White, Bill Ricketson, Enlo Gilchrist, Carl Tutt and Johnny Pruitt.

Plowing a garden with a mule in 1964

Some of the best farmland in Kentucky is in Union County and near Sturgis. Many Union County farmers have been named Outstanding Farming of Kentucky.

Thousands of acres of corn, soybeans and other crops are raised each year. Several hog and cattle raisers are located in Union County.

Harvesting corn

A snowy sunset in 1961

Top, Jim Gilchrist harvests corn. Middle, a local pig farming operation and below, cattle raising in a pastoral setting, 1963.

Sturgis Army Airfield

On October 20, 1942, the War Department officially confirmed that property south and east of Sturgis had been decided upon to be used as an Air Command Base. At this point the government issued condemnation suits for the necessary land.

A total of 1,307.2 acres (much less than originally suspected) was listed in condemnation suits.

Upon this official confirmation, work immediately began on the airfield. The railroad belonging to the West Kentucky Coal Company ran through this site, and consequently had to be relocated. It was moved to follow the lines of Cypress Creek and down Highway 60, then over to Poplar Ridge mine.

Since the construction was taking place as a wartime effort, the general public could not be kept informed of the happenings at the Base. Facts such as the approximate cost of the project, number of buildings to be constructed, and the number of men expected to be stationed at the Base were all left to speculation. Information released was that the Base would have three runways of at least 1000 feet each, forming a triangular shape. The intended use was for seasoned pilots to be stationed at the Base and to operate with the training forces of Camp Breckinridge, so those in training could learn the coordination of ground force movements with that of air defense.

The civilian guards at the Air Command Base were relieved of their duties at midnight on May 31, 1943, and the Army Air Corps then took over. No formal activation ceremony was expected or held, such as was experienced with the opening of Camp Breckinridge.

The first group of soldiers arrived in Sturgis on May 21, 1943. The group of 50-55 men traveled by train from Godman Field, Fort Knox, KY. The Sturgis Base was a sub-base of Godman Field. They arrived just prior to the activation of the Base. According to William Lista of Pennsylvania, this trip from Fort Knox involved almost a

Aerial view, 1984, fairgrounds, race tracks and three runways

week's time span. Mr. Lista recalls that upon arriving in Sturgis, their first meal was at the "Bright Spot Cafe" (later to be known as the Sturgis Cafeteria). The soldiers were then transported by trucks to the Airfield.

Upon activation, the Sturgis Army Airfield was equipped with three runways 150 feet wide and 5000 feet long. The base also had eight barracks for the soldiers, two officers' quarters, two administration buildings, a link trainer, fire house, infirmary, post exchange, recreation building, and various warehouses and supply rooms. The facility was also equipped with 17,725 linear feet of water mains, 29087 linear feet of storm, 5,400 linear feet of sanitary sewer with a sewage treatment plant, and a gasoline storage system totaling 78,000 gallons. The total construction cost of the Sturgis Army Airfield was $2,514,000.

The Sturgis Army Airfield was used by tactical squadrons for periods ranging from one week ten days for bivouac training on several separate instances. The Field was frequently used by transient aircraft for refueling purposes and for minor repairs. The soldiers stationed at the Base spent their time training in chemical warfare, first aid, camouflage, and physical conditioning. The 506th Parachute Battalion

completed their basic jumps before moving on to a new post to complete combat training. The 572nd Squadron appeared for a short time to train with B-25s. The 391st Bomb Group completed a ten-day term bivouacking in the wooded area south of the field, receiving experience in field living conditions and several mock gas attacks.

After one year of operation as the Army Airfield, the base housed 100 men and nine officials. The Sturgis Base Detachment disbanded May 1, 1944, and reorganized as the 371st AAF Base Unit under Key Field, Mississippi.

The flood that engulfed Sturgis in 1945 was the third worst recorded in the history of Sturgis. Forty-nine families had to be evacuated from the Cross Roads section and 22 families had to be removed from Boxtown to No. 1 camp. A remaining 74 families from Boxtown were transferred to the Sturgis Army Airfield. The large trucks and hard work gained from the soldiers helped to make the evacuation a very efficient process, with a minimal amount of loss. The Airfield donated several barracks and a mess hall in which to store their belongings, and to house and feed approximately 130 people who were stranded there.

By late fall of 1945, it was common knowledge that the Sturgis Army Air-

Sturgis Army Airfield, 1943

field would soon be ending its operation. Many civilian personnel received notification that their employment would end November 30, 1945. By late December, 1945, the Base was declared officially closed.

In October, 1945, 53 business and professional men and women of Sturgis met to discuss future plans for the Airfield. It was a known fact that many such facilities were being declared as surplus property since they were no longer essential to the conduct of the military.

The War Assets Administration declared the Sturgis Army Airfield surplus property in late 1946. Proceedings began to acquire the Airfield, and in January, 1948, the Union County Air Board was formed. The purpose of this Board was to acquire the Sturgis Army Airfield from the War Assets Administration, and also to maintain, manage, and operate the Airfield after acquisition. By-laws for the Air Board were adopted January 14, 1948. Offices were established by the Board; these included president, vice-president, secretary, and treasurer. Fred Alloway served as the first President of the Union County Air Board. The other charter members of the Board were Rosser Calloway, Malcolm Cason, Orville Dyer, Tyler Munford, and Wilson Rudy.

The War Assets Administration announced in March, 1948, that it was awarding the entirety of the equipment from the radio control tower, which was being awarded to the Louisville and Jefferson County Air Board. The

Sturgis Army Airfield was officially transferred without funds on Tuesday, July 13, 1948, to the Union County Air Board by Harry E. Ritter of the War Assets Administration. Tom T. Richards, County Judge, Fred Alloway, Air Board President, and Malcolm B. Cason, Secretary of the Air board were all flown to Cincinnati by James B. Norris of Ayers Flying Service for the signing of the transfer. The formal presentation of the 1,037-acre field was made to Fred Alloway and Malcolm Cason. According to the Civil Aeronautics Administration and War Assets Administration, an airfield can be transferred to any local city, county, or state if it can maintain and operate the facility. All easements pertinent to the Field were also transferred to the Air Board. This included 23 buildings of various types, such as warehouses, hangars, motor repair shops; also involved in the transfer was equipment essential to the operation of the airport, such a snow-removal, mowing, fire-fighting, and maintenance equipment. This represented several thousand dollars beyond the $2,800,000 acquisition cost of the field.

Approximately 5,000 spectators were present for the ceremonies held for the official opening of the Sturgis Airport on Sunday afternoon, July 18, 1948. Governor Earle C. Clements flew to Sturgis for this event. Approximately 150 aircraft lined the edges of the field, ranging from the massive C-47 troop carrier used by the National Guard to a number of light planes flown by mem-

bers of Kentucky's Flying Farmers. Nine F-51s from Louisville's Standiford Field performed for visitors, along with an Army F-82. A demonstration by Major D. W. Everest of the Army Air Force, in a P-80 jet-propelled "Shooting Star" was the highlight of the airshow.

Most of the changes an improvements made to the Sturgis Airport have been to the grounds rather than to the actual airfield. The Union County Fair Board was given the use of a portion of land on which was built a 1/2-mile horse racing track, exhibition hall, and grandstand, and established the area was the Union County Fairgrounds.

A major improvement came in 1973 when the Air Board was awarded a $60,000 contract, from Federal and State sources, for lighting the north-south runway. This contract included funds for the runway, taxiway, threshold lights, rotating beacon, lighted wind cone, and Vasi II.

In August, 1977, Saturn Machine and Welding purchased 4.2 acres of land from the Air Board. This area now consists of an office and shop complex that totals approximately 36,000 square feet. Saturn Machine and Welding has a 310 Cessna housed in one of the airport's hangars that is used for company business. Mr. Bill Brummett serves as the pilot for this company.

Pyro Mining Company acquired 3.6 acres of land from the Air Board in May, 1984. A $1 million building, to house some of the administrative offices, was erected on this site. The building consists of 15,000 square feet, with an adjacent parking lot comprised of 37,000 square feet. Approximately 60 employees work at this site. Pyro owns a plane for company business, and Mr. Brummett also serves as a pilot for them.

Present Members of the Air Board are:

Pete Wicks - Chairman
Bowers Wallace - Vice Chairman
Midge Blakeley
Tony Pfingston
Willis Thornsberry
William R. Pride

*Above—Cable Tow Masonic Lodge No.
79, Sturgis, KY (Circa 1954). This order
was organized and dedicated in the late
1930s. The building pictured was located
at 6th and Pike Streets, Sturgis. It
burned about 1955 and the present hall
is located at 9th and King Streets,
Sturgis. There are presently eleven active
members with the Rev. David Petty,
Worshipful Master. L to R, "Dutch"
Harper, George Greenwell, Mr. Brooks,
Doyle Anderson, Nathaniel Alvis,
Tarvin Shelton, Sherman Alderman, D.
B. Crawford, Nathan Garrett, Shelby
Garnett, Mr. McElroy, David Petty,
Clifton Adams, Howard Chiles, Thilbert
Anderson, John W. Dixon, Elmo Alvis,
S. E. Cain, Lawrence Howard. (Nine
could not be identified.) Photo courtesy
of Mildred Howard. Left —Mt. Sterling
Cumberland Presbyterian Church Gospel
Group (circa early 1950s). L to R, Mr.
Bell Providence, KY, Thomas Hughs,
Shelby Garnett, George Coffey, Wilbur
Simpson, George Rice, all from Sturgis.
Photo courtesy of Mildred Coffey. Both
photos submitted by Joel Felts-Williams.*

Old Sturgis El...

Sturgis, ...

PLATE IV

Education

FRANCES KNIGHT Wells

F. Wells

...tary School
...ntucky

Ohio Valley Baptist College

Ohio Baptist College was dedicated in 1895 on Main Street, Sturgis. It closed in 1914.

One of Ohio Baptist College dormitories which is still standing today and used as an apartment building. Main St,. Sturgis.

Graduating Class circa 1900

Standing, Carl Hibbs, unknown; seated, L to R, Bettie David, Nina McKeaig, Ethel McKeaig

Below—A group playing guitars and mandolins circa 1900. Those which can be identified are: Bottom row, #4 Shelly Bennett, #7 Linnie McMurray Rash; second row, #6 Lucy (Dyer) Rose; third row, #1 Mag King, #2 Bettie (David) Cissell, #4 Tad Gooch Simpson, #5 Sally Whitecotton, #9 Ollie (Jones) Hurley; fourth row, #1 Nina McKeaig, #2 Lille (McKeaig) Turner, #3 Katharine (Sprague) Eastin #4 Att Dyer, #5 Mrs. Mamie Sallee, #6 Fannie (Jones) Meachem

Sturgis Graded School

First Public School in Sturgis, 1906

This was both elementary and high school from its opening in 1906 until the new high school was built. The first class to graduate from the new was the class of 1922.

Historical Sketch

Building erected 1906. Approximate cost $30,000.

Mr. J. J. Watkins, Superintendent, (1906-08).
Organization of Graded School.
Increase of Faculty.

Mr. J. H. Smith, Superintendent, (1908-10).
Music introduced in High School.
Science courses with Laboratories introduced.

Mr. C. E. Clark, Superintendent, (1910-11).
Study of German introduced.
Faculty increased.

Mr. H. W. Loy, Superintendent, (1911-14).
High School Accredited Class A.
Manual Training.
Domestic Science.
Physical Culture.

Mr. C. C. Justus, Superintendent, (1914-18).
Music in Grades.
Athletics.
First Annual.
Organization of C. I. A. Mr. Justus, President.
Increase of Faculty.
Parent-Teachers' Club.
Increased Attendance.

Mr. A. L. Morgan, Superintendent, (1918-)
Spanish and French Courses introduced.
Largest enrollment in history of school.
Faculty increased.
Bond issue for erection of $30,000 High School building.
Live Parent-Teachers' Organization.

Classes

CLASS ROLL:

Ruby Caldwell	Willie B. Carter	Johnnie Mae Edwards
Naomi Hall	Robert Hagan	Louise Kern
Laureen Shipley	Naomi Shaffer	Byers Winston
	John Wynns	

History

One bright Monday morning in September, nineteen hundred and fourteen, sixteen Freshmen bashfully marched into their classroom. Embarrassed and nervous, they finally found their seats. Their awkwardness soon vanished as school continued, and before long the "Freshies" were thoroughly at home. They always took active part in the Literary Society and had, in addition, their own class society.

The Sophomore Class of nineteen hundred and fifteen numbered fourteen. At the beginning of the second term they lost one of their number, making them an unlucky thirteen. At the end of school, all were lucky but the thirteenth, who failed to make the required average.

In the beginning of the Junior year, they were a happy dozen, but had the misfortune to be reduced to ten at the end of the first semester. If the Fates are kind the remaining ten will next year take the place of the now jolly and joyous Seniors.

R. A. C. '18.

CLASS ROLL:

Letha Barbee	Ila Hinton
Henry Brooks	Lelia McKenig
Glenn Durroh	Lockett Nunn
Macola Good	Neal Quirey
Earl Hammack	Louis Shackleford
Durroh Hammack	Rebecca Simpson
Marie Hammack	Walter Quinn
Seldon Hammack	Maxwell Waters

History

When the Sturgis High School opened for work in 1915-1916, twenty-five happy boys and girls entered the Freshman Class. They were a proud and joyful lot, yet, like all "Freshies", they possessed a certain timidity and "greenness". A class meeting was called, and the following officers were elected: President, Vice-President, and Secretary. The Orchestra was organized, composed entirely of Freshmen.

As in all classes, some failed, others moved away, so that only fifteen of the original number became Sophomores. One member was gained this year. The class again contributed to the various organizations of the school, and furnished the same number to the Orchestra.

When the football team was organized, the Sophomores were prepared and willing to furnish ample material; five of the boys joined the team.

The Sophomore class of 1916-1917 will be remembered as one of the most talented and best spirited classes of Sturgis High School.

J. R. S. '19.

CLASS ROLL:

Christine Beaven	Elizabeth Ellis
Lula Barnett	Sallie T. Holt
Louise Bingham	Jeffie Holeman
Judith Bishop	Anastasia Hammack
Ferdinand Cissel	Dora Jones
Anna L. Doris	Grace Justus
Lindle Doris	Ruth Kern
Ariana Long	
Ruby McIntyre	
Lillian McGee	
Jettie McKeaig	Catherine Omer	Sarah Omer
Mattie L. O'nan	
Lowell Truitt	
Daniel Quirey	
Waller Sprague	Francis Fravel
Hugh Stevenson	Bertha Winders
Latta Smith	William Wright
Susan Shaffer	Anna Young
Elizabeth Shaffer	Edgar Wallace
John Stevens	Fount Wallace
Mary Edna O'nan	Mary L. Wallace

CLASS ROLL

Ames, Edward	Holt, Mayme
Berry, Roy	Husband, Winifred
Brill, Blayne	Kelley, Irvin
Brooks, Haleen	King, Ruth
Brooks, Myra	Latta, William
Brown, Jesse	LeGate, Vera Mabel
Chambliss, Fannie Belle	Lindle, Ernestine
Cissel, Carroll	Meachem, Eleanor
Cissel, Virginia	O'Nan, Paul
Collins, Trude	Pierson, Dixie
Delaney, Jesse	Quinn, Kathryn
Delaney, Parker	Quinn, Ottis
Durham, Lois	Quirey, Miles Austin
Hagan, Orville	Riddle, Kathryn
Hammack, Marie	Stewart, Eloise
Hinton, Claryce	Sutton, Lucile
Hinton, Kivel	Wallace, Kilburn
Hodges, Herbert	Willingham, Dorothy
Holeman, Gladyce	Woolridge, Effie
Holeman, Vyvyan	Wright, Rupert
Wynns, Nina Sue	

Sports

Sturgis High School Football Team, 1916-1917—Standing, back rwo, L to R, Coach Bobby Byars, Harry Lily, Dick Dyer, Jim Truitt, Ila Hinton, Boyd, Powell; middle row, Lowell Truitt, Bud Quirey, Louis Pritchett, Durroh Hammack, John Bishop; front row center Dick Hammack, others, unknown.

Football

This was the first year for Sturgis to try her strength on the gridiron, and taking in consideration all our drawbacks it must be admitted that Coach Byars brought forth a good team and if in the future we progress as we did during the past season we are sure to have an excellent team. We began the season with only a small number of boys out and for a while things looked blue for the 1916 S. H. S. football team, but by constant endeavor we finally got a small squad out. After about three weeks of gruelling practice we thought ourselves capable of behaving well before the teams that had a year or two advantage of us in training.

Our schedule was as follows:

TEAMS	STURGIS	VISITING TEAMS
Sturgis at Marion	0	6
Marion at Sturgis	0	7
Providence at Sturgis	6	6
Sturgis at Morganfield	0	41
Nebo at Sturgis	31	0

Although we began the season with defeat we ended it with victory. Taking in consideration that this is our first year in football we have made remarkable progress and expect in the future to be invincible.

Coach Byars came to us from Transylvania where he played for three years at halfback and end and therefore is well qualified to teach athletics as is shown by the fact that he brought forth a fighting team from raw material and undeveloped ability. With Mr. Byars as coach we are sure of a winning team in the future. It might also be added that our Coach has talent in other fields as he is champion mile runner of the state.

"Lookout for Sturgis in the future".

Girls Basketball Teams, 1916-1917. Above, the "Blacks." right, the "Golds"

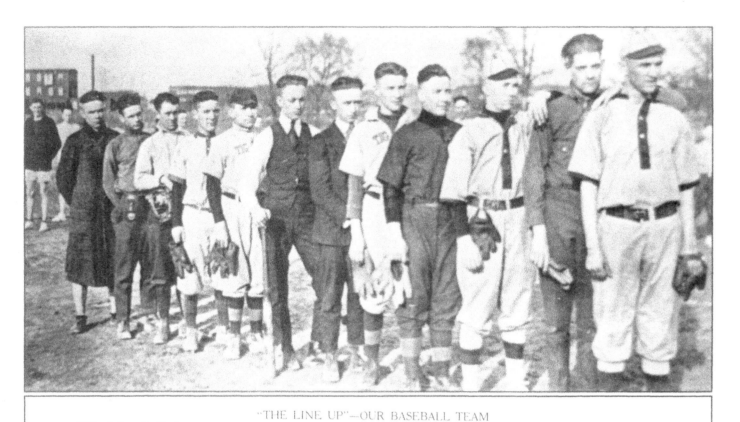

"THE LINE UP"—OUR BASEBALL TEAM

Clifford Powell, Pitcher.
Warford Watters, Catcher.
Lowell Truitt, First Base.
Howard Berry, Second Base.
First Game with Corydon High School, March 28, at Sturgis.

William Wright, Third Base.
Walter Quinn, Short Stop.
Daniel Quirey, Left Field.
John Stevens, Center Field.
Max Watters, Right Field.

Football squad, 1921

Girls basketball squad, 1921-1922—Top, L to R, Charlotte Shaeffer, Katharine Sutton, Laura Stevenson, Virginia Cissell, Juanita Wynns. Bottom row, Virginia Jones, Lena Prow, Martha Kern, Lela Prow, Doye Brown

Team and supporters depart for Marion, Nov. 25, 1921

Activities

First Annual Staff, 1917

These humorous photographs opened and closed the first "Sturgeon." The staff that year was Addie L. Winston, editor-in-chief; Ruby Caldwell, Assistant Editor; James Truitt, Business Manager; Byers Winston, Assistant Business Manager, Harry Lilly, Literary Editor; Augusta Culley, Art Editor, Emma Bishop, Music Editor, John Brown, Athletic Editor and Aline Wilcox, Humor Editor.

Orchestra, 1917— Front row, L to R, Winnie Croft, Maeola Goad, Addie Louis Winston, Rebecca Simpson and Brown Simpson. Back row, Lawrence Holt, Dick Hammack, Miss Critchfield, Lockett Nunn, Alcy Morgan, Earl Hammack and Milburn Stone

WWI Veterans were honored with this page in the 1920 Sturgeon. Pictured above are Lt. Henry D. Hammack, left, and Private First Class C. Ila G. Hinton.

High School Quartet, 1919—Pearl Morse, Sallie Holt, Anna Young, Laureen Shipley

Board of Education 1919

J. V. King *P. H. Winston* *Dr. G. B. Carr* *E. B. Jones, Sr.* *George B. Lindle*

Declaimers—Lydia Anderson, Mary E. Meacham, Virginia Jones

Orators, 1919—Miles Quirey, Barbee Simpson, Haldean Davis, Charles Young

49

Sturgis High School—1922-1937

Classes 1929

Sports

Track Squad, 1929—Front row, L to R, Wayne Reynolds, Manager, Glenn McKeehan, J. F. Springer, Unknown, Fred Stevenson, Ear McKeehan, Willis Thornsberry. Second row, Coach W. O. Wright, William Humphrey, Bill Hoerth, Delbert Floyd, Unknown, Van Allen, Dean Martin, Buster Sutton, Marvin Young, Elmo Melton

Boys basketball squad, 1929—Front row, L to R, Tom Young, Manager, Earl McKeehan, Billy Christian, Foster Peyton, Otho O'Bryan, Coach W. O. Wright. Second row, William Humphrey, John R. Bell, Dean Martin, Van Allen, Buster Sutton, Marvin Young

Girls basketball squad, 1929—Front row, L to R, Lyda Travis, Helen Edwards, Dorothy Kent, Grace Stevenson. Second row, Faye Gatten, Tim Carr, LaTrieve Sprague, Virginia Christian, Edith Kern, Jeannette Young

Sam Shipley, Sturgis, takes first in a 200 meter dash.

Girls basketball players posed for this picture in 1932. Those pictured are, L to R, unknown, Mildred Burklow, Ernestine Rehm, Mary Nell Moore, Margaret Penrod Settle, Margaret Cusic Bosecker, Louise Stanley Simpson, Rebecca Davis Kearney, Lucille Mayes, Mary Edna Below, unknown, Robert Kuykendall, Harry Quinn, Tommy Johnson and Charles Smith.

Basketball Team, 1938—Front row, L to R, Coach Ralph Horning, Clarence Houts, Harry Markham, Pete Young, Jeep Harrod and Skeets Brown. Second row, Bill Waggener, Frank Johns, Coach Morgan Christian, Danny Gregory

Basketball squad, 1940

Football squad, 1940

Basketball squad, 1946

Football squad, 1946

'61-'62 STURGIS GOLDEN BEARS
BASKETBALL SQUAD

Last Golden Bear Team—First row, David Waggener, John Whitehead, John Chapman, Mickey Lewis, David Blakeley, Keith Omer, John Robertson, Roger Omer, Larry Cowan, Bob Kellen, Steve Henshaw, Second row, David Bradford, Gary Quinn, Tom Steele, William Pride, James Vaughn, Mike Foreman, Ray Wells, Jack Henery, Mickey Pride, Dennis Walker, Billy Collins. Thirs row, Donnie Pennington, Johnny Shaffer, Slaton Sprague, Dale Higgins, Phil Young, Jack Stewart, Jimmy Bean, Danny Williams, James Inge, Larry Wright

Above left, Coaches, 1962—H. D. Holt, Jr, Ray D. Hina, Fred Lamb and Ralph Horning, head coach. Right, a manager. Left, Managers, 1964—Carl Brown, Herman Faustina, David Pettie

Cheerleaders

Top, Cheerleaders, 1946; Middle, Cheerleaders, 1948, Helen Hammack, Wanda Stewart, Barbara, Stewart, Louise Dempsey, Peggy McDowell. Right, Cheerleaders, 1962, Back row, Susan Anderson, Janice Gatlin, Connie Edwards, Joyce Gatlin. Kneeling, Harri Kay Brooks, Ona Sue Wright

Special Honors

RALPH WRIGHT.

HARRY SIMPSON

CHARLOTTE MERRITT.

DEWEY BRINKLEY.

RICHARD WATTERS

May Queen, 1927, Velma Chandler

Football Queen, 1940, Helen Shoulders

Basketball Queen, 1948, Carolyn Seibert

Football Queen, 1957, Martha Jane Kurtz

King and Queen, Sturgis High School, 1940, Ellsworth Dudley, Betty June Doerr

Basketball Queen, 1957, Judy Crowell

Golden Bear Queen, 1961-1962, Ruth Horning

Queen of 1962 Bears, Carol Ann Freer

Basketball Queen, 1962-1963, Bonnie Kearney

Basketball Queen, 1964,—Roger Omer crowns Lisa Humphrey with David Waggoner looking on. Bruce Humphrey and Judy Bell in front.

Activities

"Bear Facts" staff, 1938—Woodrow Wilson,
Editor; Dorothy Cason, Assistant Editor; Kas Wesley, News
Editor; Mary Ann Cusic, Business Mgr.; Ralph O'Nan,
Advertising Mgr.; Ellsworth Dudley, Sports Editor; W. A.
Ross, Sponsor. Assistants and reporters—Helen Oliver,
Marianna Erwin, Mary Casey Davis, Helen Barnett, Maurice
Hudson, Dorothy Nesbitt, Martha Pride, Mary Virginia
Henry, Melba Taylor, Emma Lee Logan, Martha McGee,
Marianna Holeman, Eddie Houts, Georgia Jennings, Houston
Gibson, Willie Clyde Hammack and "Skeets" Brown

Stitch and Stew Club, 1938—Mary Ann Cusic,
Mary Ben Small, Regina Paris, Helen Shoulders, Dorothy
Cason, Ruth Holeman, Lucille Dalton, Glena Edmonson,
Geneva Reynolds, Estil Hammack, Charline Reynolds, Eleanor
Ruth Erwin. Sponsor, Evelyn Hammack

FFA, 1938—Ray Andre, Joe Brown Arnold, Harold Baird,
R. W. Bell, Harold Berry, Billie Brown, Carl Couch, Bob Curry,
James Duncan, Ben Dyer, Henry D. Hammack, Joe Henshaw,
Harold Henshaw, Paul Hopper, Henry Huckeby, Billie Hugh
Johns, Earl Liles, Nace Waller Mason, Robert McCann, Charles
Morgan, Ralph O'Nan, Marshall Paris, Verlon Prince, Gus
Riddle, Gerald Schaeffer, Walter Schaeffer, Raymond Shoe-
maker, Jean Stodgill, Harold Toombs, Robert Truitt, Virgil
Truitt, Gordon Urton, J. T. Walker. Sponsor, R. E. Simons

Annual staff, 1938—Eddie Houts, Editor; Mary Casey
Davis, Assistant editor; "Skeets" Brown, Business Mgr.;
Eugene Harrod, Sports Editor; Dorothy Cason, Subscription
Mgr.; "Sonny" Jones, Snapshot editor; Billy
Wilcox,Photographer; Margaret Kirchner, Artist; Helen
Barnett, Chairman Historian; Pattie Hart, Historian; Grace
Waggener, Historian; Eugene Reynolds, Editor of Ads; Ralph
O'Nan, Editor of Ads, Emma Lee Logan, Typist

Student Council, 1940

Forensic Society, 1940

Beta Club, 1946, *Wilburn Jones, Noel Wilson, Delila Acker, Carolyn McBee, Betty Henry, Noel Wilson, Leo Boston, Mary Watson, Johnny Robertson, Garland Townsend, Ann Holeman, Virgin Logan, Warren Dortch, Wilburn Jones, Jimmy Strouse, Geraldine Cason, Margaret Wright, Don Pritchett, Ellamae Smith, Dan Berry, Edith Benson, Eva Markham, Patsy McGee, Ann McGee, Mary Ames, Charlotte Ames, Marcella Maddox, Carolyn Brantley, Betty Oliver, Betty Rigsby, Wanda Lee Tucker, Roy Hina, J. D. Sigler, Alvin Brashers, Shirley Daniels, George B. Simpson, John White, Donald Collins, Rosemary Smith, Patsy Ann Sowers, Ethel Gahagen, Dorothy Wilson, Joan Omer, Dorothy McKeaig. Sonsors, Lillie K. Peyton, H'Earl Evans.*

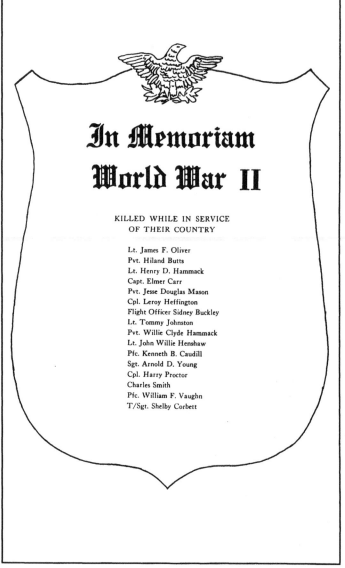

In Memoriam

World War II

KILLED WHILE IN SERVICE
OF THEIR COUNTRY

Lt. James F. Oliver
Pvt. Hiland Butts
Lt. Henry D. Hammack
Capt. Elmer Carr
Pvt. Jesse Douglas Mason
Cpl. Leroy Heffington
Flight Officer Sidney Buckley
Lt. Tommy Johnston
Pvt. Willie Clyde Hammack
Lt. John Willie Henshaw
Pfc. Kenneth B. Caudill
Sgt. Arnold D. Young
Cpl. Harry Proctor
Charles Smith
Pfc. William F. Vaughn
T/Sgt. Shelby Corbett

Memorial, 1946 annual

Class Officers, 1946

Senior

Junior

Top row, Charles O'Nan, President; Noel Wilson, Vice President; Virginia Logan, Secretary; Betty Henry, Treasurer; Warren Dortch, Reporter; Tommy Penrod, Sgt. at Arms. Second row, Daniel Berry, President, George B. Simpson Vice President, Betty Oliver, Secretary, James Herron, Sgt. at Arms; Charlotte Ames, Treasurer; Charles Quinn, Sgt. at Arms. Third row, Quentin Wesley, President; Louise Dempsey, Secretary; Helen Hammack, Treasurer

Sophomore

Annual staff, 1946, *Warren Dortch, Editor; Wilburn Jones, Assistant Editor; Aileen Morris and Shelly Omer, Business Mgrs.; Virginia Buice, Evelyn Brantley, Virginia Logan, Typists; Billy White, Jimmy Long, Jimmy Shaffer, Johnny Robertson, Advertising Mgrs.; Leo Boston, Historian; James Smith, Humorist; Carolyn McBee, Testator; Larry Deweese, Class Poet; Lillie Sue Travis, Song Composer; Betsy Acker, Art Editor; Charles O'Nan, Miscellaneous.*

Annual staff, 1948—*Gillie Irene Jones, Ben J. Quinn, Co-editors; Roy Lindle, Business Mgr.; Joan Troutt, Norma Jean Milligan, Hilda Dee Young, Ass't Business Mgr.; Quentin Wesley, Bobby Lee O'Nan, Patsy Ruth Barnard, Louise Dempsey, Circulation Mgrs.; Margaret Acker, W. B. Berry, Ralph Paris, Charles West, Art Editors; Bobbie Sue Oakley, Helen Hammack, Dorinda Nunn, Typists; Billy Wynn Omer, Guy Newcom, Sports Editors; Martha Conn, Margaret Martin, Historians; Norma Chandler, John Steelman, Humorists; Moreland McDowell, Testator; Douglas Gregory, Class President.*

Latin Club, 1948—*Fred Omer, Carolyn Burton, Carolyn Seibert, Melba Sigler, Millie Collins, Betty Dempsey, Patricia Hayes, Harold Hibbs, Mollie Moss, Dorinda Nunn, Ann Miller, Roxie Styrouse, Ann Bell, Suzanna Wesley, Ruth Glazebrook, Paul Ray Troutt, Jewell Estes, Wayne Berry, Royce Boston, Mary Ruth Holt, Barbara Holeman, Helen Hammack, Betty Jo Drury, Bobbie Sue Oakley, Bobby Lee O'Nan, Quentin Wesley.*

Band, 1948—*Director-Mrs. Ralph Alexander. Drum Major-Magaret Ann Holt. Majorettes-Mary Ruth Holt, Nell Louise O'Nan, Peggy Jo Powell, Judy Holt. Clarinets-Carolyn Seibert, Delores Oakley, Melba Sigler, Margaret Morgan, Michael Sweeney, Sarra Jean Mattingly, Donald Hines, Marcella McKinley, Donald Paris, Bobby Edwards. Trumpets-Fredie Omer, Jim Syers, Anna Sue Omer, Edwin Johnson, Dorinda Nunn, Harold Hibbs, Ronnie Omer, Paul Ray Troutt, Lowell Stewart, Dudley Hazel, Buddy Brown, Roxie Strouse. Trombones-John Steelman, K. Franklin, Royce Boston, Newt Bell, Nell Louise O'Nan Judy Holt. Baritone-R. E. Simpson, Graves Collins. E Flat Horn-Mollie Moss, Milburn Laneve. Drums-Henry Hina, Gail Carter, Junel West, Freddie Walker, Dan McCallum, Billy Tom Henshaw, Billy Wright, Jon McCallum.*

Glee Club, 1948—*Director-Mrs. Ralph Alexander. Accompanist-Lillian Martin. Soprano-Mary Ruth Holt, Peggy Jo Powell, Carol Stone, Helen June Butts, Ida Janet Woodring, Janice Elaine Roberts, Lois Baker, Ann Riddle, Betty Jean Hopper, Marcia Adamson, Ruby Mae Liles, Grace Liles, Melva Jones, Roxie Strouse, Louise Deason Olivia O'Leary, Louise Travis, Billie June Travis, Jo Adams, Boyce Dee Roy, Marie Rutherford, Melva Markham, Inez Conn, Jewell Estes. Second Soprano-Carolyn Burton, Vallie Hill, Jessie Ruth Lane, Kathrine Smith, Barbara Shoulders, Clara Ann Hines. Alto-Nell Louise O'Nan, Margaret Ann Holt, JUdy Kathryn Holt, Gloria Steelman, Mildred Collins, Carolyn Bradford, Jane Berry, Hilda Ann Collins.*

The Senior Class
Presents

At right, Senior Class Officers, 1960—Jimmy Hall, President; Sharon Stanley, Vice President; Jerry Sheridan, Sergeant at arms; Lynda Hinton, Secretary; Betty Sue Truitt, Reporter, Billy Dempsey, Sergeant at arms. 2) Beta Club, 1960. Other photos, Beta Club, 1962.

Majorettes and Drum major, 1962. Sherry Rigsby, Bobby Wesley, Suzanne Sprague, Barbara Quirey, Elizabeth Davis.

FHA, 1962

Superior Winners at State Band Contest, 1962

Senior Class Officers, 1962—Jackie Hibbs, President; Joe Woodring, Vice President; Barbara Caudill, Secretary; Steven Shouse, Treasurer; Barbara Quirey, Reporter; Harry Hina, Wayne Hooper, Sergeants at arms.

Sophomore Class Officers, 1962—Steve Henshaw, President; Gary Bell, Vice President; William Pride, Secretary; Ruth Horning, Treasurer; Ladonna Allison, Berry Ann Brooks, Bobby Kellen, Robbie Truitt, Sergeants at arms.

Freshman Class Officers, 1962—Larry Wright, President; Richard Kuykendall, Vice President; Suzzane Brinkly, Secretary; Anzie Brown Treasurer; Bonnie Kearney, Reporter,Billy Burl Collins, Mike Foreman Sergeants at arms.

MISS LILLIE PEARL KUYKENDALL
MATHEMATICS

MR. W. O. WRIGHT.
FRENCH.

MISS JEANON DAY.
SCIENCE & ENGLISH.

HIGH

FACULTY

SCHOOL

MISS NOMA DIX WINSTON.
ENGLISH.

MISS KATE HUEY.
LATIN & ENGLISH.

MR. W. D. DE HAVEN.
SCIENCE & HISTORY

Miss Carrie Eble

W. T. McGraw

Fred Shultz

"As a token of our appreciation for the years of work in our behalf, for the kind advice and deep interest in our welfare, and the esteem which we bear her in our hearts, we lovingly dedicate this volume of "The Sturgeon" to Miss Carrie Eble."

"No one can associate with our principal without absorbing some of his high ideals and love of thoroughness, which characterizes his teaching in every field of activity. In him all find a friend who is ever ready to lend his time and advice of their problems."

"As we sail over the sea of life, we meet many who leave their influence stamped indelibly upon our lives. Just such a one is our superintendent, Mr. Shultz, who has endeared himself in the hearts and lives of every individual in S. H. S.

Coaches Dehaven, Christian and Horning.

Marie Hammack

Ruth King

Lillie K. Peyton

Hazel Ray

Lillian Moss

Betty Wells

Lillian Collins

Mrs. Louis Talbott

Mrs. R. Alexander

Mrs. Ed Truman

Marie Lamb

Dorothy Stevenson

Frances Ball

Agnew Long

Ralph Alexander

Prudy Oglesby

Nettie Nall

H'Earl Evans

Mrs. T. Young

Robert R. Rehm

William DeHaven

Sue Betts

Frances Ball

Mary P. McGregor

Ralph Horning

Pauline Holt

Mrs. Lona Omer

Lillie Layman

Ernestine Lindle

Mrs. R. Horning

Mrs. L. E. Ringo

Nancy Wynn

Katharine Fletcher

72

L. B. Piercy   Malcolm Hart   Ralph Horning   Aline Gahagan   Dorothy Stevenson   Stanley Hedges

Kathryne Davis   Virginia Simpson   Margaret Berry   Wayne Reynolds   Sue Hoerth   Margaret Cusic

The photos above are some of the Junior High and Elementary teachers in 1940. On the opposite page are photos of teachers from the Graded School and the High School.

Teaching Sturgis through the years

Union County Board of Education

Parent Teacher Association

1922, officers.

1929, officers.

1948, officers. Mrs. Carles Wells. Mrs. Roy Davis, Nancy Wynns, Ruby Gatlin

1927—Mrs. Ward Carr, Mrs. J. V. King, Lillie Kuykendall and Kate Huey

Last PTA officers with last principal, H'Earl Evans. From left, Mrs. Otho Edwards, Mrs. Virgil Kearney, Evans, Mrs. Robert Truitt.

Sturgis High School, 1938-1964

1964—The last year for SHS

Since this is the last year for Sturgis High School, we, the members of the last graduating class, dedicate this yearbook to the memory of all who have associated with Sturgis High over the years.

We dedicate it to the principals, because they have through years of faithful service and guidance held its standards high, and have endeared themselves to the school and the community.

We dedicate it to all calss room teachers who have given so much of themselves in sacrificial service; who have taken an understanding attitude toward our work and play; who have challenged and stimulated within us the desire to achieve, to be up-right and to contribute to life.

The thoughts, ideals, and actions of all have made Sturgis High what it has been; and we trust that you will recapture within these pages the beautiful dreams, hopes and ambitions of your youth which the school inspired, making you proud that you were a part of Sturgis High School.

We pay tribute to each member of the fifty-eight graduating classes of Sturgis High School. May you remember and cherish the challenges, accomplishments, and firends at Sturgis High School.

That Sturgis "Spirit" brings back loyal grads wearing their "S" sweaters and joining in on the enthusiasm at the final, thrilling Sturgis High pep assembly.

Union County High School—1965 to present

Union County High School, the home of the Union County Braves and all other high school students, grades 9-12, in Union County is located about half-way between Morganfield and Sturgis on US Hwy 60. The original structure was completed in 1964 at a cost of $1,450,000. The structure was completely air-conditioned with a gymnasium which seats 3,500 persons, a separate auditorium designed in the most acoustical structure with complete lighting and stage equipment which seats 780 persons. There are 39 classrooms of traditional structure and fully equipped laboratories for various sciences, foreign languages, art, vocational home economics, vocational agriculture, retailing education and industrial education.

On the same campus, but in a separate building, is housed the trade school which offers to high school students training in Auto Mechanics, Carpentry, Industrial Electricity, Welding, and Health Careers.

Union County High School is a symbol of interest of the people of Union County in the educational welfare of the students of this school system. In those days of materialism the people of the county made a political move in 1963 in voting extra taxation upon themselves in order that their children might have the educational facilities which

Superintendent, 1964, Lewis Baker

School Board, 1964—Seated, I. C. Russell, Vernon Catlett, Eastin Wallace.. Standing, Ralph Hart, Lewis Baker, Dr. George Higginson

Hazel Brinkley

Ralph Alexander

Tony Asher

Kathleen Holt

Erma Bell

Coleman Brinkley

are paramount to the development of a strong program of education.

With the closing of St. Vincent Academy at the end of the 1966-67 school year these some 200 high school students were added to the enrollment of Union County High School. Up until the burning of the Morganfield Middle School, during the summer of 1979, Union County High School's enrollment included grades 10 through 12. At the beginning of the 1979-80 school year the enrollment changed to include grades 9 through 12 raising our enrollment to just over 1,000 students.

Union County High School reached a milestone during the 1973-74 school year in it efforts to provide an effective and interesting program for high school students. The traditional lock-step curriculum with students participating in 5 or 6 subject areas for a full year was expanded for students to participate in from 15-18 different content areas. The major complaint with this program was the lack of basic skill development. The help resolve this 9th and 10th grade students will partici-

pate in the traditional program with 11th and 12th grade student continuing in the innovative phase elective program.

In 1983 construction was completed adding a $2.5 million expansion to alleviate overcrowding. The library which is of modern design, fully carpeted now houses 15,065 volumes, 66 different magazines, 5 newspapers and 1677 different audio-visual materials with 118 different pieces of audio visual equipment. We now have an addition to the cafeteria (approximately doubling the original size), 10 new classrooms, 4 restrooms, and an elevator for the handicapped and a new physical education arena. The office area has been expanded to 10 offices with a conference room.

The first principal of Union County High School was H'Earl Evans who served from August 1964 through June of 1967. July 1, 1967 Dick Vincent was appointed principal of Union County High School. In this the 25th year (1989) of Union County High School. Mr. Vincent remains as the principal.

Richard Vincent

Roger Edmonson

Jena Davis, Mary Burgess, Honors Day, 1967

Jackie Freer, Football Queen, 1967

Union County Middle School

Union County Middle School first opened its doors for classes on August 22, 1988. The new facility, which is located on U. S. 60 between Sturgis and Morganfield, was built for $4.5 million and contains approximately 100,000 square feet of floor space. The school provides an education for all sixth, seventh, and eighth grade public school pupils in Union County. In addition to instruction in the regular academic areas, UCMS students are offered a variety of exploratory classes which include physical education, art, instrumental music, choral music, industrial arts, home economics, and computer education. Seven hundred students attended classes at Union County Middle School during it first year.

Sturgis Elementary School

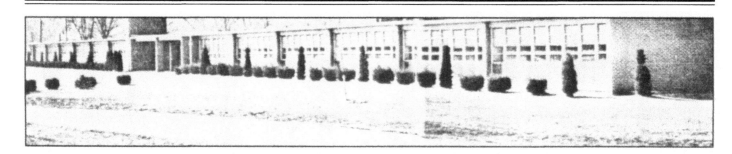

The Sturgis Elementary School was erected in 1958. For the first five years, the school housed grades one through eight. In 1964 the independent school districts of Sturgis and Morganfield were consolidated. This move resulted in the seventh and the eighth grades going to the Sturgis Junior High. Grades one through six remained at the Sturgis Elementary. Kindergarten was added in 1976. Special Education units were added in 1977. In 1988-89 the opening of the new Union County Middle School resulted in an organizational change to kindergarten through fifth grades for the Sturgis Elementary School.

Mr. Bowers Wallace became the principal when the building was erected in 1958. The current principal is Mr. John Belt. He became principal when Mr. Wallace retired in 1983.

Presently the attendance is 604. Kindergarten through 5th grades. There is a complete staff of 61, of this number 35 are teachers.

Religion

FIRST CHRISTIAN

On a knoll overlooking the canebrakes on the northeast bank of Cypress Creek sprang the Cypress Creek Christian Church in 1839. The original deed of the Cypress Christian Church was from W. K. Ball to the Trustees of the church on September 30, 1839. This reveals the existence of an organized congregation. Over the doorway of the simple log structure were the words "Christians Only." They didn't claim to be the only Christians but desired to be Christians only. The church located on the busy Morganfield-Salem Road seemed to beckon travelers on their busy east-west trail into the frontier.

Today the graves in the Cypress Creek Cemetery are a reminder of our many pioneer forefathers and their dedication to our early heritage. There are some gravestones that date prior to 1839 thus telling us there was a campground for early settlers along Cypress Creek before the church was built.

After worshipping in the log structure for 19 years the congregation decided to move to the south side of the Cypress. A historical sketch reads; "In 1858, 'before de wo,' a new church was built on this side of our Jordon (Cypress), the Jerusalem side, on a gentle slope, right on the creek bank...it faced the rising sun." Following the construction the congregation worshipped through the terrible Civil War. It survived the Ohio River flood of 1884 with just a little dry spot surrounding it. The building was sold in 1893 to make another move to more acceptable location. Some of the timber was used in the construction of the Sizemore home (now owned by the Farrs) near the spot where the second Cypress Church was located.

In the 1880s the present City of Sturgis was born. When the village was less than a decade old the Cypress Church was abandoned and the congregation moved to town. A wooden structure was erected on the best spot in town in 1893 on lots deeded to the church by George and Willie O'Nan. The location was at the corner of Seventh and Adams Street where the present brick edifice now stands.

Sturgis was becoming a progressive city. By 1912 the Christian Church was already outgrowing its present facility and in order to meet the need, as well as to keep abreast the new wave of church building enthusiasm sweeping the city, the congregation set itself to the task of building the fourth structure in its 73 year history.

The wooden structure that was on the lot was moved to where the parsonage now stands. This was used for worship while the new church was under construction. After the new church was completed it is believed the old church was moved to Boxtown.

On February 12, 1912, the building committee was appointed and immediately went to work because the contract was let on July 31, 1912. The cornerstone was laid in 1912 and the dedication was held on May 18, 1913. They had strong faith that the foundation of Sturgis was solid and would continue to grow.

Nothing was spared in the beauty of their building. The massive towers and ornate cathedral stain glass windows, which were made in Chicago, lend much to this beautiful building. The bricks were made in Sturgis and hauled by wagon from the kiln. The bell still rings from the bell tower each Sunday morning to let the people know that First Christian beckons them to the house of the Lord. A mistake was made when the church was built. They didn't build in a baptistry - one was soon added. One man fell from a scaffold and was killed during construction.

During the 1937 flood many families lived in the church basement. In July 1964 an elevator was installed and is used by many every Sunday. The interior was renovated in 1966-67. A fellowship hall with kitchen and Sunday School rooms was built in 1981. Many other changes have been made during the years.

The present building is 76 years old and has had 23 ministers during this time. Bro. George Mudd, our minister, has been with us the longest - 11 years. Jeff Bullock has served as the Youth Minister for the past 5 years.

Through the years the First Christian Church has been faithfully dedicated to the task of restoring the church to the New Testament pattern. We owe much gratitude to our forefathers for their noble heritage and hope we will always be able to fly the Banner of the Cross to the world. *Compiled from various histories of this congregation. Submitted by Shirley Brown, Church Historian*

FIRST PRESBYTERIAN

The Sturgis Presbyterian Church, to a great extent, was the child of circumstances. Thirteen years after the forming of Union County in 1811, two McGhee Brothers, one a Presbyterian and the other a Methodist, began a series of camp meetings in order for a ministry to reach large numbers of people who had been denied the advantages of higher education. These camp meetings became a rallying point for great numbers of families who year after year left their homes and attended them for a week. There were two classes of campers—those who owned their cabins and those who lived in tents or other improvised shelters during the meetings.

The meetings at Nazareth, located 2 1/2 miles northwest of Sturgis on Cypress Creek, became a religious feature of this part of the country. The first cabin holders were James Wallace, Will S. Pierson and Joseph Sprague. From these meetings the "Nazareth Society" was formed and from this beginning several churches were founded.

"The Nazareth Society" was reorganized in 1833 and a small frame church known as "Mount Ephriam" was erected on this camping ground. Among the first ministers were Rev. H. W. Black and John Barnett. From 1838 to 1879 members who affiliated with this small church totaled 314.

Throughout the old church Record we find instances where "committees" were appointed to wait on members for swearing profoundly, immoral conduct, mistreatment of wife, dancing, horse stealing, etc. We read further, "When the Brethern had maid the nesary acknowlegement, he was restored to the privaleg of the church" or "His naim is araised from the record."(sic) Members of the Session were required to give cause of absence (generally sustained), and members of the congregation as well as the Session were regularly examined on the "Docturn of the Church and the Catechism."

In 1843 by "Mutual agreement" thirty-six members petitioned for disunion and organized in the eastern boundary of Union County using the name of Union Rock Springs. This church is still located near Clay, Kentucky.

In 1866 fifteen members removed their letters and organized the Presbyterian Church of Caseyville. This organization moved to Sturgis and built a church on the lot where the United Methodist Church now stands. This property was sold when the congregation

united with the present Presbyterian Church in 1906. The building itself is still being used and is located near Clay, Kentucky.

In 1882 a new frame church was erected at Nazareth and was dedicated by Rev. B. G. McLeskey, uncle of Annie Lamb, a member of First Presbyterian Church for many years. The old building remained to be used in the camp meetings. Names of many of the older members are still legible on the tombstones in the small cemetery on the knoll behind the location where the old church once stood.

In 1890 this building was razed and moved to Sturgis. Lightning destroyed it seven years later, and a new brick church was erected.

In 1906 the General Assembly of the Cumberland Presbyterian Church decreed to unite all Presbyterian churches into the Presbyterian Church, USA. Dissention arose among the congregation resulting in many members taking their letters and forming the Cumberland Presbyterian Church of this city.

Owing to defective building materials, it was decided to tear down the first brick church and rebuild. This is the present First Presbyterian Church located at Ninth and Kelsey Streets in Sturgis, which was erected at a cost of approximately $7,050. The Rev. W. J. Darby dedicated it on March 19, 1911. The beautiful stained glass windows from the first brick church were salvaged and put in the new church. This is the most outstanding feature in our church today.

The first wedding ceremony to be held in the present church was the marriage of Kenneth G. Davis and Susan Casey Nunn on November 12, 1913, the Rev. J. F. Claycombe officiated. Many pastors have served this church since

the first one, Rev. T. M. Hurst. The Rev. Samuel C. McKee, the son of Presbyterian missionaries in China, served the greatest number of years at two different times. During the war years, we were often supplied by various chaplains from Camp Breckinridge. Also, Louisville Theological Seminary has graciously supplied us with students during interim periods when we were without a permanent pastor. This church has produced one Presbyterian minister, the Rev. Dr. Chester M. Davis, who made his confession of faith as a youth in this church. He was graduated from the McCormick Theological Institute in 1971 and served as a minister in Rahway, New Jersey for 36 years. Some pastors who were ordained and served the First Presbyterian Church are: Rev. Samuel C. McKee (1910); Rev. John H. Scott (1948); Rev. Thomas G. Atkinson (1955); Rev. James C. Erwin (1963); and our first lady minister Rev. Barbara Giltz McGarey (1978).

This church, one of the oldest organized congregations, is proud of its record as a pioneer of religion both in Union and Webster counties. In 1975, during a period without pastoral leadership, the congregation took a major step in faith when it was decided to construct a new Fellowship Hall connected to the original building. This was the culmination of a dream of our first woman Ruling Elder, Mrs. Nell S. O'Nan, who had established a building fund years before. This Hall is enjoyed by all for Sunday School classes, pot luck dinners, Presbytery Meetings and outside club use like Boy Scouts and Cub Scouts. Though the congregation remains small in numbers (under 100 active members), it tries to remain visible in the community during these times of changing values and tight economics.

STURGIS GENERAL BAPTIST

The Sturgis General Baptist Church was organized on March 6, 1949 in the old Bell building. Fourteen members went into the organization. They were James Watson, Elsie Watson, Docia Powell, A. J. McKendree, Lorene Straker, Rose Earl Neible, Sam Straker, Mary Powell, Hattie Wright, Ona Brantley, Bell Smithers, Ruby Kanipe, Jeanetta Mackey, and Bessie Yates.

The church was originally located in Curlew, a town now vanished, and the area was occupied by the Ohio River beltline of the Pitts-burg and Midway Coal Companies, Dekoven mines No. 6 and 9.

In November 1949 Mr. and Mr. Clifton Lane gave the lot on Johnson Street and one dollar toward a new church.

The pastors have been Charles Polly, William Chambliss, Earl Rinehart, B. A. Mercer, Berlan Harper, Johnny Royalty, Jim Nickleson, Larry Goldsberry, Archie Carnal, C. B. Jones, Robert Phillips, David Winders, David Townsend, J. W. Davis, and Nickey Winders.

The deacons have been A. J. McKendree, Elton Heidrich, W. D. McKendree, Earl McKendree, and Ronnie Rutter. The trustees have been James Watson, Sam Travis, Bill Duncan, Alfred Potts, W. D. McKendree, Elsie Watson, Earl McKendree, Walter Peavler, Eddie Martin, and David Simpson. The clerks have been Lorene Straker, Jeanetta Mackey, Elsie Watson, Juanice Hedgepath, and Martha Heidrich. The treasurers have been Elsie Watson and Sam Travis.

In December 1984 we added on six Sunday School rooms and two restrooms. In April 1989 we black-topped the parking lot.

STURGIS CUMBERLAND PRESBYTERIAN

The Sturgis Cumberland Presbyterian Church will celebrate its Centennial Year on August 6, 1989, which makes it a year older than the City of Sturgis, which will be 100 years old in 1990.

Cumberland Presbyterianism goes back to 1810 when several ministers in the area of the Cumberland River which is now in the states of Kentucky and Tennessee made an application to be ordained into the formal ministry of the Presbyterian Church without formal education in a seminary. The early mother church was ruled by men who were "sticklers for formal education."

Therefore, the request for ordination was denied. The group which desired to be ordained without formal education and their followers formed a new Presbytery called Cumberland. In time the group became large enough to assume the name of the Cumberland Presbyterian Church.

Sturgis became the focal point for several small groups of Cumberland Presbyterians in southern Union County. The Sturgis Cumberland Presbyterian Church was established in 1889 and a house of worship was built on the present site of the First Presbyterian Church at 9th and Kelsey Street.

However, in 1906 the status of the Sturgis Church changed when the Presbyterian and Cumberland Presbyterian churches in the nation agreed to a merger of the groups in an attempt to heal the breach between themselves. However, an "anti-unionist" group in the Sturgis congregation refused to go along with the merger and left the congregation to form a new church. This pattern was followed by many CP churches throughout the South.

The immediate problem for the dissenting group of Cumberland Presbyterians was to secure a building where they might worship. A suit was filed to nullify the action of union, but the Court of Appeals in Kentucky ruled that the property at 9th and Kelsey belonged to the merged denomination.

For a time the dissidents met in a Methodist Church located on Washington Street in Sturgis, planning all the while to construct a church home for themselves. Attempts to have them merge with Methodism sped their resolve to build a new church home.

In 1909 the Cumberland Presbyterians started building a new house of worship at 5th and Main Street, and it was completed early in 1910. Costs were estimated at $6,150, including some furnishings. Before the structure was dedicated in 1910 all but $1,000 of the needed sum had been raised.

At the dedication in 1910 five elders were functioning as church leaders. They were E. B. Jones, A. L. Hoerth, John Hughes, Eugene Whitecotton, and William Wilson. Joining the Session after the dedication were newly-elected elders G. B. Simpson, J. Y. Simpson, and O. C. Quirey.

On the third Sunday in February, 1910, the Sturgis church held its first service. The church was formally dedicated during a meeting of Princeton Presbytery in April, 1910, with Rev. A. C. Biddle moderating the service.

Two major additions plus the building of a church manse have been made to the church property in its century of existence. In 1953 an Educational Building was constructed adjacent to the sanctuary. In 1982 a nearby building was purchased to be used for classrooms and a church office. This building was named for Dr. Wayne Wiman, pastor at that time.

Pastors who have served the Sturgis Cumberland Presbyterian Church since 1899 are A. C. Biddle, J. P. Halsell, R. H. Anthony, L. M. Price, O. A. Barbee, T. C. Newman, H. M. Guynn, E. K. Reagin, E. B. Coleman, Ky Curry, J. B. McCullum, G. G. Halliburton, Cordis Womack, Thomas DeVore, J. Miller Cook, Ralph Carpenter, Gayle Keown, Hugh Kelso, J. C. Womack, John Shirey, Charles Faith, Wayne Wiman, and present pastor Joe Butler.

All surviving pastors have been invited to attend the Centennial Celebration on August 6. Acceptance letters have been received from all invited pastors except one.

But God and history do not stand still. At the present time the Cumberland Presbyterian Church is in the midst of a campaign to raise funds to build a new sanctuary and to renovate the Educational and Wiman Buildings.

Leadership in the Presbyterian form of government comes from the elders elected to the Session by the membership of the church. The present elders are Ben Brinkley, Elizabeth Nunn, W. E. White, Brenda Hardesty, Jerry Hayes, Rebecca Kearney, Barbara Sutton, Katherine Christison, J. Robert Truitt, Lana Quinton, Roger Edmondson, Robin Greenwell, Greg Collins, Joe Farmer and Ed Staton. The Moderator is Pastor Joe Butler and the clerk is Fred Lamb. Church secretary and treasurer is Clara Ann Ames.

UNITED METHODIST

The Methodist Congregation in Sturgis had its origin in the Caseyville Church which was organized in 1837. For many years Caseyville was a thriving riverport on the Ohio River and the Methodist Church flourished there. The Civil War, the periodic flooding and the coming of the railroad were factors which contributed to a shift in population. Additional churches were added to the Caseyville Charge as needed.

With the support of the Caseyville Methodist Church, a Methodist Congregation was established in Commercial Point. That congregation was most likely established in 1887 under the ministry of the Rev. James S. McDaniel. The members met in a little red brick schoolhouse that stood in a field behind what is now Pecan Street in Sturgis. The Methodist Church in Sturgis is a direct outgrowth of the Commercial Point Church.

In 1891 a building Committee was organized for a church in Sturgis. Members of the building committee were: C. B. Hatfield, Fred Alloway, Sr., William Gregg, John M. Anderson, Allen Anderson, George Gill and J. H. Beard.

Under the leadership of the Rev. P. C. Duvall a Methodist Congregation was organized in Sturgis in 1893 with twenty seven members on the roll. The congregation built a frame church on Washington Street the same year.

The Rev. Pat Davis, a well known Methodist Evangelist and circuit rider, held a revival in the little church in Sturgis about 1897. Bro. Davis is the great grandfather of Doris McAfee Oaks whose husband, David is the pastor today of the Sturgis United Methodist Church.

The Methodist congregation in Sturgis grew rapidly and by the year 1911 it was apparent that a larger and more modern house of worship was needed. Under the ministry of the Rev. R. M. Wheat a building committee was appointed composed of the following members: Fred Alloway, Sr., J. M. Stone, W. C. Smith, and Mark E. Eastin. The entire official board and membership of the church rallied to their support and by the end of the year our present church on the corner of Tenth and Adams Streets was built. The total cost was $16,000.

The church was dedicated in 1913 when the building cost was paid and the church was free of debt. Bishop E. R. Hendrix presided at the dedication on August 24. The church was presented for dedication by Peter Marquardt, on behalf of the Board of Trustees.

Many of the same families from the Caseyville Methodist Church as well as those from the churches of Dekoven, Salem, Grangertown and Commercial Point are represented in our enrollment of the Sturgis United Methodist Church. The dedication of these leaders has given us a strong foundation on which to build. We have been strengthened over the year by the addition of new members from other parts of the country.

It is our hope now, in the Centennial year of Sturgis, that the example of dedication and service shown to us by our early church leaders will continue to be a source of inspiration to us in the years ahead.

Administrative Board Chairperson - Ruth Conway; Sunday School Superintendent - John Steelman. Minister—James David Oaks, Jr.

Sunday School - 9:45
Worship Service - 10:00 a.m.

Methodist Episcopal Church, 718 Washington Street, 1893-1911

CHURCH OF GOD

The Church of God of Prophecy was brought to Sturgis in 1919 by a Kentucky Evangelist, C. L. Taylor. Bro. Taylor held a tent revival on the Grangertown school yard. From that revival the Church of God was organized on July 4, 1920, with 13 charter members. Two members of that original group are still living, Atha Hultz who lives in Illinois and Anna Daily who resides in Sturgis.

The Church of God has always been reform minded. Her leaders and members are always seeking God for guidance in all things. Because of a lack of public understanding, the church experienced persecution during the 1920s. This persecution continued for several years and in December of 1928 the church was set fire and destroyed completely. Under the leadership of Clara Miller Reese, the church met in the old Bell Building on Adams Street until a building could be completed on Commercial Point. The Church of God grew and prospered as it began to be accepted and by 1939 the membership grew to the point that once again a move was made, this time to Monroe Street in Sturgis. Property was bought from P. B. and Clara Waller and in 1940 the building was completed while Clara Reese was pastor. The church met in this building for 43 years. During that time there were many building additions and many souls were won to the Lord. In 1983, under the leadership of Kenneth Abrams, the church once again saw the need for larger facilities and a new church was built on Hwy. 60. The work of many members and friends of the church can be seen as anyone enters Sturgis. During the church's time in Sturgis there have been approximately 23 pastors to serve the people. At first the pastors were elected, but later on the Church of God adopted the Appointment system. All leaders, from the International Offices down to the local offices, are appointed and are subject to change every year. The Church of God is located in all 50 states and in over 80 foreign nations. As result of the number of ministers and other church works that have been sent out from our local congregation, Sturgis, Kentucky is known all over the world. Also the Sturgis church is known as the Mother church to several congregations in our area. Henderson, Morganfield, Marion, Wheatcroft and Providence. We feel that our church, like Sturgis, has gotten better over the years, and we have our eyes on the future to continue to grow and serve our city. We are serving God as we serve and help meet the needs in our community.

FIRST BAPTIST, GRANGERTOWN

The First Baptist Church of Grangertown was started as a mission of the First Baptist Church of Sturgis after a series of meetings conducted by Rev. J. R. Kelley.

On February 18, 1919, nine members of the First Baptist Church of Sturgis, Rev. Kelley and Rev. H. H. Wallace, pastor of the home church, met with 16 who formed the original church. Seven joined by transfer of letters and nine by baptism.

In 1920, a church home on the bank of Tradewater River was started and completed in 1922. Services in the little church were monthly until 1949 when preaching twice a month began. This continued until 1952 when the church voted to go fulltime. By this time, it was necessary to remodel the one-room building and add five Sunday School rooms. This was completed September 9, 1961. Again it was

necessary to enlarge and ten more rooms were added in 1963. Then the church voted to relocate on Highway 109. Dedication services were December, 1976. In 1985, the church purchased a parsonage, also on Highway 109.

Rev. Kelley preached from February 18, 1919 until September 23, 1922. Pastors succeeding him were: E. C. Woodall, 1923-41; N. B. Sizemore, 1942-51; John Coble, 1951-56; James R. Brown, 1956-57; R. Truett Miller, 1958, interim 3 months; Charles Harris, 1958-62; Charles Simmons, 1963-65 and Donald J. Collins, 1965.

In 1989, on the 70th year of the church, there are 361 resident members and 94 non-resident members. Value of the church property is $310,000.

Quoting from a letter from Mrs. Mabel Kelley, 1952, "I am glad you are so interested in missionary work. That is really the work Jesus organized the church for - to go into all the world and let everyone know they have a Saviour. He gave us that commission nearly 2000 years ago."

FIRST BAPTIST, STURGIS

First Baptist Church
Eighth & Adams Streets
Sturgis, KY 42459
333-2691

Sunday
Sunday School 9:45 am
Morning Worship 11:00 am
Evening Worship 7:00 pm

Wednesday
Bible Study 7:00 pm

The First Baptist Church of Sturgis was organized on December 6, 1888, in the Odd Fellows Hall, located on the second floor of the corner building on Adams and Sixth Street.

There were thirteen charter members, and in 1889, the church reported 23 members with $100.00 a year set aside for the pastor's salary.

The lot for the church building was donated in April 1890 by Col. Jordan Giles, a founder of the city of Sturgis.

By 1914 the church had outgrown the original white frame church. It was torn down and in 1915 a new white brick building was erected.

In 1947 additional property was purchased and in 1951 the first educational building was occupied.

In 1964 the church voted to build a second educational building and, when feasible, to build a new sanctuary where the old one then stood. The cornerstone to the new educational building was laid in 1965, and in 1971 the new sanctuary was dedicated.

Down through the years the church has grown and prospered from the first thirteen members that met in an upstairs room over a bank to the modern church complex that is now used for worship, Bible study, and ministry through music, mission study, recreation, and fellowship. Whatever one's age, FBC of Sturgis is a place to worship, study and serve.

ST. FRANCIS BORGIA

St. Francis Borgia Church was dedicated September 30, 1952, by the Most Reverend Francis R. Cotton, D. D., Bishop of Owensboro, Kentucky. The name of the church stems from the donors, Mr. and Mrs. F. L. Lewis, through the Catholic Extension Society.

The church structure, on the corner of 13th and Adams Street was built on property donated by the James L. Long family and has a seating capacity of 168 persons. In the beginning, St. Francis was a mission of St. Ann's Church in Morganfield.

In 1963, the rectory was added and in 1969, the Parish Hall was built. An addition of 3,760 square feet, a joint effort of St. Francis and St. Ambrose, was added to the Parish Hall in the fall of 1986.

The first Sunday Mass was celebrated on October 5, 1952. The first

marriage was between James L. Long and Nancy McDonald, October 11, 1952. The first baptism was James David Conn on October 19, 1952. The first Holy Communion Class was May 31, 1953 and the first

funeral was for Catherine Ann Mills, infant daughter of Jim Fred and Martha Mills.

The current pastor is Fr. Albert A. Reed, C. PP. S., appointed September 1, 1989.

STURGIS BAPTIST

The Sturgis Baptist Church which was originally named the Tabernacle Missionary Baptist Church was established on December 9, 1934 with sixty-eight members and the pastor being W. W. Bullis.

The members met at the New Princess Theater until a church could be built. Mr. and Mrs. C. W. Pugh deeded the church lot on Adams Street which is the present church site. The new church was completed in 1937 and the first worship service was held in it on Easter Sunday.

The old hotel property being adjacent to the church was purchased and used as an Educational Building. A parsonage was purchased at 1121 N. Main Street in 1943.

The name of the church was changed from the Tabernacle Missionary Baptist Church to the Sturgis Baptist Church in 1962.

The former pastors include: W. W. Bullis, Harry A. Ross, John W. Kloss, Charles H. Warford, J. T. Hall, and I. Houston Lanier.

In 1968 C. C. Hinton became pastor and in 1970 under his leadership the church left the Southern Baptist Convention to become an Independent Missionary Baptist Church.

On November 24, 1970 the church building was destroyed by fire. Members then met in the old Pugh's Variety Store building, until a new church could be built. The church was completed and dedication ceremonies were held on August 15, 1971.

C. C. Hinton was the pastor until 1973 when Bob W. Watson became pastor. He was the pastor until 1982 when Herbert Williamson became pastor.

The fall of 1983 the Sturgis Christian School was established using the A.C.E. curriculum.

A Fellowship Hall was built the same year and dedication ceremonies were held on September 4, 1983. It was named in honor of senior deacon Wesley Heffington Jr.

In 1986 the church purchased property at 1117 N. Main Street to house Mr. and Mrs. Phillip Braddy, who teach at the Sturgis Christian School.

The same year over 49 acres of land was purchased in Mack's Creek, Missouri for the establishment of the Mack's Boarding School for Troubled Youth.

In July of 1988 the church purchased the Bible Church property in old Shawneetown, Illinois and a mission was started called the Old Shawneetown Baptist Mission with Paul Skinner preaching. Services are held twice a week.

The Sturgis Baptist Church has to date 109 members and supports over 40 mission projects monthly with the total of over $63,000 given in missions last year. There are also two church families serving as missionaries on a foreign field, Mr. and Mrs. Paul Pritchard in Brazil, and Mr. and Mrs. Gordon Downs in Canada.

Matthew 16:18 says "...upon this rock I will build my church; and the gates of hell shall not prevail against it." To God be all praise, honor and glory!

STURGIS CHURCH OF CHRIST

The Sturgis Church of Christ was first envisioned in the fall of 1961 when four families from rural congregations decided there were some advantages to meeting in town. It was hoped that in this way the needs of more people would be more easily served. On January 7, 1962 services were first held at the American Legion building on Monroe.

Those families present for that first service included those of Darrell Kanipe, Harry Brown, Benny Griggs, Roy O'Leary, Bobby Griggs, Noble Denton, Prentice Troutman, Robert West, Mrs. Betty O'Neal, and Edd Finch. Brother Finch served as minister for the group and for three years they met weekly at the American Legion Hall.

In 1964 the group bought the property at the corner of Eighth and Monroe and began a building program. They met in their new building the first Sunday of 1965. Rolls show that 35 met for Bible Study and 70 for worship that first Sunday. They continue to worship in that same auditorium.

Edd Finch continued to Preach for the congregation until late in 1971 at

which time the church bought a house and Elwood Jones was hired as minister. Brother Jones continued with the church until he became ill in 1974. In the fall of that year he was forced to give up work and Daniel Askew came to preach for the congregation. He continues with them in 1989.

In 1980 a group of six or seven families left the Sturgis congregation and began a new work in Morganfield. Among this group were Charles Miller and Bill Kimble who had served as the first elders of the Sturgis congregation.

With the full support of the Sturgis Church of Christ the Morganfield congregation stands now ready to serve that community.

An addition to the building was begun in 1986 and completed in 1987. This addition enabled the congregation to have ample classroom space as well as providing a multipurpose room for large church groups and activities.

During all its history the church has held God's word and allegiance to it as our prime objective. And so may it ever continue. *Submitted by Daniel Askew*

DeKOVEN CHURCH OF CHRIST

Services were first held in an old school house in Independence Valley about a mile from Dekoven in 1902. The first building was located on a hillside just north of the existing building on land donated by Mr. Henry Rehm in 1905.

In 1949 Mrs. Jim Boettiger offered the present site to the congregation for the taxes due upon it. Members donated their skills and time to build the church. Some labor was paid in cash, and the total cost was about $8,000.00. Here at the junction of Highways 1508 and 492 services were held in the simple frame building for the first time on February 5, 1950, by Lawrence Taylor of Henderson, Tennessee. Attendance at that service was 39, with membership reaching high in the 60's.

Some historical comparisons were noted in a crumbling record book dated July 31, 1904, to July 31, 1905. Receipts were $30.26 with $11.08 paid to a Brother Black for unspecified services, and operating costs included a dime for coal oil for the lamps, 35 cents for a bucket and a nickel for a dipper.

Changes to the building over the years included the addition of classrooms, a baptistry, restrooms, and exterior brick.

Decisions were made by the members to start congregations in Sturgis and in Morganfield, so the nucleus for these endeavors came from the Dekoven congregation.

Many men have filled the pulpit. At present the minister is Alan Stanley who comes to the church on Sunday morning for Bible study, the Lord's Supper, and preaching.

Although the membership is small, the church still supports a half-hour radio program on W.M.S.K. at Morganfield. They also support the "ChildPlace" program at Jeffersonville, Indiana, and sponsor several missionaries in foreign fields. *Submitted by Catherine Omer*

MT. STERLING CUMBERLAND PRESBYTERIAN

The Mt. Sterling Cumberland Presbyterian Church is located on the corner of Seventh and Like Streets, Sturgis, KY. It was originally constructed there in 1890 at the crossroads. In 1909 plans to build another church were laid out with completion in the year 1913. This church was hit by three floods with the flood of 1937 being the worst. The water almost completely covered the church and did much damage. All of this contributed to the deterioration of the building, and eventually to the plans and preparation of a new church would become a reality 75 years later. (Today!)

The new, present church was constructed and dedicated August 27, 1988. Persons who served as committeemen and who worked out the plans and details for the new church were: Sharon Combs, chairperson, George Greenwell, treasurer, Margaret Burks, secretary, Robert Greenwell, Larry Burton and Elliott Shelton. These persons are also the Church Trustees along with its elder and deacons.

The oldest member of Mt. Ster-

ling is Sister Christine Shelton, who is also the church historian. She came over with the church from "Crossroads." Another cornerstone of the church is sister Beluah Greenwell. She has been like "Mother Greenwell" to every child and adult in Mt. Sterling. Every member of Mt. Sterling has really been supportive. We have worked very hard.

A list of the pastors for Mt. Sterling is as follows, beginning with Rev. Oscar Powell, Sr., our present pastor, Rev. Clark, Rev Hardison, Rev. Riley, Rev. Kersey, Rev. Richards, Rev. Tinsley, Rev. Ray and Rev. Shelby Garnett.

Mt. Sterling is very proud of the progress which it has made over the past years. God has truly been good to its flock there. We, as a membership, are proud to be a part of the great history of this book. *Submitted by Sharon Combs.*

NEW SALEM BAPTIST

The New Salem Baptist Church was organized in 1896 under the leadership of the Rev. Willie Lewis. The floods of 1913 destroyed the church building, then located in Crittenden County; the Rev. Garret was minister. In July 1913 fire drove parishioners from downtown churches in Sturgis, when flames leveled all buildings on Main Street between Fifth and Sixth Streets.

In that year, New Salem Baptist Church relocated to Sturgis and first met in a tent in the vicinity of Sixth and Monroe Streets. Property was acquired on Sixth Street for a church site and the present church was buildt in 1921, during the ministry of the Rev. J. F. Drone. Dedication services were on June 22, 1924 under the direction of Pastor G. W. Coleman.

Pastors has included the Reverends C. L. Ward, L. W. Jackson, Gaines, Haskins and Grinstead.

Those ordained among the congregation were the Reverends William Tyler, Sam Reed, Burt Nichols and Lawrence Howard.

Deacons have been Jim Barner, Manzello Wallace, Jim Ed Wallace, Curtis Williams, Preston Ward, Elmo Alvis, Herman Garnett, Leonard Moore, Luther Tapp, Eugene Lawrence, Gabe Summers and Marshall Hughes.

Many improvements have been made through the years by the active and dedicated members.

The present pastor is the Rev. Frank Cowan and the oldest church members is Mattie Willis, who celebrated her 102nd birthday this year. *Material provided by Mrs. Velorice Cole. Submitted by Joel Felts-Williams.*

E.M.B.A. building, erected by West Kentucky Coal Company in the early 1920s.

Farmers S
Sturgis,

PLATE V

FRANCES KNIGHT WEЦS

F. Wells

te Bank

Kentucky

Businesses, Organizations and Tributes

Al Shipley
"Grocer"

Staple and Fancy Groceries   *Courteous Treatment*

We appreciate your patronage

STURGIS, KY   **PHONE 106**

OUR POLICY

FIRST: To Carry Merchandise of Good Quality

SECOND: To Sell at Small Profit

Third: To Give Our Customers Polite Attention
and a Square Deal

93

Farmers State Bank

In the year 1913 the present site of the Farmers State Bank was occupied by the First National Bank of Sturgis, Kentucky. During that year the entire business block was destroyed by fire. After the fire, the First National Bank of Sturgis was rebuilt on the same location. On August 10, 1916, the First National Bank of Sturgis was sold and rechartered as the Farmers State Bank of Sturgis, Kentucky.

Many people may not know that there was also a Bank of Sturgis operating on the corner of Sixth & Adams Streets. On July 1, 1937, the Bank of Sturgis merged with the Farmers State Bank.

The building with its beautiful columns remained the same until 1940. The interior was changed by adding modern fixtures, and in 1950 the bank underwent a complete remodeling and offices were built onto the front. A new facade in 1954 gave the institution a more contemporary appearance and started a wave of improvements on the city's main business thoroughfare. In 1958 additional interior improvements were made and a new acoustical ceiling with recessed lighting was installed.

By 1963 the bank had acquired the building formerly occupied by the Sturgis Specialty Shop, thus doubling the floor space of the bank. The wall that divided the buildings was torn out and a complete remodeling and refurnishing again took place on the inside. It was at this time that the full glass front and vertical metal louvers were constructed. The old Red Front Grocery was acquired in 1976 and converted into the present Loan Department, giving much needed space in the rear for our Bookkeeping Department.

In keeping with the time, Farmers State Bank opened a Drive-In facility on the corner of Fifth and Main in 1967. Traffic increased so much in the next decade around this facility that in 1977 a better location at the north end of Main Street was acquired and a new Drive-In Branch was opened that summer.

Representative of the continuity of our growth is the fact that we remained a solvent and growing institution even through the Depression years of 1929 to 1935. Beginning with an original capitalization of $25,000, it is interesting to look at the Statements of Condition throughout the years and track the growth to the present $57,000,000 (as of 1989) in assets. The Farmers State Bank many times takes a leading role in civic functions and encourages the support of the local community.

In March of 1984 a one-bank holding company, the Farmers BanCorp of Sturgis, Inc., was formed and acquired 100 percent of the outstanding shares of the Farmers State Bank. The same Directors serve on both the bank and the holding company Board of Directors.

The original officers and directors are: Chairman of the Board, J. B. Holeman; President and Trust Officer, Garland Certain; Executive Vice President, Billy Joe Evans; Vice President, I. Dix Winston; Cashier, Charles N. Wells; Vice President, Gary Logan; Vice President, Greg Collins; Vice President and Assistant Trust Officer, Ruth Conway; Assistant Cashier, Janice Adamson; Assistant Cashier, Betty Lamb; Branch Manager, Connie Shaffer; and Marketing Officer, Sandy Arnold; Directors are: Charles Pyro, Jr., I. Dix Winston, J. B. Holeman, James D. Syers, Robert E. Morgan, William R. Sprague, Joseph Sprague, Billy Joe Evans, and Slaton Sprague.

Morganfield National Bank
Sturgis Branch

Our Sturgis Branch opened as a full service branch bank March 25, 1977. Located just north of Sturgis on U.S. 60 the modern facility offers all bank services as a walk-in bank plus the added conveniences of a drive-in bank with two drive-in windows. A community room is also available to serve the needs of area civic groups and organizations.

Bank Staff include: Fred Q. Alloway - Manager and Assistant Cashier, Anna Chambliss - Assistant Manager and Assistant Cashier, Melanie Collins - Teller, Joy Engle - Teller, Tara Benfield - Teller.

BANKING HOURS
Mon.-Thursday—8:30 am—4 pm
Friday—8:30 am—5:30 pm
Saturday—8:30 am-12 noon
Branches only
Member FDIC

MORGANFIELD NATIONAL BANK

MEMBER OLD NATIONAL BANCORP
130 North Morgan • Morganfield, KY 42437

Pyro Mining Company

Pyro Mining Company Offices, Sturgis Airport

Pyro Mining Company has operated under many names as well as several owners since coal was first extracted from its holdings in Hopkins, Union, and Webster Counties over 40 years ago.

Pyro began its operations in Webster and Union Counties in 1963 when its owner expanded into a strip miner operation in Wheatcroft, Kentucky; opened its Pyro Number 1 underground mine and established Pyro Mining Company. The administrative offices and other facilities were situated on the Webster/Union County line where the operations office and three preparation plants are still located. The underground operation of Pyro Number 1 mine proved to be a profitable undertaking, and its success led to the development of Pyro Number 2 and Pyro Number 9 mines during the early part of the 1970s. In 1976, Pyro was bought by a large corporation with its accompanying new management team.

The growth and expansion of Pyro really began in 1978 when the newly assigned management team put together the first of a series of five-year plans. Over the years, these plans have developed from projections to realities. For instance, Pyro now used conventional, continuous miners an a longwall machine to extract coal from the Number 9 seam in Webster and Union Counties. Reserves are also available in the Number 6, 11 and 13 seams. Three preparation plants for washing and blending coal and a pellet plant, for transforming previously difficult to handle coal fines into easily handled stoker size pellets are in operation.

Pyro has ready access to transportation through its affiliated company Tradewater Railway, and through its modern dock facility on the Ohio River just South of Caseyville, Kentucky. From these facilities it provides quality coal to major utilities in the Tennessee valley and throughout the southeastern United States.

During the late 1970s the different departments and offices were operated from trailers and small buildings, and in 1981 many of its offices were located in Sullivan. In December 1984, the newly completed Headquarters Building located at the Sturgis Airport and Industrial Park was occupied by the Administrative Departments of Pyro Mining Company, and Sturgis became headquarters for one of the largest coal companies in Kentucky.

At the present time Pyro employs approximately 1,000 employees, produces approximately 6 million tons of coal annually and produces an annual payroll of approximately $35,000,000.

Saturn Machine & Welding Company, Inc.

Saturn Machine is the major designer and manufacture of coke oven end closure and end closure cleaning systems in North America. Saturn, owned by William Ray Baird and his son, Billy Carr, was established in 1964 at the Sturgis Airport.

Since 1964 Saturn has serviced several industries including the local underground coal mines. The major effort has been toward the design and development of equipment to contain toxic emissions at coke oven plants that operate in conjunction with steel mills.

Saturn designed coke oven equipment including doors, door cleaners, jamb cleaners, door extractors, and standpipe lids have been provided to most all of the major steel producers in the United States and Canada. A small amount of Saturn equipment is also in operation in the Federal Republic of Germany.

Saturn holds both domestic and foreign patents on several items of equipment. The development and introduction of innovative coke oven equipment, to include a computer controlled jamb cleaner and an emission proof coke oven door, has helped Saturn gain international recognition as a leader in the area of controlling toxic emissions at coke plants.

The Saturn facility comprises approximately 40,000 square feet of production and office space equipped with the latest computerized engineering and production machinery. Saturn's location at the Sturgis Airport has served in many ways to enhance its growth and prosperity.

Saturn averages approximately 45 employees which represent its greatest asset.

Sturgis Pharmacy

1900-1989

Kearney and James L. Long purchased the pharmacy from Mr. Cason's daughters and heirs, Dorothy and Juliet. Mr. Kearney and Mr. Long changed the name of the business to Sturgis Pharmacy.

One year later Virgil Kearney purchased J. L. Long's interest in the business and continued to operate the Sturgis Pharmacy until July 1, 1963 when he sold one-half interest to Thomas Roe Frazer, pharmacist, from Marion, Kentucky. Tom Roe is the son of Ted Frazer, one of the previous owners of the drug store from 1925-1927.

Virgil and Tom worked together for six months at which time Virgil became a silent partner in the business for two years.

Thomas Frazer purchased Virgil Kearney's interest on January 1, 1966 and continues to own and operate the Sturgis Pharmacy as a full service drug store.

"Thank you" to Lawrence Holt, Virgil Kearney and Dennis Kirchner for their collaboration to an accurate, chronological history of the Sturgis Pharmacy.

Eastin Seagraves opened Seagraves Drug Store somewhere around 1900. He owned and operated the drug store until his death in 1923. Following the death of her husband, Mrs. Seagraves employed Vernon Royster who managed the business for two years.

In September 1925, three men from Marion, Kentucky formed a partnership and purchased Seagraves Drug Store from Mrs. Seagraves. Gleaford Rankin, Ted Frazer and George Orme, all pharmacists, owned and operated the store until February 1930 as Rankin Drug Company. Mr. Rankin managed the drug store and Mr. Orme and Mr. Frazer were silent partners.

The Rankin Drug Company was sold to S. M. Jenkins February 27, 1930. Mr. Jenkins renamed the business "The Golden Rule Pharmacy" and operated the pharmacy for two years.

West Kentucky Coal Company bought the "Golden Rule Pharmacy" from S. M. Jenkins in 1932 and employed Malcom Cason, a pharmacist from Paducah, to manage the business. The drug store was renamed WesKo Pharmacy.

Twelve years later, in January 1944, Malcom Cason and Waverly Robards, a pharmacist from Madisonville, purchased the WesKo Pharmacy and changed the name to "The R-C Pharmacy." The business was operated in this manner until 1947.

In 1947 Malcom Cason bought out Waverly Robards interest and continued to operate the store under its new name "Cason's Pharmacy."

Virgil Kearney came to work for Mr. Cason in November 1945 and continued in his employ until his death in August 1954.

After Mr. Cason's death Virgil

1970

Sturgis Pharmacy
523 Adams
Sturgis, KY
Since 1963
Tom Roe Frazer, Pharmacist

Patricia's Country Clothes
517 Adams
Downtown Sturgis, KY
Patricia Frazer, Manager
Specializing in Ladies' Clothing

Whitsell Funeral Home

Whitsell Funeral Home was established in 1921 by J. F. Whitsell. Located in the Sturgis Masonic Building on Washington Street. In 1929 J. N. Whitsell joined the staff and in 1935 the Morganfield Funeral Home was opened. The two funeral homes have been in operation ever since.

The new facility in Sturgis was opened in 1970.

The Bargain Barn

Furniture—Waterbed, and Mattress Outlet

517 Adams Street
Sturgis, Kentucky.

Guaranteed lowest prices on all name brand home furnishings.
Save everyday 30% to 70% off retail prices.

Queen Annes—Regular $289.60 our price $169.00.

Recliners—Name brands, always a large selection, $89.00—$289.00.

Dining Room Suites—$99.00 to $599.00 over 50 different styles and finishes.

Bedroom groups starting at $199.00

Also a large selection of Lamps, Sectionals, Bookcases, Gun cabinets, Waterbeds, Entertainment centers.

Bargain Barn will beat any competitor's price on all name brand furniture.
We also offer free delivery, 90 days same as cash, financing, along with instant credit. Layaway for your shopping convenience. If you have any questions, or problems, we'll be here to help you personally and promptly.

Tommy & Kathy Fulkerson, Owners of Bargain Barn

Brown's Welding Service

L. to R. William Brown, Sr., Wm. E "Pete" Brown and Wm. "Bill" Brown

In 1938 William Brown, Sr. purchased a small blacksmith shop in Sturgis from Farmers State Bank. Mr. Brown, a Clay resident, sold his team of horses, which he used on his small Webster County farm, to purchase the business.

In 1964, after serving in World War II, William "Bill" Brown, Jr. came to work with his father.

After William's death Bill continued to operate the expanding and changing business. They were doing more welding and farm equipment repair and less blacksmith work.

In 1964, William Ellis "Pete" came to work with his father in the business. Expansion has been more rapid in the past twenty-five years. There are now twelve employees at Brown's Welding Service.

Hites' Imperial Printing

Congratulations to the past and present residents of Sturgis for a job well done in making Sturgis what it is today, and best wishes to the future caretakers of this beautiful community. Thank you so much for being our friends through the years.

Bob and Jane Hite, Owners

Staff: Rachel Collins, Tom Hite and Francis French

Hite's Imperial Printing
Court Street at 128
Morganfield, KY 42437

Holts

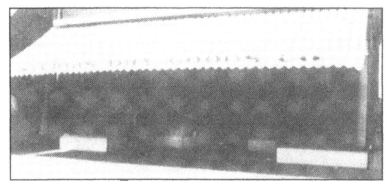

From 1982 . . . to 1990
Serving Union County for 98 Years

Holts Department Store, Sturgis

Holts Furniture, Sturgis

Holts Department Store, Morganfield

Minesafe Electronics, Inc.

Minesafe Electronics was started in 1975 primarily to service the local mines in this area. We service the electronic safety equipment used in the mines. Mine communications equipment is manufactured in our facility and sold through distributors to the major mining areas in the East and West. FM Two-way radio equipment is sold and serviced for many farmers, public service organizations and businesses in this area. After 14 years in business Minesafe Electronics is striving to maintain our present markets and diversify into other fields in electronics.

Quinn Lumber & Building Materials Co.

Whitfield, Mike Gorman, Tommy Markham, Rod Pogue, Jeff Brooks, Kim Davis and Carl Thurmond. Charlie's daughter, Teresa Quinn Vaughn and son-in-law, Bruce Humphrey manage the company.

Charlie Quinn married Betty Newcom and they have four children: Becky, Teresa, Lisa and Charlie Wayne. Charlie Quinn died October 31, 1988.

Charlie Quinn started working at the Alloway Lumber Company in 1947 and worked his way to the position of Manager and Plans Estimator. Charlie opened the Charlie Quinn Lumber Company and Building Materials on July 1, 1971, carrying a full line of building materials.

Charlie began with the following employees: Wayne Armstrong, Shelby Garnett, Betty Newcom, John McCollum, Eddie Bealmear and Virginia Borders. Current employees are: Wayne Armstrong, Bob

In Memory
Charlie Quinn

George B. Simpson

Attorney at Law

Available are biographies and social and church history:
(by George B. Simpson unless otherwise stated)

Rev. John Withers - Baptist (1811-1858) - $14.95
Rev. W. W. Wynn - Cumberland Presbyterian (1839-1900) - $19.95
Rev. J. T. Barbee - Cumberland Presbyterian (1838-1921) - $19.95
Judge Peter Casey (1760-1825) (Union County) - $19.95
Cypress Creek Christian Church and Cemetery List (1833-1859) - $14.95
Mt. Ephriam Cumberland Presbyterian Church and Session Minutes (1833-1880) - $19.95
Memories of Eighty Years (1821-1905) by Judge George Huston - $14.95
Early Union County Roads - $5.00
Early Union County Militia - $5.00
Volume I - Caseyville River Merchant Trade/Sale Records (1854-55) - $37.50
Volume II - Caseyville River Merchant Trade/Sale Records (1854-55) - $37.50
From Pride Station to Pond Fork to One Eye Ridge (1930 to 1955 in South Union County) - $24.95
From Heath Mountain to Anvil Rock and The Bell's Mine Clerk Records and Notes (early coal mining on the Tradewater River) - $24.95
Abe Lincoln's 1840 Kentucky Political Speech and the Whig Presidential Campaign to 1840 in Southern Illinois - $24.95
From Blueberry Hill to Sturgis to Blind Mule Crossing (1930 to 1955 in South Union County) $24.95

514 Adams Street
P. O. Box 303
Sturgis, KY 42459

Office—(502) 333-5337

George B. Simpson, wife, Sandra and children, Will and Jeannie.

V. I. Soni, MD

Office: Highway 60 North

Congratulations Sturgis!

Sureway Grocery

Congratulations Sturgis on your 100th Birthday

We're glad to be a part of the community. Having served this area for 25 years. Quality meats, fruits, vegetables, and dairy products.

Sturgis Clothing Company

The clothing factory in Sturgis, located at 6th and Main, was first realized when several businessmen banded together in what was known as the Sturgis Industrial Corporation, raised $18,000 among themselves and interested a Mr. Mercer Lowery and some associates to come here and start a pants factory. Their first production payroll was March, 1946. The following year, the Richman Brothers Company of Cleveland, Ohio—one of the nation's largest manufacturers of mens clothing—became interested in the plant and began operating here. In 1969, F. W. Woolsworth Company bought the Richman enterprise and it is now known as Richman/Anderson-Little - the latter plant is in Fall River, Massachusetts.

Richman's sent Mr. Earl Runkel to Sturgis to superintend the plant. He retired in 1963 and was followed by Burtis Christison. Since his retirement in 1977, the plant has been managed by Dan O'Leary.

The plant draws its work force primarily from Union County with additional employees coming from Crittenden and Webster Counties. The plant is the city's largest industry and adds much to the economy. The company offers many benefits, including vacations, pensions, life insurance and other opportunities.

For many years, the original part of the factory building was used as a garage and during World War II was a USO Center for men and women of the 83rd Division located at Camp Breckinridge, Morganfield and 101 Airborne Division. In the early part of the century parts for Model T Fords were shipped by rail to the local depot, transported to this building and assembled. After the war the building was turned into a Youth Center.

Since 1947, the building has been

remodeled and expansions added in 1959, and 1983. Many inside improvements have been made and the latest in pressing and sewing equipment acquired.

Richman/Anderson-Little sells its products only through their own stores which number approximately three-hundred throughout the United States.

The Sturgis News

Thornsberry Insurance Agency, Inc.

Thornsberry Insurance is probably the oldest continuously operated agency in Union County. The agency was started by D. A. Brook, Jr. and Company in Caseyville in conjunction with his wharfboat coal dealer and U. S. Mail business. At that time he represented Aetna Fire and Inland Insurance Companys.

The agency was later moved to Sturgis and Mr. James L. Long became an affiliate. Mr. A. L. Thornsberry joined Mr. Long after World War II and remained a partner until the time of Mr. Long's death.

Willis Thornsberry and Gary Thornsberry merged with A. L. Thornsberry in 1973. The agency then merged with Milton Pullen Agency in 1977, and in the Riggs Agency in 1981.

The agency now is a market for several companies, including automobile, homeowner, commercial fire, inland marine, excess liability, bonds, life and health, commercial liability and aviation.

Whitehead Electric Co.

Congratulations, Sturgis on your 100th year!

*Celebrating
25 years
of service . . .*

Whitehead
Electric Co.
Sturgis, KY

Arnold Chiropractic

Chiropractic is the second largest health care industry in Kentucky and in the nation. The term chiropractic was coined back in the 1800s by a man named D. D. Palmer. Chiro is a Greek term for hands, and practic is a term for to practice. Therefore, the chiropractic uses his hands to manipulate or adjust the spine and all related tissue. However, manipulation was used during the times of kings and great philosophers. For example Hippocrates wrote "in disease look to the spine."

In 1916 the first professional chiropractic organization was started in Kentucky. In the early 1930s chiropractic was introduced to Sturgis by Dr. A. E. Niese (Doc). In 1970 after graduating from college and spending two years in the U. S. Army Dr. John A. Arnold, Jr. (Dr. John) became associated with Dr. Niese. Dr. Niese and Dr. Arnold were both active in civic, local, and state organizations and also worked to see that their patients receive similar benefits as patients of other health providers.

Dr. John Arnold would like to congratulate all the fine people who have worked on this centennial publication. Thanks.

Buzzard's Cafe

Buzzard's Cafe, formerly known as City Cafe, was opened in 1976.

Ann and Ricky McPherson own and operate the business. Their three children, Preston Buzzard, Brian Buzzard, Jennifer Buzzard Ratley and grandchild, Ashley Ratley all very much a part of this family place.

The cafe is located at the Four Way stop at Main and 5th Streets in Sturgis. Many activities are scheduled throughout the year: music, flea markets, and the Amish selling their goods.

We try to present a friendly place to our town. Fourteen years of business has given us lots of good memories and lots of friends. Many who have come and gone will always be remembered. Thanks for your years of business.

Kentucky Utilities

Kentucky Utilities Company, of Lexington, Kentucky, purchased the electrical system of Sturgis in 1926 from West Kentucky Electric Power Company. At the time of purchase, the population of Sturgis was 2,154. Kentucky Utilities Company provided twenty-four hour electric service through a steam generating plant.

The K.U. office in Sturgis was located on Adams Street and was moved to its present location at 415 Main Street in 1969. The property for the new office building was purchased from the City of Sturgis. At the time of purchase, the Police Department and Fire Station were located on the property.

Former Managers of Kentucky Utilities were: W. W. Whitfield, Harold Blanks, Inas Stallins, Henry Moss, R. W. Burrow, Maurice D. Mills, John S. Williams and Ken Sheridan. The present manager is Robert D. Teague, who is also District Manager of the Morganfield District.

J. & J Service Center

On December 17, 1986, John and Mary Anna Ashby purchased the Service Center located on 1425 North Main Street, at Public Auction.

The service station was built by Sam and Bill Sizemore in the late 1940s or early 1950s.

In June 1988 the Ashby's son-in-law, Chris Glazebrook joined the business.

They offer complete auto repair with friendly and courteous service.

John, Mary Anna, Kathy (their daughter), and Chris appreciate the fact that you, the public, have helped to make the business successful.

COME VISIT US FOR YOUR AUTO REPAIR

Kozy Kitchen

The Kozy Kitchen Restaurant was established on March 15, 1989, by David and Cheryl Farthing.

Kozy Kitchen, 511 Adams Street, downtown Sturgis, features a country-home type atmosphere with breakfast, hot and cold sandwiches, salads, pies, and hot plate lunches.

Kozy Kitchen is operated by the Farthings, along with their sons, Jason and David and four employees Jill Stone, Betty Blackburn, Mary Crawford and Wanda Mudd.

The building which houses the restaurant underwent major renovations beginning in October of 1988.

Many different businesses were located here. Beginning with Sturgis Grocery Company and Rudy's Bakery. Others which followed were Advance Refrigeration, Pete's T.V., Mike's Lawn and Garden, Family Video, and U. C. Movies Galore.

Kozy Kitchen invites you to come by and visit and dine with us.

Land-O-Nan
(Now Circle-O-Farm Center)

Land-O-Nan Warehouse was conceived and began in Nov. 1949. It began in the old Sturgis Implement and Hardware store warehouse on Kelsey, owned by Garve Davis and Edd O'Nan, Sr. Its was started by Edward O'Nan, Jr. with seed cleaning and bag fertilizer the main items of service. In 1950 a contract was signed by Edward O'Nan on the old Standard Oil Plant on 2nd and Monroe. This was the first fertilizer blending plant built in Kentucky. In 1955 O'Nan purchased the old Sturgis Ice Plant and the seed cleaning equipment was moved there. The business expanded and a Hot Mix Liquid Fertilizer Plant was built in Morganfield, also a first liquid plant in Kentucky.

In 1964 the Spencer Chemical Co. purchased the assets of Land-O-Nan and then Gulf Oil Corp. purchased Spencer. After a few years the Morganfield and Sturgis plants merged and is now at a location between Morganfield and Sturgis near the Union County High School.

In 1972, after Edward O'Nan had left Gulf Oil, Circle-O-Farm Center was born in Marion and then moved a branch to Sturgis in 1975 in the Ice Plant. Circle-O-Farm Center is still in operation managed by Dennis O'Nan, the oldest son of Edward O'Nan.

Meacham Hams, Inc.

Founder William Meacham began curing country hams and bacon for farm workers and family in the 1930s; using the process that was handed down to him by his Grandmother Meacham.

In 1948, William moved to the present location near Sturgis, and constructed a small concrete block building for curing hams in 1960. Hams sales grew to 300 hams per year and in 1970 the plant was expanded to a capacity of 1500 per year.

In 1982, the firm was incorporated and William's son, Rodman joined the business after graduating from the University of Kentucky. Plant expansion continued to accommodate growing sales.

Today, Meacham Hams, Inc. occupies approximately 6000 square feet. Projected production should reach 10,000 country hams by 1990. In addition, a full line of country meat products; including bacon, sausages, smoked cheese and smoked turkeys is marketed nationwide.

Mill's Florist

Before there was a florist in Sturgis, Tib Nunn was an agent for Shaw's Flower Shop of Henderson, Kentucky. Orders for small arrangements were delivered by Shaw's to Tib's home. Large arrangements were delivered to Tib's Newstand; Tib then delivered these flowers on her bicycle. The first florist in Sturgis was known as The Sturgis Flower Shop. It was started in 1946 by Belle Jenkins in the home of her sister Cora Lee Lamb. In 1949 the business was moved to Mrs. Jenkin's home on Kelsey Street where it remained until 1958 when it was relocated to its current location on Adams St. Mrs. Jenkins married C. J. (Buck) Brown and sold the business to Maurice and Bessie Mills on January 1, 1972. The florist was renamed Mills Florist and is still operating today under Bessie's management and the help of her daughter Nancy Berry and Mary Ashby. Also helping are Belle Brown (former owner,) Joyce Grounds, Norma Jean Collins and daughters, Donna Hollis and Connie Sheffer. Maurice Mills manages the fanacial affairs and oversees the "special occasion" deliveries. The Mills have made many good friends while in business, and they want to continue to serve the people of Sturgis and the surrounding communities. *Submitted by Bessie Mills*

The Petal Pushers

The first flower shop to open at 116 W. 6th was the "Blossom Shop" owned and operated by Janie Kuykendall from Sept. 1980 to Jan. 1984.

The business was purchased in Feb. 1984 by co-owners Leroy Farmer and Jerry Borders and was named "The Petal Pushers." Leroy Farmer remained as head designer for Marianne until Dec. 1987.

Remodeling enhanced the atmosphere—laying new carpet, painting and papering. With flowers, hanging plants, floor plants and special treatment of seasonal scenes in the window, Petal Pushers Florist creates the charming appearance of a flower garden.

Favorite time and special services offered are Weddings, Christmas, affordable custom designs for beloved homes and special designs for churches.

Customers are provided professional assistance in sales and delivery by the faithful employee, Anna Gibbens. Mary Borders has been added as designer. Full support and helpful hands of family and friends are often used to deliver and to do other chores.

With a motto of "Pushing to Please" Marianne's joy of the business is being able to cheer and delight people of the community with God's loveliest creation—FLOWERS.

Tradewater Railway

In Dec. 1981 Illinois Central Gulf Railroad announced that it would no longer serve the Sturgis, Morganfield area and abandon several miles of track including that from Pyro Mining Co. to Providence and Princeton. Pyro Energy Corp. explored purchasing the abandoned tracks.

After a great deal of study and lots of encouragement from area businesses, it was decided to lease with an option to purchase the 92 miles of track. In March 1982 the Tradewater Railway Co. officially became a short line railroad and in Dec. 1982 the out right purchase was completed.

The Tradewater's first shipment, in March 1982, consisted of three cars of grain from Union Co. Grain, Sturgis. In years to follow, along with grain, more than 10 million tons of coal has been transported from Pyro to the CSX Railroad at Providence, for delivery into FL, TN, AL and KY.

The Tradewater has five locomotives and 300 rail cars. Most of the railroad's equipment, fuel and materials is purchased from local businesses.

All of Tradewater's employees live and raise families within Sturgis and the surrounding areas. If a community is to grow and prosper, it must have good rail service and Tradewater Railway stands ready to provide that service.

Sturgis Furniture

Sturgis Furniture Company began in 1932 when Mr. and Mrs. William Payne and Mr. and Mrs. Carroll L. Seibert purchased it from Walter Hoe, Providence, Kentucky. The store had been managed by Forest Northern, Sturgis, Kentucky and was located at it's present location.

Mr. Payne and Mr. Seibert were partners in this business for 13 years. Then in 1945, the Seiberts purchased the Payne's interest. These present store buildings housed in earlier years the following: Culley's Tavern, Quirey's Hardware Store, the Picture Show - this was formerly the old Rakes Picture Show, Ed Johnson's Bowling Alley, City of Sturgis Post Office, Lil Wesley's Shoe Store, Mrs. W. W. Wynn's Purity Ice Cream Parlor & Sandwich Shop (with dance hall in the back).

In 1949, Thomas Dalton, a Sturgis boy, came to work at the furniture store. In 1950, marrying the boss's daughter, he became part of the store. With the exception of four years off for military service, Thomas was with the firm. In 1967 following Carroll Seibert's illness, Thomas became the manager of the store. He and his wife later purchased the store from her father and worked forever after.
Submitted by Carolyn Dalton

Sturgis Speciality

The business started as a small dress shop about 35 years ago by Nannie C. Vaughn (MAM), her daughter Alma V. Quirey (Bobbie), and Bobbie's husband Coyrtney C. Quirey, Sr. (C. C.)

The store is presently operated by O. V. Quirey, one of Bobbie and C. C.'s sons.

514 Adams Street
Sturgis, KY 42459
(502) 333-4629

"CLOTHES FOR THE ENTIRE FAMILY"

Tib's News Stand

In 1929 Elizabeth (Tib) King was given the management of the magazine and newspaper section of her father's drug store (King Drug Company). After her father's death the drug store was sold. January 1, 1935 Tib moved her magazines, newspapers and popcorn popper to a corner in Gordon McKeaig's Bright Spot Cafe. Within a short period of time Tib's News Stand moved to the building where C. S. Welch had a Jewelry Store. Tib expanded her services by becoming an agent for Evansville Courier and Press and Louisville Courier-Journal with home delivery. As the years have passed much has been added to better serve the reading pleasures of the people of Sturgis and surrounding areas. Newspapers, magazines, best seller books—both paper and hard back - Bibles, inspirational and Bible Study books are available everyday. Always a special service, as Tib says "If we do not have it we can get it." *Submitted by Tib K. Nunn*

Modern Cleaners

Modern Cleaners has served the dry cleaning and laundry needs of Union County since its founding by Abe Wicks in 1929. The Wicks family operated the business until December 1988 when it was purchased by Wear Care, a partnership formed by Jack and Joel Felts-Williams and Bill and Merilyn Gillespie Felts.

At its peak, Modern Cleaners had locations at Camp Breckenridge, Morganfield and other towns in Webster and Crittenden counties, and ran three shifts daily during WWII.

In the past three decades, all but one o these locations had ceased to operate. Since purchasing Modern Cleaners, Wear Care has established pickup stations in Shawneetown, IL and Clay and Marion, KY with two other sites in the planning stages.

A shoe repair service is offered at some locations. Future plans call for the installation of another operational plant somewhere in the Tri-county area, with added pickup stations. *Submitted by Joel Felts-Williams*

Modern Cleaners, established 1929, L to R, Jack E. Williams, Merilyn Gillespie Felts, William P. Felts, Joel Felts Williams

Wear Care Partnership. Seated, William P. Felts. Back row, Jack E. Williams, Joel Felts-Williams, Merilyn Gillespie Felts

I. O. O. F. Lodge No. 307

The original Lodge Hall was purchased from Cumberland Iron Company September 3, 1904, at a cost of $6,000.00.

Sturgis Lodge #307 Independent Order of Odd Fellows (I.O.O.F) was instituted on June 18, 1892. The Grand Master of Kentucky W. G. Simpson presided. Four of five Charter members were elected as officers: B. F. Ford, Noble Grand; W. A. Hicks, Vice Grand; A. M. Benedict, Secretary, and Jon H. Bailey, Treasurer. J. F. Cartwright, Charter Member, was also present. The Grand Officers present were G. R. Woodring, Grand Warden Pro-Tem; Jon K. Wall, Grand Secretary, W. F. Mart, Grand Treasurer; T. P. Joffrey, D. G. M. After election of officers the Grand Master waived all rules and read petitions from eleven candidates, named a committee, the committee signed the petitions and the Lodge voted on and accepted all delegates. Later on petition of A. W. Omer was read, accepted and voted on favorably. The initiatory first, second and third degrees were put on the candidates and they were enrolled in the Lodge the same night. The Lodge continued to grow and at one time had around three hundred members. It now has twenty-three members.

On July 6, 1913, the Lodge burned. At the meeting of the Lodge July 11, 1913, a Motion was made to build a new building on the site where the old building had burned. J. B. Lamb, R. L. Holt and R. L. Benedict, Trustees, were named as a building committee to have said new building erected. The Trustees were empowered to do all things necessary to erect the building and to pledge building and lots to secure sufficient monies. The new building was completed and the first meeting was held on January 16, 1914. Each member could invite a lady and the Lodge furnished a barrel of apples and box of cigars to celebrate the new Hall. Bonds were sold and the building mortgaged to

Bottom, L to R—George A. Jackson, treasurer, Robert E Kellen, Noble Grand, Everett W. Miller, Sec'y, Charles C. Olden, chaplain; Top, B. E. Milligan, Vice Grand, Robert Truitt, R. S. Noble Grand, Milton Carter, warden, George B. Simpson, member.

cover cost of building ($5,000.00).

In 1942 Boxville Lodge #222 merged with Sturgis #307 and all property including David Rest Cemetery became property of Sturgis #307. In 1971 the Lodge turned the operation of the Cemetery over to a committee.

On February 21, 1947, Ark Lodge #86 Caseyville consolidated with Sturgis Lodge #307. The Caseyville Cemetery which was owned by Ark Lodge was put in the hands of a committee of former Ark Lodge members. One thousand dollars was set aside for upkeep of the cemetery. After consolidation, the cemetery was to remain in the hands of the committee.

Part of the Sturgis Lodge Building was leased to Austin's Food Market for five years beginning in 1965. In 1971 Austin's had gone out of business, and this portion was leased to Farmers State Bank on a long-term basis. The Lodge Room is upstairs and we have just completed renovation (1989) including painting, bathroom fixtures, carpet on the stairway and ceiling repairs

and painting the ceiling.

The American Order of Odd Fellows was established in April 1819. They are the only Order that has the honor of placing a wreath on the Tomb of the Unknown Soldier in Washington each year.

We believe God, our church and our families are the most important things in life. Also, we are committed to visit the sick, take care of the widows and orphans, encourage youth programs and to help in the community. Each year youths are selected by various lodges in the U.S. and set on an all-expense paid two-week tour to visit the U. N. Assembly in New York. They stop at various historical points along the way including Washington, D. C., spend a week in New York and go on to Niagara Falls on the return trip. We have two going from Sturgis this year. Robert E. Kellen, Noble Grant of Sturgis Lodge #307, has been the Kentucky State Chairman for this program for five years. *Submitted by Robert E. Kellen, Special Deputy Grand Master of all I.O.O.F. Lodges in Western Kentucky*

Kelsey Lodge No. 659

The Masonic Lodge at Sturgis was chartered October 6, 1891 and named Kelsey Lodge #659.

Kelsey Lodge derived its name from Dr. Percival Gates Kelsey an influential leader in Union County at that time. Dr. Kelsey graduated from the Medical College of North Western University of Chicago. He was a Civil War Veteran of 1862.

After the war Dr. Kelsey migrated to DeKoven, Kentucky. He abandoned his medical practice in 1869 and entered the business world. In 1873 he managed the Shotwell Mine of DeKoven and was later promoted to President of the Ohio Valley Coal, Coke and Mining Company of DeKoven.

Dr. Kelsey was influential in establishing a railroad that would give an outlet to shipments of coal and coke. A line connecting Sturgis and DeKoven that connected with rail facilities from Chicago to New Orleans was built.

Dr. Kelsey died in 1921 leaving these monuments of progress to his name from which Kelsey Lodge #659 took its name.

The first officers were: Thomas N. Given, Master; A. J. Berry, Senior Warden; J. D. Harris, Junior Warden; W. W. Pierson, Secretary; J. J. Bradburn, Treasurer; George H. Whitecotton, Senior Deacon; H. J. Wallace, Junior Deacon; J. H. Beard, Steward and Tyler.

The first Master Masons were: Albert J. Berry, William M. Berry, James T. Bishop, James J. Bradburn, Johnson H. Beard, John H. Bailey, John W. Cross, Thomas N. Givens, Thomas P. Gilchrist, Joseph D. Harris, Samuel Hughes, Jesse J. Jones, Alexander King, Will W. Pierson, Mortimer Quirey, Reuben Reasor, Rev. S. B. Withers, Hiram J. Wallace, George H. Whitecotton.

Fellow Craft - Benjamin H. Price; Entered Apprentice - William I. Martin.

The first lodge hall was upstairs at the Bennett and Winston General Store located in the Lindle Block. Meetings were held the second and fourth Tuesday of each month.

With visions of owning a building of their own, in 1921 plans were drawn up for building a Masonic Temple. The plans included renting to other tenants to bring in revenue on the investment. These plans never materialized because of financial stress of the times.

During the great depression many members were suspended for non-payment of dues. The membership dropped to twenty seven. Instrumental in keeping the lodge functioning during the years of the depression were: J. T. Lamb, O. H. Wilcox, Mark Eastin, D. A. Brooks, Gilbert Lamb, Clifton Lamb, Robert Hagan, W. R. Givens, H. H. Chancellor, J. J. Martin, Frank Steelman, L. C. Quirey, C. S. Welch, J. T. Hughes, W. S. Wilson, M. P. Brooks, H. O. Barkley, T. C. Montgomery, K. L. Holt, and others.

It was during these years that oyster suppers and smokers were favorite social activities. The lodge furnished cigars for the smokers.

On March 29, 1922 fire destroyed the Bennett and Winston General Store resulting in the Lodge losing its meeting place, its charter and all records.

A new charter was issued by Grand Lodge on October 18, 1922 with a membership of 146. The IOOF Hall was rented and meeting held there until purchasing the Morehead Building on Washington Street on February 3, 1948, for $12,000.00. This included the feed store stock worth $4,500.00. A balance of $7,500.00 had to be raised puls $2,000.00 needed for repairs.

Twelve thousand dollars was borrowed from the bank at five percent interest. By December 1948 they owed only $1,545.00. At this time the membership had grown to 230.

The Lodge moved to this location in January 1949. Brothers Oscar Reynolds, T. C. Montgomery, R. S. Dunlop, Leslie Nesbitt and others made the necessary repairs to ready the building for occupancy. Trustees were Albert Thornsberry, Wilbur Shields, and L. C. Quirey.

This hall was dedicated at a meeting held at the airport on August 27, 1949. Over 250 Master Masons attended representing all lodges in the surrounding area, as well as Illinois and Indiana.

Sturgis Chapter #444 Order of Eastern Star was chartered October 24, 1944. Officers were: Margaret K. Holt, Worthy Matron; Roland Lamb, Worthy Patron; Irma S. Bell, Associate Matron; T. C. Montgomery, Associate Patron.

March 1951, a faithful brother, J. J. Martin, told the Lodge if they would provide, in his home, for his needs during his old age, he would deed his property in Sturgis (house and lot on Fourth and Monroe) to the Lodge. Assuming a $1,300.00 mortgage along with the property the Lodge agreed to this. Brother Marign expired July 8, 1951. The property sold on September 5, 1951 for $4,500.00. This made the Lodge debt free with money in the treasury to be used for improving the property.

In 1951 with a membership of 247, a degree team was formed to confer the third degree. Composing the team were: Raymond O. Young, James E. Gilchrist, Pete Wicks, Jim Syers, Fred Alloway, Leslie Nesbitt, Roy Waggener, Johnnie Robinson, Wilbur Shields, Doug Gregory, Dorris Lee Kanipe, Willard Hall, Sgt. Merl Stanley, George N. Holt, Jack Wright, Ed Ames, Bob Christian, Weldon Collins and Ralph Alexander. John Steelman was the director. This team conferred its first work for seven candidates in March 1952. Ninety-one Master Masons were present.

In October 1952 a plot of ground behind the hall was rented to Mr. C. W. Pugh to erect a storage building. The terms were a ten years lease with $20.00 a month rent.

A past Masters Night was held June 1953 with twenty past masters in attendance. Brother O. H. Wilcox was the oldest past master, having been in the lodge fifty-five years. June 1955 a room was furnished in the new Sturgis Community Hospital for $650.00. This was done in memory and honor of J. J. Martin.

Because of the need for funds, in June 1963, the lower part of the Lodge Hall was rented to an auto parts store. This type store under different managements has continued to operate in this location.

January 24, 1981 the first open installation of officers was held. Installing officers were: James. E. Gilchrist, Master; Wilbur Shields, Marshall.

In 1981 the parking lot was paved and rented to the Chamber of Commerce.

Membership in 1989 stands at 135 and Lodge meets the fourth Tuesday night of the month.

Officers for 1989 include: Kevin Vaughn, Master; James E. Gilchrist, Senior Warden; Fred Williamson, Junior Warden; Tony Collins, Senior Deacon; Larry Taylor, Junior Deacon; Arthur Collins, Secretary; Glen Layman, Treasurer; Wilburn Vaughn, Tyler; James Rayburn, Chaplin; Jon McCollum, Senior Steward; Chris McCollum, Junior Steward.

Kelsey Lodge has supplied four District Deputy Grand Masters who represent the Grand Lodge at Lodges in Henderson, Union and Webster Counties. They were: Kenny Holt, 1944-1945; Leslie Nesbitt, 1960-1961; James E. Gilchrist, 1966-1967; Maurice Garrett, 1977-1978.

Grandmasters who have visited the Lodge are John T. Taylor, 1931; Joe L. Tigue, 1945; Albert Hanson, 1947; J. Herber Lewis, 1952; Earl W.

Adams, 1955; C. J. Hyde, 1961; Joe C. McClanahan, 1965; Davie J. Smith, 1957; Thomas E. Dicken, 1974.

Past Masters of Kelsey Lodge #659 are:

1891 Thomas N. Givens
1892 George H. Whitecotton
1893 John H. Bailey
1894 John H. Bailey
1895 Joseph D. Harris
1896 Daniel A. Brooks, Jr.
1897 Algernon S. Winston
1898 Fred Alloway
1899 William Wilson
1900 W. C. Hieronymous
1901 W. C. Hieronymous
1902 George H. Whitecotton
1903 George H. Whitecotton
1904 W. C. Hieronymous
1905 James Mack Thompson
1906 W. C. Hieronymous
1907 Mark E. Eastin
1908 William D. Wallace
1910 Daniel A. Brooks, Jr.
1911 Philip Harris Winston
1912 Henry R. Dyer
1913 John Thomas Lamb
1914 Mark E. Eastin
1915 John Thomas Lamb
1916 Mark E. Eastin
1917 John Thomas Lamb
1918 Jeptha Lee Townsend
1919 Jeptha Lee Townsend
1920 Philip Harris Winston
1921 William Shearer Williams
1922 William Shearer Williams
1923 Orlando H. Wilcox
1924 Givens Christian
1925 William R. Givens
1926 Clifton Lamb
1927 John T. Lamb
1928 Herbert H. Chancellor
1929 William R. Givens
1930 Clifton Lamb
1931 John T. Lamb
1932 William R. Givens
1933 John T. Lamb
1934 John T. Lamb
1935 John T. Lamb
1936 John T. Lamb
1937 Gilbert Lamb
1938 Gilbert Lamb
1939 Gilbert Lamb
1940 Orlando H. Wilcox
1941 F. L. Steelman

1942 F. Y. Simpson
1943 K. L. Holt
1944 K. L. Holt
1945 C. C. Wright
1946 John Robert Bell
1947 Clyde Lynch
1948 D. D. Syers
1949 J. D. Smith
1950 Wilbur Shields
1951 R. O. Young
1952 W. O. Reynolds
1953 Dorris Lee Kanipe
1954 R. O. Young
1955 Leslie Nesbitt
1956 James E. Gilchrist
1957 Wayne Wicks
1958 Wilbur Shields
1959 James E. Gilchrist
1960 John H. Roberson
1961 John H. Roberson
1962 Roy D. Waggener
1963 John W. Steelman
1964 John W. Steelman
1965 John D. McCollum
1966 John D. McCollum
1967 Leslie Nesbitt
1968 Wilbur Shields
1969 Arthur Collins
1970 Virgil Collins
1971 Perry Adams
1972 Maurice Garrett
1973 Arthur Collins
1974 Mike DeMoss
1975 Maurice Garrett
1976 Richard Young
1977 Arthur Collins
1978 Clarence DeMoss
1979 Mike DeMoss
1980 Arthur Collins
1981 Jon McCollum
1982 Arthur D. Stewart
1983 Larry T. Taylor, Jr.
1984 Mark Taylor
1985 James E. Gilchrist
1986 Kevin Vaughn
1987 Jon McCollum
1988 Jon McCollum
1989 Kevin Vaughn

Researched and submitted by James E. Gilchrist, May 1989

Kiwanas

The Sturgis Kiwanis Club was chartered on May 22, 1922 with W. J. Kern as the first president. None of the original 53 chartered members survive today.

The goal of the Kiwanis is to render voluntary service to youth, community, and nation. Its membership is to reflect a cross section of the community. The original members were a mixture of occupations: businessmen, farmers, physicians, and surgeons, publishers and reporters, coal miners, postal employees, school officials, insurance agents, barbers, and jewelers. They were Fred Alloway, Sr., Fred Alloway, Jr., A. N. Barker, J. S. Berry, C. E. Bradburn, Tom Christian, Jr., Dr. G. B. Carr, M. W. Cusic, J. F. Doge, J. E. Dalton, C. G. Davis, S. W. Ezell, Charles H. Ellis, Herman Foyer, Jim Hargis, B. F. Humphrey, J. T. Holt, B. F. Hall, E. R. Holt, W. A. Jones, E. B. Jones, Sr., E. B. Jones, Jr., T. E. Jenkins, W. J. Kern, J. V. King, E. H. Long, J. O. McCauley, Sherman Melton, J. J. Martin, C. S. Prtichett, C. C. Quirey, Davis Read, T. B. Rhodes, Math Rich, C. F. Richardson, M. O. Ross, J. C. Stone, E. Seagraves, Clarence Sisco, J. B. Stevenson, James A. Sutton, T. L. Stanton, Al Shipley, G. A. Wallace, T. C. Williams, O. H. Wilcox, C. T. Wallace, C. S. Welch, P. H. Winston, J. F. Whitsell, J. G. Wynn, W. L. Winston, and I. D. Winston.

Through the years the club has prospered and with their prosperity the Sturgis community has reaped many benefits. At the sixty year celebration, John Young Brown, Sr. was the guest speaker.

M. Y. Nunn, who has been a member since 1935, remembers some of the highlights of the club's activities.

The Club started sponsoring a Drag Race program in 1956 at the Sturgis Airport each Sunday to give local boys an opportunity to drag race under controlled conditions rather on the city streets endangering many lives.

"We had between eight and nine thousand people that biggest Sunday," he said, "Dragsters were here from Nashville, Louisville, Booneville, In., Bowling Green, Carbondale. We had an awful drawing. We were first.

Nunn said, "There was a professor from Minneapolis-St. Paul (Minnesota) city schools who wrote a book, and devoted a whole chapter to the Sturgis Kiwanis sponsored drag races."

The Sturgis Kiwanis was well known all over Kiwanis International for its drag race program, Nunn said, because the club made over $400,000 during more than a 10-year period. It ended up because of competition, Nunn said. Drag strips had opened up in Paducah, Harrisburg, Illinois, Marion, Illinois and towns above Evansville, reducing attendance to a point where it was not profitable.

The money made from the program went toward building the Kiwanis pool and retiring the debt on the Kiwanis building, which was dedicated in 1950.

The building was to serve as a meeting place for the club as well as a meeting place for other organizations which had difficulty finding places to meet.

He started the club thinking about it when he was president in 1940.

Nunn said the cost of the building was cut in half. "By contributing our labor and materials. Everybody who was in the electrical business could order wiring and lights. Everybody who was in furniture business, Carroll Siebert, ordered chairs and windows, and anything in his business he could order at cost."

Nunn's wife, Tib, owned the lots where the Kiwanis Building stands. He said that the Kiwanis bought seven lots from her for $100 a piece.

Then the club had the distinction of being the only one which had its own meeting place. Before in 1950, the club had been meeting in church basements and other places such as the Humphrey Building.

When Nunn represented District 10 at the Kiwanis International's convention in New York in 1953 at the Old Astor Hotel, he "was introduced as the lieutenant governor and former president of the club, the only club in Kiwanis International who had built their own building."

"I was real swelled up with pride there in New York as the only club in the United States, Canada and they named all of the places where they had opened some new clubs," which had its own building.

Today the club building is used for Boy Scouts, the senior citizens nutrition program, family reunions, and church gatherings.

The Kiwanis Club of today follows in the tradition of the past years. Through its efforts a swimming pool was built in 1957 and two tennis courts were built in 1962 and 1975. Both facilities in addition to the building are used extensively by the community.

The bridge joining Union and Crittenden Counties is called the Kiwanis Bridge after the Kiwanis Club. The road is also named after the Kiwanis Club.

The Kiwanis sponsors a mini-basketball league each year as well as the men's basketball league. In addition they are involved with fund raising activities such as the yearly apple sale and the pancake breakfast.

Kiwanis, in the language of the Otchipaw Indian tribe, means "We gather together-We make a big noise." The motto of the Kiwanis International is "We Build," which has been the guiding word for the Sturgis club through the years.

Sturgis Library and Woman's Club

The old Sturgis Library was torn down to make room for a modern new building which is more than twice the size of the former building.

Since 1927 Sturgis has enjoyed some form of a library when the Sturgis Women's Club obtained the first 90 volumes at a tea and book shower held in the city hall.

It was, in fact, the need for a library that was the motive behind the formation of what is today known as the Senior Woman's Club of Sturgis.

Organized in 1925 for the expressed purpose of obtaining some form of a library, the club met in homes and began gathering a few volumes. Then when the tea netted 90 volumes the project really began to roll.

To house the books, which now numbered close to 200, Mr. Carroll Welch gave the ladies free space in his store. This was soon outgrown and the library was moved to two rooms in what is now the Neal Quirey home on Washington Street. When the house was sold, (as it was not Mr. Quirey's at that time) the Library moved to the George Simpson Store, a grocery, and later as it grew it moved again to the Al Shipley store. All of these merchants donating space for the cause of literature and reading.

The big move came in 1938 when the former structure on 7th Street next to the hospital was purchased from Dr. Humphrey.

It had formerly been his garage, and when his home burned, all that was left was this building which was purchased with a down payment of $500.

It took another $400 to fix it up, and shortly thereafter, with approximately 1200 volumes the Woman's Club hung out their sign, "Free Public Library."

The building was 18 x 18 feet, and as it grew, and grew, and grew, it became apparent to one and all that something had to be done.

To write a complete history of the Sturgis Woman's Club and its Main project—a free public library—would require much more time and space than is allotted to us.

Go back forty years in the spring of 1925, when twelve women under the leadership of Mrs. Jones Quirey organized a Woman's Club with two purposes, first to start a study club for the women of Sturgis, and second, to estab-

lish a library for the community. We met in the homes and had many worth while programs and all the time adding a few volumes to what we called "A Book Collection." About twenty-five good books were given to us by a "Younger Literary Club" and other interested citizens contributed. To raise money for books we had soup suppers, rummage sales, plays, booths at the fall festival and many other projects. A real beginning was made toward the library in 1927 when at a tea and book shower, in the city hall, ninety books were added. To house these books we were given free space in Mr. Carroll Welch's store. eventually we out grew this space and two rooms were rented on Washington Street, now known as the Neal Quirey Home.

This home was sold and Mr. George B. Simpson furnished us shelves at his grocery store as did Mr. Al Shipley at a later date.

On July 27, 1938 we purchased the building we now occupy. The down payment of $500 was given us by the trustees of the old Y.M.C.A. which had been discontinued. An additional $400 was needed to remodel. The building was ceiled, painted and stuccoed. The floor was raised eight inches to keep out the street water, shelves, lighting, heating and furniture were added. Again we resorted to ice cream suppers, street dances, and food sales. Shortly after moving in we could boost 1200 volumes. Then with pride we hung out our little shingle—Free Public Library.

And other early interests of the Woman's Club were beautification of Highway 60 and of the city park. Trees were planted along the highway beyond the cemetery and in the park a water fountain was erected, walks were laid, flowers planted, lights installed and the band stand remodeled. This

was in cooperation with the Music Club.

Years ago we brought in a book mobile to serve Union County. Through the efforts of the Senior Woman's Club and interested citizens we passed a property, library tax, being the first county in the state to pass such a tax. As a result we have a much larger book mobile and we will have 1000 sq. feet of space added to our present 400 sq. feet. The architect's drawing of the building is a thing of beauty. We will receive a grant-in-aid of 64% of the cost from the state—how grateful we are for the interest and aid given by our state workers.

We feel that the building will be completed before the end of 1966.

Having worked under many difficulties these 40 years, we the Sturgis Senior Woman's Club with the aid and cooperation of many citizens who believe in books as a Key to Knowledge, are happy to bring to our community a Public Library and all its many advantages which are offered through its facilities.

It has been a pleasure and a privilege for our club to serve our town and community in this most worth while project.

This article on Sturgis Public Library and Sturgis Senior Woman's Club, was written in 1965 for the Sturgis Diamond Jubliee Celebration. The new, and modern Library, pictured above is one of which Sturgis can be proud. The Sturgis Senior Woman's Club is no longer active but their good work lives on, in the beautiful educational Library that stands as a monument to their dedication. What had been a dream, came true for Sturgis through the hard work and inspiration of those faithful women.

Garden Club

One bright October afternoon in 1940 a meeting of twelve ladies was called by Mrs. Davis Read to discuss organizing a Garden Club. The first meeting of the Club was held at the home of Mrs. B. N. Holt on November 13th.

As temporary Chairman, Mrs. Holt recognized the Nominating Committee and their presentation of names for Club Officers and unanimously accepted.

These officers were: Pres. Mrs. Davis Read; V. Pres., Mrs. Frank Alloway; Sec'y, Mrs. Clarence Wilson; and Treas., Mrs. William Williams.

The meetings were held monthly and through the years plants, bulbs, and all sorts of flowers, birds, and other of Nature's beauty spots have been studied, in an effort to beautify our community and our individual homes.

In fall 1942 the Club disbanded for five months to help in Red Cross work making bandages. Donations have been given the Red Cross and other worthy causes.

The Club gave its first Flower Show at the Service Center, May 11, 1945 and many lovely flowers were displayed and a very entertaining program of music and songs was enjoyed by a large audience, both afternoon and evening.

In the spring of 1950 permission for planting four beds of Canna bulbs at the Fair Grounds was granted.

The Club was asked by the Fair Board to sponsor the Flower Show which was to be held at the Fair and to make a list of flower arrangements .

Each year since, the Club has sponsored the Flower Show at the County Fair, and for the past two years has shared the sponsorship with the County Homemakers, each Club having charge of the flowers for two days.

Three charter members are still in attendance. These are Mesdames J. L. Pritchett, C. L. Seibert, and Frank Alloway.

The present officers are: Pres., Mrs. J. L. Pritchett; V. Pres.t, Mrs. A. D. Sprague, Sr.; Sec'y and Treas., Mrs. N. O. Denton; and Reporter, Mrs. H. L. Patton.

We believe that "One is nearer to God's heart in a garden than anywhere else on earth."

The above was written by Mrs. Alloway in 1965 in Celebration of Sturgis Diamond Jubilee Anniversary.

Up-date - 1990 Centennial Year— The Sturgis Garden Club continues the original custom of having 12 members. Each member hostesses , has a program and devotional once a year. The Club uses the same type programs and is still interested in helping to make Sturgis more beautiful. Club members are helping on several programs of City beautification at this time. We have one charter member still active in the Club, Mrs. Anne Willie Seiber.

The present officers of the Garden Club are: President, Rebecca Kearney; Vice President, Katherine Christison; Secretary and Treasurer, Amila Callaway; Reporter, Jane Gilchrist.

Collectors Club

The Collectors Club was organized December 1970 at a breakfast meeting at the home of Mrs. Rebecca (Willie) Baird. The original members were Marily Andre, Rebecca Baird, Jimmie Nell Cooper, Alma Greenwell, Peggy Hibbs, Mary Jane Holeman, Johnye Knight, Jane Kurtz, Blackie McLeod, Betty Rayburn, Hazel Waggner, Marianne Wesley, Beulah Williams.

The purpose of the club is to become more knowledgeable in the field of antiques and collectable. Each member is responsible for hosting the club and presenting a program once a year. The club has no officers and keeps a membership of twelve.

The members of the club in 1989 are Nadine Baldwin, Shirley Brown, Amelia Callaway, Jane Gilchrist, Alma Greenwell, Mary Jane Holeman, Jane Kurtz, Blackie McLeod, Jane Shipley, Louis White, Martha Williams.

Others who have been members at one time are Emmabelle Baird, Liz Brown, Pat Steelman, Ginny Lou Wells, Dot Willet, Kathryn Woodring, Suzanne Woodring.

Tours have included trips to antique shops and malls in New Harmony, Newburgh, and Evansville in Indiana, Shawneetown, Illinois, Nashville, Tennessee, and in Kentucky to Paducah, Murray, The Kentucky Lake Area, Providence, Marion and Owensboro.

Information has been used on a variety of subjects for program content. It has ranged from pottery to fine china, including ironstone, Blue Ridge Pottery, Hull, Bennington and Kentucky pottery, Staffordshire, Royal Copenhagen and Haviland. Silver plate to sterling silver has been discussed. Glass including Carnival, pressed, Mary Gregory, Venetian, Fostoria, Fenton and cut glass. Also, stained glass and Tiffany.

Art work from Pennsylvania Duth Folk Art and Indian art to Chinese art. Artist and art included Norman Rockwell, Paul Sawyier, and other Kentucky artists, Currier and Ives and Tom Clark, a wood sculpturer. Figurines of Hummel and Precious Moments.

Collectables include old bottles, canning jars, pipes, guns, knives, granite ware, crockery, pottery (Roseville, Hull, Majolica), Kitchen wares, tin, mugs, country store items, advertising tins and wooden boxes. Plates, stamps, coins and Hallmark Christmas ornaments are the more modern collectables.

Miniatures, dolls, toys and paper dolls, hat pins, thimbles, sewing equipment, buttons, old linens and handwork added to the variety of information.

A history of quilts and a beautiful display of pieced, applique and patchwork quilts provided a kaleidoscope of fascinating designs and colors.

Other programs included jewelry from rhinestones, Indian and Cameos to beautiful antique jewelry.

Miscellaneous lessons on old books, greeting cards, paper collectables, early American lighting, lamps and candlesticks, bells, paperweights, photography, clocks, baskets and Christmas decorations have been examined.

The club continues to explore avenues of information for sources of topics for the program each month. Members can be found attending auctions and sorting through boxes hoping to find "the very thing" they had been looking for to complete or add to their collections.

Junior Homemakers

The Sturgis Junior Homemakers club was organized in the year 1950. The first meeting was held at the First Christian Church with 12 members present. The County Extension agent was Helen Stevens. The club is a continuing education group under the direction of the Cooperative Extension Service of the University of Kentucky. This service just celebrated it 75th year of existence.

The club currently has 15 members which meets on the second Wednesday of each month at the Morganfield National Bank, Sturgis branch. We receive landscaping notes, a timely lesson, recreation, devotional, and a potluck meal. Visitors are always welcome.

Since the year 1950 we have accomplished many things. One of our first activities was a County Style Show in 1950 in which several of our members participated. In 1952 we held a county home tour. Mrs. Charles O'Nan, one of our members, displayed her home for the tour.

There are many activities that our club sponsors on an annual basis. We donate money and time as leaders to the local 4-H Club. Each year our members sponsor a program at the Sturgis Rest Home. The Club also donates monies to help organizations like the American Cancer Society and the Union County Junior Miss Program. We also sponsor a scholarship each year for a college-bound student. At Christmas we leave our regular meeting place for the home of one of our members to enjoy a special day of food, fun, and exchanging of gifts. In the summer we enjoy a picnic with our children at a local recreational spot or at a member's home. During International month we treat ourselves to a foreign meal at a restaurant of our choice.

Our present officers are Dot Willett, President; Jan Baird, Vice President; Marilyn Baird, Secretary/Treasurer; Marguerite Morehead, Devotional Leader; and Mary Ebelhar, Recreational Leaders. Our current extension agent is Linda Young. As of date we have three chartered members: Marquerite Morehead, Liz Brown, and Dottie O'Nan. *Submitted by Liz Brown and Brenda Stevens*

Senior Homemakers

The Sturgis Homemaker Club was organized in 1927 in the basement of the First Christian Church with Mrs. Cella Sprague president. Other members were Mrs. Lillie Griffin, Mrs. Eberley Davis, Mrs. Kenneth Davis, Mrs. Nell O'Nan, Mrs. Jess Brown, Mrs. Dan Shouse, Mrs. Arthur Kelley, Mrs. John Reynolds, Mrs. Annie Willie Seibert, and Mrs. Lona Omer.

Our first County Agent was Miss Dixie Lewis who served from 1930 to 1933. Agents following were: Miss Sadie Wilgus, Miss LaRue Nance, Miss Dorothy Hill, Miss Helen Stevens, Miss Emma Lou Johnson, and presently Mrs. Linda Young.

There are eleven clubs in the county.

The Sturgis Homemaker Club now has seventeen members - President, Mrs. Elvira Kellen; Vice President, Kathryn Christinson; Secretary, Lillie Layman; Treasurer, Belle Brown; Devotional Chairman, Glenna Davis; and Recreation Leader, Dorothy McGee.

Other members are: Agnes Bradford, Frances Anderson, Ruth Hinton, Annie Willie Seibert, Jewell Holeman, Louise Hooper, Marie Lamb, Velma Simpson, Aredrue Taylor, Ruth Henry, and Lona Omer.

They meet on the second Thursday of each month in the Recreation Room of the Farmers State Bank.

During these years the clubs have carried projects in food preparation, nutrition, home improvement, home management, clothing, landscaping, school lunches, reading, speech, etiquette, and style trends.

The clubs, also do nice work in citizenship, development of leadership, encouraging wholesome recreation, and many other phases of work.

The Henshaw Club was the first Homemaker Club in Union County and recently celebrated their 60th anniversary. A member of this club, Mrs. Nannie Brown, supplied much of this information.

The first Union County Homemaker Association's meeting was held at Morganfield Presbyterian Church November 4, 1925. One hundred and twenty people attended. The speakers were Miss Myrtle Weldon, State Leader from University of Kentucky and Miss Zelma Monroe, Assistant Leader, Rep. G. L. Drury, and Senator J. K. Waller.

The first officers of the county organization were President Mrs. C. B. Waller of Boxville, Mrs. Newman Wheatley of Waverly, Vice President, and Mrs. Earnest Hart of Grove Center Secretary-Treasurer. *Submitted by Lona Omer*

The Mort Quirey Family

(Circa 1910) Top row, Winston Quirey, Waller (Quirey) Bodell, Clore (Quirey) Markham—a daughter, William Markaham, Edna (Markham) Gregory, Lucille (Doss) Hughes, Will Hughes. Middle row, Amial Hoerth, Mary (Quirey) (Doss) Hoerth—a daughter, Mort Quirey, Molly (Nunn) Quirey—his wife, Otho C. Quirey—a son, Sophronia (Curry) Quirey. Bottom row, Mort Hoerth, Dixie (Markham) Dorroh, Sue (Hoerth) Betts—the baby, Louis C Quirey and Wallace Quirey. Absent from the photo are Mort and Molly's other two sons, Jones and George Hugh Quirey.

Eastern Star

Sturgis Chapter #444 Order of The Eastern Star
Organized October 24, 1944 Sturgis, Kentucky

List of Charter Members

Margueriette Allen	Martha Nunn	Louise Wright
Mayme Holt	Maeola Holt	Robert Bell
Mildred Allen	Lillie K. Peyton	Givens Christian
Velma Holt	Minnie Reynolds	H. C. Dedman
Eva C. Christian	J. B. Small	K. L. Holt
Jewel Lamb	Will Wright	H. D. Holt
Martha Montgomery	Dorothy Stevenson	Ewell Johnson
Katie Dedman	Nannie Strouse	Roland Lamb
Nora Davis	Mildred Sweeney	Tom Montgomery
Frances Nunn	Maude Sloan	R. W. Powell
Margaret Holt	Bessie Wright	Oscar Reynolds
		C. C. Wright

When the Chapter was organized 1944: Margaret Holt, Worthy Matron; Roland Lamb, Worthy Patron; Irma Bell, Associate Matron; T. C. Montgomery, Associate Patron; Lutie K. Dunkie, Worthy Grand Matron; Mills R. Thocker, Worthy Grand Patron; Ella M. Mount, Grand Secretary.

Sturgis Chapter #444 Order of the Eastern Star Officers 1988-89 (58 members)

Worthy Matron, Marguariette Owen; Worthy Patron, Charles C. Owen; Associate Matron, Bonnie Bogart; Associate Patron, Jon D. McCollum; Secretary, Kathleen Whitehead; Treasurer, Martha Omer; Conductress, Mayre Sherer; Associate Conductress, Virginia McDowell; Chaplain, Ella Mae Fitzgerald; Marshall, Mary K. Chandler; Organist, Helen McKeaig; Adah, Pauline Jenkin; Ruth, Ruth Greene; Esther, Barbara E. Shelton; Martha, Ruby Roberson; Electra, Reda K. Jenkin; Warder, Gladys Suits; Sentinel; Guy McDowell

Peace Rebekah Lodge

Peace Rebekah Lodge No. 22 I. O. O. F. was instituted December 11, 1947 with twenty-seven charter members. The Lodge started with its first meeting January 8, 1948 with Mrs. Fannie Sue Taylor Voss as the first Noble Grand. Five of the charter members are still members of the Lodge. Peace No. 22 is a member of District 13 where many of the members have served as officers through the years. Peace No. 22 is also a part of the Rebekah Assembly of Kentucky I. O. O. F. where several of the members have served and are serving as Assembly officers. Peace No. 22 meets in the I. O. O. F. Hall on Sixth Street twice a month on the second and fourth Tuesdays at 7:30 p.m. The present Noble Grand is Mrs. Barbara Milligan.

Sittin' Pretty

The Sturgis Sittin' Pretty Community Group was formed August 1, 1988, by nine Sturgis residents. The group's primary purpose is to spruce-up and enhance the appearance of Sturgis, especially downtown and in areas of high visibility. The group maintains close contact with other civic organizations to help accomplish their goals. Membership and monthly meetings are open to all Sturgis residents.

The group's name was suggested by Donna Certain and received the members unanimous approval. The generous donation of $500.00 was made by U.M.W.A. Local #2550 to help launch the group's first projects. Officers were selected by the eight members who attended the first meeting. Nadine Baldwin (Co-Chairman), Rev. Joe Butler (Chairman), Donna Certain, Helen McKeaig, Cindy Owens, Joe Owens (Treasurer), Annie Willie Seibert, Patsy Ruth Steelman, and Sharry West (Secretary).

Tribute
Walter John Kern

Sturgis has benefited in many ways form the enterprising spirit and constructive labors of Walter John Kern. With a 4th grade education he became a newsboy in Cincinnati, Ohio, and left home at the age of 11. He worked for the Edison Light Company of New York electrifying the street railway system. He was the first man to operate a streetcar in Lexington, Kentucky. After working for an Ohio firm helping construct buildings for the World's Columbian Exposition in Chicago, he became an engineer for Owensboro Electric Light Company. In 1910 he went to Calhoun, Kentucky, and constructed the plant of the Green River Light & Water Company, which he sold in December 1910. In January 1911 he began work on the Sturgis Ice Plant, and he opened a laundry in 1922, and also planted and owned the Hillcrest Orchard just outside Sturgis. He served as Mayor of Sturgis for 3 terms, was the first President of the Sturgis Kiwanis Club, also serving as Lt. Governor of the Kentucky-Tennessee Kiwanis District, and was Vice President of the Iceman's Association of Kentucky. He was an active Mason and Shriner, a Presbyterian, and was instrumental in getting asewage system in Sturgis. He died in 1929 just after agreeing to run for a fourth term as Mayor. *Submitted by Sandy S. Arnold and Jane S. Young*

Family Histories

ily Quilt

ALLEN - CORNWELL

Van McGarvie Allen (Garvie) was born July 5, 1886 in Union County, KY. Louetta Miranda Cornwell was born March 27, 1889 in Allen County, KY. They married on Nov. 15, 1906 in Sturgis, KY. They were employed on farm's, Garvie supervised, working in the fields, Louetta cooked and fed the farm hands.

They moved to Sturgis and eventually made their home at 901 Grant Street where they lived the rest of their lives. There they raised their five sons and one daughter. Garvie worked as a mechanic and salesman at Bradburn's Ford Garage, later he became the Fire Chief of Sturgis' volunteer fire department, this was the only position that the city fire department paid a salary. Louetta worked at home raising the six children.

As it was for many folks, times were hard on the Allen's. Garvie worked odd jobs when possible, often in trade for fruits and vegetables for his family. Louetta made the best of the family garden, canning and preserving what she could.

Believed to be taken in 1921. Pictured are Garvie, Louetta, Toy, Van, Elsie and Barney

After several years Garvie suffered a stroke, and was unable to work. Louetta worked odd jobs, staying nights with the sick, anything she could find. During WWII they even took in boarders. Friends and neighbors were always wonderful and shared with the Allen's, often lending a hand when needed. Many Sturgis residents may recall them in the porch swing when they passed the corner of Ninth and Grant Streets. Garvie passed away Sept. 9, 1963 and Louetta passed away Feb. 7, 1975.

Allen Children; Toy Walker was born Sept. 4, 1907, married Mae (Sullivan) Mason, a widow with a son, J. D. They lived in Paducah, KY for a while where Toy worked in a bakery. They returned to Sturgis and Toy was the Chief of Police, and later worked at Thornsberry's Grocery for many years. J. D. died in WWII. Toy passed away April 9, 1969. Mae passed away Dec. 16, 1978.

Van McGarvie was born Sept. 4, 1907. He migrated to Kansas working the wheat harvests. He settled in Wichita and married Iline Powers on April 12, 1942. Van was a Dairy Inspector for the County Health Department. Van passed away July 17, 1976.

Elsie Rae was born May 16, 1914, and moved

to Evansville, IN, to work in a factory. She married Robert McCullough on Jan. 1, 1940. He worked for Ford Tractor and they moved frequently. They raised two daughters Mary Louise, and Etta Rae. Elsie passed away November 24, 1983.

Barney Morgan was born Sept. 9, 1919, he married Dorothy Scott and they made their home in San Antonio, TX. They had two daughters, Miranda Coran and Karen Iline. Barney passed away Aug. 24, 1969.

Claude Leslie was born March 13, 1922. He settled in Los Angeles, CA and married Kathryn Gallette on July 13, 1947. They had a son, Leslie Wayne and two daughters, Kathryn Louise, and Sandra Rae. Kathryn passed away Feb. 28, 1972. Claude has retired from Lockheed Aircraft, remarried to Janet Crawford and lives in Meadow Vista, CA.

Ben Humphrey was born July 13, 1925. He married Erika Dalitz. He is retired from the FAG Bearing Company and they live in Neosho, MO. *Submitted by Leslie Wayne Allen*

ANDRE

The Andre family came to the Sturgis area in 1910. They lived in and around DeKoven. Sadly, there was never a reunion until 1979. A lesson to be learned is start early working on your family history and keep researching. It is rewarding.

1986 Andre Reunion, Ray Andre and Wm. Andre Alvey

Parents of Nicholas Andre were Marie Barbe Semet and George Jacob Andre. Nicholas was of Donnersberg, Germany and married Lowesa Weber of Winchberg, Baveria. They came to America in 1832 and located in Pennsylvania. In 1855 they moved to Connersville, IN and bought a farm. They had eleven children. They died in 83 and 84 and are buried in Connersville. Information from Fayette County Library states they were Alsatians from Alsase-Lorraine. It also gives much information on one of their sons, David. In 1876 he had the Andre Opera House built in Connersville. The structure covered ground 48 x 80 and was two stories high; on the second floor was a room with a stage 21 x 46 feet and a seating capacity of 600 people. Fully equipped with sets of scenery for plays of all kinds. The cost of the building was $20,000. It was destroyed by fire in 1958.

Nicholas and Lowesa were great grandpar-

ents of Clarence and James Andre of Sturgis. James and Clarence were cousins. Clarence Bailey Andre married Anna Stella Henshaw and they had a son, Ray, and a daughter, Hazel. His parents were Lee Adam Andre and Rose Ella Smithers. She died in the great influenza epidemic of 1918 and is buried at Caseyville.

James Carroll Andre married Francis King and they had a daughter, Jean, and a son, William. His parents were David Oliver Andre and Elizabeth Winterfred Smelser.

Lee and David Andre were sons of Nicholas and Lowesa Andre, who was the son of James Monroe Andre. The family members here in Sturgis still attend reunions and research family history. Francis, James and Clarence have died. Stella lives out of Sturgis on a farm near DeKoven. History states our ancestors were Alsatians, but we are very glad they made us Americans. *Submitted by Hazel A. Niese*

ARNOLD

John Alloway Arnold, Sr. (Alloway as his friends call him) was born May 12, 1909, in Arnold Station, KY, the son of John Samuel and Lena (Pride) Arnold. He traces his family back to Thomas N. Arnold, a pioneer of Owen County who married Elizabeth Frear of Virginia and Colonel Wilson Hunt, a War of 1812 hero who married Margaret Shotwell of Virginia. They were the parents of Samuel and Mary (Hunt) Arnold and came to Owen County from North Carolina. Samuel Arnold's son, Newton Arnold was born March 26, 1851, and moved to Union County in 1875 when he was young.

Newton Arnold was first a farmer and later a grocery owner. He married Nancy R. Holeman on Nov. 20, 1877. The children born to them were John Samuel, Molly, Ella, Fred Alloway, Audie Lee and Addie. Until 1906 the area now known as Arnold Station was a few farmhouses. Then the Morganfield and Atlanta Railroad came through and most of the right-of-way obtained was on Newton Arnold's farm. Hence Arnold Station was the name given to that community. A railroad depot was built and John Samuel and Fred Arnold and Bain Holeman established a general merchandise business.

J. Alloway Arnold and Justine B. Arnold

John Samuel Arnold who was born in 1879 and died in 1962 married Lena (Pride) who was born Dec. 21, 1878, and died Jan. 1, 1974. She was the daughter of Jim and Molly (Christian) Pride. They became parents of six children: Floy Christaine who married Dennie Brown, Mary Katherine who married John White, Rebecca Watson who married George Brown, John Alloway who married Justine Blackwell, Jimmy Leah who married Bob Ohning and Martha Blanche who married Raymond Smith. Martha A. Smith is deceased.

Alloway grew up in Union County and farmed until 1973. He married Cleo Justine Blackwell on Dec. 11, 1930. Justine was born on Oct. 14, 1912, the only child of Loyd and Pearl (Woodring) Blackwell. Loyd Blackwell's family were farmers in Webster County, John Breckinridge Blackwell and Rose Mae (Fryer) Blackwell. Pearl Blackwell's family were farmers in Union County and they were John Woodring and Kitty (Wright) Woodring.

Alloway and Justine are both very active Senior Citizens members and stay on the go. They are parents of two children Raymond Durwood Arnold and John Alloway Arnold, Jr. (see Durwood Arnold and John Arnold for more information). *Submitted by Sandy S. Arnold*

JOHN ALLOWAY ARNOLD, JR.

John Alloway Arnold, Jr. is the younger son of John Alloway Arnold, Sr. and Justine (Blackwell) Arnold. John was born on Aug. 23, 1944, in Webster County, KY. After graduating from Sturgis High School he went to Indianapolis, IN, and graduated from Lincoln Chiropractic College. He married Sandy Stevenson on Aug. 13, 1966.

Dr. John Arnold, Sandy Arnold and John Arnold III; Alisa Beth Arnold

After college and two years in the U. S. Army he returned to Sturgis and went into practice with Dr. A. E. Niese in 1970. John and Sandy have two children: Alisa Beth Arnold who will be a senior at the University of Kentucky and John Alloway Arnold III who will be a senior at Union County High School.

John has been a city councilman and Mayor of Sturgis. He is actively involved in legislative affairs for the chiropractors in Kentucky and is a member of the Sturgis Economic Development Foundation, who are actively seeking new industry for the City of Sturgis. Sandy is a secretary and Marketing Officer for Farmers State Bank and enjoys working with young people such as the 4-H group. *Submitted by Dr. John and Sandy Arnold*

RAYMOND DURWOOD ARNOLD

Raymond Durwood Arnold, son of John Alloway Arnold, Sr. and Justine Blackwell Arnold was born April 26, 1939, in Webster County. Durwood was reared on the family farm in the Pride/Bordley area. Durwood entered farming operations with his grandfather, Loyd Blackwell in 1957 where he remained until 1987. Durwood was appointed by Governor Wendell Ford to fill out the remainder of the Magisterial position left vacant by the death of Austin Strouse in 1976. He later won the seat in an election where he served for one full term. Durwood has worked as an Emergency Medical Technician (EMT) for both the county and the hospital.

On March 17, 1957, Durwood married Jackie McKown Arnold in Shawneetown, IL. Jackie was born Feb. 25, 1939, in Moline, IL. Her parents, Shelby G. McKown and Hilda (Presley) McKown moved to Clay, KY, in 1945. Jackie and Durwood graduated from Clay Consolidated High School in 1957. Jackie has worked as a secretary and bookkeeper for the Union County Area Vocational Education School from 1976-1988.

Durwood and Jackie moved to Sturgis from the family farm in 1987. They purchased the Bob Bell home on the corner of Highway 60 and 270 E. They opened a business in the basement of their home in 1988. Their business, "The Basement" specializes in prints, framing, and stained glass windows and gifts.

Durwood and Jackie are the parents of four children: Annette Arnold Logan, 30, is the wife of Gary D. Logan and lives in Sturgis. They have two children Ryan D. and Rachel P. Annette works for Regional Medical Center in Home Health Care and Gary is Vice President at Farmers State Bank. Ellen Denise Arnold 27 lives in Bloomington, IL, and works as a field technician for Nixdorf Computers. Raymond Andrew Arnold married Catherine Cavins Arnold and lives in the Pride area. He is employed by Agri Tech Cattle Company of Marion, KY. He also manages the family farm. Erin Lynn Jenkins, 18, married Thomas Lee Jenkins, Jr. who is a member of the united States Armed Forces and is planning to make a career in the Air Force. *Submitted by Jackie M. Arnold*

HARRY AND FANNIE SUE BARKLEY

Harry Oldham Barkley, son of David Maple Barkley and Georgeana Carroll (Owen) was born Nov. 14, 1872 in Princeton, KY. Harry worked for 50 years as a Grocery Department Manager for the West Kentucky Coal Company stores in Sturgis. He was a Masonic member of Kelsey Lodge #659 F.&A.M. and received his Fifty Year Button and Gold Life Membership Card in January, 1960. Fannie Sue (O'Nan) Barkley was born May 10, 1877 on a farm near Sturgis. Her parents were Dennis O'Nan and Eliza Blue (Ralph) O'Nan. Harry and Fannie Sue Barkley were the parents of two children. Harry Oldham Barkley, Jr., who died in infancy and a daughter, Eliza Carroll (Barkley) Heavrin, who lives in Evansville with her husband, Burbie Lewis Heavrin. They have one son, David Wayne Heavrin. Harry Oldham Barkley's father, David Maple Barkley, attended the Medical Department of the University of Louisville where he received his Diploma and Degree of M.D. in 1861. He moved to Princeton, KY, where he practiced his profession and occupied the chair of the Greek and Latin in the Princeton , KY College. He later moved to Caseyville in Union County, KY, where he continued to be an M.D. for 38 years (History of Union County). Fannie Sue (O'Nan) Barkley's parents were successful farmers in Union County and were faithful members of the First Christian Church. Her father was a friend and counselor to the young and had the friendship and respect of every true citizen he came in contact with in his daily life. (O'Nan Book - Treasure Up the Memory). *Submitted by Eliza Carroll Heavrin*

BARNARD

The Barnard family is of Dutch origins moving to the United States in the mid 1800s. they settled in Tennessee near Fountain Head. Wallace Barnard was born March 13, 1904 to Atlas Eldon and Minnie Hulette Barnard. When Wallace was three months old, his mother died and he was raised by his Aunt Sally Barnard. Atlas (At) Barnard was a blacksmith and moved to the Sturgis area where he was employed at the coal mines for several years. At and Wallace played the fiddle and mandolin at many social events during this time. At Barnard later returned to Tennessee where he spent his remaining years.

While in Union County, Wallace married Iva Lillian Hinton, daughter of Mr. and Mrs. W. A. Hinton of Arnold Station. Two children were born to this union. Patsy Ruth and Wallace (deceased). During the depression, Wallace worked as a farm hand for 25 cents a day

Mr. and Mrs. Wallace Barnard and daughter, Patsy Ruth

with the WPA. He later worked on the construction of Camp Breckenridge. He finished his working career as a Coal Miner and retired from the Pleasant View Mine near Madisonville in 1962.

Lillian Barnard died on August 15, 1945. Her wish was to live until World War II ended and on that day her life quietly ended with the news that the war was over.

Wallace lives in the Grangertown Community with his wife Dona Neible Barnard. Their children are Patsy Barnard Steelman, Jackie Stewart Edens and Tommie Stewart along with six grandchildren and six great grandchildren. Wallace enjoys drinking coffee at Buzzard's Cafe and visiting with old friends.

KELLY AND CHARLOTTE BEAVER

Kelly and Charlotte Beaver moved to Sturgis in April of 1981 when Kelly assumed the position of Minister of Music and Youth at First Baptist Church of Sturgis.

Charlotte, whose maiden name is McGuffey, was born Jan. 8, 1951 in Berea, KY, where she grew up. She was first employed Gibson Greeting Card Co. in Berea. She has done kindergarten and day care work in churches in Sylvania, GA, Louisville and Shelbyville, KY, and is currently employed as a clerk at Holt's Department Store in Sturgis.

Kelly and Charlotte Beaver

Kelly, born April 27, 1949, is a native Georgian. He received his undergraduate training at Piedmont College in Demorest, GA (1971) and earned a Master of Arts in Education degree (1972) at Eastern Kentucky University in Richmond, KY. After graduation Kelly served as Minister of Music and Youth at First Baptist Church, Sylvania, GA.

Kelly met Charlotte while living in Richmond and they were married on Jan. 6, 1973. They continued serving the church in south Georgia until the summer of 1976 when they moved to Louisville, KY where Kelly entered the Southern Baptist Theological Seminary in pursuit of a Master of Church Music Degree.

While at seminary and for two years following graduation, he served as Minister of Music at Mt. Pleasant Baptist Church in the Todds Point Community of Shelby Co.

Kelly supplemented his income from the part-time church position by working as a floral designer at Betsye's Flower and Gift Shop in Simpsonville, KY and also with Griffith's Decorating Service in Shelbyville, KY where he installed wall covering, draperies and window treatments.

Kelly's interest in music composition has led him to compose several cantatas, songs and hymns, including a centennial hymn for First Baptist Church, Sturgis, a centennial hymn for the Ohio Valley Baptist Association, and a centennial song, "Sturgis, Our Home Town," for the centennial of the city of Sturgis, KY.

Kelly and Charlotte are both active in the community. Kelly has served as director for both Community Chorus, a mixed choral group, and Community Chimes, a handbell group. He is a member of the Union County Ministerial Association and is a volunteer chaplain with the Pastoral Care Committee of the Union County Methodist Hospital.

Kelly and Charlotte reside at 1117 Washington Street where they have ever since moving to Sturgis.

WILLIAM CARROLL BENSON

My grandparents were the late William Carroll Benson, son of William Morgan Benson and Sally Jane Benson born on July 25, 1887 died Jan. 7. 1958. Carroll Benson married Mayme Magadeline O'Leary Benson. Mayme was the daughter of Daniel and Ollie O'Leary. They were married in the old Little Bethel Church in 1926. They had nine children; Violet Elaine Benson, Edith Pearl Benson Carver, William Arnold, Rev. James Louis, Shirley Freeman, Ollie Jane Benson Ammerman, Marion Eugene, Bobby Ray, and Ella Louise Benson Renje.

Wm. Carroll Benson and Mayme Magadelene (O'Leary) Benson

My grandparents lived in the Grove Center area and the Salem area. My grandpa was a farmer until World War II then he went to work at Camp Breckenridge. Then my grandparents moved to the Pond Fork area where they lived 14 years and attended Bethany Baptist Church. My grandmother worked in restaurants and in homes caring for the sick, Mayme worked for Dr. and Mrs. McKinney, 25 years. The Benson's have 24 grandchildren, 17 great grandchildren. Mrs. Mayme Benson died June 27, 1983. *Submitted by Patricia Gean Carver*

JONES BERRY

Jones Berry was born Aug. 21, 1889, the second child to be born in Sturgis before its incorporation and one of nine children of Albert Judson and Mollie Nunn Berry. Albert was the first police judge in Sturgis. Jones was born in the first house built in Sturgis. The house was built in 1874 by Pete Casey who was his mother's (Mollie Nunn Berry) brother-in-law.

Jones Berry

Jones married Mary Shaffer and they had one son, Tom Berry. Tom and his wife Ruelene had one daughter, Renee, and they currently live in the same house located at 1119 E. Sixth and Monroe Streets. Jones passed away Jan. 19, 1970. *Submitted by Mrs. Ruelene Berry*

THOMAS BOSTON

Thomas Boston, son of Jesse T. and Permelia E. (Quick) Boston, born near Sturgis, KY, May 20, 1862; died Sturgis, April 7, 1935; married (at bride's parents' home, Nov. 2, 1887) Mary Sue Young, daughter of Andrew Jackson and Narcissus (Davis) Young, born Union County, KY, March 4, 1869; died Sturgis, Aug. 2, 1937; both buried Little Bethel Baptist Cemetery. He was a farmer.

The Boston Family

Children (born Sturgis, Union County, KY): Ora Ellen, b. Feb. 8, 1889; mar. Henry C. Paris; John Wesley, b. April 16, 1890; single; farmer, res. Sturgis, KY; Nonnie, b. Jan. 29, 1892; d. March 12, 1920; single; (David) Edgar, b. Feb. 16, 1894; d. New Orleans, LA Oct. 29, 1959; mar. Johanna Santas; no children; barber; Ivan Jackson, b. March 4, 1896; d. in infancy; Thomas Virgil, b. Aug 27, 1897; d. 1963; mar. Geneva Travis; William Earl, b. Aug. 31, 1899;

d. March 9, 1952; mar. Anna L. Mimms; Clarence Marion, b. March 23, 1902; d. Nov. 17, 1957; mar. Vurbelle A. Fleig; Infant, b. and d. Jan 24, 1903; Robert Gorden, b. Dec. 28, 1903; d. Aug. 12, 1923; Lucile Nunn, b. Nov. 4, 1905; mar. Robert H. McCaw; Anna Carmen, b. July 9, 1908; mar. John T. Paris; Nannie Justine, b. July 29, 1910; mar. Franklin Wright; Virginia Lee, b. May 8, 1912; d. July 18, 1916.

BRADDOCK

Joseph Augustin Braddock came to Uniontown, KY as a Federal Marshal on the Ohio River in 1857. He travelled up and down the river helping catch cattle thieves, etc.

He met and married Lucy Waggner and moved to Morganfield, KY in 1884. He worked at several construction jobs and one we best remember was helping build Highway 60 through Union County. They had two (2) sons, Leo Joseph and James. When the sons grew up, they opened a Shoe Shop and Poultry House in Uniontown, KY.

Back Row L-R: Leo, Annie, Juel (Braddock) Benson, and Leonard. Front Row: Mary Frances (Braddock) Holmberg, Gordon, T. P. and Bertha (Braddock) Gary

In 1912, Leo met and married Annie Laura Lefler. They moved to Sturgis, KY in the Hazel Ben community in 1913. They had three (3) daughters and three (3) sons: Agnes Jewel, Joseph Leonard, Mary Frances, James Gordon, Theodore Patrick and Bertha Ann. The older children attended Mount Pleasant School and the younger children attended the Sturgis schools. Leo worked in several mines and farms during his lifetime.

Leo and Jimmy married sisters, Annie and Ida Lefler.

Agnes Juel Braddock married Lester Benson in 1933. Lester was employed by the Bill Holt farms near Sturgis, later by the Syers Service Station and at Camp Breckinridge. They had four children, Howard, Morgan, Patsy and Kathaleen.

Joseph Leonard Braddock married Anna Kathryn Markham in 1941. Leonard worked at Camp Breckinridge, farmed and at a saw mill before going to the coal mines in 1955. They have three children, Mary Ann, Leonard Thomas and Linda.

Mary Frances Braddock married Ben Holmberg of Chicago in 1945. Ben was in the armed services and was wounded twice while serving in the Pacific. They have two sons, James and Scott.

James Gordon Braddock married Isabelle M. McCauley of Chicago in 1949. Before going into the armed services in 1942 Gordon worked in Chicago and at Camp Breckinridge. After serving in nine countries he came home in 1945 and worked for the Sturgis Hardware before going into the mines in 1953. He worked there for 31 years. They have five children, James Patrick, Shelia Marie, Vincent Joseph, Theresa Ann and Brendan Allard.

Theodore Patrick Braddock married Ruth Fox of Sturgis. T. P. worked about 38 years for Whirlpool Company. He served in the Army from 1943 to 1945 in Europe. He was wounded twice and received three medals. T. P. and Ruth have a combined family of four children: Nancy, Sharon, Theodore and Peggy.

Bertha Ann Braddock married William Gary in 1942. Bill served in the armed services and worked at Camp Breckinridge. Bertha Ann and Bill had one son, William Richard. Bertha Ann died in 1946 as the result of a tragic coal stove explosion.

ELI BRANTLEY

On May 2, 1922 Eli, 1875-1968, and Nora Reynolds Brantley, 1878-1946, moved their children, two horses, three pigs, four crates of chickens, one dog, a screen wire cage containing nine cats, and a square grooved piano from their farm near Blackford to 701 Grant Street in Sturgis.

With boys sitting on the back of the coupling poles, leading two milk cows, the train of five wagons, piled seven feet high contained every necessary item to feed and bed down nine family members that night, and to introduce us to the ways of town living.

Eli and Nora (Reynolds) Brantley

Our house was built for one of the Illinois Central Railroad bosses when those tracks were laid and was still painted their colors, yellow with red trim, when we bought it with $110.00 of borrowed money. It had three porches, five rooms, one small closet that held all our clothes with space to spare; no electricity, but it did have a wide path out back.

The two bedrooms contained two double beds each, dressers and chairs. A leatherette davinette in the living room opened to make a bed, and a tall folding bed in the dining room

let down to make another one. When other families visited us; the lid of the square grand was folded down, a feather bed put on the top of it, and that slept four kids, crosswise. The pedals came off, and another feather bed was put under the piano and four more slept there crosswise—we feuded over who would get to sleep where. Company was welcome and we always had room for one more.

The Brantley's parented eleven children: Claude, Ben, Genie, Archie, Bert, Herb, Ina Pearl, Ruby, (Abe) Alpha, Cella and Helen. We were reared on Christian principles, the belief in hard work, and to walk in the opposite direction when trouble arose. We slept with the windows open and the doors were never locked for we considered everyone to be our friend. Eli and Nora are the grandparents of 18, the great grandparents of 28, and the great, great grandparents of four.

Eli Brantley was a loyal and faithful employee in the West Kentucky Coal Company's Machine Shop at Mine Number Two until his retirement. The most money he made was 66 2/3 cents per hour, but with that he gave his family shelter, clothing, food and all the education that any of his children wanted. He was so grateful that he has never had to be on the Government Relief program or work on the W.P.A.

Nora Reynolds Brantley's hands were never idle. She was devoted entirely to the comfort and welfare of her family, to helping with the sick people in her neighborhood, and to feeding the hungry hoboes who came to her doors during those "Depression" years. She never turned a deaf ear to any person's needs.

Sturgis was a wonderful place to grow up in for we said "Howdy" to everyone. It's also a wonderful place to grow old in for it's people still care about each other. The memories we have of this place warms our hearts to this day, and we shall always be happy to call it "Home."

BRINKLEY

Mary Lucile Hall born Sept. 1, 1910. Married Dewey Clifton Brinkley on June 30, 1928 (born Aug. 19, 1907). Three children: Janice Hall Brinkley, born Feb. 5, 1935, married Henry Ramey on Nov. 20, 1952. Four Children: Vicki Maureen Ramey, born July 15, 1953, David Henry Ramey, born Aug. 15, 1955, Douglas Alan Ramey, born May 19, 1959, Karen Fay Ramey, born July 19, 1960.

Ida Ann Brinkley, born Jan. 3, 1939, married Frank Waggoner on June 30, 1957 (born Dec. 2, 1936). Two children: Teresa Jane Waggoner, born March 9, 1959, married Craig Owen Manley on Dec. 22, 1979. Two children: Derek Manley, born April 11, 1984, and Jay Manley, born Dec. 9, 1986.

Robert Frank Waggoner, born Sept. 13, 1962, married Amy Byars on June 27, 1986.

Martha Kay Brinkley, born April 13, 1947, married Dwight Paul Little on June 15, 1968 (born Aug. 7, 1946). One child: Paul Bryan Little, born July 18, 1970.

JAMES EDWARD AND SHIRLEY BROWN

James is a farmer in the Pride Community where he was born July 9, 1926. He married Shirley Ann Daniel, born Sept. 3, 1929, on Nov. 18, 1956, at the Broadway Christian Church in Lexington, KY.

He is the son of Dennie Gist Brown, born Sept. 10, 1903, died Sept. 1, 1982, buried in Pride-Bordley Cemetery, and Floy Arnold Brown, born April 28, 1902. They were married November 14, 1923 in Webster County, KY. He has a sister, Betty Jo Brown and a brother Charles "Sammy" Brown. His paternal grandparents were Charles Caldwell Brown, born Oct. 10, 1860, died Nov. 10, 1945 and Ada Jones Brown, born in Dawson Springs, KY on Oct. 13, 1871, died Sept. 1, 1915. His great grandfather was the Rev. W. W. Brown, a Cumberland Presbyterian preacher, who ministered for many of the churches in this area. Arnold, born Dec. 21, 1878, died Jan. 1, 1974. They operated a store at Arnold Station for many years.

L-R: James, Nancy and Shirley Brown

Shirley is the daughter of George Leslie Daniel, Sr., born Aug. 1, 1897, died June 15, 1970 and Beulah Holt Daniel, born March 8, 1896, died Aug. 15, 1980. Both are buried in Pythian Ridge Cemetery. (Listed under Daniel-Holt).

They are the parents of one daughter, Nancy Ann Brown, born Oct. 10, 1960 in Evansville, IN. She graduated from the University of Kentucky in 1982 with a B.S. degree in Journalism and Sociology. At this writing she is External Communications Coordinator for St. Joseph Hospital in Phoenix, AZ.

James began farming at an early age. He purchased his first farm in partnership with his Dad in 1945. He took two years from his vocation to serve his country during the Korean Conflict in 1954-56 and spent 14 months of that time in Alaska in the Tank Division. He is a member of the First Baptist Church where he has taught Sunday School. He is also a 40-year member of the Masonic Lodge. Before marriage Shirley was employed by the Farmers State Bank. She is a member of the First Christian Church and the Daughters of the

126

American Revolution. In politics they are both Democrats. *Submitted by Shirley Brown*

JOHN FRANKLIN BUSH SR. AND SUSAN A. BUSH

John Franklin Bush Sr. son of Loranzo Dow Bush and Alymra (Greenwood) Bush was born Jan. 17, 1891 in Trigg County, KY. Susan Albine (Tuggle) Bush was born July 4, 1895 in Tuggleville, Trigg County, KY. She was the daughter of Abner Tuggle and Susan (Wilson) Tuggle. John Franklin Bush Sr. died May 27, 1966.

They were married in Cadiz, KY, Oct. 15, 1915. Frank Bush was working in Blackford, KY for the I. C. Railroad. They moved to Sturgis around 1920.

He worked as a foreman at the car shop for the West Kentucky Coal Company in Sturgis until his retirement in 1956.

L-R: John Franklin, Benjamin, Mrs. Sudie Bush, Frank Sr. and Mary (Watson) Bush

He also had one of the largest blacksmith shops in Union Co. from the late 1920s till early 1930s. This was during the depression years.

At the blacksmith shop he shoed the little mine mules for the #2 mines, at Sturgis. He also built wagons, wagon wheels, and did all types of general blacksmithing.

Frank Bush Sr. and wife Sudie had two sons - John Franklin Bush Jr. born March 30, 1923 and Benjamin Ravdin Bush born Dec. 10, 1926.

Both sons served in the Armed Forces in World War II. John Franklin Bush Jr. served in the U. S. Army Air Corps from Feb. 5, 1943 to March 1946. Benjamin Ravdin Bush was in the Air Force Engineer Corps and served from April 1946 to March 1947.

John Franklin Bush Jr. is married to Virginia (Logan) Bush and they are the parents of three children - John Franklin Bush III, Cathy Susan Bush, and Robert Scott Bush.

He worked as a foreman in the die-cast department of Gamco in Henderson, KY until his retirement in 1986.

Bejamin Ravdin Bush married Mary (Watson) Bush and they had four children, Ben Bush, Frank Allan Bush, Elizabeth Ann Bush, and Diana K. Bush.

He attended the University of Kentucky and graduated from the Louisville School of Pharmacy.

He was a partner in a drugstore at the Paoli, IN Clinic at the time of his death Feb. 23, 1981.

CALLAWAY

John Maxwell Callaway born in Campbell Co. VA in 1832 came to Union County, KY, with his family in 1873 from Bedford County, VA. He served under Robert E. Lee, Battery B. 10th VA heavy artillery, surrendered with Lee at Appomottax Court House. He married Ariana Maria Rosser, she was born Botetourt County, VA, Dec. 2, 1834 m. Bedford County, VA, Oct. 21, 1852, she died DeKoven, KY, July 19, 1882. They had 11 children, 6 lived to be grown. Thomas William, Ariana Cralle, Nancy Logwood, Virginia Long, Margaret Marcella and Louisa Maxwell, who was born in Kentucky.

Row 1 - Margaret O'Nan, Grand-papa Callaway, Helen Lowery on lap, Mildred O'Nan, Mary Va. Callaway, row 2 - Wm. P. Donan, Eleanor Newman, Louise Callaway, Eleanor and Virginia O'Nan, Rosser Callaway Jr., John and David Donan, row 3 - Frances Newman, William and Maxwell Callaway, Aug. 6, 1924

Thomas William came to Union Co. with his parents, was born Lynchburg, VA, Aug. 6, 1853 m. Louisa (Lou) Long at White Sulphur Springs, KY, Dec. 5, 1876. He died Dec. 26, 1928, Sturgis, KY buried Pythian Ridge Cemetery. Lou was born Nov. 29, 1850, died May 5, 1896 after lifting a churn, breaking a blood vessel. Daughter Eleanor 18 years old took over care of the children. She is buried Mt. Pleasant Cemetery, near Sullivan, KY. Callaway's were Presbyterians. She was the daughter of Albert Gallatin Long and Maria Kenner Cralle. Long's came to Kentucky from Campbell Co., VA in 1836. Armistead Sr. officer in American Revolution was given a land grant of several thousand acres. Armistead Jr. and Albert Gallatin and families came and settled White Sulphur Springs, KY. Callaway's and Long's were friends in Virginia.

Thomas William and Lou had 6 children Eleanor Long m. Obediah Newman, of Morganfield, John Maxwell m. Mayme Waskom, Adeline Jones m. Dr. D. C. Donan, Morganfield, KY. Mary Louise m. Leonard Lowery, Rosser William m. Katherine Christison and Ariana Wyndham m. Walter Sturgis O'Nan. Thomas William m. (2) Hattie Williamson after children were grown. He was a farmer and mine owner, later selling the mines to son Rosser also owned a garage. *Submitted by Virginia Thornsberry*

BENNIE AND EDITH CARVER

Mr. Bennie Carver was born in Elk Valley, KY, to David Taylor and Daisy Castel Carver. He married Edith Pearl Benson who was born in Union County to William Carroll and Mayme Benson on July 9, 1929.

The Carvers married on July 20, 1946 at Pond Fork Baptist Church. Bennie Carver worked at Popular Ridge and Tom Henry Mines at Sullivan, KY. They later left Union County and moved to Dawson Springs, KY, where he worked at Dawson Daylight and Marsh Brother's for 17 years before retiring from mining. They moved to Vincennes, IN where Bennie Carver worked as maintenance superintendent of Park Recreation for 15 years. Mr. Carver worked at Kemmell Park Camp Site for 10 years in Vincennes, IN before retiring and moved back to the quiet country side of Sturgis, KY, where life is quiet and the people are friendly. Mr. Carver now spends his time working with flowers, fishing and hunting and with his wife Edith enjoying their 20 grandchildren.

Bernie and Edith Carver and children

Mrs. Edith Benson Carver attended Grove Center Grade School, Salem Grade School, Sturgis Junior High and Sturgis High School where she was in the Beta Club, Latin Club. She won 1st Place in track when attending Sturgis Jr. High. While Edith lived in Vincennes, IN, she worked at the White Kitchen and Executive Inn for 15 years before she and her husband moved back to Sturgis. Edith has worked at Union County Hospital for 10 years. Edith attended and graduated from University of Southern Indiana for continuing education. She is a certified Dietary Manager and a member of D.M.A. Association since 1986.

The Carver's have 7 children; Patricia Carver, Owensboro, KY; Bernie Carver, Sturgis; Donna Carver Marsh, Sturgis; Ann Carver Marsh, Sturgis; Steve Carver, Mitchell, IN; David Carver, Sturgis; Mayme Carver Sinclair, Windsor, VA. All four sons of the Carver's were in the Armed Forces as well as a son-in-law. Mr. and Mrs. Bennie Carver are members of the Sturgis Missionary Church. Mrs. Carver

worked with Sturgis Girl Scout program five years. *Submitted by Patricia Gean Carver*

DAVID AND RENEE CARTER

Dawn Renee West Carter, daughter of Robert and Sharry West was born March 7, 1956 in the old Sturgis Hospital.

She is a lifetime resident of Sturgis and a graduate of Union County High School.

Renee is married to David Wayne Carter son of Julius and Jean Carter, former minister of the Methodist Church in Sturgis.

David, Renee, Chad and Dawn Carter

They are the parents of two children, Chad Wayne age, 14, and Stacy Dawn age 13.

Renee and David are former owners of the J & J House of Jewels Jewelry Store, which was located at 501 Adams Street in Sturgis opening in March 1977 and were in partnership with his parents until it closed its doors for business in December 1984.

David is presently employed in Carmi, IL at the Patiki Mines.

Renee maintains and operates the Little League Concession, where both children are active in sports.

They presently reside in DeKoven, KY. *Submitted by Renee West Carter*

JULIUS AND JEAN CARTER

Julius and Jean Carter moved to Sturgis in 1972, where he was appointed Pastor of the united Methodist Church. They are the parents of 3 sons, Roger Dale, Larry Earl and David Wayne, and have 5 grandchildren.

As a former watch repairman, Brother Carter and Dr. John Arnold of Sturgis formed a partnership and opened a retail jewelry store in March 1977 under the name of J & J House of Jewels.

After about 1 1/2 years later, their son David bought John Arnold's half of the business, thus making it a family operation.

David Carter is married to the former Renee West, daughter of Robert and Sharry West.

In 1978 Bro. Carter was appointed to Brandenburg, KY in Meade County. David and Renee then became the managers of the store.

Julius and Jean moved to Cadiz, KY in June 1980, after being appointed to the Cadiz Church. While living in Cadiz, J & J House of Jewels bought another store in Princeton, KY, formerly known as Lucille's Jewelry. Jean managed the store in Princeton under the same name of J & J House of Jewels.

The store in Sturgis did a large volume of business for a town its size, but because of the substantial loss during an armed robbery on Dec. 3, 1980, the store was never able to recover and on Dec. 30, 1984 the store closed its doors for business.

Julius and Jean presently reside in Louisville, KY, where Julius is Minister at the Epworth United Methodist Church. *Submitted by Jean Carter*

CERTAIN

Wilbert and Ethel Certain. Wilbert Certain, son of Charles E. and Lucy Henry Certain was born October 21, 1909 at DeKoven, KY. Wilbert helped his father in construction work and later went to the coal mines. When the depression hit the country he went to work on the Davis Brother's farms near Sturgis. He later went back to the coal mines and worked there untill his health forced him to retire Aug. 17, 1969. He was a coal miner for 34 years.

Ethel McKendree Certain was born near Henshaw, KY, Dec. 30, 1911. Her parents were Arthur J. (Pete) McKendree and Lucy Luellen Gibbs. Ethel graduated from the DeKoven High School.

They are the parents of four children, two sons and two daughters, and seven grandchildren. The oldest is Joyce married to Kenneth Price of near Clay, KY. They own their farm and Kenneth is a school bus driver. After school Joyce worked at Sturgis Grocery Stores. Then went to Farmers State Bank and worked there from 1954-1983.

Harold, their oldest son, started at the Sturgis Rexall Drugstore at age 15. After high school he went into Pharmacy School. After college he came back to Sturgis, then back to Lexington. He is now vice president of Super-X Drugs in operations. He married Judith Brewer. They have one son and one daughter. Son Douglas is with Caldwell Bankers, Residential Sales. Their daughter, Carmen is at Kansas University in Lawrence, KS. Harold's home is at Cincinnati, OH.

Son, Garland, is married to Mary Catherine Holloran. He has one daughter Cindy who lives at Henderson, KY. His son David lives at home. Garland worked in Union County School System for a few years. He is now

President of Farmers State Bank. Their home is in Sturgis.

Daughter Sherrie is married to Stanley G. Williams. They live in Richland, WA, where Stanley is minister with the Richland Church of Christ. They have three children, Kerry Wayne, Melanie and Jarrod.

Mr. Certain departed this life January 13, 1971. *Submitted by Ethel Certain*

GEORGE MASON CERTAIN

George Mason Certain was born March 30, 1915 at DeKoven, Kentucky the son of Charles E. and Lucy Henry Certain. Virginia E. Certain was born April 21, 1915 at DeKoven, KY the daughter of Robertson and Mary Nash Campbell. The Certains were married Dec. 25, 1940 at Morganfield, KY.

In the early years of their marriage, Mason worked in the farming area. When the Earle C. Clements Center was being built, he worked in construction. Later he went to Evansville, IN and worked at Servel Inc. When World War II was declared he worked at the Ship Yards making L.S.Ts.

Mason Certain Family

The last twenty years before retirement he worked for Island Creek Coal Company at Uniontown, KY. He retired in November 1975.

Virginia has always been a homemaker, except for a short time, when she worked for Ben Franklin and Thread & Thimble.

They have four children, Judith Ann who is an elementary school teacher in Madisonville, KY and is married to Robert Harrison, principal of the Hall St. School in Madisonville. They have two daughters, Hope, a sophomore at the Community College, Heather, a senior at North Hopkins High School.

Gary lives in Forest, MS and is self-employed. He is married to Betty Herron who is a Speech Therapist in the Forest City School. They have two children Faye and Mason both middle school students.

Connie Sue is employed by the Union County School System. She is married to Terry Moore, a Civil Engineer for Kentucky Utility. They have two sons, Jonathan at Middle School, and Marc, fifth grade at Morganfield Elementary.

Bonnie is a busy housewife. She is married to Steve Curtis who works for Texas Gas in Owensboro. They live in Madisonville, KY.

They have two children, Andrew, second grade, and Ginny Sue, kindergarten. They attend school in Hanson, KY.

All the children graduated from the Sturgis High School.

July and Gary both have degrees from the Western Kentucky University in Bowling Green.

Virginia was in the last graduating class of the DeKoven High School 1934.

Mason and Virginia still live in DeKoven, "the little city among the hills." *Submitted by Virginia Campbell Certain*

CHRISTIAN

This picture was taken in 1889 when Thomas Fountain Christian was about one year old showing him standing beside his father, Robert Granville Christian. His grandparents, John Granville Christian and Rebecca Givens Christian are seated in front of them. The other side of the picture shows his mother, Virginia Hammack Christian and seated in front of her are her parents, Thomas Hammack and Elizabeth Montgomery Hammack. The two young boys on the front row are his brothers, John and Charlie G. Christian. The girls at the sides are his sisters, Tippie and Maggie who died in their early teens. Two brothers, Robert Spurlin and Montgomery Givens Christian had not been born when this picture was made.

John Granville Christian was the son of Robert Black Christian; his father was Matthew Christian, who was the founder of the Christian family in Union County. Matthew Christian was the son of Patrick (Paddy) Christian of Augusta County, VA. Patrick was a soldier in the Revolutionary War and was present at the surrender of Cornwallis at Yorktown.

Thomas Fountain Christian was born in 1888. He married Inez McCann in January 1910. They had six children: Harold Elsworth Christian, deceased in 1981; William Granville Christian, Nashville, TN; Marilyn Christian (Omer), Marietta, GA; Kathryn Christian (Fletcher, Sturgis, KY; and twins, Dorothy Christian (Stiles), Charlotte, NC and Charles Franklin Christian, Bethpage, TN.

Submitted by Kathryn C. Fletcher and William G. Christian

CICERO SMITH COLEMAN

Cicero Smith Coleman (Sept. 15, 1839 - Jan. 2, 1927) and his wife, the former Mary Ann Adams (April 24, 1851 - April 1, 1931) and their young baby girl, Eliza Eleanor Coleman, moved to Sturgis from Bordley, KY. Their home was one of the first houses built in Sturgis before the town actually existed.

Mr. Coleman extended two rooms on the front of their home planning a general store, as he expected "Monroe" to be the main street of town. He did do business there for a time. In later years the two front rooms were taken off the house and it has remained that way to this day. The house still stands today at 305 Monroe Street.

Women on ends unknown. Starting with man on left, Cicero Smith Coleman, Eliza Coleman, Mary Ann Adams Coleman, Nell Harris Coleman.

Original House - 305 Monroe Street

Two children were raised in this home; Nell Harris Coleman Royster (Jan. 5, 1892 - Aug. 22, 1974) and Eliza Eleanor Coleman Hunt (Aug. 10, 1889 - Jan. 23, 1976). Mr. Coleman, a graduate of Georgetown College, built the first school in Sturgis on Pike Street, one block over from their home on Monroe. Mr. Coleman, who was a teacher, owned the land. In the 1890s he not only taught his children but all other children in the area who were able to come. He was an active participant in establishing a form of government for the betterment of the community. Also, every Sunday he could be found in the first pew of the First Baptist Church.

Mr. Coleman's wife, Mary Ann Adams, was a graduate of Bethleham Academy near Louisville, KY. She majored in Art and Music and gave music lessons for many years in Sturgis. Their daughter, Eliza Eleanor, graduated from the first graduating class of Sturgis College

Conservatory. She married William Haden Hunt (Dec. 25, 1887 - Feb. 6, 1962) on Nov. 1, 1909. Haden Hunt was the son of Daniel Hunt (1865 - 1947) and Eugenia Nix, also early settlers of Sturgis. Daniel Hunt worked in the coal mines just outside Sturgis.

Haden and Eliza Hunt had three children, Ruth Haden Hunt (April 1, 1911) Horace Hunt (Sept. 19, 1912 - 1980), and Mary Eugenia Hunt (May 12, 1915). Eliza Coleman Hunt was an accomplished pianist and played for all the silent movies at Rakes Theater in Sturgis. Her specialty was ragtime music. Haden Hunt worked in the West Kentucky Coal Company stores in Sturgis and Wheatcroft. Later he returned to Sturgis to work for George Simpson's General Store. In 1918 the family moved to East St. Louis, IL, where Haden went to work for the B. & O. Railroad until his retirement.

Nell Harris, the Coleman's younger daughter, graduated from the Sturgis College Conservatory and went to work for the Bank of Sturgis until it closed. She married Vernon Royster on May 28, 1925. Vernon was a pharmacist and managed Segreaves Drugstore for many years; the favorite afternoon social stop for fountain favorites, especially Coke. Nell and Vernon moved to St. Louis after the bank closed and she was employed by Stix, Baer & Fuller. Vernon was a pharmaceutical salesman until his retirement and lived until 1959. Nell maintained the original home at 305 Monroe Street, totally modernizing it during her summer vacations. She returned home to Sturgis to live out her life until her death in 1974. *Submitted by Ruth Haden Hunt Schmisseur and Mary Eugenia Hunt Hodges*

JOHNATHAN CATLET TAYLOR COLLINS

Johnathan Catlet Taylor "Cat" Collins was born in Union County, KY, Sept. 29, 1858. Son of Phillip and Amanda Francis Smith Collins. He had 6 brothers and 5 sisters. Two older brothers, James W. and Louis B. died in their middle 20's. John B. died in infancy, leaving Catlet the oldest surviving son.

Catlet was married April 28, 1880 to Martha Isabelle McKinley, born Dec. 17, 1855. They had 4 sons and 2 daughters, rearing their family on their farm now known as the Bill Yates place. Their children: Charles Albert married Annie R. Collins; Addie Jane "Jennie" married John Van Cleave; Ben Raymond married Ida Bell Johnson; George Noel married Olevia Urton; Mary Magdaline married Claude Collins, and John Wickliffe who died in infancy. Widowed in 1905, Catlet lived with his son Raymond, often visiting his other children. He was known throughout Union and surrounding counties for his "horse-trading" and as stock buyer for Alf Johns of Henshaw, always traveling on his "spotted pony."

Catlet's brother Phillip Otto, born July 27, 1865 married Martha Elizabeth "Mattie"

Johnathan "Cat" Collins

McMain born August 17, 1866. They had 8 children. Phillip died of typhoid fever in 1905. Said his grandson, Harold E., "Grandfather was greatly liked and was a great loss to grandmother. When her first child was born, there was an old slave cabin on the place with the remnant of a family who used to 'belong' to the family. An old negress came to grandmother and offered to help for 'she had at all the other family births.' Grandmother remembered seeing an Indian traveling through the countryside when she was a girl."

Third surviving son of Phillip was George Simpson born Jan. 23, 1869. He married Rose Ellen Veach in 1890. They had 9 children, sons Joseph Edgar, Basil Jerome, Sylvester "Red" Ambrose, and Henry Lester Nunn "Skeet." In the Collins' musical family George played the fiddle.

John Wickliffe "Wick" born Feb. 1, 1871, youngest son of Phillip married Mary Magdalene "Molly" Veatch. They had 5 sons: Ben Gilbert, Frederick Owen, Martin Andrew, and Harry. "Wick" played the bass fiddle.

Catlet was the fifth known generation of the Collins family. His grandfather, Jeremiah W., born 1788 in Virginia, married Sarah Young born 1790 in Kentucky, daughter of Christian Young. Jeremiah W. was the son of James, born 1755, Orange County, VA, and Mary Herndon. Brothers of Jeremiah (from his father's Will) were John who married Nancy Young (sister of Sarah), Edward G., and Dr. James W. Collins who married Eleanor Ann Pittman. James was the son of Edward and Jane Jones Collins, Spotsylvania County, VA.

Jeremiah W., Dr. James W., John, and Edward G. were active in the founding of Little Bethel, Highland, and other local Baptist Churches. Catlet donated the land on which Old Bethel Church now stands.

It is believed the Collins acreage originally amounted to more than 2,000 acres. It was gradually divided among the many children, or sold to Voss', Clements', Gardiners, etc. *Submitted by Jane VanCleave*

TAYLOR AND JULIA E. COLLINS

Taylor Collins was the third child of Jeremiah Adam Collins (1850 - 1927) and Sarah Elizabeth Smith Bass Collins (?). He was born Jan. 24, 1881 in Union County, KY. He married Julia Ellen Markham, the third child of William

Catlet Markham (1854 - 1928) and Emily Kate Collins Markham (1865 - 1955). Julia Ellen Markham was born August 31, 1892 in Topeka, KS. Her family moved to Union County, KY when she was a year old. Taylor and Julia were united in marriage the 16th day of May 1909, by J. W. Milspaugh in Shawneetown, IL. Their witnesses were Will McMain and Taylor's sister, Emma D. Collins Mackey.

Taylor Collins, known to his family as Pa Taylor, was a well known fiddle player and he and Julia, known as Ma Taylor, went to many a dance where he played the fiddle and she would dance every set. He also played for her many a night as she would cook meals for their family. Their family began with a daughter born March 5, 1911. She was given the name Effie Kate. Two more daughters were born, Edna Gertrude Dec. 7, 1912 and Kempie Louise Jan. 28, 1915. Next were five sons, Virgil Winston born May 3, 1917; Davis Harlen born June 7, 1919; Robert Max born June 13, 1921; Wilburn Taylor born June 2, 1924 and Jerry Add born March 19, 1926. A daughter, Virginia Irene was born April 24, 1928. To complete their family, a set of twin boys were born on Sept. 26, 1931. They were given the names of Arthur Lee nad Luther D.

Taylor and Julia Collins Family 50th Wedding Anniversary, May 1959

Five of their sons served their country and all five of them returned to their family which was considered a great blessing. Serving during World War II were Davis, Wilburn Taylor, and Jerry. Arthur and Luther served during the Korean War.

Another wonderful celebration occurred for Taylor and Julia when they celebrated their 50th wedding anniversary in May of 1959. Nearly all of their family was in attendance and all had a wonderful time. However, this was to be the last time they would all be together.

Taylor Collins passed away Feb. 4, 1961 at his home on King Street; Sturgis, KY. He is buried at Old Bethel Cemetery; Union County, KY.

Julia lived on by herself in the home place on King Street until her death Nov. 30, 1980 at Union County Hospital. She is buried along side her husband, Taylor at Old Bethal Cemetery, Union County, KY.

Now, we the decedents of this great couple must carry on with the faith, love, honesty, and

JOSEPH E. AND HELEN (COLLINS) CONN

Helen (Collins) and Joseph Conn

Joseph E. and his wife, Helen (Collins) now reside on the farm. They have five children. Michael at home. David is married to Anna Danhauer. Cynthia teaches school in Bowling Green, KY and is married to George Cole. Constance Marie is a registered nurse in Bowling Green, KY and is married to Joe Daniel. Joseph A. is married to April Holeman and lives in DeKoven, KY.

WILLIAM TRAMMELL CONN

William Trammell "Billy" Conn was born in Jefferson County, KY, Oct. 25, 1831 to John and Ann (Oliver) Conn.

His great grandparents, Hugh Conn and Mary Trammell Conn lived in Loudoun County, VA, and did not leave there. His great, great grandfather, Hugh Conn, was born in Macgilligan, Ireland in 1685, graduated from the University of Glasgow. He was a Presbyterian minister, died in Bladensburg, Prince George County, MD, June 28, 1752.

William Conn married Susan Bean, daughter of James and Matilda (Conn) Bean in Louisville, KY in September 1862. They returned to Jefferson County (Pee-Wee Valley) in 1865. They remained there until 1870, returning to Union County. Seven children were born. The survivors are Mattie Ann, John David, William Lee, Joseph, and Archie. Mrs. Conn died June 10, 1882, buried in Cypress Creek Cemetery.

Mr. Conn owned approximately 465 acres of fine farm land. He erected a large brick mansion on the hill above his bottom land in 1873. It was one of the show places of Union County. As the many visitor arrived, they would drive through a grove of Walnut trees that lined the driveway on each side. This brick home burned in the early 1900s. Marie Simpson Curry, a granddaughter, remembers this event. A large frame house was built in 1912. This home was torn down around 1960. A seed house was built in its place. Many of you farmers have had your seeds cleaned there. The homeplace is owned by two grandsons, Joseph E. Conn and Arch Conn, Jr.

130

Mr. Wm. T. Conn married Olivia Powell (1859-1935), daughter of Thomas W. Powell, Henderson County, KY, April 18, 1888. Mrs. Olivia was a school teacher. One son, Thomas Powell Conn was born August 19, 1891 and died October 9, 1956.

Mr. Conn was a member of the Christian Church for many years and was known as a prosperous man, one of few words, each one of great weight. He and Mrs. Olivia are buried in Pythian Ridge Cemetery. He died Oct. 25, 1917; she in 1935.

The bottom land is owned by Thomas Conn's four daughters, Martha, Inez, Linda and Anna.

Martha married Marlin Watson Jan. 5, 1951. They have 2 children: Marlene Blue and Larry Watson, also 3 grandsons, John Sayles, Jerad Sayles, and Bill Tom Watson.

GEORGE C. (PETE) AND RUTH MITCHELL CONWAY

Pete and Ruth were married in 1948 and at that time made their home in Sturgis. Pete's parents were Hugh and Paschal Conway. They moved to Sturgis from Grove Center in 1946. Hugh was a partner in and managed the union County Grain Company. Ruth's parents were Leonard Leslie and Onie Page Mitchell. After Ruth married, her mother, a widow, moved to Sturgis from Clay, KY. Ruth has two sisters, Betty M. Davis of Sturgis, and Sarah M. Richardson of Columbia, SC, and one brother, Leonard T. Mitchell of Henderson.

Prior to his serving in World War II in the U. S. Coast Guard, Pete was a school teacher and principal of the Sturgis Elementary School. Both Pete and Ruth attended Western Kentucky State University. After World War II, Pete and his brother, Hugh G. Conway, were partners in the Sturgis Milling Co., a wholesale feed mill, until they liquidated the business in 1978 and retired. Ruth is employed at the Farmers State Bank.

They have three children: Peter Mitchell, Ruth Leslie and Ellen Page. Peter is a surgeon in Louisville, KY. He married Lorrie Smith of Flint, MI. They have two children: Christopher Robert and Margaret Smith. Leslie is a teacher in the Math Department of Apollo High School, Owensboro, KY. She is married to George E. Carpenter, Jr., formerly of Bowling Green, KY, and they have a daughter, Kathryn Conway. Ellen is employed at First National Bank in Henderson, KY. *Submitted by Ruth M. Conway*

MARY LUE AND LOUIS COURTNEY

Mary Lue (West) Courtney was born, Sept. 23, 1938, the only daughter of Willie and Thelma West. She has four brothers, Willie Jr., Robert, James, and Harold. She graduated from Sturgis High School in 1956. On August 14, 1955, she married Louis Gilbert Courtney, son of John and Ziel Courtney of Morganfield.

Mr. and Mrs. Louis Courtney and family

Louis has worked in the coal mines for 26 years and does some farming.

Mary and Louis live on Monroe Street. They are the parents of four children, Bridget, Louis Jr., Daren, and Karen. Bridget was born April 26, 1959 and married to Jeff Winders. They have two sons, Kris and Shawn. Louis Jr. was born May 22, 1962 and married to Vicky Morris. They have two daughters, Ashley and Emily.

Daren was born June 28, 1966 and married Tonia Piper. They have a son, Jacob. Karen, a twin to Daren, was born June 28, 1966. She is married to Jeff Bradford and is a teacher at Sturgis Elementary School. *Submitted by Mary Lue Courtney*

FREDERICK J. COWAN, JR.

Mary Virginia Wesley, daughter of Roberta Wynn Wesley and Charles Wesley, was born "on the hill" in a little white house located between Pride and Sullivan. She attended Templeton one-room school for eight years. Two outhouses, one for the boys and one for the girls stood in the back of the school house. A large pot-bellied stove kept the children warm; a well with a pump gave them good cool water.

Mary graduated from Sturgis High School in 1935 and went to Louisville to business school. In 1939 she married Frederic J. Cowan, a native of New York. To this union was born Roberta Marie, Frederic Joseph, Jr. and Charles Wesley. After a divorce in 1953, Mary moved with the children to Sturgis. The next year the family moved to Louisville where the children attended school and were graduated from Atherton high School.

The Fred Cowan, Jr. family

Roberta Marie married Glenn F. Chesnut and they had two children, Anna Grace and Benjamin Thomas. This union ended in divorce in 1978. Roberta is a graduate of Southern Methodist University and Oxford in England. She is currently a professor at Candler School of Theology at Emory University in Atlanta. She is married to Richard Bondi.

Frederic Joseph Cowan, Jr. went to Darthmouth College with the help of a scholarship. After Darthmouth he served with the Peace Corps in Africa for two years. After returning to the states he worked as a consumer advocate in Little Rock, AR, where he met and married Linda Marshall Scholle, an attorney. The next year, they moved to Boston where Fred attended Harvard Law School. After graduation Fred joined a law firm in Louisville where he became interested in politics and subsequently was elected state representative from the 32nd district in Louisville, serving for six years. In 1987, he was elected attorney general of Kentucky with a large majority of the vote.

Fred spent many summer vacations in Union County with his Aunt Kas and Uncle A. D. Sprague and their four children. He has said many times that his most pleasant childhood memories go back to the good times on the farm.

Charles Wesley Cowan is a graduate of the University of Kentucky and has a doctors degree in anthropology from the University of Michigan. As a small child he searched for arrowheads in the fields behind his grandparents' house. These finds kindled his desire to look back into native American Indian culture. He is currently Curator of Archeology at the Museum of Natural History in Cincinnati. He is married to Shelly Gertzog. They have two children, Samuel Withers and Anna Riva. "Sam" was named after his great, great grandfather Withers who was a Confederate soldier in the Civil War.

THOMAS AND CAROLYN DALTON

William Thomas Dalton, son of Henry Lively and Lulu Maude Eddings Dalton of Clay, KY, was born Nov. 30, 1929. After his mother's death of typhoid fever, he and his father moved to Sturgis to live. Thomas attended the Sturgis Schools and was graduated from Sturgis High School in 1947. He attended college at Union University, Jackson, TN, and Georgetown College, Georgetown, KY.

During his childhood days after school and on Saturdays, Thomas would work at Talbotts 5¢ and 10¢ Store where he would sweep the wooden floors and assist the clerks. They would make their own floor sweep getting sawdust from Alloway's lumber yard and added red oil. Working there, during World War II with it's sugar rationing, he remembers when rare shipments of candy would come in, they would be saved until Saturday, then he would help the clerks wait on all the many

people that would come in and purchase it all on that day. He also had his regular "coal customers" filling coal buckets for people and emptying ashes from their coal stoves and fireplaces each day.

L-R: Thomas and Carolyn Dalton, Stephen and Rozanna Dalton Thompson, Daphne and Kelli Crooks Dalton. Front: Leslye Ann, Brian Christopher and Erick Dalton

Thomas married his childhood sweetheart, Carolyn Seibert, in 1950.

Carolyn Ann, daughter of Carroll Leslie and Annie Willie Callender Seibert was born on Dec. 26, 1931. She attended the Sturgis Schools and was graduated in 1949. She attended Georgetown College in 1950.

One of her remembrances of Sturgis was the large crowd of people that were in town on Saturday night filling the sidewalks. Some would come to town and park their car early in the morning so they could sit in it later and watch the people. The store would stay open until after 10 p.m. or when the show was over for someone might come by and make a purchase.

Thomas served the U.S. Navy for four years 1952-1956, then returned to Sturgis to live. He joined his father-in-law at the Sturgis Furniture Co. and later upon Mr. Seibert's retirement managed the firm.

Thomas and Carolyn are parents of three children, Rozanna, Brian Thomas and Daphne Ann.

Rozanna Dalton Thompson, wife of Attorney Stephen Price Thompson, lives in Louisville, KY. Rozanna was graduated from Union County High School in 1971, Georgetown College, Georgetown, KY and The Southern Baptist Seminary School of Music, Louisville, KY. From 1980-1982 she served as a missionary Journeyman to Brazil. Rozanna is on staff at Kentucky Opera, Louisville, and is a freelance harpist.

Brian Thomas Dalton was graduated from Union County High in 1973. Brian is married to Kelli Lynn Crook Dalton and they have three children, Christopher Thomas, Erick Timothy and Leslye Ann. Brian and Kelli live in Sturgis in the house where four generations of his family have lived and his mother was born. He is employed with Pyro Mine.

Daphne Ann was graduated from Union County High School in 1984 and Carson-Newman College, Jefferson City, TN. She is an Interior Designer and is employed with a

Design Firm in Nashville, TN. *Submitted by Carolyn Dalton*

G. L. DANIEL-HOLT

George Leslie Daniel was the son of George Oliver Daniel, born Oct. 1, 1874, died Oct. 16, 1947 in Evansville, IN and Emma Sue Omer Daniel, born Dec. 29, 1876, died Dec. 22, 1962. They were married Sept. 17, 1896 in the parlor of St. George Hotel, Evansville, IN. His paternal grandparents were Thomas Jefferson Daniel, born in Louisville, KY on Nov. 18, 1849, died in Union County, May 4, 1914, and Jennie Williamson Daniel, born in Jefferson County, KY, Feb. 27, 1852, died Jan. 31, 1924. They married at the bride's home on Feb. 20, 1872. Both are buried in Pythian Ridge Cemetery. His maternal grandparents were Thomas D. Omer, born March 20, 1845, died May 16, 1918 and Sarah Henry Omer, 1845-1885.

Less, as he was known to his friends, was born on a farm in the Pond Fork Community on Aug. 1, 1897, died June 15, 1970. He was a farmer and during the winter months he operated a slaughter house and was known throughout this area for their homemade country sausage. He was a deacon in the Christian Church.

He married Beulah Holt on Oct. 17, 1922 in Morganfield, Kentucky. She was the daughter of James Harrison Holt, born Aug. 26, 1857, died Jan. 1, 1931 and Lucy Whitecotton Holt, born May 15, 1960 died March 31, 1901. Her paternal grandparents were Peter C. Holt, born in Spencer Co., June 22, 1826, died March 30, 1888, and Sarah Reasor Holt born in Jeffersonville, KY, on April 2, 1837, died May 7, 1932. Peter C. came by flatboat to Uniontown, KY to claim his bride on Dec. 13, 1853. The Holts and Reasors were among the pioneers of Kentucky. Her maternal grandparents were George W. Whitecotton, born Oct. 27, 1802 in Virginia, died July 19, 1889 in Union County and Sarah Smith Hobbs Whitecotton, a widow, born Oct. 18, 1818, died April 3, 1870. Both are buried in the Caseyville Cemetery.

Beulah was born March 8, 1896, died Aug. 15, 1980. She had a twin, Eula and they were born and raised along with two sisters and two brothers on a farm that is included as part of the Sturgis Airport. She was a member of the First Baptist church.

They had four children: Dorothy Sue, born Aug. 29, 1924, married Douglas L. Miller, born Jan. 17, 1921, on Oct. 14, 1957 in Louisville, KY where they reside - no children; Shirley Ann, born Sept. 3, 1929, married James Edward Brown, born July 9, 1926, on Nov. 18, 1956 and reside in the Pride Community - one daughter, Nancy Ann, born Oct. 10, 1960; James Owsyn, born Oct. 11, 1932, married Mary Kate Hudson June 17, 1961 in Walnut, MS - one daughter, Laurie Daniel Heinz, born Sept. 29, 1962 in Texas and now lives in Memphis, TN. James, a Capt. in the U.S.A.F., was killed July 9, 1964 in the Smokey Mountains near Elli Jay, GA, while piloting a jet plane, buried in Pythian Ridge; George Leslie, Jr., born July 9, 1936, married Sylvia Carter, born Nov. 27, 1936, on April 11, 1960 in Sturgis - two daughters, Leticia Gayle, born Sept. 2, 1964 and Dana Danielle Daniel, born March 13, 1974. They reside in Evansville, IN.

THOMAS JEFFERSON DANIEL

Thomas Jefferson Daniel (1849-1914) a son of Joseph G. and Mary Daniel of Louisville, KY married Jennie E. Williamson (1852-1924) on Feb. 20, 1872 in Jefferson County, KY. They had five children, Annie May, George Oliver, Emma Belle, Thomas Jefferson Jr., and Clyde Simpson before they decided to move westward. In March 1880, when young Clyde was only six weeks old, they journeyed down the Ohio River by boat and entered Union County through Uniontown and settled down on a farm just north of Morganfield. Thomas and Jennie had six more children, Cordie Ella, Roy Everette, Bessie Roser, Ruby Earl, Dora Jackson, and Hester Katherine. Three of these eleven children, Thomas Jefferson Jr., Cordie Ella and Hester Katherine, succumbed to childhood illness. The other eight children grew up and married into Union County families such as Markham, Omer, Ames, Hughes, and Montgomery. The oldest son, George Oliver, married Emma Sue Omer, daughter of Thomas Daniel and Sallie Crocket (Henry) Omer on Sept. 17, 1896. George was a farmer in the Pond Fork area of southern Union County and he and Emma Sue had four children, George Leslie, Oswyn Omer, Jennie V., and Clarence Earl. Their daughter, Jennie V., was courted by and married Wallace Burns Quirey, the youngest son of Otho Carter and Sophvonia Ecton Quirey of Sturgis on Nov. 20, 1921. Wallace Burns and Jennie V. Quirey had three children, Alla Burns, Earl Daniel, and Otho Carter. Alla B. is a retired office supply salesman, single, and living in Sturgis. Earl Daniel is a retired Federal Employee, married to Ann (Lynch) Applin, daughter of Claude and Mary Lynch, and they also live in Sturgis. Otho Carter is an ironworker, married to Dollie Anglin, and they are living in Paducah, KY. *Submitted by Earl Daniel Quirey*

CHARLES CAUDILL DAVIS

Charles Caudill Davis married Betty Carolyn Mitchell at the United Methodist Church in Sturgis, on Oct. 21, 1950.

Betty was born in Clay, KY, on Oct. 14, 1928, the daughter of Leonard Leslie and Onie Page Mitchell. Charles (Chic) was born in Union County, KY, on April 2, 1927, the son of Charles Eberley Davis and Cappie Caudill Davis. Charles is the fourth generation of the Davis family born in Union County. His great grandfather, Dr. Ila Metcalfe Davis, was born in Union County on Jan. 22, 1827. Dr. Ila was the great grandson of Ishmail Davis, who was

132

born in Wales in 1745 and immigrated to Maryland, United States. Dr. Ila's eldest son, Charles Metcalfe Davis (born March 9, 1862), married Josephine Carolyn Eberle (born May 13, 1864) on March 4, 1885, in Caseyville, KY. Josephine Carolyn was the middle of five children born of the marriage of Charles Eberle and Katherine Leibenguth. Mr. Eberle was born in Rosemeyer, France in 1838, and Ms. Leibenguth was born in Welshback, Germany, on Jan. 2, 1843. They married in Caseyville in February, 1861.

Charles Eberley Davis was born on April 5, 1893, the seventh of eleven children of Charles Metcalfe and Josephine Carolyn Davis. He married Cappie Caudill, of Poorfolk, KY on Feb. 22, 1895. Eberley and Cappie had four children: Rebecca Ann Davis (Clegg), who was born November 17, 1925 and died in July 1982; Charles Caudill Davis; Robert Metcalfe Davis, born Sept. 10, 1932; and Alice Eberley Davis who died at birth on Nov. 22, 1935. Charles Caudill and Robert Metcalfe ("Bob") have farmed for many years as Davis Brothers. Their farm is located approximately three miles west of Sturgis and two miles north of Caseyville and includes much of the farm that was originally acquired by their grandfather, Charles Metcalfe Davis.

Charles and Betty are the parents of five children. Sarah Page was born May 8, 1952, and married James R. Ricketts Jan. 9, 1971. They built a house on the farm in 1978 where they live with their two sons, Lance Davis and Charles Matthew. Sarah is a teacher at the Sturgis Elementary School and Jim is in management with Peabody Coal Company at the Camp Complex.

Alice Anne was born Jan. 19, 1955 and is married to Thomas Keith Hancock. They live on St. Ambrose Road, with Anne's seven year old son, Charles Randall. Anne is a teacher at Sturgis Elementary School and Keith is employed by Tradewater Railway Company.

Richard Eberley was born March 5, 1957, and married Margaret ("Meg") Riggs on Aug. 11, 1984. They live on the farm in the family home where Eberley's grandfather were born. They have one daughter, Sarah Margaret ("Maggie"). Eberley is a lawyer and was recently elected Union County Attorney. Meg formerly taught at Sturgis Elementary School and is now a housewife.

Mary Carolyn Davis was born March 23, 1959. Mary lives in Peoria, Illinois, where she teaches school and is the head girls' coach in basketball, volleyball and soccer.

Charles Metcalfe was born Jan. 23, 1964, and married Kim Stanley Henshaw on July 27, 1985. Charlie and Kim reside on Highway 109 near the family farm. Charlie is an accountant with York, Neel & Company in Morganfield, and Kim is employed by Charlie Quinn Lumber Company.

ROBERT DAVIS

Sturgis High School 1950 Classmates,

Suzanna Wesley, daughter of Roberta Wynns and Charles R. Wesley, and Robert Metcalfe Davis, son of Cappie Caudill and C. Eberley Davis, were married March 9, 1952. They are life-long farmers and members of the First Presbyterian Church in Sturgis. They live in the "Old Brick House" located on Highway 109 and 492. This house was the first brick house built in Union County. They have three children:

Laura, a graduate of U.K., married Robert Louis Holt on Aug. 17, 1974. They have three children, Heath Davis, Benjamin Forrest, and Katherine Suzanne Holt. They own and operate a family clothing store in Greenville, KY.

Randolph Blane, a graduate of Mississippi State University, married Gayle Braunecker of Jasper, IN, on March 26, 1988. They live in Plainfield, IN, and are in the insurance business.

Robert Hunter, a graduate of U.K., married Vickie Ann James of Ohio County, KY, on March 9, 1984. They have two children, Jonathan Robert and Lauren Suzanna. Hunter is a registered Professional Engineer and licensed land surveyor and is employed by Pyro Mining Company. They live on the family farm in the house once occupied by Charles Metcalfe Davis, Hunter's great grandfather.

ROY B. DAVIS SR.

Roy Burnett Davis Sr. was born Oct. 8, 1897 to Mr. John Buchannan Davis and Rebecca Sprague Davis. John B. Davis was the son of Miles Davis and Jane Barnes Davis and Rebecca Sprague was the daughter of Joseph Sprague and Plexona Winstead Sprague. Both the Miles Davis family and Joseph Sprague family were early settlers in Union County. Roy B. Davis married Glennie Hawes Davis on July 29, 1917. Glennie Hawes was the daughter of Samuel P. Hawes and Amy Elizabeth Ford Hawes of Ohio County, KY. The Hawes and Ford families were early settlers in Ohio County.

Roy B. Davis Sr. and Glennie Hawes Davis were the parents of four children, Rebecca, Roy B. Davis Jr., Amy Elizabeth, and Robert Hawes.

Rebecca Davis married Virgil Kearney of McKenzie, TN and they have one daughter Bonnie Kearney Edmondson and one granddaughter Rebecca Deane Edmondson.

Mr. and Mrs. Roy B. Davis Sr., in center of picture celebrating their 50th Wedding Anniversary. Sons, L-R: Robert Hawes Davis and Roy B. Davis Jr., Daughters, Rebecca Davis Kearney and Amy Davis Truitt

Roy B. Davis Jr. married Mary Jean Perry and they had one daughter Elizabeth Ann Davis Martin and two grandchildren Michelle and Melanie Martin. Roy B. Davis and Mary Perry Davis are both deceased.

Amy Elizabeth Davis married James Robert Truitt of Crittenden County and they have two children, Sue Truitt Brinkmann and Robert Davis Truitt. The Truitts' have 4 grandchildren, Amy Elizabeth Truitt, Bradley Truitt, Jennifer Brinkmann, and Daniel Davis Brinkmann.

Robert Hawes Davis married Louise Dempsey of Sturgis and they have two daughters, Jena Davis Coker and Joni Davis Thomas. Robert and Louise have 3 grandchildren, Audra Coker, Elyse Coker and Robert Spalding Thomas.

Roy B. Davis Sr, died January 1974. Glennie Davis is 92 years old and lives in Sturgis at this time in the year 1989.

Mr. Davis was manager and Bookkeeper in the garage owned by his brother-in-law Frank Cissell and operated by Bernie Brashear, in the thirties and early forties. In 1946 Mr. Davis opened the Sturgis Motor Parts and operated it until he sold the business to his son-in-law, Virgil Kearney in 1963.

Mr. Davis was City Treasurer of Sturgis under three mayors. They were J. B. Holeman, Willis Thornsberry and Charlie Pryor.

Mr. Davis was a charter member of the present Sturgis Cumberland Presbyterian Church and was church treasurer for 20 years before his death.

In 1956, Mrs. Davis was chosen by Sturgis Kiwanis Club as "Outstanding Citizen of the Year." This honor was based on the work she had done as President of Sturgis Parent Teacher Association. Mrs. Davis served two different terms as P.T.A. President. One term was served during the World War II Era. She helped seal and can food, especially meats such as sausage, fried chicken and other various types of meats to be sent to the soldiers overseas. The cannery where this was done was located at the Sturgis schools and operated by the former Mr. Ralph Alexander, who was the school's agriculture teacher. Mrs. Davis helped there for many years and the

"Victory Garden" grown by many people during the war years, and the farmers produce, made the cannery a very busy place.

Mrs. Davis also helped keep the school cafeteria going during the war years when the women started working outside the home.

Mrs. Davis is a member of the Cumberland Presbyterian Church and has served as a Sunday School Teacher, choir member, president for many years of the Missionary Auxiliary, and continues to teach a Sunday School class and attends church regularly. Mrs. Davis has served as Presbyterial President of Princeton Presbytery Missionary Women. Mrs. Davis worked many years in C. P. youth camps at Ashland Camp near Clay, and at Morgantown, KY Camp.

In 1980, the Cumberland Presbyterian Denomination established a "Golden Patron Membership" honor certificate to be given away only to women who have served in the C. P. Church for 50 years, and a recommendation from her church accompanied by $150. Mrs. Davis had the honor of being the first woman from the local C. P. Church to receive this membership. This also made her the first woman in Princeton Presbytery to receive the honor. Mrs. Davis has received Life and Perpetual Membership in Missionary Auxilianess from Princeton Presbytery and local church.

RAYMOND KELLY DAY

Raymond Kelly Day was born on Jan. 17, 1929 to Naomi (Walker) Day and Ernest Day in Union County. He was the grandson of Kelly and Ava Walker of Caseyville and James and Alice Day of Illinois. Raymond Kelly Day married Bettye Delorse McGee on July 19, 1948 when Raymond was nineteen and Bettye was sixteen. Raymond worked on river barges as a deck hand for thirteen years, then he worked as an underground miner for Island Creek Coal Company for 23 1/2 years. Raymond and Bettye had 5 children and adopted one when she was 17 months old. Their six children are: Rayma Lee (Day) Hollis, Richard Gordon Day, Rhonda Gayle (Day) Hollis, Ryan Chester Day, Russ Kelly Day, and Monica L. (Day) Foster. Raymond and Bettye now have 9 grandchildren now living and 3 grandchildren dead.

Raymond lived all his life in Union County, he was an active member of the Grangertown

Baptist Church where he played the flat top guitar and sang with his wife Bettye for church benefits and at one time he was an active member of the DeKoven Baptist Church where he was Sunday School Director. Raymond put together a country music band called "The Day Family" where he and Bettye sang and he played the guitar along with his sons in the group, the band played for different organizations and benefits in the county. After Raymond retired because of Black Lung in 1983 he began work on his fish market, in Caseyville where he lived, where he fished everyday on the Ohio River to sell fish to his family and friends. Raymond Kelly Day died at the St. Mary's Hospital on Feb. 21, 1987 in Evansville, IN of a massive heart attack and was brought back to the Whitsell Funeral home in Sturgis where his services were held and over 500 people attended. Raymond died when he was 58 years old and if you go to Caseyville, KY to the Ark Lodge Cemetery where he was buried and look at his head stone you will find engraved a guitar in the center of the stone. Raymond was buried in that cemetery along with his grandmother, grandfather, mother, and father. His lot number is 18 and 19. *Submitted by Bettye M. Day*

N. O. DENTON

In March 1942, Mr. and Mrs. N. O. Denton and his father, G. T. Denton, moved to Sturgis from the McClure's community having purchased the house known as the Fred Alloway home. They moved from their country home and farm because it was taken by the government when Camp Breckinridge was being built during World War II.

Mr. G. T. Denton died in February 1949 at 92. Later in the year after moving to Sturgis Noble Denton bought the West Kentucky Coal Company farm. In 1959 that farm was bought by Alcoa Aluminum Company and Mr. Denton retired from farming. Then he enjoyed gardening, caring for the lawn, and keying up the house.

Mr. and Mrs. N. O. Denton

Mary Denton enjoyed her home, entertaining her friends and was a member fo the Garden Club, Homemakers, Canasta Club, and enjoyed any kind of game.

Mr. and Mrs. Denton were members of the Church of Christ and attended regularly as long s they were able. Mr. Denton died in 1981 at age 96. Mrs. Denton died in 1987 at age 98.

The Denton's two children were employed out of the county at the time their parents moved but thy were in Sturgis often. Tom Will Denton retired from government employment in 1974 and came back to make his home with his parents.

Dorothy Denton met her future husband in Sturgis after the war ended. She and Robert (Bobby) Sprague were married in 1947. He died in 1967 while they were living in Salem, KY. They had three sons.

At present, Dorothy and Tom Will live at the family home in Sturgis. *Submitted by Dorothy Denton Sprague*

DYER

"Locust Hill" has been the home of the Dyer Family since 1861. "Locust Hill," located two and one half miles north of Sturgis KY, was first home to John Mason Dyer and his wife Sophronia Jane Pierson Dyer. They were the parents of ten children. John Mason Dyer was a farmer and owned 800 acres of farmland. He was an enterprising farmer owning the first riding plow and stump digger in the county. John M. remarried after the death of his first wife. John M. and his second wife Mary Elizabeth Welch had three children.

The Civil war touched the lives of the Dyer Family. Although Kentucky was a neutral state, John M. was a southern sympathizer.

One experience the Dyer family had was when the Union Army came to the farm to requisite the mules and horses on the farm for use of the Union Army. There were so many Union soldiers that they filled the avenue that led to the house. Union soldiers also looted the house for firearms. Another time a captain of the Union Army ordered a meal to be prepared for him and his officers. The other enlisted men with him helped themselves to the milk in the milk house and robbed the orchard. The hill in front of the dyer home is one of the highest points in the county and was the perfect place for the rebel soldiers to camp. When the rebel soldiers camped on the hill John M. had large pans of biscuits baked for them.

Locust Hill, 1936

John M. died in 1887 and the farm was divided between his second wife and his children.

The second family to make their home at Locust Hill was Benjamin Wright Dyer and his wife Martha Williams Dyer. Ben was the fifth son and seventh child of John Mason Dyer.

Ben and his brother Orville Dyer bought out their brothers and sisters share of the farm. Ben was a bachelor for many years, but in 1918 he married Martha Williams of Providence, KY. When Ben was fifty-seven and Martha forty-six they became parents of their only child, Benjamin Wright Dyer, Jr.

Benjamin Wright Dyer, Jr. and his wife Charlotte Henshaw Dyer made their home at Locust Hill from 1948 to 1971. Ben graduated from the University of Kentucky in 1948 and returned to the family farm. Bens' heart was not in farming and he eventually rented the farm out. Ben was a talented musician and enjoyed rebuilding old pianos. Ben and Charlotte are the parents of ten children. They are: Benjamin Wright Dyer, III, Martha Dyer Williams, Bryan Williams Dyer, Robert Cameron Dyer, William Henshaw Dyer, Jan Dyer Conway, Anna Dyer Hunter, John Mason Dyer, Mary Alane Dyer, and Jennifer Lyn Dyer.

In 1976 Ben and Charlotte built a home across the road from Locust Hill. Although the home is across the road it is still part of the original farm. Ben died in 1980 after a long illness. In 1987 William Henshaw Dyer (Billy) and his wife Cindy York Dyer bought the home from Charlotte Dyer. Billy and Cindy are the parents of three children: Gary Thweatt, Lucas Wright Dyer, and Elizabeth Ann Dyer.

Benjamin Wright Dyer, III and Susan DeWitt Dyer are presently making their home at Locust Hill. Benjie (as most people know him) graduated from Murray State University in 1971 and returned home to farm. Benjie and Susan bought the farm from Ben and Charlotte in 1979. Ben raises hogs, cattle, corn, wheat and soybeans. Ben has won several county and state awards for corn, soybean, and swine production. Ben serves on various agriculture associations both in the county and in the state. Susan is also involved in agriculture as she is employed by the United States Department of Agriculture as a program assistant for ASCS. Ben and Susan are the parents of three children: Stephanie Jo Dyer, Angela Sue Dyer, and Benjamin Wright Dyer, IV.

Locust Hill has provided the Dyer family a way of life for over one hundred and twenty-five years. Hopefully the Dyer family has been able to share some of the blessings they have received.

True Charity

Without true charity everywhere,
The world, would be hopelessly bare,
Without its kindness and its love,
That God has given us from above,
We should spread it far and near,
And always be ready with good cheer,
To help some unfortunate person,
Each day of the year.
Written by Benjamin Wright Dyer, Jr., Jan.

17, 1936, age fourteen. *Submitted by Susan DeWitt Dyer*

CARRIE EBLE

Carrie Eble was born June 27, 1874 in Nebo, KY the daughter of Andrew and Emma Hartman Eble. Mr. Eble was born in Baden, Germany.

Charles Eble, Carrie's brother was born Feb. 13, 1877 in Hopkins County. Charles married Cora B. Davies. Cora and Charles did not have any children. Charles enlisted in the Army and rose to the rank of Captain and served in the Philippines. Charles died in 1926.

Carrie Eble

Andrew Eble, Miss Carrie's father, was a salesman. Mr. Eble's work made it necessary for him to move his family from time to time. The Eble family lived in Nebo and Greenville, KY and Boonville, IN.

Before the year 1900 the Ebles moved to Caseyville where they were in the hotel business. While the family was living in Caseyville Carrie returned to Boonville where she boarded and completed high school.

Mr. Eble died in 1904. Sometime after that Mrs. Eble and Carrie moved to Sturgis where they lived on Kelsey Street.

For a while, including the years 1919 and 1920, Miss Carrie was the proprietor of a variety store on Adams Street named "The Ten Cent Store." Miss Carrie's mother clerked there. Toys were advertised as a speciality and every article "new and up to date."

Miss Carrie attended Butler College, Irvington, IN. In Addition she was a graduate of Lockyear's Business College, Evansville, IN. Later she continued her education at Murray State College.

Miss Carrie began her long teaching career in Union County in 1911 in the Sturgis School. By the year 1917 she was Assistant Principal according to the commencement program for that year.

The 1919 Sturgeon was dedicated to Miss Carrie and refers to her as teacher, friend and advisor. These attributes show the high regard in which Miss Carrie was held. She was an outstanding teacher and set high standards for herself as well as her students.

At the peak of her career Miss Carrie Eble had the distinction of serving as Superintendent of the Union County Schools from 1922-1930. After Miss Carrie's tenure as superintendent she returned to Sturgis High School where she served as librarian.

Miss Carrie Eble retired in 1944 at age 70. For many years after official retirement Miss Carrie continued as a substitute teacher.

One of Miss Carrie's special talents was coaching students for speech competition. Many area residents will remember the long hours of preparation under Mis Carrie's guidance. Miss Carrie's ability as a coach was proven time and time again when her speech students excelled at the District and State levels.

In addition to coaching speech students, Miss Carrie was always ready to help boys and girls with their lessons. For many years students would come to her home to be tutored in algebra, history, reading or whatever subject needed more work. Miss Carrie was glad to be of help and usually did it without pay.

Former students will agree that time spent with Miss Carrie left a lasting impression . Miss Carrie is remembered as an exacting but fair teacher who held a continuing interest in her pupils long after they left the classroom. Sources: Conversations with Miss Carrie, conversations with her former students, Sturgis High School yearbooks and Eble family records. *Submitted by Mallie Moss Lobb*

FELTS-PROCTER

George Hamilton Felts, Sr. was born in Simpson County, near Franklin, KY, June 20, 1897, son of John Morgan and Sally Rutherford Felts. He married Annie Belle Procter in 1915 and they honeymooned at Lookout Mountain, TN. Annie Bell, born June 22, 1898 was the daughter of Dr. William Adolphus and Dr. Annie Forrest Chick Procter, whose ancestors came to KY from Wales by way of Virginia.

In 1923 George moved his family from Simpson County to Sturgis where he had accepted employment in the coal fields. They also operated the Skinner Hotel on Main Street from 1929-34. In 1941 George, his sons Procter and George, Jr. and Mrs. Ernie Berry built a two story home on property along Highway 60 north which he named Blue Berry Hill (presently the George B. Simpson home). The Felts' opened Blue Berry Inn during WWII, which provided sleeping rooms and a dinner restaurant until 1944-45.

George was the owner/operator of the Sturgis Feed and Produce Company on Washington Street from 1944-48, when he left Sturgis and operated businesses in Louisville, Elizabethtown and Buffalo, KY. At his death Feb. 2, 1968, he was farming in Larue Co., KY. Annie Belle passed away July 15, 1946 and both are interred in Pythian Ridge Cemetery, Sturgis.

Four children were born to this union: Evelyn Lorraine Felts Quinn b. Sept. 7, 1916, Arthur Procter b. Jan. 28, 1919, George Hamilton b. June 24, 1922 and Carolyn Josephine

Felts Howell b. May 12, 1924. The two sons served their country in the Armed Forces during WWII. George, Jr. was imprisoned in Germany during 1944-45 and Arthur Procter served on the homefront. All 4 children were educated in the Union County School System. *Submitted by Joel Felts-Williams*

FELTS-VANCLEVE

Arthur Procter Felts b. Jan. 28, 1919 in Orlinda, TN, son of George Hamilton Felts, Sr. and Annie Bell Procter Felts, and Mary Kathryn Rosina VanCleve b. March 10, 1919 in DeKoven, KY, a daughter of Joseph Joel VanCleve and Mary Edna Syers VanCleave, were married in July 1938 in Henderson, KY.

Proc graduated from Sturgis High School in 1936 and worked the coal mines most of his adult life, although for a time, he operated a gas station on the corner of Main Street and Hwy. 109 in Sturgis. He served in the United States Army during WWII.

Katie graduated from Grove Center High School in 1936 and attended the Lois Glynn School of Beauty in Bowling Green, KY where she received a degree in cosmetology. After rearing her family, she realized her life-long dream of serving in the nursing profession. She was employed at the old Sturgis Hospital and the Union County Hospital.

Three children were born to this union: Joel Ann Felts (see Williams-Felts) b. March 30, 1939, Sturgis; Georgia Kay Felts Reisz, b. June 30, 1941, Sturgis, currently of Louisville, KY; son, John Simpson Nall, Jr. (deceased); William Procter Felts, Sr. b. July 23, 1943, Sturgis, now in Winnemucca, NV, married Merilyn Joyce Gillespie, Sturgis, children: Jennifer Michele Felts and William Procter Felts, Jr.

The Felts' mining employment took them West to Colorado until 1980 when they retired back in Kentucky. Katie passed away Aug. 14, 1984 and is interred in Pythian Ridge Cemetery. Proc currently resides in Southern Illinois and spends his time visiting the three children and tending his bountiful gardens. *Submitted by Joel Felts-Williams*

CARROLL FINNIE

The Finnie family traces its roots in Union County to Captain James Finnie who, with his brother Colonel John Finnie, moved here in 1810. Carroll Finnie was born in Caseyville in 1893 (died 1980). He married Virginia Kellen, born near Smith Mills in 1896 (died 1977). Their four children, Thomas Carroll, Gordon, William H., and Nadine were born at home in Caseyville. The family moved to Lexington in 1935. Carroll was Chief Engineer for the American Barge Line Company until his retirement in 1950. He and Virginia returned to Union County in 1948.

Thomas Carroll married Evelyn Warren and they have two sons, Thomas Warren and

William Carroll. Thomas and Evelyn live in Cambridge Shores on Lake Barkley. Thomas served as an Army Engineer Officer in New Guinea, the Phillipines, and Japan during World War II. He retired as Deputy Director of the Defense Mapping Agency after 35 years of Government Service. Thomas is semi-retired and does Systems Engineering consultant work. Their son, Thomas Warren, is Deputy City Manager in Charlotte, NC where he resides with his wife Kay and children Allyson and Thomas Cummins. Their son William is Director of Strategic Planning at Anheuser Busch, Inc. and adjunct Professor at Washington University in St. Louis, MO where he resides with his wife Glenda and sons John and Steve.

Gordon married Madge Johnson and they moved to Sturgis in 1948. They had four children; Patricia, Michael, Ginny Lou, and Elizabeth Ann. Madge died in 1979. Gordon retired from the Island Creek Coal Co. in 1983 and resides in Sturgis. His son Michael and wife Dreama have two children, Jennifer and Patrick. Michael is the Senior Special Investigator for Mine Safety and Health Administration, District 8 and lives in Vincennes, IN. Patricia is a Special Education Teacher at St. Charles Elementary School, and she and her husband Lyndle Vaughn and two daughters, Melanie and Emily, live in Madisonville. Melanie and her husband, Kevin McGlothlin, live in Madisonville with their son Kevin Blake. Ginny Lou and her husband Kris Stegelman live in Madisonville with their two children Sarah and Daniel. Elizabeth Ann is Secretary/bookkeeper for her husband's building contractor business, and she and her husband Donald Beal live in Sturgis with their sons Jonathon and Robert.

William H. married Rachel Williams and they have five children; Richard, Nancy, Julia, Rebecca, and Roger. William owns an Engineering firm and he and Rachel reside in Lexington. Their son Richard is manager of William H. Finnie and Associates. He and his wife Ellie and children William, Kara, and Megan live in Lexington. Nancy and her husband Dr. Terry Estes live in Bristol, TN with their children Jonathan, Geoffery, and Gregory. Julia and her husband Dr. Gerald Pratt and their son Robert live in Monticello, KY. Rebecca and her husband David Bouchey and their son Michael live in Palmyra, VA. Roger works at William H. Finnie & Associates. He and his wife Donna and their daughter Sarah live in Lexington.

Nadine married Robert C. Baldwin Jr. of Danville and they had two sons; Robert Calmes III and John Carroll. Nadine was a Personnel Manager with National Cash Register Co. in Orlando, FL. She retired and moved to Sturgis in 1985. Her son Robert is manager of Southeast Development at the Aberthaw Co. He and his wife Mary and daughters Sarah and Emily reside in Orlando, FL. John Carroll works at Stromberg Carlson Engineering Co.

and lives in Orlando, FL. *Submitted by Nadine Baldwin*

FRAZER

Thomas Roe Frazer and Patricia T. Frazer moved to Sturgis in July, 1963. Tom is the son of Ted Frazer, Sr. and the late Melba Williams Frazer of Marion, KY. Also, he is the grandson of the late Dr. Atchison Frazer, well-known physician from Marion. Patricia is the daughter of the late Joseph Bernard Teasley and Mable Hall Teasley of Bradshaw, WV. The Frazers are the parents of three children, Thomas Roe Frazer II, Jackson, Mississippi, Joseph Atchison Frazer, Louisville, KY, and Robin Lynn Frazer of Atlanta, GA. Roe Frazer II is married to Sandra Roderick from Green Bay, WI, and they are the parents of Chelsea Collins and Thomas Roe Frazer, III. Joseph Atchinson Frazer is married to Laura Maxwell from Rumsen, NJ.

L-R, front, Thomas Roe and Patricia; standing, Roving, Joseph and Roe

Tom Roe is a registered pharmacist and owns and operates Sturgis Pharmacy which he purchased from Virgil Kearney in July, 1963. Patricia has worked at the Sturgis Community Hospital and the HCA Union County Hospital as a registered nurse. Also, she taught nursing at Henderson Community College, Henderson, KY from 1976-1984. Currently, Patricia is the manager of "Patricia's Country Clothes," a ladies clothing store which the Frazers purchased from the Al Holt family in October, 1984.

Tom Roe is a member of the Sturgis Kiwanis Club, the Sturgis Chamber of Commerce, and the Sturgis Merchants Association. The Frazers are active members of the United Methodist Church of Sturgis.

GILCHRIST

Robert James Bayard Gilchrist (1798-1866), one of the first settlers in Union County came from Virginia prior to 1811. He owned approximately 4,000 acres of land in the Highland Creek area bordering Henderson County.

Gilchrist served on the first court in Union County that convened at Jeremiah Riddle's on May 27, 1811, well as the first Board of Trustees of Union County Academy in Morganfield in 1821.

Gilchrist married Henrietta Maria Ross, Feb. 4, 1833. Eight children blessed this union. they were: Robert R.; Leonard W.; Henry C.; Thomas Page; Francis Marion; Edward Marshall; Mary Ross; and Julia I.

Thomas Ray Gilchrist

R. J. B. Gilchrist sold and traded the above mentioned land for land in the Pond Fork and Sturgis area.

Marriages and Children: 1866, Henry C. to M. R. Niblace; 1879, Robert C. to Julia C. Jones; 1879, Thomas P. to Maria Crutcher - eight children; 1879, Francis M. to Emma Taylor Davis; 1886, Edward M. to Nannie Puryear; Julia I. to Jim Gill - 2 children; Leonard W. to unknown; and Mary Ross never married.

Thomas Page Gilchrist owned 42 1/2 acres in the Pond Fork area where the Sturgis Aiport is now located. He raised a family of eight children here. The children were: James Ross (1879-1963); Arch David (1881-1973); Stephen B. (1883-1963); Susan Ramey (1887-1946); Ruth Frances (1888-1971); Thomas Enloe (1890-); Henrietta (1892-1976); Gilbert Crutcher (1894-1950).

Marriages and children:

In 1903 James R. to Susie Holdman - one son - Jesse Ross Gilchrist.

Arch D. to Fannie Quirey (1890-1944) - three children - Dixie, Arch D. Jr., and Thomas Marshall. Fannie died in 1944. Arch married Lela Gunter in 1956. She died in 1970.

Stephen B. to Mayme Crowder - one son - Kenny M.

Susan Ramey to George S. Sears - no children. Following the death of Sears she married a Mr. Crowell.

Ruth Frances to Rowan Waskon - one daughter - Louise.

Henrietta to a Mr. Beers - no children.

In 1926 Gilbert C. to Mabel White (1894-1927) one son - James Edward Gilchrist.

Thomas Enloe remained a bachelor.

In 1900 Thomas Page Gilchrist traded his 42 1/2 acres in the Pond Fork area for 318 acres on the Trade Water River in Union County. He and his wife lived here until their deaths. Sons Thomas Enloe and Arch D. bought the farm. Later Arch D. sold his part to Thomas E. who owned the farm until 1974 when he sold it to James Shaffer and Jim Syers and moved to Sullivan. He lives here at the present time at the age of 98.

I, James E. Gilchrist, have farmed since 1949 in partnership with my uncle W. W. White and cousin W. E. White. This partnership started in the Hazel Bend area and moved tot he Henshaw community in 1958.

On February 12, 1966 Martha Jane Jones and I were married. We have no children. We continue to live at the Henshaw location and still engaged in farming. *Submitted by James E. Gilchrist*

GOAD

John B. and Rebecca Gatlin Goad came to Union County in eighteen fifty five. They had one son William Burnett. They were farmers in Union County. W. B. married Lula Harris, born to them were two daughters, Maeola Harris and Nancy Burnett.

Maeola married H. D. Holt, born to them were H. D. Holt Jr. and Barbara Harris (deceased).

H. D. Holt Jr. married Pauline Brown (deceased), born to them were two sons, Steven Delaney and Henry Bruce. They also have three granchildren, Summer Lynn, Tara Sue and Chase Delaney.

Barbara Harris married Jack Chambliss, born to them were three children, Bill Holt, Jane Delaney and Joe Harris. They have one grandson, Walker Chambliss.

Nancy Goad maried Rives Hall, and they had no children.

W. B. and Lulu Goad built a home at corner 8th and Main and moved to Sturgis in 1903. They were Baptists and very active in community organizations. He was connected with the Bank of Sturgis. On occasion he served as interim mayor and served as a councilman with every mayor.

The surviving duaghter, lives in the home 8th and Main, only home she has ever known, at this writing eighty two years. The memories are great!

GRIGGS

Bobbie and Ida Griggs were former Camp Breckinridge residents. Bobbie Griggs, born Feb. 25, 1893, was the fourth of ten children born to John Minor Griggs and Mary Virginia Cromwell, who were married in 1890. The Griggs family orginially came from England. The Cromwell family came from Scotland. John Minor Griggs died Feb. 17, 1942. The family, upon returning from the funeral, found a notice posted on their farm from the U. S. Government stating that their home and land was being taken from them to facilitate the building of an Army post, namely Camp Breckinridge. One of Bobbie Griggs' brothers,, Willie Griggs, died in France during World War I. The Griggs - Alvey American Legion Post at Morganfield was named after him.

Ida Delora Allinder married Bobbie Griggs March 15, 1916 in Evansville, IN. Their attendents were Goldie Allinder and Starling Sut-

Bobbie and Ida Griggs' 50th anniversary

Dotty, Debby, Kim, Beth and Suzy Hall

ton. Ida was the daughter of William Lora Allinder and Rosa Lynn. Before Bobbie and Ida moved to Union County, Bobbie Griggs worked as a conductor on a streetcar in Evansville, IN. After their move to Union County, Bobbie and Ida were life-long farmers. Bobbie and Ida Griggs' children were Lulu Evelyn Schieber, Willie Clara Griggs, John Robert Griggs, Margaret Eleanor Wilkerson, Mary Ruth Griggs Henshaw and Benjamin Louis Griggs.

Mary Ruth Griggs and James Kenneth Henshaw, Sr. were married May 30, 1947. The children of Mary Ruth Griggs Henshaw and James Kenneth Henshaw, Sr. are James Kenneth Henshaw II, Pamela Sue Henshaw Braddock and Jerry Lee Henshaw. Ruth and Kenneth have five granddaughters, Lissa Ruth Braddock, Kenna Kay Braddock, Kimberly Ann Henshaw, Mary Elizabeth Henshaw and Faith Anne Henshaw. *Submitted by Ruth Henshaw*

HALL

Alex and Gleeda Hall moved from Benton, IL, to Sturgis, KY, in July 1970 with their six children, Dotty, Debby, Kim, Scott, Beth and Suzy. They are originally from Eastern Kentucky and had lived in Benton for 4 years.

Alex began working for Island Creek Coal Co., Hamilton #1, May 1970 and continued working for them until Hamilton #1 began closing in Dec. 1982.

Seated, Alex and Gleeda; standing, Scott, Beth, Suzy, Dotty and Kim

In 1970 Dotty and Debby enrolled in Union County High School, Kim and Scott in Sturgis Junior High, and Beth and Suzy in Sturgis Elementary. All six children graduated from U. C. H. S.

Dotty went to Freed Hardeman College, Henderson, Tennessee, for a year, returned to Sturgis and worked for Attorney George B. Simpson for several years and later on for Pyro Mining Company. She now lives in Marion, KY with her husband Steve Short, their children, David, Jeania, Heath Lovell, Wesley Lovell and Stephanie. Steve is employed by Green River Coal Co. in Madisonville, KY.

Debby attended David Lipscomb for a short period before joining the Air Force and beginning a career in aerospace. She left the Air Force after starting her family but has continued her career and now works as an electrical engineer for Assurance Technology Corp. in Carlisle, MA, near Boston. She and her husband Jerry Akerson and children, Lindsay, Jarrod and Stacy, have lived mostly in Lompac, California, and will reside in Massachusetts until Jerry graduates from MIT in Boston in 1990.

Kim graduated from Freed Hardeman College with an AA Degree in social work. She met her future husband Eddie Morris at Freed and they married after graduation. Eddie is a wildlife biologist and Kim has worked in various positions until their two sons Matthew and David were born. Due to Eddie's career, they have lived in several different locations. They currently reside in Milwaukee, WI, but will move to Gainesville, GA this summer.

Scott worked for Genault in Morganfield, KY after graduating from high school and before moving to San Francisco, CA. He worked for I. Magnin for several months before starting his career with Pacific Bell Telephone Co. where he has been employed since 1981 as service representative.

Beth, after graduating from high school, worked for Sturgis Specialty Shop and Western Auto in Sturgis. She has also attended Henderson Community College part-time. Beth has worked for Pyro Mining Co. for the past six years and lives in Sturgis at the present time.

Suzy went to Freed Hardeman College for one year before returning to Sturgis to work at Shelter Insurance Co. She moved to Nashville, TN, in 1983, stayed in the insurance business, and has been employed by Coroon and Black Insurance Co. for the past four years as service representative. She now resides in Brentwood, TN.

Alex and Gleeda are members of The Church of Christ in Sturgis. Since retirement, they spend as much time as possible traveling to different states to visit with their children and their families. *Submitted by Gleeda Hall*

A. R. HAMMACK

William Hammack, a Revolutionary soldier, born 1760, great grandfather of A. R. Hammack (1871-1959), received a government grant after the war and came to Union County, KY in 1790.

He married Nancy Brown, born 1770. They had 8 children. William and Nancy are buried one mile from old Salem Church.

One of their sons, Morgan Brown, married Margaret Bishop in 1823. They had 8 children. Five members of their family died during a scourge of typhoid fever.

Their son, Daniel B., born 1842 married Alice Maria Davis, formerly of Maysville, daughter of Elizabeth Whittington and George Washington Davis, who had just moved to the Pond Fork area.

A. R. Hammack was the oldest of six children born to this couple. The others were Tom, Rudell, Iva, Floy, and Georgie, who died at 18 months.

Mr. Hammack, also called "Gus," was a well respected and progressive farmer, who lived between Sullivan and Pride.

He was a deacon and active member of the Southern Missionary Baptist Church.

In 1895 he married Nannie McGill, daughter of S. C. and Eliza McGill. They had one son, Richard Seldon, whose mother died about 2 months after his birth.

Seldon, known as "Dick," a mining engineer, married Virginia Jones, in 1924. Their son, Dick, Jr., was a veteran of World War II. He went to California to live, where he was recognized as an outstanding teacher in that state. He is now deceased.

Seldon later married Theda Ward of Dawson Springs. Their daughter, Sherry Kay, married Jon Pierce of Mobile. They live in Walnut Creek, California and have 3 children: Lesley, Julie and Brad. Seldon died in 1962.

Twelve years after Miss Nannie's death. Mr. Hammack married Ethel McKeaig, daughter of Willis Abram and Mattie Lockhart McKeaig and a graduate of Ohio Valley Baptist College. They have three daughters: Evelyn, Julia Dixon, and Geraldine. Their mother died at the age of 36 years. Mr. Hammack lived to 88 1/2 years old.

Evelyn married Lowell Hurley, a veteran and farmer, son of Ollie Jones an Oliver Hurley in 1946. They have two daughters: Gayle and Jean.

Gayle was married to Shelby Woodring in 1967. Their children are Maria, Laurel, and Eric. Now Gayle is married to Tom Lempeke. They live in Saginaw, MI.

Jean was married to Dave Walton of Nashville in 1977. She has an excellent position in Nashville with Northern Telecom.

Julia Hammack after College, graduated from American Conservatory of Music, studied at Indiana University and two years in Europe.

She taught piano at Bessie Tift College, choral work in Union University, and Gary Model High School, and taught private piano. She spent 2 years in Germany during World War II and U. S. O. Director and has traveled extensively.

Geraldine, known as Jerry, married James F. Hughey, Martin, TN, a dentist, in 1941. They live in Tuscaloosa, Alabama.

Their children: Jim, a lawyer in Birmingham; Greg, an industrial engineer, in Orange, VA; Elaine, a banking consultant in Nashville; and David, a dealer in antiques, woodworking, and real estate, Tuscaloosa.

DANIEL HAMMACK

Daniel Hammack was born in Union County on Jan. 14, 1842. He was the son of Morgan B. and Margaret (Bishop) Hammack. His education was five or six years of schooling, "off and on," in Union County. During the Civil War he was a non-combatant, but he lost the only horse he had at the hands of the guerrillas.

On Nov. 20, 1867 Daniel Hammack married Alice Davis, daughter of George W. and Elizabeth (Whittington) Davis. Alice was born Dec. 23, 1843 in Maysville, Mason County. She came to Union County by flatboat. Alice Davis had loved dancing, but when she became Alice Hammack her dancing ended, as Daniel's Baptist religion forbade it. Her brother, Howard Davis, was a lawyer in Morganfield.

Floy, Ivy and Earl Hammack

Daniel Hammack had a farm of two hundred and seventy-three acres and only one horse to work with. His principal crops were corn, wheat and hay. His residence, which was part log and part box weather-boarded, was built in 1874 upon rising ground near the road. In politics Daniel Hammack was a Democrat, and held the office of School Trustee. He was a member of the Baptist Church for twenty years.

Six children were born to Daniel and Alice. George died young; the five surviving children were Augustus Reese, Thomas Earl, Rudelle, Ivy Pearl and Margaret Floy. Ivy Pearl Hammack married James William

138

O'Nan in a double wedding with Will's brother Reeves O'Nan and Ruth Henry at Princeton, KY. They went by train to Princeton.

Will and Ivy resided on the O'Nan family "homeplace" near Sturgis. They had three children: William, who died in infancy, Margaret Frances, and James Frederick, who died at age twenty-three from strep throat. Fred's death came one year before the use of penicillin.

Margaret Frances O'Nan married Ralph Coleman Hart in Akron, OH on June 24, 1934. Frances was an elementary school teacher for thirty years. They have two daughters, Barbara O'Nan and Fredericka Jean.

Barbara was born April 10, 1935. She married Henry Bernard Hina. Their children are Henry Bernard Hina, Jr., born June 15, 1963 and Ralph Ernest Hart Hina, born June 21, 1966. Unfortunately, the marriage later ended in divorce.

Jean was born on Feb. 21, 1941. She married Edwin Dale Stadelman of Chicago, IL. Ed was killed in a tragic airplane crash on May 8, 1976. They had two children: Benjamin Edwin Stadelman, born Oct. 30, 1967 and Frances Helen Stadelman, born June 16, 1970. *Submitted by Frances Hart*

PETER HAZEL

The Peter Hazel family moved to the Territory of Virginia in what is now known as Union County, KY following the Revolutionary War. They were among the first white settlers in the Sturgis area and had received a land grant and purchased and additional one thousand acres of land. Peter Hazel was a relative of Caleb Hazel, one of Abraham Lincoln's first school teachers. Peter and his wife had nine children, one of whom was Fielding Hazel.

Fielding and his wife Martha Collins had nine children. One of the children, James Ira Hazel and his wife, Lela Lucy Berry, had two children, Robert Vanderbilt and Kenneth Rockerfellow. James Ira or, Dick, as he was called purchased his brothers and sisters share of their fathers estate, following Fielding's death. This land that had never had a deed issued in anything but the Hazel name was still owned by the two brothers, Van and Kenneth, when Alcoa Aluminum purchased a large section of the area in the 1950s. Currently approximately two acres of this land is still owned by the Hazels and has a building lot and a family cemetery on it.

Kenneth had one son, Kenneth Dudly, who makes his home in Mount Juliet, TN. Van and his wife, Willia Nell Hoffman, of the Hoffman's from North Carolina, had two daughters, Ruth Wayne and Norma Jean. Ruth and her husband, Robert Joseph Long, had one son, Robert, Jr., who now lives in Huntsville, AL. Norma had four children, Robert Scott Quinn, Anthony Allen, Patricia Anne and Alphonse Enu Bartolotto, OL. There

James Ira "Dick" and Lela Lucy Berry Hazel c 1910; Robert "Van" and Kenneth "Red" Hazel, 1917

is an area known as Hazel Bend, a bridge over Highway 109-85 at Hazel's Branch and several other landmark areas attributed to Peter and his decedents. The first quarter horse race track in this area was located behind the Hazel Cemetery, one of the first preachers at the Bell's Mine Church was a Hazel. The original home place was built in a Walnut grove after the first selected site was found to be inhabited by a band of Indians when they arrived to start construction. Prior to the purchase of the land by Alcoa there were three untouched Indian grave sites on the last one hundred acres owned by the Hazels. Legend has it and was still being told by older residents in 1988 that Canille Hazel killed a bear in a knife fight near the Tradewater River area of the farm and one of Peter's sons went to California during the gold rush of 1849. He returned by boat that brought him into Louisiana where he completed the journey home over land. The complete trip home took nearly a year. Over the years three coal mines have been located on the farm with the last coal being used for family and tenant consumption in the 1940's. The original family farm was self sustaining with grain, tobacco, hemp for rope, sugar maple trees for sugar, every vegetable and over ten different fruits being raised along with sheep for wool, goats, cows, horses, mules, chickens, turkeys, and ducks. This area ended with the demise of small farms.

BURBIE AND ELIZA CARROLL HEAVRIN

Burbie Lewis Heavrin, Son of Thomas Handley Heavrin and Sophia Agnes (Urton) Heavrin was born April 9, 1915 in Evansville, IN.

His father, Thomas H. Heavrin, was a carpenter and built the Cross with the figure of Jesus that is in St. Ambrose Cemetery. The Cross was erected in 1927 and Burbie acted as water boy during it's construction.

Burbie graduated from Sturgis High School in 1933 and was employed in the Accounting Department of the West Kentucky Coal Company. He was also Assistant Secretary of the Employees Mutual Benefit Association working with O. H. Wilcox, Secretary of the E.M.B.A. In 1936 Burbie became a Representative for Metropolitan Life Insurance Company in Boonville, IN and later worked in Evansville 36 years for Metropolitan. After retirement, he worked for seven years as a Realtor in Evansville. Eliza Carroll (Barkley) Heavrin was born on a farm near Sturgis. Her parents were Harry Oldham Barkley and Fannie Sue (O'Nan) Barkley. Eliza graduated from Sturgis High School in 1934. She worked as a Dental Assistant and a Lab Technician at Welborn Clinic in Evansville. They are parents of a son, David Wayne Heavrin, who is employed by the Evansville Printing Corporation in Evansville. He and his wife, Nancy (Hayes) Heavrin, have three daughters, Jennifer Genet, Julie and Janna Heavrin and two granddaughters Kendra and Lindsey Genet. Burbie is a member of Downtown Kiwanis in Evansville, IN and was the Kiwanis Club's Secretary for 17 years. He is a Masonic member of Reed Lodge #316, F. & A. M., the Ancient Accepted Scottish Rite, and Hadi Shrine Temple all in Evansville. Burbie's grandparents, James R. Heavrin and Bridget (Fitzgivens) Heavrin were farmers living near St. Ambrose Catholic Church and John Urton and America (Collins) living near Old Bethel. John Urton owned a Thresher and traveled in Union County threshing wheat for the farmers. Burbie lived several years with an Uncle and Aunt, Noel and Olevia Collins, on Talbott Street in Sturgis. Eliza Carroll (Barkley) Heavrin's grandparents were Dennis O'Nan and Eliza Blue (Ralph) O'Nan, farmers of Sturgis, and Dr. David Maple Barkley was a Doctor in Princeton and Caseyville, KY. He traveled by Horse and Buggy and treated his patients in their homes. He was a Doctor for 38 years. Additional information may be obtained from O'Nan Book - (Dennis O'Nan) - Treasure Up The Memory. David Maple Barkley - History of Union County, KY. *Submitted by Burbie Lewis Heavrin*

JOSEPH DIXON HENRY

Mary Levina (Mollie) b. 7/24/1866, d. 12/7/1958 married Charlie C. Shaffer b. 5/6/1863 d. 2/11/1909. Born in Louisville area - died in Sturgis. Livelihood: carpenter - lived at 13th and Washington Street, Sturgis. Children: Raymond m. Verna Holeman; Ora Pearl m. C. W. Woodward; Walter m. Mattie Johns; Mary m. Jones Berry; Naomi m. Willis Benson; Susan m. W. H. Cobb; Elizabeth m. John Bishop Stevens; Charlotte m. Ernest Pettigrew (div.) m. Chase Ballou; Marth m. Ottrell Miller.

Sallie b. 1868 d. 12/1958 m. William B. Brooks b. 1859 d. 1931 in Sturgis. Livelihood: Preacher - resided on Monroe Street near 5th Street, Sturgis. Children: Mary, Myra Boyce m. Frank Holt (Deceased) m. Collins; Ethel m. Hugh Goodman, Ruth m. Jack Lynch, Eva m. Peck Nesbitt.

Ida Effie b. 10/31/1869 d. 1953 m. John Thomas Slaton b. 1869 d. 1941. Livelihood: furniture business in Morganfield and farming in Pride Community. Resided in Pride area. Children: Emma m. Nace Williams, Lilly

L-R: Marson Henry, Effie Slayton, Mollie Shaffer, Sallie Brooks, Mattie Bingham, Ruth O'Nan and Herman Henry

m. Orvil Williams, Maltie m. Wade Pride, Joe m. Mary Elder and Luke m. Laz Duncan.

Chester Henry m. Mary Maxwell, born in Salem Community. Livelihood: dentist - resided in Sulphur, OK. Children three.

Lutha b. 1883 d. 1934 m. James E. Dalton b. 1878 d. 1935. Livelihood: furniture business. Lived at Monroe and 6th Street. Children: Forest and James.

Ora b. 12/22/1885 d. 1/19/1906 m. Mr. Nunn.

Rose b. 1878 d. 1943 m. Horace Smith b. 1877 d. 1939. Livelihood: West Kentucky Coal Company and farmed. Lived on Adams at 12th Street until the house burned in the 1920s; then moved to farm in Pride Community. Children: Latta m. Christine Sparks, Mason Venner m. Nancy Jean Cottingham, H. H. Smith Jr. m. Lois Ruth Holeman.

Mason C. m. Sadie Brewer. Livelihood: banking and farming. Resided in Dixon, KY on N. 41 Highway.

Mattie m. Hal Bingham. Livelihood: farming in the St. Ambrose neighborhood and retired in Henshaw, KY.

Children Ruby m. Bill O'Daniel, Louise m. Harry Stevens, Agnes m. John Reid, Henry (Jack) m. Ceclia.

Herman b. 1/13/1885 d. 10/1971 m. Georgia Thomason b. 10/21/1885 d. 8/24/1972. Livelihood: dairying and farming. Born and resided in Salem Community. Children: Dorothy Brinson m. Mr. Cissell (dec) m. Mr. Ritchie, Marietta m. Henry Manning, Kathryn m. Jack Waller, J. D. m. Ruth Chancellor.

Ruth b. 12/18/1886 d. 9/5/1986 m. Reeves O'Nan b. 9/25/1884 d. 1/15/69. Born in Salem Community. Livelihood: Dairy - resided at Sturgis City limits on Kiwanis Road. Children: Rebecca m. Melvin Brooks, Lucille m. Walter Clarke, Bill m. Ida Mae Harbison, Ralph m. Betty Miller. *Submitted by J. S. Kurtz, 1989*

SHELBY JOE "JACK" HENRY

Shelby Joe "Jack" Henry was born November 2, 1908, in Webster County, KY. He was the second son of Ursie Marian Phillips of Crittenden County, Rosebud, KY, and Thomas W. Henry of Webster County, Blackford, KY.

Shelby J. Henry

"Jack" had an older brother Thomas Lynn (1907-1968), and a younger brother Wilbur Raymond "Billy) (1910-1938), and a sister named Jesse Louise (1915-1969).

"Jack's" grandparents were William G. Henry of Union County and Frances E. Omer, also of Union County. His mother's parents were Lynn Boyd Phillips and Mary Davis of Bells Mines, Crittenden County, KY. Mary Davis' family came from Wilson County, TN, near Cherry Valley.

"Jack" and his family were raised near the Blackford Church Road in Crittenden County, near the Tradewater River and the Nunn-Switch Community. His father worked as a waterman for the I. C. Railroad.

Trains were to have a great impact on the Henry Family. Brother "Billy" was killed by one when he was 28 years of age. "Jack" also lost part of one of his legs due to an infection from a railroad injury.

Thomas L. married Mildred and lived in Sullivan, and later near the Sturgis area. He served in some political offices such as fire marshall for the district during the 1960s.

Tom had two children, they include Betty (Nichols) of Lexington, KY, and Jerry Henry of New Mexico.

"Billy" Henry married Irene Vaughn and had one child who died in infancy.

Jesse married Albert Eugene Lewis and they lived in Sullivan, KY. Jesse and Al had seven children; Eugene Shelby who resides in Paducah, KY; Wilbur Ronald who lives in Louisiana; Roger Neil who has served as an elected judge in Northern Kentucky; David Michael who is an attorney (and has served as assistant Commonwealth Attorney in Louisville), and now resides in Texas; Gregory who now resides in Amarillo, TX; and Joe Henry Lewis who lives in Texas; Leslie Ann the only girl, married a Camboni and lives in La Grange, IL.

"Jack married Margaret Helen Shields of Pride in December, 1941. He was not eligible to served in WWII because of his amputation, so he traveled the states in order to help construct a gas pipe line. He worked as a heavy equipment operator. Richard Lee, his first son, was born in Houma, LA, during this time, and Jacquelin Sue was born in Houston, TX.

They returned to reside in Sullivan, KY and had another son, Robert Joe Henry.

"Jack" became a successful businessman in

Sturgis when he formed a construction company with Mr. Easley and I. C. Russell.

"Jack" died of heart failure in Sullivan in August of 1951.

Richard presently is employed for the State of Florida in Tallahassee. Robert Joe is a C. P. A. in Katy, TX, near Houston. Jacqueline is living in the St. Louis area and is employed at Deaconess Hospital. *Submitted by Jacqueline Sue Henry Terrell*

GEORGE T. HENSHAW - LILLIE BROWN HENSHAW

George T. Henshaw married Lillie Brown and 9 children were born to them.

Daughters: Lulu Henshaw married Gip Berry. Their 6 children were: George Edward, Marvin, Clyde Morris, and Harold. Two daughters: Virginia Helen Semlow and Dorothy Jean Adamson.

Emma Henshaw married Lee Harris. Their 6 children were: Daughters, Lucille Harris Sharp and Georgia Marie Harris. Four sons: Rowleigh Harris, Marion Harris, W. L. Harris and Curtis Harris.

George T. and Grandpa Henshaw, Otha Biggs, Emma Harris, William Henshaw and Lulu Berry; Mary Agnes Henshaw

Otha Henshaw married Dr. F. H. Beggs. Their 6 children were: Lillie Dean Beggs Jackson, Eva Mae Beggs Eckiss, Anna Lee Poland and Etta Jayne Beggs. Sons: T. J. Beggs and Hugh Gerald Beggs.

Sons: Felix married Pearl Davis, Wilson married Gertrude O'Brien, William married Edith Henshaw, Mason married Hazel Opperman and George B. married Agnes Mattingly. One son, Arthur, died in infancy. George Berry Henshaw married Agnes Mattingly and 3 children were born to them.

Agnes Viola married Charles H. Bradford. They had 7 children: Charles David married Linda Bye, Rebecca Ann married Larry Wallace, Clarence Roger married Shelia Solloman, Pamela Kaye married Sam Prichett, Robert Paul married Patricia Nagel, Phillip Wayne married Pamela Walker, Deborah Ann died at age 3.

George Thomas Henshaw married Viola Detraz.

Ben Edward Henshaw married Agnes Detraz.

The George Berry Henshaw-Agnes Mat-

tingly Henshaw family settled in the Shiloh Community about 1928-29. At this time the Church at Shiloh was closed with no pastor and no services. Being a God-fearing woman, Agnes Mattingly Henshaw desired that her three children be brought up in Church, so she obtained the key to the Church, canvassed the neighborhood and invited the people to Church. It took ingenuity and determination to bring the services back into being. So...she started a contest, named the two sides red and blue, and before long the Church boasted 100 in Sunday School. When she died at age 46 the Church would not hold all the mourners. Mr. Bill Young and her nephew Harry Mattingly preached her funeral. She is buried in the Masonic Cemetery at Morganfield, KY. She would be proud to know that services are still being held at the Shiloh Church, with additions plus a parsonage, new office and nursery onto the front of the Church. *Submitted by Agnes Bradford*

JAMES I. HENSHAW

Ruth and James Ila Henshaw were married in 1903 and farmed and reared their family near Sturgis. she was the daughter of Emma Dobbins and William Van Cleave. He was the son of Alodia Dodge and Thomas Henshaw. Thomas's father was Jim and Jim's was Adam Henshaw.

James I. is pictured with their Family Tree. It was made in 1964 by a granddaughter. Ruth and James are deceased and eldest child has the Tree and keeps it up to date. This Tree has six limbs, one for each child. Their children are Stella Andre, Edith Wallace, Emma Mason, Morton, John Willie (killed in Normandy Invasion) and Kenneth. In addition to six children, there are 15 grandchildren, 37 great grandchildren, 20 great, great, grandchildren and 2 great, great, great grandchildren.

James I. Henshaw with "Family Tree"

The Henshaw family has always taken part in community activities. All the children attended Sturgis High School. As a young man James went to Ohio Valley Baptist College in Sturgis. The Ohio Valley College Dormitory founded in 1895 still stands on Main Street.

James and Ruth were members of the Henshaw Christian Church. Since her death in 1947, there is a Ruth V. Henshaw Ladies Circle of the Henshaw Christian Church in her

honor. Following is a direct quote from their circle program. "In 1903 at the age of 16, she became the bride of James I. Henshaw. They raised her brothers and sisters and part of his family, along with six children of their own.

Mrs. Henshaw joined the Henshaw Christian Church in 1923 and was baptized in the Alf Johns Fish Pond on the Shaffer Farm.

She was always a virtuous lady, interested in her husband, children, home, and church.

James and Ruth are buried in Phythian Ridge Cemetery along with a brass plate honoring John Willie who is buried in France. All other children live in or near Sturgis. *Submitted by Stella Andre*

ERNEST HINA

Ernest Hina is the son of George and Elmer Culley Hina of the Bell's Mines community, Crittenden County.

Ernest's grandfather, Joseph Anton Hina came from Germany in 1853 and settled at Bell's Mines in 1855.

Ernest married Mary Ellen Glenn of Louisville, KY. They had nine sons and one daughter.

George, (deceased) married Daisy N. Babbs. Born to them was three sons, Danny, Steve, Paul and one daughter, Mary Diane. They have one granddaughter.

Roy married Margie Berry, and they have two daughters, Holly, Laurie, and a son, Denny. They have two grandsons.

Clara Ann married W. H. Winders, (deceased) and they had two daughter, Donna Kay, Nancy Ellen, and a son, Jeffrey Wayne. She later married Wesley Ames and they have a son, Kenny. They have seven grandchildren.

Henry married Barbara Hart, and they had two sons, H. B. and Ralph. He later married Bonnie Shockley.

Bill married Scotty Heathscott, (deceased), they had two daughters, Mary Martha and Susan Lee. They have one granddaughter. He later married Charlsie Abel.

Charles, married Mary Ann Armstrong and they had one daughter, Joy. They have two granddaughters.

Fred married Nancy Parrish (deceased) and they had a son Fred, and a daughter Amy. They have two grandchildren. He later married Ruth Haley.

Harry lives in Atlanta, GA.

Rupert lives with Ernest, who will be 84 years old on June 17. Ernest still attends church (Cumberland Presbyterian) where he has been a member for over 50 years.

CARL OWEN (PETE) HINTON

Carl Owen Hinton (Pete) was born April 18, 1911 in Union County, KY. He was the son of William Aubury and Priscilla Shaffer Hinton. He attended Sturgis Elementary and Sturgis High Schools. Pete Hinton met and married Reba Truman Reynolds in 1937.

Pete worked as a cashier in the West Kentucky Store at Wheatcroft, KY. In the early forties he farmed near Pride, KY. Later Pete owned Hinton's Restaurant in Sturgis at the Corner of Fifth and Adams Streets. After that time Pete went to work in the coal mines where he was employed for twenty years.

G. B. Mackey and Carl Owen Hinton

Pete and Reba Hinton have two sons, William (Bill) and Jerry. Bill resides with his wife Phyllis in Pewee Valley near Louisville, KY. Bill and Phyllis have two children, Heather and Mark. Jerry Hinton and his wife Martha live in Paducah, KY. Jerry and Martha have one child, a daughter Marcie.

Pete Hinton enjoyed people. In his later years he loved to meet wih this friends at their favorite gathering places, such as the Farmer's State Branch Bank which was located on the corner of US Hwy. 60 and Fifth Street. There the friends would trade and swap stories. The bank presented Pete and his buddies with a decorated cake in appreciation for their removing the flag at the end of the day.

Pete died at age 66 on July 30, 1977.

Reba continues to live in Sturgis where she looks forward to visits from family and friends. *Submitted by Phyllis Hinton*

WILLIAM TAYLOR HINTON

William (Bill) Taylor Hinton, son of Pete and Reba Hinton, was born January 38, 1939 near Clay, KY.

Bill's family moved to Sturgis shortly after WWII. He attended Sturgis Elementary School and graduated from Sturgis High School in 1957.

Bill Hinton, Navy, 1962; Bill, Mark, Phyllis and Heather Hinton

Bill Hinton joined the Navy in 1958 and served nearly five years. Bill traveled exten-

sively and returned to Kentucky in 1962 to complete his college education. In 1963 he married Phyllis Mullins whom he had met while in the Navy. After completing college in 1966 he worked for General Electric briefly and after that for the Xerox Corporation for seventeen years.

Today Bill is President of HFH Inc., a real estate development company which he founded in 1986. He lives in Pewee Valley, a suburb of Louisville, KY. Bill and his wife Phyllis have two children, Heather and Mark.

Bill looks back fondly on his years in Sturgis, and enjoys sharing many stories of the fun times he experienced with childhood friends. *Submitted by Phyllis Hinton*

W. A. HINTON

The W. A. Hinton family had their origins in England. They immigrated to the United States in the early 1800s. The family settled in Virginia and later in Mitchelville, TN. The Joe Hinton family of Mitchelville, were farmers and storekeepers. Their children were, Charles, James, William Aubry, Josephine, Maybelle and Albert.

William Aubry Hinton came to Arnold Station, KY and ran a General Store and Blacksmith Shop. This was an important service to the people in this area as the trains came through Arnold Station twice daily to deliver goods and pick up produce. He married Prudy Priscilla (Cilla) Shaver, daughter of Jake and Susan Shaver in 1900 at Morganfield, KY. They had five children, Jack Celesta Pearl, Carl (Pete), Iva Lillian and Mildred Kathryn (Kate). Mr. Hinton worked in later years at the No. 2 Mine shoeing the mine mules.

Mr. and Mrs. W. A. Hinton

The family members still in this area are Celesta Pearl (Mrs. Harry) Turner, Sturgis. Ruth Polley (Mrs. Jack) Hinton, Sturgis and her sons Jackie, New Hope, AR, and Way, Princeton, KY. Reba Reynolds (Mrs. Pete) Hinton, Sturgis and her sons Bill, Louisville and Jerry, Paducah. Patsy Barnard Steelman, Sturgis daughter of Iva Lillian. Jamie Holt Saladino, Louisville daughter of Kate.

After retiring, Mr. and Mrs. Hinton resided in Sturgis their remaining years.

JAMES RUSSELL HOLEMAN

James Russell Holeman, son of Houston

Holeman and Drucilla Broadus Holeman, was born February 22, 1896. Russell worked on the family farm, in the coal mines, and a few years at Camp Breckenridge. but Russell always liked working, with an repairing automobiles, so that was really his life's work.

Onabel Cartwright Holeman was born September 30, 1896 to William Archibald Cartwright and Sue Day Cartwright. Onabel was a school teacher. She loved teaching and working with young children. She began her teaching career early, in the school at Grangertown, then Old Bethel, and Little Bethel. She also taught some in the Sturgis schools, at Shepherdville, KY and at Weaverton and Corydon in the Henderson County School system. After she retired from the public school system she taught some at St. Peter's in Uniontown. Onabel finished her college education by attending summer school at Western State Teachers College, and graduated at age 60. Her father W. A. Cartwright was born in 1829 and served in the Civil War.

Russell and Onabel Holeman c. 1960

Russell and Onabel were both born on farms in the Boxville area of Union County. They were married December 25, 1915. They lived a few years in Morganfield and then moved to Sturgis about 1920.

They were the parents of nine children; Marjorie, Helen and Hazel (twins), James, Ruth, Allen Houston, Anna Carmen, Louis Gordon, and Shirley Jean.

Ruth A. (deceased) and her husband Robert E. Kellen have four children: Hannah Jo, Mary Virginia, Robert E. Jr. (deceased), and Karen Sue.

Russell H. and his wife Lucille (Brown) have three children: Russell N. (Nicky), John Gordon, and Mary Lucille.

Anna C. and her husband Harold D. (Poss) Hina have four children: Martha Virginia, Harold D. Jr., Frances Elaine, and Linda Carol.

Louis G. and his wife Clara Jean (Strause) (deceased) have five sons: Louis G. (Butch), William Lynn, Steve, Clyde and Brett.

Shirley J. and her husband Donald R. Lester have three children: Tonia, Donald R. Jr., and Amber.

In 1947 Russell and his son Russell H. built a repair shop and went into partnership together. They named the business Holeman and Son Garage. It is now owned and operated by grandson Nicky.

Russell and Onabel's ancestors came from Virginia in covered wagons. The Holeman's settled first in Caldwell County and then moved to Union County. They are of German, Scottish, Irish and English decent.

Onabel was a distant cousin of Jefferson Davis, President of the Confederate State.
Submitted by Russell and Lucille Holeman

THOMAS HOLEMAN

Thomas Holeman came to Union County in 1926 to drill power holes for the #1, #8 and #9 mines. He is the son of the late William Thomas and Sallie Rankin Holeman of Crittenden Co. Mattieleen McGee Holeman is the daughter of the late John Riley "Buck" McGee and Lillie K. Cross McGee of Union County. Tom and Mattieleen were married 12/2/27 and have been married 61 years.

Tom retired from the Coal mines in 1969 after working there for 42 years. They have five children: Lorene McCann deceased in 1960 mother of Mike McCann who is married to Connie Smith and they have 2 children Heath and Dava.

Thomas Holeman Family

Barbara Freer, divorced and mother of Jackie Freer Oakley who is married to Kenneth Oakley. They live in Cadiz, KY and have 2 children Tara and Brad.

Edward Holeman who works for Frontier Kemper has three children Leslie married to Chippy Peltier and have 3 children Jason, Lindsey and Danny. They live in Franklin, LA.

Debbie married to Ramah Guess, they have 3 daughters Misty, Talitha and April and they live in Franklin, LA.

Ed's son Tim married Cathy and they have two daughters Cassey and Megan and they live in Gonzales, LA.

John W. Holeman married to Linda Michels and have 5 children, Jay and Laura live with their mother Louise Marshell, Mike married to Carolyn and have 1 son Caleb live in Radclife, KY.

Steve and Jona Lynne Holeman of Vine Grove, KY. Sondra Kathryn Holeman lives at home with her parents and sister Barbara.

WILLIAM AND SHERYL ROSE HAZEL

Sheryl Rose Belt was born Oct. 1949 in Kut-

tawa, KY. Her parents are George and Elizabeth Belt; brothers Jim, George "Porky," and sister Emma K.

February 1971, Sheryl married William H. "Junior" Hazel, a Sturgis native. His parents are Loren and William "Dub" Hazel (deceased). Brenda Hazel Walls is Junior's only sister. Sheryl and Junior have two children - Lori Beth, born Dec. 1971 and William Caiep "Will" Hazel, born Dec. 1975.

Junior is a brickmason and Sheryl works for Fran's Country Crafts in Sturgis. The family are members of the Sturgis First Baptist Church. *Submitted by Sheryl Hazel*

GEORGE NEWTON HOLT

George Newton Holt was born on a farm near Sturgis, Nov. 4, 1896. Mr. Holt's ancestors, both paternal and maternal, were among the pioneers of Kentucky coming to Union County in its early days. He was the son of Peter Franklin and Barbara A. Delaney Holt. He had two brothers and a sister: Henry Delaney, Burnett Milburn, and Clara Elizabeth. Mr. Holt served in the Army during World War I in Germany. he married Lillie Ann O'Bryant, daughter of Otho and Annie Shaw O'Bryant, Mortons Gap, KY, Nov. 19, 1924. He was employed by West Kentucky Coal Company, First Christian Church of Sturgis, Union Electric Company, The Sturgis Furniture Company, and the Union County Board of Education. Mr. Holt was well known for his quickness of step, abundant energy, ready laughter, and whistling while he worked. Seven children were born to George and Lillie:

Mrs. Herbert Allen Dorley (Elizabeth Ann), Nashville, IL. Two children: Gary Allen and Kathryn Ann. Gary Allen, his wife Susan, Aaron, Amy and Amanda live in Scottsdale, AZ. Kathy and her husband Allan Kiifner, and Chad and Kyle live in Franklin, IL.

Nancy Shaw, Otho Franklin, Judy, Mary Ruth, George Newton and Lillie, Dorothy Helen, George, Jr. and Betty

George N. Holt, Jr. and his wife Virginia (Buice), Carbondale, IL. Three sons: Mark Raymond, Craig Delaney, and David Lee. Mark, his wife Linda, and Krislina and Stephen live in Carbondale also. Craig and his daughter Jennifer live in Tulsa, OK. David and Jamie have just recently married and live in Westerville, OH.

Mrs. Shelley Allen Omer (Dorothy Helen), Lexington, KY. One daughter, Susan Holt who is single and lives in Lexington also.

Mrs. Bryon M. Brady (Mary Ruth), Elkhart, IN. Three children: Edwin M., Kimberly A., and Nicholas J. Edwin (Ted) and his wife Joyce, and Megan and David live in Chicago, IL. Kim and her husband, David Miller, live in Kansas City, MO. Nick is single and lives in Elkhart.

Julia Kathryn, who married George Randall Jones, Atlanta, GA. Two children; George R. Jones, Jr. and Rebecca Ruth. Randy and his wife Gayle and Brent live in Tucker, GA. Becky is single and lives in Marietta, GA.

Otho Franklin, and his wife, Barbara (Thomas), live in Altus, OK. Three children: Karen of Napa, CA, and Gregg and Barry of Altus. All three are single.

Mrs. Ronald Luckett (Nancy Shaw), Baton Rogue, LA. Two sons: Brian and Michael who are both single and also live in Baton Rouge.

Mr. Holt, a member of First Christian Church at Sturgis, died June 7, 1978 and is buried at Pythian Ridge Cemetery in Sturgis. Mrs. Holt, a former secretary for West Kentucky Coal Company and reporter for the Sturgis News, still lives in Sturgis and continues at the age of 86 to be active in First Christian Church. She is an inspiration to her seven children and their families which include 16 grandchildren and 11 great grandchildren. *Submitted by Dorothy H. Omer*

JOHN THOMAS HOLT

John Thomas Holt, son of Peter C. Holt, was born November 12, 1859. He was married April 9, 1881, to Bettie Sue Smith, daughter of Christopher Smith and Sarah Hall. He was reared on his father's farm in Pond Fork area, and worked at a general store in Caseyville, at that time a city of some size. In 1892 with two partners, C. S. Wallace and Fred Dyer, they started a store on the south side of 4th and Main Street known as The Sturgis Dry Goods Company. Later the store was moved to its present location at 6th and Adams Street. the fire of 1913 destroyed the building, but the bricks were cleaned and used as lining the present store, and the store was extended to the alley. Mr. Holt bought out his partners and it became known as Holts, and he ran this business until his death at the age of 73 when he died of a heart attack.

Mr. Holt had 7 children: Lila, Earl, Leslie, J. T. Jr., who died as a baby, Lawrence, Mayme, and Robert. The business was carried on by the children - Earl, until he moved to Dallas, TX, in 1936; Lila, Mayme and Robert. Robert's son is the present owner.

Mr. Holt's grandparents were pioneers of Kentucky. Harrison Holt of Virginia and Harrett Belmer of Maryland, his wife, were the parents of Peter C. Holt, born in Union County in 1826. Peter C. married Sarah Reasor of Union County in 1853. Twelve children, two of whom died at an early age, where born to this union. Peter owned 170 acres of land on the Bordley-Commercial Point Road. He was considered a steady businessman, a thorough Christian, a kind father, and a popular neighbor. He died in 1888 leaving a legacy of industry, honesty, and friendship. Mr. Holt was a member of Knights of Pythias, Sturgis Kiwanis Club, but his greatest love was for his church. He was saved and baptized into the First Baptist Church, and was later ordained as a deacon where he served until his death March 14, 1933. He was noted for his kindness, his generosity to the poor and needy, his honesty, his morality, and his loyalty to his church.

LESLIE E. "SONNY" AND PAULINE "POLLY" HOLT

Leslie E. "Sonny" Holt, son of George Leslie and Hallie Davis Holt was born, in Sturgis, Feb. 11, 1927. Sonny owned and operated Sonny's Home Appliances from 1958-1968 and retired in February 1989, as Sales Engineer, from National Mine Service Company, Madisonville, KY. "Sonny" as he is known to his many friends, in the mining industry, was sent to Germany, by his company, for special training on Mine Rescue Breathing Apparatuses and has been training throughout the United States, mining companies, Federal and State Agencies during the past 17 years.

Polly Newcom Holt, daughter of Ila "Pete" and Jennie Rutherford Newcom was born in the Bells Mines Community of Crittenden County, Nov. 10, 1923. Polly helped her husband in the appliance business and in 1968 went to work for the U. S. Postal Service and retired as Postmaster of Sullivan, KY, July 1, 1988.

Sonny, Adam and Nick Holt; Becky and Barry Holt

They are both graduates of Sturgis High School and were married Aug. 4, 1945 in North Augusta, SC, while Sonny was serving with the U. S. Army in Augusta, GA.

They are the parents of one son, Barry, born Aug. 22, 1955. Barry is presently employed at AlCAN, Sebree, KY and owns and operates B & B Satellite Systems from his home. He is married to the former Becky Hagan, daughter of Joe and Juanita Hagan of Waverly, KY. They have two sons Nicholas Earl "Nick" age 11 and Adam Joseph, age 7. They all reside on 12th and Kelsey Streets, Sturgis.

Sonny is the grandson of the late John Thomas and Betty Sue Holt. He had one brother, James Thomas (deceased) and a sister Norma Jean Haney.

Polly is the granddaughter of the late Gus and Ida Rutherford. She has a sister Ilene Gatten who is married to Charles M. "Buster" Gatten.

Polly, Sonny, Barry, Becky, Nick and Adam are all active members of the First Presbyterian Church on Kelsey Street in Sturgis.

ROBERT C. HOLT

Robert C. Holt was the youngest son of J. T. Holt and Betty Smith Holt. After graduating from Sturgis High School, he attended University of Kentucky, and afterwards worked in the family store until World War II, where he served in Europe with the 80th Division. After the war, he rejoined his brothers and sisters in Holt's Store until his death in 1969. Robert was noted for his friendliness and was especially faithful to Kiwanis, one of his special interest being the Sturgis Pool. He also loved First Baptist Church where he was a deacon and was regular in support and attendance.

Kathleen R. Holt, daughter of Louis Elbert Ringo and Mellie Elaine Hudson Ringo, graduated from Blackford High School, and received an A. B. Degree from Western Kentucky University, and an M. A. Degree for Peabody College, Nashville, TN. As a Civil Service employee, she worked at Camp Breckinridge and Fort Campbell. She was also a teacher in Webster County, Clarksville, TN and the Union County School System until her retirement. Kathleen's greatest interest outside of her family and friends is First Baptist Church. She has taught a Sunday School class, has sung in the choir, worked with WMU or its younger organizations, and worked in VBS ever since she came to Sturgis in 1942.

The Robert C. Holt Family

They are the parents of four sons: Thomas R., Robert L., David H. and John Phillip. Thomas, after graduating from Murray State University, worked in the family business until 1981 when he became owner of Holt's Furniture Store in Sturgis. He is married to Mary Brown Holt. They have a daughter, Margaret Elaine, and a son, John Thomas. Robert attended University of Kentucky and has stores in Greenville and Madisonville, KY. He is

married to Laura Davis Holt. They have 2 sons, Heath and Benjamin and a baby daughter Suzanne. David received his B. S. Degree from Western KY University, and operates a store in Union County Shopping Center, Morganfield, KY. He married Cathy Eden, and they have a daughter, Jennifer, and a son Logan. Phillip Holt, who has a BS Degree from University of Kentucky, owns the original family business. He is active in civic and community affairs, but his greatest interest is First Baptist Church where he is a deacon. The four boys have continued the business traditions that were started by their grandfather beginning in 1892 and were passed down by their father.

WILLIAM HENRY HOLT, JR.

The William Henry Holt, Jr. family has pioneer roots, with some branches of the family settling in Kentucky before it was a state and in Sturgis before it was a town.

One branch of the family stretches over nine generations—from the one-year-old great grandsons of William Holt and Velma Holt Simpson, back to Michael Reasor, a revolutionary soldier born in 1760. By reason of Michael Reasors service in the Revolutionary War, 1777-1781, his descendants are eligible for membership in the Sons and Daughter of the American Revolution. The Reasor family's connection with Sturgis came in 1852, when Michael Reasor's grandson, Thomas Reasor, moved from Shelby County, KY to the Lindle Precinct of what later became Sturgis. The daughter of Thomas and Rebecca Reasor, Sarah Elizabeth, married Peter C. Holt (the grandfather of William Holt) in December 1853.

William Holt was born in Sturgis in 1902, the son of William Henry Holt, Sr. and Annie Marie (Smith) Holt, daughter of Christopher C. and Sarah (Hall) Smith. William attended Sturgis Schools in the Class of 1921 and was a lifelong member of the Sturgis Methodist Church. His family moved to his mother's homeplace, the Christopher Smith farm in rural Sturgis, where William later engage in farming and raised horses. William named the farm Oaklawn.

In 1931 William married Velma Ruth Small of Sturgis, the daughter of Joseph Benjamin and Margaret (Love) Small. (The J. B. Small family history is described elsewhere in this book.) To this union were added one daughter and two sons—Margaret Anne in 1932, William Joseph in 1935, and Kenneth David in 1937.

In 1938 William became terminally ill and the family moved from the farm to a house on Washington Street in Sturgis, where William died in 1939, leaving his wife and three small children.

Velma took over the management of the farm on William's death, and engaged a series of tenant farmers to live on the farm. In 1947,

Velma and the children returned to Oaklawn when she married Leiter H. Simpson, the son of George B. and Octa (Barbee) Simpson of Sturgis. Leiter Simpson died in 1978, and Velma remains on the farm today.

Velma has been active in musical circles in Sturgis from the early 1920 to the present. She served as organist and pianist at the First Baptist Church in Sturgis for many years until she moved her membership to the Cumberland Presbyterian Church with her husband in 1971. Velma taught music in Sturgis for most of her life, and several of her piano pupils later became successful professional musicians.

Margaret Anne Holt married John Burton Chapman, a career military officer from Euclid, OH in 1956. Lt. Colonel Chapman retired from the U. S. Army Chemical Corps in 1977 in Washington, DC, and is now an international defense consultant. Margaret is director of the U. S.-Soviet trade program for a Washington public-policy organization. Margaret and John Chapman are both graduates of Ohio State University. They have two sons, Christopher John and Scott Edward. Christopher is the General Manager of Kinetic Sports, Inc. in Arlington, VA and Annapolis, MD. Scott is married to Vicki Elizabeth Small and lives in Manassas, VA. Scott is Eastern District Systems Engineer for Fortune Computer Company and Vicki is a ballet teacher associated with The Cuppett Performing Arts Studio.

William Joseph (Bill) Holt married Patricia Adams of Mayfield in 1957. Bill received B. S. and M. A. degrees from Western Kentucky University and did further graduate work at Indiana University. He is on the faculty of Murray State University. Patricia is a graduate of Western Kentucky University and is associated with Lindsay Jewellers in Murray. They have two daughters, Margaret Allyson and Amanda Ruth, and one son, William Joseph (Will) Holt, Jr. Allyson is married to Charles Steffan, Jr., a Professor of History at Murray State University, and she teaches at Murray High School. Amanda is in advertising and promotion with Arbys, Inc., in Atlanta, GA, and Will is a student at Murray state University and employed at Briggs.

David Holt married Vicki Loa Griggs of Louisville in 1960. David is a graduate of Western Kentucky University and is in the insurance business in Sturgis. Vicki also attended Western, and is a casework specialist with the State of Kentucky's Cabinet of Human Resources. They have two daughters, Michael Lauren and Hilary Anne. Michael is married to Barry Kent Fisher of French Lick, IN, an agronomist with the State of Indiana at Greencastle, and she is a high school are teacher. They are the parents of one year-old Benjamin David Fisher. Hilary is married to Fred Lamb Hooper II of Morganfield and both are students at Henderson Community College. They are the parents of one-year-old Miles Douglas Hooper.

JOHN HANLEY HOOPER

James Hooper was born in 1740's in North Carolina. He was related tot he William Hooper who signed the Declaration of Independence. Hooper moved to South Carolina and fought in Colonel Williamson's Cavalry Brigade during the Revolutionary War.

Around 1802 James Hooper migrated to a part of Henderson County which later became Union County. In 1811 he receive a land grant for property near what is now Grove Center. He died there in 1813.

Samuel Hooper, son of James, married Susan Slocumb in 1815. Their son, Isaac Hooper (1818-1859) married Mary Anderson Hannah. His second marriage was to Nancy Henshaw Stone in 1852.

John Thornton Berry Hooper (1850-1924) was a son born of the second marriage. John Hooper married Florence Bell Funk in 1873, and was a prominent farmer of the Grove Center Community.

John Walter Hooper (1879-1955) was first married to Lola Perkins, and secondly to Daisy Likens. Lola Perkins was the daughter of Doc and Martha Johns Perkins.

John Hanley (Pete) Hooper was born in 1916. He married Pansy Prince, daughter of Henry and Ella Pierce Prince, in 1934. Pete Hooper holds the distinction of truly being a self-made man. He has attained business success and financial security while never having worked for another man.

The children of Pete and Pansy Hooper are: Donald Eastin (deceased), Peggy Jo, Patsy Lola, Ella Jean, Wayne Gordon, and Martha Justine Hooper.

Peggy Jo Hooper married Elmer Kirchner. Their sons are Dennis A. and Gregg D. Kirchner. Dennis married Karen Bickett and has a daughter, Kara Dawn. Gregg married Susan Harris, a descendant of Union County Pioneer Solomon Blue. They have three daughters, Natonya, Katy, and Laura.

Patsy Lola Hooper, unmarried, is well known for her christian charity and family devotion. Through hard work and perseverance she earned a college degree in mid-life, a notable accomplishment.

Ella Jean married Reuben Hawkins, of Cobden, IL. He farms and teaches at the Shawnee Junior College. They have one son, Reuben Andrew.

LEE ANDREW HUDSON

Lee Andrew William Hudson (b. 1-7-1873, d. 1-20-1945) was born in Pee Wee Valley, (Oldham Co.) KY. He was the son of William Allen (Jack) and Mary 3. Taylor Hudson. His family moved tot he Seven Gums area of Union Co. in 1880, and later to a farm straddling the Union-Webster Co. lines. Pyro Mining Company's #11 High Wall Mines is now located on the old farm. Lee Andrew married Willie Truman Wallace (b. 9-14-1880, d. 9-19-

1945), daughter of James Daniel and Laura Belle Wallace on No. 17, 1898. Their marriage produced twelve children.

The first child, Earl Ecton Hudson (b. 8-23-1899, d. 1-19-1979) married Floella Taylor (b. 9-11-1900, d. 3-10-1977). They lived most of their lives in Detroit, MI and had no children.

Cora Lee Hudson (b. 9-23-1900) was the second child. She married Dewey Marlin Lamb (b. 10-23-1899, d. 5-22-1971) on October 28, 1922. They had one daughter, Wileta Lamb. (b. 10-22-1926). They lived in Sturgis most of their lives.

Arthur Posey Hudson (b. 1-17-1903, d. 6-18-1986) married Marguerite Miller (b-2-8-1908). They had three children: Jack Lee (b. 8-6-1928, d. 12-17-1986), William Arthur (b. 2-12-1930) and Kay Annette (b. 6-21-1939). They lived in Detroit, MI.

The fourth child, William Daniel Hudson (b. 3-31-1905) married Ida Belle Driver (b. 12-12-1909, d. 11-13-1977). They had no children and lived in the Wheatcroft area.

The fifth child lived to be only three months old. She was named Mary Beatrice Hudson (b. 6-3-1907, d. 9-19-1907).

James McClain (Mack) Hudson (b. 3-30-1909, d. 5-20-1977) married Mary Eloise White (b. 9-4-1905). They had three children: James David (b. 9-4-1935), Donald Earl (b. 1-11-1940) and Darrel Douglas (b. 10-24-1945, d. 10-27-1945). They lived most of their lives near Patoka, IN.

Mabel Kathryn Hudson (b. 4-17-1920) was the seventh child. She married Roland Ray Baker (b. 8-13-1904, d. 12-19-1974) and they had four daughters: Helen Adelle (b. 4-13-1928), Kathryn Rhea (b. 1-3-1930), Wilma Ann (b. 3-29-1932) and Regina Beth (b. 5-15-1941). They lived on a farm just a short distance from Sullivan.

Wallace McClure Hudson (b. 6-20-1912, d. Aug. 1912), was the eight child. He lived to be only six weeks old.

The next child born was Thomas Wickliff Hudson (b. 12-15-1914, d. 6-15-1950). He was married to Kathryn Hina (b. 6-26-1919) and they had one child, Diana June Hudson (b. 6-13-1938). Tom farmed the family farm until his death.

The tenth child was Virginia Belle Hudson (b. 1-19-1916). She married Carol David Jenkins (b. 4-1-1909, d. 12-19-1956) and they had three children: Patricia Ann (b. 5-29-1936), Barbara Nell (b. 5-4-1938), and Thomas Lee (b. 6-28-1941). Belle and Cora Lee Lamb opened the Sturgis Floral Shop in 1946 and operated this business until Dec. 31, 1971.

Dortha Truman Hudson (b. 2-22-1918) married Wilburn Carol (Water Boy) Morgan (b. 4-8-1919), they had two children: Richard Hudson (b. 10-2-1940) and Dortha Carolyn Morgan (b. 7-30-1943). They have lived most of their lives in the Sturgis area.

The last child was Rebecca Mae Hudson (b. 2-19-1920). She married Elvis Roscoe Holt (b. 3-8-1916) and they had five children: Jackie

Roscoe (b. 8-14-1938), Daniel LaRon (b. 11-19-1939), Virginia Ann (b. 2-4-1944), Laura Yvonne (b. 9-1-1946), and Ecton Keith (b. 7-5-1952).

Many of the children, grandchildren, great grandchildren and great, great, grandchildren still live in the Sturgis area.

HUMPHREY

From the Commonwealth of Virginia to Nelson County, KY to Union County, arriving prior to the Civil War (we think), John Burr Humphrey settled in the Seven Gums area to farm and raise his family. Some of that land remains today in the family's name, being in the Dr. William Humphrey Estate and lived on by Bruce Humphrey, great grandson of John Burr.

John Burr (1833-1923) married Cordelia Nall (1837-1916) in December 1856. From that marriage nine children were born. John died young. Of the boys, Perry and Tom left Union county, while Walter and R. E. Lee stayed on the farm and Benjamin Franklin returned to Sturgis to practice medicine following graduation from the University of Louisville medical school. This was around 1901. Le remained a bachelor, farming the home place and living with his sisters Sallie and Bess until each in turn died. The third sister was Lutha, who married Thornton Berry and lived in the Seven Gums area.

In 1903 Ben married Lillian Russell from paris, Texas. They met when she came to Kentucky to visit her Henry grandparents. For two years, we are told, her father came from Texas to Kentucky on horse buying trips; on the dirst trip he met Anne Richards Henry, and when he made the second trip, he took home a bride as well as horses. We think they traveled in a covered wagon.

Dr. Ben and Lillian lived for many eyars in a house where Thornsberry Insurance now stands. His office and the stables were adjacent in his early medical days, but burned in about 1926. They then bought the house at 912 Adams Street, where they lived until their deaths, both in 1947.

The children born to them were Dorothy Russell (1903) and William Perry (1913). Dorothy married Thoms Ford, an Ohioan whom she met at college, and had a daughter, Anne Russell, who married Gerald Shaffer and lives in Evansville. Dorothy later married H'Earl Evans, long-time Sturgis school teacher and principal. At this time she resides at the Community Rest Home.

William Perry was known as "Son" growing up, then as "Young Doc Humphrey" when he joined "Old Doc" in medical practice following his graduation from Louisiana State University School of Medicine during World War II. His marriage was to Georgia Coker from Crittenden County. Their children are Ben, living in Colorado Springs, CO; Lisa now Mrs. Dan Hogan of Waverly; Dottie, residing

in Henderson; Brian an accountant in Nashville, TN; and Bruce, married to the former Lisa Quinn and involved with her family's business, Quinn Lumber Company. *Submitted by Anne Shaffer*

HURLEY

Ollie Jones, daughter of Josie Creas and Eddie Jones was married to Oliver Hurley, son of Martha Wooldredge and John Hurley of Marion in 1906. They lived in several places, operated several theatres, owned a grocery in Providence, then farmed in Union County. They had 3 children.

Katharyn was married to Dr. H. Grady Ketchum, a Southern Baptist Minister at Jackson, AL for 37 years. Their children are Karolyn Coulter, Los Alamos, NM; Rosalyn Palmer of Linden, AL; and Grady Wayne of Jackson.

Lowell is a retired farmer, World War II veteran, deacon of Strugis First Baptist Church, married in 1946 to Evelyn Hammack, a Union County teacher, daughter of Ethel McKeaig and A. R. Hammack. They have two daughters, Gayle and Jean.

Gayle was married to Shelby Woodring, son of Catherine Whalen and Charles Woodring, in 1967. Their children are: Maria, a student at Murray State; Laurel of Terre Haute; and Eric of Saginaw. Gayle is now married to Tom Lembeke. They live in Saginaw, MI.

Jean was married to Dave Walton of Nashville in 1977. She workds with Northern Telecom.

Lee Roy married Virginia Connaway, daughter of Baptist minister, Rev. Z. T. Connoway, and his wife, Jessie.

Their son, Lowell Taylor, was married to Carol Hughes. They have a son, Jeff. Later he was married to Patty Farmer Pruitt. Their children are Kimberly, Jon, and Chance of Evansville.

JOHNS

The Johns family was an active agriculture and commercial family in the St. Ambrose community during the late 1800 through the 1900s. Carl Friedrich John b. 5/31/1811 a tanner, woolcorder and grist mill operator by trade left Delsnitz, Saxon (Sacken) Germany for America where he changed his name to Charles Fredrich Johns and married the younger Nancy Austin b. 4/18/1829 in Delaware on his way to Kentucky. Charles and Nancy Johns purchased 315 acres between Henshaw and Sturgis and their great granddaughter, Jane Shaffer Kurtz now live on the farm with her husband, George. Evidence of Charles' grist mill are visible on the farm in two grinding stones and the stone lined well in the front yard of the Kurtz home. Seven children were born to Nancy and Charles Johns, the most memorable of whom were Alfred and Charles (History of UC 1886 page 810). While

Charlie was a bachelor, "Alf" married Annie Catherine (Katie) Stevens b. 8/10.1871, a Posey County, IN native, who was educated at St. Vincent Academy.

Alf Johns was a livestock farmer who used modern equipment by threshing wheat with a separator and steam engine, filling silos with a corn chipper and blower, bailing hay with a stationary baler powered by mules or gasoline engine and making hay stacks with a lift rake and horses. He was an order cattle buyer and sold more fat cattle on the Chicago market in 1916 than any other farmer.

The daughters of Annie Catherine and Alf Johns, Lela, Mattie and Alice

Since Alf's farming operation had grown to several hundred acres, work was given to every one who came and wanted employment. The John's had many horses and mules and could outfit each man with a team, disk, cultivator, cultipackor drag or harrow. These teams would go in and out the land by the home at Henshaw several time a day and the dust was fine and deep. With the windows raised, it was dusty inside and out. Katie and the three surviving daughter fought dust and fed field hands. Lela married Hugh G. Davies and died in child birth in 1918. Their son lives in Wilmington, NC. Alice (see William Henry (Harry) Stevens) married Harvey Jones and had three children.

Mattie drove a horse and buggy and later a car, farm to farm, while her father filled cattle orders. She once broke her arm while cranking a 1917 Model T Car. Mattie married Walter Mason Shaffer b. 9/4/1894, a West Kentucky Coal Company electrician and bookkeeper and lived in Sturgis for a short time before returning to Henshaw to assist Mr. Johns in supervising the Johns farm. Mattie was a charter member of the Henshaw Homemaker and worked to get the Kentucky Farm Bureau established to improve Kentucky farm markets. Mattie and Walter had one daughter, Jane Shaffer Kurtz m. George M. Kurtz and three sons Gerald (m. Anne Ford), Dugan (m. Jeanne Minor), Jim Shaffer, deceased, (m. Marty Hackworth). *Submitted by J. S. Kurtz*

EDWIN AND ELEANOR JOHNSON

Edwin, "Eddie," Johnson was best known in Sturgis as the picture show man. He operated the old Ritz Theater until the new Victory Theater was built in the EMBA building in 1940. Many will remember the home movies he made of people on the streets of Sturgis and showed them in the theater to a packed house on Thursday nights.

Eddie was born in Morganfield on March 31, 1899. Two years out of high school, in 1920, he started a long and successful professional baseball career. He played right field for the Washington Nationals (later called the Senators) when Babe Ruth played the same position for the Yankees. In fact, his first professional game was in Yankee Stadium and he was awed when Ruth passed him going to the field and said, "Hi kid."

He returned home in 1931 and married Eleanor Long, the daughter of Edward and Virginia Long. They made their home just west of Sturgis in the Long homestead on Midway Street. Eleanor was born in Sturgis Feb. 3, 1897. She worked along side her husband in the theater business, selling tickets at the Ritz and Victory theaters. After the Victory Theater burned in 1958, the Johnsons in partnership with Dr. William Humphrey built the Sunset Drive-in Theater near Waverly. Later they also managed the Broadview Drive-in near Morganfield.

In addition to the theater business, Edwin Johnson was also involved in other business which provided recreation and services to the people of Sturgis. In the 1940s and early 1950s he also owned a bowling alley, a pool hall, and a Western Auto Store.

The Johnson's had one son, Edwin Jr. born in 1935. He is known as Johnny Johnson to his friends in Sturgis. He attended Sturgis High School and played on Coach Ralph Horning's football team that won the Western Kentucky Conference in 1952. After playing college football and studying pre-engineering at Western Kentucky College for two years, he went to the University of Kentucky to get his engineering degree. At Western Kentucky he met Rosemary Richardson, who was born in Bowling Green, KY. They were married in December 1956. Johnny took a job with NASA at the Kennedy Space Center in Florida and was involved in checkout of manned spacecraft form Project mercury to the Space Shuttle flights. He retired from NASA in 1986 and is now working for McDonnell Douglas Space Systems Company in Huntington Beach, California. Rosemary and Johnny had five children, Steven, Kathy, David, Michael, and Randy. Kathy, utilizing some of the inherited athletic ability of her grandfather, won a silver and a bronze medal in the 1984 Olympics in gymnastics.

Edwin and Eleanor Johnson spent some of the happiest days of their lives visiting their grandchildren in Florida, but Sturgis was always home and they always returned. Edwin died in Sturgis in July, 1975 and Eleanor lives in the Sturgis Rest Home today.

MARY ALICE JOHNS JONES

Mary Alice Johns, daughter of Alfred Johns and Annie Catherine Stevens, was born Dec. 24, 1894, near Henshaw, Union County, KY.

Mary Alice Johns and her two sister,s Lela Catherine Johns, born March 4, 1893, and Mattie Pearl Johns, born Feb. 8, 1896 attended Henshaw School, grades 1 through 6, and Metropolis, IL, school, grades 7 and 8. They lived with their Uncle Richard and Aunt Sylvia Austin in Metropolis while attending school there.

On Feb. 6, 1915, Mary Alice Johns married Harvey Cornelius Jones in Union County, KY. Harvey Cornelius Jones graduated from Bowling Green, KY college; then taught school at Mt. Olive School, located on Mt. Olive Road, near Henshaw. Harvey Cornelius Jones was employed by DeKoven Coal Mine as bookkeeper and shipping clerk from 1920 to 1926. He farmed, raised crops and livestock for more than 50 years.

Harvey Cornelius Jones and Mary Alice Johns Jones have three children: Robert Alfred Jones - b. Aug. 6, 1916 at Henshaw, KY, d. July 3, 1980, m. Helen Byrne, 1943. WWII U. S. Army, Airplane Mechanic in Panama.

Mildred Floreda Jones - b. Nov. 18, 1918 at Henshaw, KY. Married William Hildreth Harms(b. oct. 22, 1916, Green Co., IL), June 14, 1941. WWII - U. S. Navy, Okinawa

Richard Cornelius Jones - b. April 12, 1923 at DeKoven, KY, d. April 24, 1988 near Henshaw, KY. WWII - U. S. Navy, m. Gladys Merrill Self April 12, 1958, WWII - U. S. Army, France.

Mary Alice Johns Jones, age 94 years, resides at Sturgis Community Rest Home. She is a life member of Henshaw Christian Church and now attends Sturgis Christian church.

Subject's father, Alfred Johns, born Feb. 2, 1861, near Henshaw, KY, is the son of Charles Johns and Nancy West Johns. Alfred Johns was an extensive farmer. He raised corn, grain, pastured and fed cattle and hogs. The livestock was herded down the dirt road to Henshaw, loaded into railroad cattle cars and shipped to Chicago and St. Louis stockyards.

Mary Alice Johns Jones is the maternal granddaughter of William H. Stevens, who was born Sept. 7, 1840, in Vanderburgh County, IN and on Oct. 2, 1862, in Mt. Vernon, Posey County, IN, married Elizabeth Carson, born Nov. 24, 1841, in Marrs Twsp., Posey County, IN. William H. Stevens and Elizabeth, his wife, also have a son, Paul J. Stevens. On March 29, 1881, William H. Stevens and Elizabeth, his wife, purchased form Robert Spalding and Ellen M., his wife, 110 acres of land situated in Union County, KY, on the waters of the Ohio River (Deed Book 32, p. 32, 33). On May 10, 1883, William H. Stevens purchased form J. W. Quick 60 acres of land situated in Union County, KY on the waters of the Ohio River (Deed Book 33, page 589).

William H. Stevens died March 27, 1914. Elizabeth Carson Stevens, his wife died Aug. 8, 1916. They are buried in Caseyville Cemetery, Union County, KY.

VIRGIL AND REBECCA KEARNEY

E. Virgil Kearney, son fo E. J. Kearney, Sr. and Lillian (Stafford) Kearney, was born Jan. 19, 1918, at Trezevant, TN (Carroll County). The family moved to McKenzie, TN in 1925. He graduated from McKenzie High School in 1936.

He married, Rebecca A. Davis, of Sturgis, KY on Aug. 27, 1939. She is the daughter of Roy B. and Glennie Hawes Davis. (See Roy B. Davis)

Rebecca graduated form Sturgis High School in 1936, and entered Bethel College (a Cumberland Presbyterian Church College) in McKenzie, TN in the fall of 1936. Here is where Virgil and Rebecca met.

Virgil and Rebecca moved to Memphis, TN and lived there until Aug. 1941, when they moved to Sturgis. Virgil entered the Army in December of 1942 and was discharged Oct. 25, 1945.

While Virgil was in the service, Rebecca was employed in the payroll Dept. of West KY Coal Company for a year. When Camp Breckinridge was opened Rebecca worked in the Finance Dept. there until mid - 1946.

After Virgil's discharge from the service, he returned to Sturgis and was employed by Malcolm Cason at the Sturgis Pharmacy (formerly Wesco Pharmacy) in November of 1945. He worked there until Mr. Cason's death in 1954.

After Mr. Cason's death Virgil and Rebecca bought the store from Mr. Cason's daughters and operated it until July of 1963.

They sold the Sturgis Pharmacy to Tom Roe and Patricia Frazier, in July of 1963.

The Kearney's then bought the Sturgis Motor Parts Company form Mr. Roy Davis, who was retiring. They operated the store until January 1980, and then sold it to Earl and Sue (Truitt) Brinkmann.

Virgil and Rebecca have one daughter, Bonnie, born March 15, 1948.

Bonnie graduated from Union County High School in 1966, and from the University of Kentucky in 1970, and is presently teaching at Union County High.

When Bonnie started college, Rebecca went to work for the State Dept. of Economic Security. She was employed with the State for 12 1/2 years.

Virgil and Rebecca are presently retired. Both are active members of the Sturgis Cumberland Presbyterian Church.

Daughter Bonnie, married Roger A. Edmondson, son of Carrol and Estine Edmondson, on June 4, 1971.

They have a daughter, Rebecca Deane, born Sept. 9, 1976.

The Kearneys reside at 319 - 3rd Street, where they have lived for over 40 years.

They celebrated their 50th Wedding Anniversary on Sunday, Aug. 27, 1989. *Submitted by Virgil Kearney*

ROBERT EARL KELLEN

Robert Earl Kellen, son of Add Young Kellen and Mary Elizabeth (Reddick) Kellen, was born Jan. 11, 1916. His brother James A. born 9/21/17 is retired, lives in Paducah, KY. His brother Joseph Melvin born 8/04/21 is retired and lives in Millersburg, MI. His brother Leslie Evans born 8/23 died Sept. 1923.

Bob attended grade school at DeKoven five years and Clay Elementary the next three years. His mother died while he was in the Eighth Grade at Clay. He then lived in Caseyville with his grandparents, Thomas James Kellen and Hannah Graham Kellen. he attended DeKoven High School three years and walked both ways every day for two of those years. His dad remarried in 1933 (Nellie Lane Brown) and moved to Morganfield. Bob lived with them and graduated from Morganfield High School in 1934. His dad's marriage lasted two years after which Bob either boarded out or lived with his paternal grandparents. His dad died on June 6, 1946.

James Henry and Lidie Ellen Graham Lancaster

Thomas James and Hanna Graham Kellen

His paternal grandparents, Thomas J. Kellen and Hannah Graham Kellen, moved into Union County from Smith Mills, KY. His maternal grandparents, Joe Reddick and Anna Stevenson Reddick, moved into Union County from Norris City, IL. From 8/02/35 until 3/31/36 Bob served in the C.C.C. in Paducah. He worked for Union Sand & Gravel Co., Fred Alloway Lumber Co. and Dept of Agriculture Farm Program. In 1943 he accepted a job with the government at Camp Breckinridge where

he worked for nineteen years. During this period he also worked two short periods at Fort Knox and approximately two years at Ohio River Ordnance at Henderson. He then transferred to Ft. Knox, KY in 1963 and lived in government quarters during the week, returning home to Sturgis on weekends via Greyhound Bus. Bob was Head of the Major Items Section and Chief of Customer Assistance Branch for all Army Units. Bob retired in 1975 after 31 years service. During the 12 years I commuted to Fort Knox and lived in government quarters, I became acquainted with Leroy Brown. I lived next door to him in our quarters and rode to work each day with him. I did not have to have a car of my own. We still communicate and travel with each other.

Robert E., Add Y. and Thomas James Kellen; Mary Reddick Kellen

In 1941 Bob married Ruth A. Holeman, moved to Sturgis where they had four children—Hanna Jo born Aug. 23, 1942; Mary Virginia born June 20, 1944; Robert E., Jr. born Jan. 14, 1947, and Karen Sue born Jan. 29, 1950. In September 1955 Ruth A. (Holeman) Kellen was killed in a car wreck. Bob kept the children together (three were in school) and continued to work. On March 21, 1959, he married Elvira Elizabeth (Wright) Hughes who was born and reared in Caldwell County, KY. She was the daughter of George W. and Nannie E. Wright and the widow of Baxter Barbee Hughes who died April, 1956. Bob and the children moved out to her farm. Elvira worked for Human Resources Division, State of Kentucky, in Morganfield. She helped rear the children and worked for 36 years before retiring in 1973. In 1974 Elvira sold her farm and they moved into town.

Robert E. and Elvira Kellen

Hanna Jo Kellen married Larry W. VanHoose, moved to Michigan, later divorced,

and she is now employed by General Motors Corporation in Detroit. They have two sons and one daughter—Dr. Lisa Ann (VanHoose) Bartolotto of Lascassas, TN, Billy Earl VanHoose of Taylor, MI, and Robert Lynn VanHoose located in Germany with the U. S. Army. Robert has a wife (Missy) and two small sons—Robert, Jr. 2 1/2 years and Stephen, 10 months old.

Mary V. Kellen, who still lives at home and works for the State of Kentucky, Human Resources Division, Morganfield, KY has a part-time Catering Service as a hobby.

Karen Sue (Kellen) Brantley married Marlon Bruce Brantley of Crittenden Co., KY, and they have two children—Christy Lynn Brantley, 10 years old. Karen Sue's husband Marlon is employed by Pyro Mining Company.

Robert E. Kellen, Jr. was married to Donna Briody of Evansville, IN and was later divorced. They had two children, Tammy Lynn Kellen born Dec. 20, 1966, and Robert Gerald Kellen, born May 23, 1969. Robert E. Kellen, Jr. burned to death in a private home in Harrisburg, IL on Jan. 2, 1975. His children continue to live with their mother who has since remarried.

Hanna Jo Kellen; Mary V. Kellen

Karen Sue Kellen; Robert E. Kellen

Bob Kellen is a member of the Caseyville United Methodist Church for 58 years. He served on the Sturgis City Council for six years (1980-1985). He is a member of Sturgis Economic Development Foundation and Board of Adjustments. He is a Mason, Scottish Rites and Shriner, Past Master and now Treasurer of DeKoven Lodge #577, F&AM. He is Noble Grand of Sturgis I.O.O.F. Lodge #307, Member of Patriarchs Militant and Encampment Degrees of this Lodge. He holds the rank of Captain (retired). He is Special Deputy Grand

Master for all I.O.O.F. Lodges in Western Kentucky and in 1988 was awarded its highest honor—the Meritious Medal of Honor. He is also Past Grand Chaplain, Grand Marshall and District Deputy Grand Master of I. O. O. F. A member of the Sturgis Kiwanis Club and Chamber of Commerce, Bob also served four years as a member of the Sturgis Air Board. He is now retired and lives with his wife Elvira and one daughter in the City of Sturgis at 12th and Grant Street.

KERN

A successful Sturgis businessman who believed in pushing forward the wheels of progress and working hard was Walter John Kern. He was born May 16, 1872, in Ohio. His parents were John and Agnes (Tabelman) Kern. Agnes Kern was born May 18, 1852, a daughter of John and Lizetta (Kuhlman) Tabelman and died on Aug. 5, 1896. John Kern was born Sept. 1, 1849, in Bremen, Germany, and learned the wood-turner's trade; he died in 1903. The John Tabelman's were natives of Berlin, Germany. John Tabelman was born in 1829 and became a retailer and manufacturer of cigars. mrs. Tabelman was born Nov. 25, 1825, and died in 1909.

Walter John Kern first came to Lexington, KY, while connected with the Edison Electric Company of New York. After working in the engineering and electrical field in Owensboro and Calhoun, he moved to Sturgis and began work on the Sturgis Ice Plant in 1911. He also opened a laundry and planted and owned the Hillcrest Orchard. Walter John Kern served as the first President of the Sturgis Kiwanis Club. He served as the mayor of Sturgis for three terms and died October 21, 1929, prior to running for a fourth term.

Walter John Kern; Leota B. Kern

Walter John Kern married Leota Hall Bradley, the daughter of James M. and Dorcas (Gregory) Bradley. A native of Ireland, her father was a building contractor, a Baptist and a merchant in Cloverport. James Bradley died Sept. 3, 1902. Dorcas (Gregory) Bradley was born Jan. 16, 1832, and died May 29, 1911. Their daughter Leota Bradley Kern was born Nov. 25, 1874, and died in June 1941. The Kerns became parents of ten children: Alma Lillian Kern born March 24, 1896, lived for four days. Margaret Agnes Kern b. Sept. 1, 1897, d.

March 31, 1965, married Kenneth L. Holt and had no children.

Louise Lizetta b. October 16, 1899, d. 1966, married C. C. Wright, resided in Louisville, KY, and hd one daughter Patsy Bell Teson.

Ruth Scott Kern b. Sept. 3, 1901, d. Oct. 1, 1987, married William C. Davis and had three children Fred Davis, Jane D. Taylor, (deceased) and William Kern Davis (deceased) and later married Rash Wells of Madisonville, KY.

Martha Jane Kern (Possum) b. Sept. 13, 1903, d. 1945, married M. Y. Nunn and there were no children.

Mildred May Kern (Toadie) b. May 14, 1907, d. Oct. 1979, married B. L. Turner, resided in New York and had two children Camille Turner Lynn and Cheryl Turner Ottaviano.

Annette Loretta Kern b. June 1909, d. in the 1950s, married Lou Torcaso and resided in Ohio and had no children.

Edith Elizabeth Kern b. April 16, 1911, d. in the 1970s, married Ligon Beshear of Dawson Springs and had one daughter Karen Beshear Zeh.

Dorothy Leota Kern b. June 23, 1912, d. Nov. 14, 1981, married Fred Willis Stevenson and had three children Nancy Sandra Arnold, Martha Jane Young, and James Frederick Stevenson.

Walter John Kern, Jr. (son) b. Jan. 29, 1915, m d. March 30, 1941, married Betty Varden of Evansville and had one daughter Ann Varden Ehrenclou; Betty later married W. A. Riley and resides in North Carolina.

The Kern home, on the corner of Ninth & Washington Streets, was quite a gathering place in the community. As you can imagine with 8 girls many young men came calling. Mrs. Kern often stayed up late at night playing cards or cooking country ham and biscuits for the girls and their beaus. The Kern's and all of their children are now deceased. The only family remaining in Sturgis are the grandchildren, Sandy Arnold and Jane Young, and the great grandchildren. *Submitted by Sandy S. Arnold, Jane S. Young*

JAMES VAUGHAN KING

James Vaughan King married Lena Berry June 8, 1904 in Sturgis, KY. J. Vaughan was born in Waverly, KY, Aug. 31, 1876. He was an accountant, bookkeeper, and salesman for Tradewater Coal Co., Sturgis, KY. In 1910, he bought J. S. Wilson's interest in Wilson and Meacham Drug Store. He studied pharmacy, passed the State Board and was a registered pharmacist. In 1927, he bought J. E. Meacham's interest, and operated King Drug Co until his death Aug. 8, 1932. From 1932 until January 1935, the store was managed by his daughter, Elizabeth (Tib) King when the store was sold to West Kentucky Coal Company.

James Vaughan King was the son of Alexander and Mary Alice (Vaughan) King. Alexan-

der was the son of James H. and Carolyn (Brinkley) King. Mary Alice was the daughter of Stephen F. and Elizabeth (Jennings) Vaughan. James H. King was a miller and merchant, and the founder of King's Mill in Henderson County, where Alexander was born.

Alexander King was a merchant in Waverly, KY. From Union Co. History 1886, Page 649, "In Mr. King's store, which is a large 20" x 80' room, there is a well stocked and fine assortment of dry goods, boots, clothing and notions." In 1889 Alexander sold his business and home in Waverly and moved to Sturgis where he was proprietor of Sturgis Hotel and secretary of Cumberland Iron and Land Co., the company that platted the city of Sturgis. Alexander died in 1910.

Lena (Berry) King, born Oct. 29, 1879, was the daughter of Albert Jutson and Mollie (Nunn) Berry. Albert Jutson was the son of Thornton and Elizabeth (Edwards) Berry. Mollie was the daughter of Hugh and Martha (Whitecotton) Nunn. Albert Jutson was a building contractor. He was the first Police Judge of Sturgis, Jan. 1, 1891, to Jan. 1, 1893. After four years, he was re-elected and served until his death in August 1899.

James Vaughan and Lena King were parents of three daughters. Ruth King married Richard C. Fry of Clarksville, TN. Ruth taught in Clarksville City Schools and is now retired, living in Clarksville. Ruth and Richard had one son, James R. Fry, who married Constance Jasper. They have three children, Jeremy, Joshua and Jennifer.

Mary Proctor King married E. P. Littlepage Jr., of Mart, TX. She is still active as Vice-President of the family business, Littlepage Furniture Co. and Littlepage Funeral Home. Mary Proctor and E. P. had one son, Paxton King Littlepage, who married Rose Ann Hart. They have two children, Laurie Elizabeth and Mary Susan.

Elizabeth H. King married Mark Y. Nunn. Mark Y. Nunn was born in Niagra, KY grew up in Marion, KY. He owned and operated Texaco Service Station in Sturgis, KY, from 1951 to 1978 when he retired. Mark Y. Nunn was active in all church and civic affairs. He was a member of Cumberland Presbyterian Church, Kiwanis Club, Masonic Lodge, City Council, the first County Fair Board, American Red Cross. He died Feb. 14, 1989. Elizabeth is now owner and operator of Tib's News Stand, Sturgis, KY. *Submitted by Tib Nunn*

OSCAR KNIGHT

On January 14, 1910, Oscar Phillip Knight was born in St. Charles, KY. He was the son of William H. Knight (10-12-1852) and Ora E. Knight (8-11-1880). He had one sister, Mary Viola (9-15-1914). When he was twenty-five, he married twenty-two year old Johnye Eleanor Christopher, (-22-1912). They married in Dawson Springs, KY on April 8, 1935. Her family came from Murray County, TN. She was the daughter of Oscar Christopher (1-12-1880) and Anna Morgan Christopher (8-14-1894) and the granddaughter of John Morgan and Laura Frances Morgan (4-17-1867).

During the beginning years of their marriage, Oscar and Johnye moved to Sturgis and he began working t Poplar Ridge Coal Company. He later worked as an electrician for other area coal mines until his retirement. He provided well for his family, loved to hunt and fish and became known in the area for his beautiful hand crafted furniture and clocks. He was an active member of the City Council and served as Mayor of Sturgis for several years.

The Oscar Knight Family

Johnye was the proud Mother of the four Knight children, two boys and two girls. She was a member of the Cumberland Presbyterian Church and a Collectors Club member. Employed part time at Tibs, she is remembered for her friendly smile. She was a stitchery artist, creating beautiful crocheted heirlooms. For forty years, the family home located at 118 King Street displayed the work of Johnye and Oscar, two extremely talented people. The children that were born into this family during the period of 1936-1942 were Joyce Eleanor, Mary Frances, Phillip Dean and William David.

Joyce married Donald L. Smith, son of the late Bailey Smiths of Sullivan. They reside at 5560 Leesway Boulevard, Pensacola, FL, 32504. After a career with the Air Force, Don is Building Services Director at Baptist Hospital in Pensacola and Joyce is employed with Weight Watchers, Inc. They have three daughters, Kathy, Jennifer, and Rachel, and two grandsons, Christopher and Matthew.

Frances lives at 909 Main Street, Sturgis, and is the mother of two grown children, Fawn Wells McDonald and Jason Slaton Wells. Their father is Charles N. Wells, son of Charles E. and Virginia Wells, all of Pride, KY. Frances is a graduate of Murray State University and is a professional artist and art instructor at Union County High. Fawn and husband, Rob live in Lincoln, IL, and Jason lives in Sturgis.

Phillip married Jeanne Marie Cusic, daughter of the late James D. Cusic and Mrs. Cusic, who still lives in Morganfield. Phillip has a Doctorate from Vanderbilt University, and has a position with Kodak in Rochester, NY. They

have one son, Jon Morgan Knight, a college student, and live at 10 Wincanton Drive, Fairport, NY 14450.

David married Anne Christian Fletcher, daughter of Wayne and Katherine Fletcher of Sturgis. He is a graduate of Murray State University and is with an Insurance Firm in Houston. He and his family reside at 3914 Vintage Valley Drive, Houston, TX 77082. He and Anne have two grown daughters, Shannon and Shawn, and two son, Timothy and Patrick.

Oscar Phillip Knight died on Sept. 5, 1982 and his wife Johnye Christopher Knight died on Dec. 2, 1984. They are buried at Pythian Ridge, Sturgis, KY. *Submitted by Frances Knight Wells*

KURTZ

Jane and George met at the University of Kentucky in 1937 when he was a Senior and she was a Freshman. They married September 27, 1938 at her home near Henshaw, KY. George M. Kurtz, Garrad County, KY and Jane from Union County, Henshaw, KY were from farm families and had heard of each other through 4H Club work. George was president of the Kentucky Association of 4H Clubs in 1933. Jane showed the Grand Champion Hereford Steer at the Louisville 4H Fat Stock Show in 1929.

After graduation, George served as Assistant County Agent in Winchester, KY and that is where they lived after their marriage. Later they were transferred to Casey County, then later as County Agent in Edmonson County in Brownsville, KY. George's total time in Agricultural Extension work was five years.

In 1942, George and Jane moved to the farm near St. Ambrose Church in the Sturgis area where they still reside. George raised hemp seed for the United States Government in 1942 and 1943.

Jane and George Kurtz

George and Jane lived in an old log home built by her great grandfather, Charlie Johns in 1866 at the end of the Civil War. While the family attended the Union County Fair, the house burned to the ground with all contents in July, 1958. They lived in a trailer placed under walnut trees near the original location where the Bedford stone house was being built. When the last walnut hit the roof of the

trailer in late December, the family moved into the new house in 1958.

On the farm they grew corn, tobacco and hay. Their main business was Aberdeen Angus Cattle, having annual sales each fall.

George attended the Reppert School of Auctioneering in the fall of 1945, and later founded the Kurtz Auction Realty Company. During his early auction career, much of his time was spend selling purebred livestock (mainly Angus Cattle) in 18 different states. Many people have helped to put Sturgis on the map, and in selling at auction for 45 years, George has tried to help in this respect. George judged cattle at many county fairs and shows, and judged one year at the State Fair in Louisville. George was on 4-H judging teams and also on the team at the University of Kentucky that own the Southeastern Judging contest in 1936. This proved to be good training for selling purebred livestock.

Kurtz Auction Realty Company now has four offices in the Ohio River Valley including Marion, Morganfield and Owensboro in Kentucky and Evansville in Indiana. Jane served as clerk for years at auction sales. There are about 45 people working with Kurtz including auctioneers, clerks, cashiers, real estate brokers and salespeople.

George and Jane have four children, three of whom operate the various offices; Martha Williams in Marion, KY, Kelly Goetz in Morganfield, and Bill Kurtz in Owensboro and Evansville, IN. Julia Tackett is an attorney, and is now serving her third term as District Judge in Lexington, KY.

Each child has two children making eight grandchildren. Martha's daughter, Molly Sherrell, and her husband Tony are the parents of Chelsea Evan, June 16, 1989 is our first great grandchild. Molly has enough hours at the University of Kentucky Community College to be a Junior and expects to get her degree. Martha's second child, Nancy Dean, a junior in the Kentucky School for the Blind is interested in music, and for a number of years has been a member of the Crittenden County Country Club Swim Team. Bill's two children are Beth Kurtz who graduated Summa cum laude from the University of Kentucky, May, 1989 and was initiated into Phi Beta Kappa her Senior year, and John Kurtz who will be a Junior at Indiana University, Bloomington in the fall of 1989. Julia's two children are John Lindsay who enjoys playing Babe Ruth baseball and Sarah who is looking for a mate for her cocker, "Charlie Sunshine." Both children have been in the cast of "Singy's Saga" and "Charles Dickens' Christmas Carol" in the Children's Theater held in the Opera House in Lexington. Kelly's children are Sidney Jane and Nicholas Goetz, both play soccer and have been placed in State Tournaments and Marshall County Invitationals. In Burns school track, Sydney won first in the mile relay and in the 800 meter race. Also, they are in the Talent Development Curriculum.

George served as president of the Kentucky Auctioneers Association in 1963 and in 1989 was admitted to the Kentucky's Auctioneer's Association Hall of Fame.

George and Jane have been members of the Sturgis United Methodist Church since moving to Sturgis in 1942.

They travel some and enjoy it. The children gave them a trip to Mackinac Island in Northern Michigan that included lunch at the Grand Hotel in September, 1988 for their 50th Wedding Anniversary. The Kurtzs are big University of Kentucky sport fans, attending basketball and football games every year and have attended several Final Four Basketball Tournaments.

The Kurtz daughter-in-law is Sharon Ling Kurtz and the sons-in-law are Robert M. Williams, John W. Tackett and Jim Goetz. *Submitted by G. M. Kurtz*

LADD

The Ladd family moved to Sturgis from Dawson Springs, KY on May 26, 1924. Perry M. and Fannie Brashear Ladd moved to Number 9 mining Camp of West Kentucky Coal Company where Perry had a job. They brought their two sons, Gerald Edward and James Estel with them. The boys attended the Sturgis schools and both are graduates of Sturgis High School. They became members of the United Methodist Church in 1934. When World War II broke out both boys joined the armed forces. Gerald entered the service in June 1941 and James entered several months later in November 1941. After returning from the service both sons helped form the Veterans of Foreign War Post 5486. Gerald became the charter president and served in 1945-1946. James later served as Post Commander in 1970-1971. Perry, Fannie, Gerald and James were all made Kentucky Colonels in the year 1970.

Gerald married Lelia McKeaig in 1946. They had two children, Dorothy Jean born on April 22, 1950 and Gerald Wayne born on December 5, 1951. Dorothy married Gary Gebhard in 1974. Gerald Wayne married Charlotte Russell in 1972. They had two girls, Julie and Lisa. Lelia died in 1976 and the daughter died in 1979.

Perry and Fannie Ladd

James married Mary Ann Brown in 1947. They had two daughters, Carolyn and Nancy. Carolyn married Jerold Thurston in 1971. They have three children, Michele, James and Cari Ann. Nancy married Wayne Hunt in 1970. They have three daughters, Kim, Mary Ellen and Jenny.

Perry died in November 1976 and Fannie died in February 1980. They are both buried in Pythian Ridge Cemetery. Their sons, grandchildren and great grandchildren all still live in or around the Sturgis area. *Submitted by Gerald and James Ladd*

JOHN H. LAMB

Near the turn of the 20th Century, two young people lived on adjoining farms at the foot of Holeman Hill near the village of Cullen, KY in Union County. A neighborhood romance gradually developed and led tot he marriage of the ancestors of one branch of the Lamb family in Union County.

John Henry Lamb, son of John Simeon Lamb and Nancy Ann Potts Lamb, was born on Feb. 25, 1884. He took as his bride Julia Haynes Pride, who was born to James Pinkney Pride and Mary Isabella Christian Pride on Oct. 31, 1890. The wedding was solemnized on March 10, 1910. The Pride and Christian families were very prominent in the early development of the Pride and Bordley communities in Union County.

John and Julia Lamb

The Lambs lived in Cullen for three years as John continued to farm, but their lives changed abruptly in 1913 when a disastrous fire destroyed the business district of Sturgis, a larger town in southern Union County. John, Julia, and their three children moved to Sturgis where John worked as a carpenter helping to rebuild the town. For the remainder of his life John Lamb was wedded to wood and family, both of whom he dearly loved.

When Sturgis was restored, John was employed by the Alloway Brothers Lumber Company as head of its carpentry shop. The firm later became the Fred Alloway Lumber Company, and John remained as shop foreman until the coming of World War II.

In 1942 John left the Alloway firm to work in the construction of Camp Breckinridge primarily as a cabinet maker. Later he moved to the Sturgis Airport, where he was in charge of the carpentry shop. After the war, John opened his own shop which he constructed adjacent to the Lamb home on Pike Street.

Julia remained the helpmate of John and the mother of their six children. James Franklin Lamb, born Jan. 16, 1911, was city clerk of Sturgis when he died on Dec. 9, 1958. John Granville "Peck" Lamb, born April 24, 1912, died in Jacksonville, FL, on Jan. 21, 1974. Anna Louise Lamb, born Sept. 6, 1913, married Douglas Hooper and still lives in Sturgis in the Lamb family home. Reburn Christian Lamb, born Feb. 14, 1917, died the day after Christmas in 1939, at the age of 22. Fred Alloway Lamb, born July 24, 1923, is a retired school teacher-counselor who still resides in Sturgis. Margaret Grace Lamb, born Feb. 18, 1925, married Charles Price of Earlington, where the Prices still live.

John Lamb served as a member of the Sturgis City Council for several years under the administration of Mayor E. C. "Bud" Calman. He was a longtime member of the International Order of Odd Fellows. He also was a very active member of the First Baptist Church, having served as church treasurer for a number of years.

Julia was a people person. The Lamb yard and a couple of adjoining vacant lots were used for football, basketball, track, and even miniature golf, a craze in the 1930's in the United States. Julia had two rules for the neighborhood kids: "no cussing, no fighting" and she ran a tight ship!

Being located near the railroad tracks, south Pike Street had more than its share of hoboes during the depression of the 1930's. Julia Lamb could always find a bit of food for good people who were victims of an economic situation not of their making.

The couple from Cullen left their mark on the history of Sturgis. They cared for people!

LATTA

Bill was the son of A. S. Latta and Lula Moffett Latta, born in Corydon, KY. He was one of four children. Bill was a graduate of Sturgis High School. He was a prominent businessman in Sturgis associated with Latta's Restaurant for over 30 years, working with his father and brother, Rodgers Latta. AT the closing of the restaurant, he devoted his time to the buying and selling of livestock. Bill was a former Mayor for the city of Sturgis. He was appointed to complete the unexpired term of E. C. "Bud" Calman, serving from December 1947 to December 1949. Bill was a life-long member of the Sturgis First Christian Church. he was at one time the only member of the church who attended Sunday School every Lord's Day for 26 years in the Sturgis Church. He was a loving, and loved husband, father, grandfather and great grandfather.

Louis Berry Latta was born on a farm in rural Union County near Seven Gums Baptist Church. Her parents were Thornton I. Berry and Lutha Fontaine Humphrey. She was one of nine children. Louise graduated from Sturgis High School and later attended college at Western Kentucky University in Bowling Green.

Louise Latta, William E. "Bill" Latta and Nilda L. Schleifer

Bill and Louise are the parents of two children: Nilda L. Schleifer and Billy Berry Latta, who died at the age of three months. Nilda and her husband, Fred, are the parents of five daughters: Faun S. Fishback, Berry S. Hammermeister, Marie S. Fowler, Kathy S. Byrns, and Jhan S. Luttrell, and one son, Frederick William Schleifer who died shortly after birth. There are ten grandchildren.

When the Western Kentucky Coal Company held dances in the 1930s, Bill and Louise were awarded the title of King and Queen of Waltz of Sturgis. In 1939 at the Sturgis High School Alumni Association banquet, they were requested to participate in the entertainment and performed an old fashioned waltz to the delight of all present. *Submitted by Louise Latta*

JAMES E. AND HELENA LEFLER

James E. and Lena Lefler married and moved to Route 2, Sturgis, KY in 1888.

Lena Lefler, Florence Caldwell, Annie Braddock, Eddie Lefler, Pearl Braddock and Agnes Pease

Lena wove carpets, swing sets, rugs and peddled milk, cream, eggs and chickens in order to raise her eight (8) children as her husband passed away at a young age. The children were Ida, Annie, Florence, Eddie, Gennie, Pearl, Agnes and Theodore. *Submitted by Gordon Braddock*

LINDLE

On July 24, 1911 Elmo and Virge Lindle each contributed $250 and borrowed $100 to buy the Butcher Shop of pet Marquardt. Up to this time Elmo had been driving "Old Beck" on a farm and Virge was working in the mill.

Their first meat was purchased on credit from T. V. Pritchett and H. L. Culley and delivery was made on foot with a market basket. That business was good was show by the fact that ten days was the longest the best pair of shoes they could get would last.

The Lindle Family

In 1912 the Lindle Brothers bought out local butcher A. L. Hoerth and added a bicycle for delivery. Included in the deal with Hoerth was an orant brass cash register which the Lindles continued to use in their store for many years.

At the time of the great Sturgis fire in 1913 the business was located in the Voss building which presently houses the Ace Hardware. The fire ruined only the doors and windows of the store. The brothers were able to reopen in the morning and were ready for business at eleven.

In 1914 the Lindles erected a building next to the present mine safe electronics. In 1919 they moved into an addition next door on the corner of the block. From 1920 to 1930 they operated a motion picture theater on the second floor of that building.

No history of the Lindles would be complete without mention of "Old Barney," a horse included in the original deal with Pete Marquardt. The horse was used to bring meat from their slaughter house at 15th and Washington, and would be seen coming down the street with its load of beef or hogs but without a driver. the horse had memorized his route. Old Barney was a valuable asset to the business until he died at the ripe old age of 32 years in 1923.

In the late 1930s a Kroger store was opened in the corner Lindle building and the brothers moved their business tot he smaller building next door. In 1948 Elmo's two sons, Elmo "Poss" and Roy, took over the business. In 1959 the Kroger Store closed and after remodeling, the Lindle Brothers moved back into the corner building. In 1966 the Lindles built a modern, spacious new store on North Main Street. Being civic minded, they donated use of their old store building to the Sturgis Teen Center and later sold the building to the group.

Roy retired in August of 1983 and sold his half of the business to Poss. Then in August of 1987 Poss sold to the Sureway chain of grocery stores. For the first time in over 75 years there was no Lindle Brothers Market in Sturgis.

Virgil Lee Lindle was born in 1874, retired in 1941, and passed away on Dec. 1, 1955. Elmo Roy Lindle retired in 1948, was born in 1883, and passed away on Feb. 24, 1958.

Elmo Poss Lindle was born on Dec. 25, 1926 and married Virginia Lynch on Sept. 25, 1949. They have a son, Elmo Rance, born on March 17, 1966.

Roy Lindle was born on Aug. 4, 1930. He married Zelma Roberts and they have a daughter, Evelyn June.

ELBERT CLIFTON AND LALLIE LEE LOGAN

Elbert C. Logan was born Nov. 15, 1887 to John Wesley and Mary (McElroy) Logan in Allen Co., KY.

He was married to Lallie Lee (Dalton) Logan on Oct. 19, 1915.

She was the daughter of William Thomas and Estella (Conner) Dalton. She was born Oct. 31, 1889 in Allen Co., KY.

L-R: Estella (Logan) Webber, Pauline (Logan) Chandler, Emma (Logan) Lyons, Mrs. Lallie Logan, Jewell (Logan) Edds, Frances (Logan) Bumgardner, and Virginia (Logan) Bush

The Dalton and Logan families both moved to Union Co. about 1911 from Allen Co., KY.

Elbert worked in the coal mines until he was killed in a mining accident in 1934. He was struck by falling debris in West Ky. mine #8 and died soon after in a hospital in Evansville, IN.

His daddy John Wesley Logan and all of his brothers - Carlie, Charlie, Thurman, Raymond, and James worked at or for the mines in and around Sturgis.

Elbert and Lallie Logan were the parents of six daughters and a son who died in infancy.

The daughters were - Mary Estella, Estil Pauline, Emma Lee, Jewell Bell, Ora Frances and Virginia Helen. The sons name was Clifton Bural.

All of the daughters graduated from Sturgis High School, and all had Miss Marie Hammack Lamb as a first grade teacher.

Mary Estella Logan was married to Bill Webber and they had three children - Wilma Lee, Nancy Evelyn, and Daniel Owen Webber. Mary Estella died Jan. 20, 1984.

Estil Pauline married Edd Chandler and they had four children - Dlifton Hollis, Edwin Gayle, Polly Lee and Michael Wayne Chandler. Estil Pauline died March 20, 1986.

Emma Lee married Darnell Lyon and they had six children - Barbara Jean, Billy Elbert, Tommy Jack, David Lee, Patricia Ann, and Virginia Beth.

Jewell Bell married Beverly Edds and they had two children - Hubert Wayne and Janet Carol.

Ora Frances married John Bumgardner and they had five children - Sandra Jean, John III, James Randall, Robert Edwin and Lori Anne.

Virginia Helen married John Franklin Bush Jr. and they had three children - John Franklin Bush III, Cathy Susan, and Robert Scott Bush.

EDWARD HENRY LONG

Edward Henry Long, son of Albert Gallatin Long and Maria Kenner Cralle Long, was born July 28, 1848 in White Sulphur Springs, Union County, KY. His family moved to Caseyville when he was a small child. As a young man he began farming on land in Commercial Point, which was later incorporated with Sturgis. He continued farming all his life. In 1884 he engaged in the manufacture of brick and tile which was one of the important industrial assets of Sturgis for nearly forty years.

On Oct. 2, 1888, he married Virginia Long Callaway, daughter of John Maxwell Callaway and Ariana Maria Rosser Callaway. Mrs. Long was born Oct. 19, 1865 in Bedford County, VA. Her family came to Kentucky just after the Civil War and located in Union County.

E. H. Long home shortly after completion in the early 1900s with the brick factory to the right in the picture

To their marriage were born seven children of which only four lived beyond infancy - Eleanor Long Johnson, Elizabeth Long McBee, Ariana Long Parker, and Edmund Randolph Long.

Edwin and Eleanor Johnson operated the Ritz and Victory Theaters in Sturgis from the early 1930s until a fire gutted the Victory in the E.M.B.A building on Nov. 27, 1958.

Edmund Randolph Long and his wife, Joye

Smith Long returned to Sturgis from Texas and Oklahoma in 1948. Randloph Long and D. D. Syers entered into a partnership to establish and operate the first bulk propane business in Union County under the name of Western Kentucky LP-Gas Company. Such partnership existed until the death of D. D. Syers, at which time Randloph Long assumed sole ownership of the company and operated the business for 30 years until his retirement in 1978. *Submitted by Carolyn McBee Moske*

JAMES L. LONG

Dr. Burgess Mason Long came to Caseyville in a covered wagon from Lynchburg, VA with his wife, Mary Virginia Rosser. From that marriage there were eight children.

Dr. Long had served the Confederate Army as a surgeon with Morgan's Cavalry.

His wife died in 1879 and eleven years later he married Ruth Dolly Lamb of Sturgis. From that marriage they had two children, James Lamb Long and Opie Elizabeth Long.

James L. Long was born in 1897 and spent his first eleven years in DeKoven. The house he was born in still stands. His education came from both Sturgis and Evansville schools.

On Dec. 28, 1927 he married Regina Catherine Heavrin from Flournoy, KY. From that marriage they had two children, James L. Long Jr. and Robert Joseph Long.

James Long was well known in Sturgis. He was active in the insurance business for over forty years until his death in 1964.

Among his interests were Long and Thornsberry Insurance Agency, Sturgis Pharmacy, Sturgis Hardware, Long's Department Store, a six hundred acre farm, No. One Camp, Long Addition, the old West Kentucky Coal Company building, and many others.

His wife, Regina, still resides at 918 Kelsey Street in the house he built in 1923. At that time it was only 20' x 30'. Since then it has been enlarged several times and now is known by a lot of people as "The Pink House."

Jim Long Jr. graduated from Sturgis High School in 1946 and the University of Notre Dame in 1951. While serving in the Air Force during the Korean War he met and married Nancy Sue McDonnell of Great Falls, MT. From that marriage came nine children, Karen, Jim III, Michael, Regina, Nancy, John, Matthew, Christopher and Paul. Jim Long moved from Sturgis in 1969 and is now in real estate in Albuquerque, New Mexico.

Robert J. Long graduated from St. Vincent High School in 1951 and attended the University of Notre Dame. He married Ruth Wayne Hazel of Sturgis and had one child, Robert J. Long Jr. He was active in farming for many years with his father, James L. Long. Bob died in 1975.

ROBERT HAYNES MC CAW

Robert Haynes McCaw, son of Robert

McCaw and Catherine (Coffman) McCaw, was born Aug. 27, 1901 in Union County, Sturgis, KY.

Lucille (Boston) McCaw, was born in Union County in the Old Bethel Community on Nov. 4, 1905. Her parents were Thomas Boston and Mary (Young) Boston, farmers in the Old Bethel Community.

Robert and Lucille McCaw

They were the parents of ten children, six living, with four living in Sturgis, KY. One lives in Paducah, KY, and one in Harrisburg, IL.

They had eleven grandchildren and thirteen great grandchildren. *Submitted by Helen McCaw Gray*

MC GEE

Dorothy Ann Buchman McGee is the daughter of John Hamilton Buckman and Lillie May Sheffer Buckman. She is a life long resident of Union County Kentucky and was married to James Claire McGee, son of Joseph Henry McGee and Margaret Estella Ball McGee.

In his early years, Joe McGee came to Sturgis from Carthage, TN. He farmed and raised Tennessee Walking horses. Claire McGee was a local farmer and also was employed at Camp Breckinridge, KY for several years.

James Claire McGee and Dorothy McGee

They have four daughters. Jean Wilson of Paris, TN, began her career as a teacher at Sturgis Elementary. She is married to Russell Wilson, and they had two daughters, Jeanne and Kathleen. Anne Pemberton of Evansville, IN was secretary to the county agent at the court house. She is married to Jack Pemberton, and they have three daughters Rebecca, Debbie and Donna. Mary Hoagland of Henderson

KY began her career as a nurse at Sturgis Hospital. She is married to Robert R. Hogaland, and they have three children Rob, Anne, and Cathy. Laura McDowell of DeKoven, KY is currently manager of Union County High School cafeteria. She is married to Bill McDowell, and they have two sons Billy and Kenneth.

Dorothy McGee graduated from Morganfield High School. She was organist at Salem Methodist Church for years and is a member of Sturgis Methodist Church. Dorothy served as manager of Union County High School Cafeteria for seventeen years until retirement. She is currently a member of the Chapter of the Daughters of the American Revolution. She is a direct descendent of Henry Helm Floyd for whom the chapter is named.

Henry Helm Floyd was born on Sept. 21, 1761 of Scotch Irish descent. In the fall of 1804, he brought his family down the Ohio River on a flatboat. They settled near Waverly, KY (known as the Floyd settlement). The old Floyd Cemetery remains there.

Later, Henry Helm Floyd served as a lieutenant under George Rogers Clark in the conquest of the Northwest, and in the War of 1812 was a colonel with Jackson at the Battle of New Orleans. He died on Sept. 8, 1850. A cedar tree planted by his son marked his grave. The tree was blown down years later during a windstorm. Colonel Hansford L. Treklkeld, descended from the daughter, Elizabeth Crosby Floyd, gave to the DAR Chapter, named in her father's honor, a beautiful silver-bound gavel, appropriately inscribed, made from the cedar tree which had marked Henry Helm Floyd's grave. The local Daughters of the American Revolution currently uses this gavel. *Submitted by Mary Hoagland and Anne Pemberton*

JOHN HARDWICK MC KEAIG

John Hardwick McKeaig (1922-1983). After a bout of the dreaded disease Polio at an early age, with the help of Dr. Sloan he overcame it with therapy and cod liver oil without crippling results. After graduating from Sturgis High School he worked at Camp Breckinridge as electrician in its erection. He served in WWII Jan. 9 1943 to Feb. 1946 in European Theater of Operations with 110th Port Marine Maintenance as Mechanic, Marine Engine and Electrician in Southhampton, England. He married Helen Margaret Reed, Sept. 8, 1945 in Bardstown, KY who was formerly a resident of Sturgis, but at the time was living in Birmingham, AL.

They purchased the Hopewell property on the corner of 7th & Washington Street in 1946 and his widow still resides there to the present date. On Dec. 3, 1958 their daughter Judith Helen was born. She is married to Benny Alan Griggs, son of the late Benny and Lois Griggs. John and his dad operated the Exchange Milling Company and Helen as traveling salesman

until they sold the mill. He was employed by Pittsburg Midway Coal Co. for nearly 15 years until it closed. The McKeaig family worked together and played together. He helped his dad with the West Side Crocery. We all belonged to the First Christian Church on the Pythian Ridge Cemetery Board and were avid fisherman. John, Helen and Judy operated a Chicken (Egg) Farm for several years and then a Worm Farm, shipping worms to all parts of the United States. He lost the business due to a fire and rebuilt on a smaller scale, later selling the farm due to bad health.

Helen, Judy and John McKeaig

Helen was Past President of the Jr. Womans Club, Past Matron of Order of Eastern Star Chapter #444 (44 year member), Secretary of Pythian Ridge Cemetery and still bowls on leagues and tournaments, camps at her trailer at Barkley Lake, loves to travel and make all the Flea Markets with her daughter Judy and son-in-law Benny. She was the first woman to run for City Council in the City of Sturgis on "Bud" Calman's ticket.

JOHN GORDON MC KEAIG

John Gordon McKeaig (1894-1958) a lifelong native and resident of Sturgis. His parents were Levi Clarence and Carter Hardwick McKeaig. In 1918 he married Ora Lee Holt (1895-1966) of Clay, KY.

Gordon and John McKeaig, Hattie Omer Roberts and H. D. Holt, Sr., in the Bright Spot Cafe

He served in WWI from May 15, 1917 to April 7, 1919. He was first assigned to 3rd Ky. Infantry and later with 149th Infantry when he served in England and France. After discharge he worked for the West Ky. Coal Co. many years and then joined the ranks of a businessman, operating the Bright Spot Cafe and later

years Exchange Milling Co. and West Side Gro. They had one son, John Hardwick McKeaig.

WILLIS ABRAM MC KEAIG

Willis Abram McKeaig, from Spencer County, son of Sarah Ann Smith and John Hays mcKeaig was married to Mattie Lockhart, daughter of Permelia and James R. Lockhart. They lived in Sturgis, where they had a restaurant about 1900.

He was a magistrate, became a farmer in Pond Fork neighborhood, a deacon in Bethany Baptist Church and served on the board of trustees of Ohio Valley Baptist College from which several of his children were graduated.

W. A. McKeaig Family

This couple had seven children; Lillie was married to Henry Turner. They had two boys, Glenn of Sanford, deceased and William Abra of Metropolis.

Iva was married to Ed Holeman. Their boys were Austin and Waldeau both deceased, and Vivienne Matthews and Gladyce, both of Memphis.

Ethel was married to A. R. Hammack. Their daughters are Evelyn of Sturgis, Julia Dixon of Indianapolis, and Jerry of Tuscalausa.

Nine was a homemaker.

Emma died when a young adult.

Howard was band director in Mayfield and Morganfield, part-time farmer, and deacon at Bethany Baptist Church.

JERRY BYRNE MCKENNEY

Jerry Byrne McKenney, son of Tipps McKenney and Garnett Jennings McKenney, was born Jan. 11, 1926 in Lexington, KY. He graduated form Lafayette High School in Lexington and served in the Army Air Corps in World War II. He received a B. S. degree from the University of Kentucky and his M. D. degree from the University of Louisville, where he was a member of Alpha Omega Alpha, Medical Honorary. Dr. McKenney's ancestors came from Ireland and England; among them was Salmon P. Chase, Chief Justice of the U. S. Supreme Court under Abraham Lincoln.

Dr. McKenney has been a practicing physician in Sturgis since opening his office in 1956. At this time he admitted patients to the Sturgis

Community Hospital; a few years later, it became the first small hspital inthe U. S. to be fully accredited. Later, he admitted patients to Union County Hospital. Dr. McKenney is an elder at First Christian Church, where he is a Sunday School teacher. He holds a private pilots license for single-engine aircraft, with instrument privileges, and an amateur radio license. For several years, he was a member of the Union County Airboard.

Elizabeth (Betty) Katherine Ford McKenney, daughter of Robert Harvey Ford and Elizabeth Elliott Ford, was born in Louisville, KY, on Jan. 26, 1930. Her father was County Agricultural Extension Agent in Union County from 1939 to 1947 and Betty graduated from Morganfield High School. She received a B. S. from the University of Kentucky, where she was a member of Phi Upsilon Umicron, home economics honorary. She received her Master's Degree from Murray State University. Her paternal ancestors came from England to the U. S. about 1650 and some later served in the Revolutionary War. In the early 1800s, they settled near Fordsville, KY, in Ohio County. On her mother's side ancestors came from England and founded Brampton, Ontario, Canada in the early 1800s. Betty was a homemaker for a number of years and is presently an elementary school teacher.

The couple are the parents of four children. Jerry John McKenney is a graduate of the University of Kentucky, where he is a member of Alpha Zeta, agricultural honorary and Farmhouse fraternity. He holds a law degree from Salmon P. Chase School of Law at Northern Kentucky University. He is an agricultural Missionary to Haiti.

Jan McKenney Hill is a graduate of Indiana State University. She holds a Master's Degree from Kent School of Social Work, University of Louisville, and is a counselor at a privat charity in Evansville, IN. Jane and her husband, Gary have two children, Christy Leigh and Chase.

Mary McKenney Faulhaber is a graduate of th eUniversity of Kentucky, where she was a member of Phi Upsilon Omicron, home economics honorary, and Alpha Gamma Delta sorority. She received a Master's Degree from the University of Kentucky. Mary was a home economics extension agent and is now a homemaker for her husband, Paul and their two children, Carrie Anne and Amy Carol.

James Elliott McKenney is involved in construction and he and his wife, Jamie, have a daughter, Kara.

MC PHERSON

Ann moved here in 1976. She was born and raised in White Plains, KY. Graduated from South Hopkins High School, attended Bethel Baptist College.

She went into business in 1976 into what was at one time the City Cafe and is now known as Buzzard's Cafe. She remarried in 1982 to Ricky Joe McPherson.

154

Ricky and Ann McPherson

Ricky is the son of Buel and Bea McPherson from Princeton, KY. Ricky has spent most of his nine years in Sturgis driving a coal truck. In slow time he helps manage and maintain the restaurant.

ann's parents Mildred and Sterling Rickard moved here in 1965. They resided in 811 Adams Street. Her father worked in the mines until he retired and moved back to White Plains.

They have three children, their oldest son Preston Buzzard is 23 years old. He works at Rayloc, and resides at 910 Adams Street. Their middle child a son, Brian Todd Buzzard is 21 years old. He is serving four years in the Navy and is stationed in Norfolk, VA. Their youngest, a daughter, Jennifer Lee Buzzard Ratley is a senior at Murray State University. OUr only grandchild is Ashley Nichole Ratley is 3 years old and lives in Murray with her mother Jennifer.

JOE AND LOUISE MACKEY

In this day and time, most of us know something of our genealogy. I am proud to say there have been six generations of Mackeys living in or near Sturgis, up to and including this time. Thanks to hard work, determination and the persistance of Mrs. Amy Paris, I can trace most of my ancestors as far back as the late 1700s.

My name is sheena Mackey Hosch. I am the second of four children born to Joe and Louis Mackey. my dad, "Little" Joe was the youngest of five children born to "Old" Joe and Mattie Mackey. Most of my relatives were poor, proud, hard-working Irishmen. Some were small farmers, most were coal miners and we all seem to have a great love for Kentucky, especially Union County.

Joe Mackey and Louise (Bingham) Mackey

I left Strugis my Junior year at the age of fifteen to go to the mountains of West Virginia to care for my eldest sister Mina. That is where I met my husband, Ronald Steven Hosch. he was born and grew up in a small coal mining community about the size of Sturgis. After graduating, my dad brought us back to Kentukcy where we were wed 24 years ago. Here is where we chose to make our home.

I gave birth to two children, a son Ronald Keith in 1966 and a daughter, Tabatha Joe in 1968. They both died in a tragic fire in 1972, along with my nephew Patrick Michael Terry. By the grace of God and the goodness of this community we survived. The U.M.W.A. Coal Miners in this community took it upon themselves to pay the expenses of the funeral. We will be eternally grateful to the men for their kindness.

Five years later we adopted our daughter, Michelle Lee (Shelly) in 1977. Again this community rallied around us and made this event a shared one, with showers, gifts, visits and newspaper interviews.

Shelly is twelve years old now and a student at the Union County Middle School. When she studied Kentucky Hisotry in the fifth grade, she was amazed to find there were so many important places to see and things to do in the Bulegrass State. We decided to let her tour Kentucky the following summer. It was one of the most enjoyable vacations we have ever taken. Most everyone across the state showed warm hospitality and good southern manners. People make the community, and I believe the best folk ever are in this State and this small town of Sturgis. *Submitted by Shenna Hosch*

CHARLES WILLIAM MARAMAN

Charles William Maraman, son of George McKeaig McGruder Maraman and Verna Lee Omer Maraman was born June 7, 1904. Charlie worked at the coal mines for approximately 34 eyars ehre in Sturgis. mr. Maraman passed away June 25, 1950.

Ruth Lillian Collins Maraman was born Nov. 4, 1906 here in Sturgis, KY. Her parents were William Henry Harrison Collins and Mary Helen Stephens Collins.

Ruth Maraman

Mr. and Mrs. Charles William Maraman were parents of four children: Charles Reginald Maraman, Darhl Hugh Maraman, Helen

LaVern Maraman Brown, and Georgiana Maraman Lashbrook.

Charles Reginald Maraman married Lois Adkins and they had three children, Alan, Virginia, and keith. Mr. Maraman was a Baptist Minister and he died Sept. 15, 1979. They lived in Mountain View, MO.

Darhl Hugh Maraman married Sue Powers and they had two children, Cindy and Lary. They live in Camden, TN.

Helen LaVern Maraman married Charles Samuel Brown, and they had two children, Sherri Ruth and David Pryce. They live at R. R. 1 Clay, KY. Sherri is a Dentist and she married Mark Steven Osteen. They reside in Augusta, GA. They have one daughter, Samantha Jean Osteen. David married Angela Cowan and he is a partner in their family farm business. David has two sons, Dennie Alan and Landon Nicholas Brown.

Georgiana Maraman married Daniel Lashbrook and they have had three children, Randy of Los Angeles, CA, Joe and Stephen of Camden, TN.

Ruth's grandparents were Lucinda Malinda Watkins Stephens born Dec. 18, 1835, died April 14, 1908 and Henry Clay Stephens. Mr. Stephens wa a Methodist Preacher and they lived inLyon County. Lucinda was a sister to John Watkins who lived in Sturgis with his daughter Miss Dora Watkins who taught school here for several years and was a tax collector. Ruth was never able to see her grandparents because of transportation and distance in those days. *Submitted by Ruth Maraman*

OTTO LEE MARKHAM

Otto Lee Markham, son of Jessie Eli H. Markham and Sara Ellen Hinton Markham was born Sept. 8, 1904 in Blanco County, TX. At the age of 2, his family moved by wagon to Sturgis. Otto worked in the coal mines around Sturgis since the age of 18.

Rosa Belle Vinson Markham, daughter of Wiliam Vinson and Clara Belle Plumlee Vinson was born Sept. 25, 1909 in Crittenden County, KY.

Standing: Melva, Eugene and Duel; Center: Rosa Markham; Seated: Kenneth, Doyle and Gerald

They were married Oct. 12, 1929 and they have 7 children 6 boys, including a set of twins and 1 daughter. Otto also had a son by a previous marriage to Ruth Penrod Markham. They are as follows:

Allen Lee Markham married Elizabeth Vaughn Markham of Sturgis, KY. They have 5 children David Lee, Donald Allen, Margaret Ruth Markahm Miller, Martha Ann Markham Garver and Ricky Dale. Allen was in the Army and then worked on a farm until his death in October 1985.

Douglas Eugene Markham has worked for Sprague and Sons since the age of 12.

Melva Louise Markham Daugherty married Donald Eugene Daugherty of Morganfield, KY.. She has one son Raymond Keith Markham.

Doyle Markham married Alice Dixon Markham of Simpson, IL. They have 3 children Kathy Jean, Lester Otto and Patricia June. He worked at Caterpillar Corp. in Peoria, IL then left for the Army and then later return to Caterpillar where he retired.

Duel Markham married Reba Ruth Wright Markham of Sturgis, KY. They have 3 children Eddie Lee, Roger Dale and Tanya Sue. He also worked for Caterpillar in Peoria since graduation and is now retired from there.

Kenneth Alvin Markham married Mary Lee Woolever Markham of Morganfield, KY. They have 4 children Rosa Lee Markham Elsey, Kenneth Alvin Jr, Danny and Sherman Douglas. Kenny worked as a farmer, mill worker and coal miner.

Gerald Wayne Markham married Pamela Ann Clark Markham of Uniontown, KY. They have 2 children Thomas Wayne and Christina Eve. Gerald worked at Movac in Morganfield, KY and is now a coal miner.

Daniel Kerry Markham married Margart Rebecca (Becky) Barnes Markham of Sturgis, KY. They have one daughter Kerry Jean. Danny was in the Armyu, worked for Eaton Axle in Henderson, KY and is now a coal miner.

Rosa and the late Otto Markham have 19 grandchildren and 25 great grandchildren. *Submitted by Melva Markham Daugherty*

WILLIAM TANDY MEACHAM

William Tandy Meacham, son of Charles Mayfield, Jr. and Annie Hammer Meacham, was born and raised on the farm that was a Revolutionary War landgrant to the Hammer family. He graduated from Morganfield High School, attended the University of Kentucky and has been engaged in farming all his life. In 1952 he began producing country hams commercially. At the present time he is president of Meacham Hams, Inc.

In 1940 William married Jane Elgin Dudley, daughter of Ralph Emerson and Camille Lackey Dudley of Sturgis. Jane graduated from Sturgis High School, attended Christian College, Columbia, MO and graduated from the University of Kentucky. She taught school briefly and later worked with the Kentucky Department for Social Services. Both William and Jane are active members of the United Methodist Church. Jane is a member of the Hnderson Community Methodist Hospital Board.

In 1948 William and Jane moved to the Morgan farm, three miles north of Sturgis. His maternal great grandfather, Springer Morgan, came to Union county in 1850 and built the house where william and Jane live.

William and Jane are the parents of four children: Ralph Ellsworth, Margaret Hammer, Rodman Tandy and William Elgin.

Ralph graduated from Sturgis High School adn attended the University of Kentucky. He was very active in the 4-H and FFA and is presently engaged in farming. He is married to Evelyn Shouse, daughter of James O, and Marietta Futrell Shouse. Evelyn graduated from Union County High School and Western Kentucky University. She is a teacher at Union County Middle School. They have two children Amanda, a Junior at UCHS and Charles Mayfield, IV (Chuck), a Sophomore at UCHS.

Margaret graduated in the last class from Sturgis High School. She attended Tennessee Wesleyan College, and the University of Kentucky where she was a member of the first class to complete the Major in Computer Science program. She is married to Robert Louis Shirel, son of Louis, Jr. and the late Nadine Urton Shirel. He is an accountant and an executive of South Central Communications in Evansville, IN. They have two children, Matthew Louis, Junior at Reitz High School, and Susan Elgin, in the 6th grade at Helfrick Middle School.

Rodman graduated from UCHS and the University of Kentucky where he majored in Agriculture Economics. He is Vice President and General Manager of Meacham Hams, Inc. He is married to Ann Elizabeth Elder, daughter of Damien and Mary Catherine O'Nan Elder of Morganfield. Ann, a graduate of UCHS and Murray State University, is a Speech Therapist at Sturgis Elementary School. They have three children, Lindsay Michelle, age 8, Kyle Damien, age 6, and Stuart Tandy, born March 1, 1989.

Bill graduated from UCHS and the University of Kentucky with a major in Agriculture Economics. He lives in Madisonville, KY and is a District Sales Manager for Pioneer Hy-Bred International. He is married to Susan Horn, daughter of Morris and Jane Mitchell Horn of Campbellsville, KY. She is a teacher at South Hopkins High School. Both Susan and Bill are very active in church and community activities. *Submitted by Jane S. Meacham*

SHERMAN MELTON

Sherman Melton (1880-1965), born in Sebree, KY, was married to Jessie Lee Wall (1890-1968) of Manitou, KY in 1906. Seven children were born of this marriage. "Sherm" was chief electrical engineer of the West Kentucky Coal Company for forty five years and, upon retirement acted as consultant engineer for the alexander Stone Company for ten years. The Meltons resided in the two story house now standing at 1113 Washington Street. He was a member of the Kelsey Masonic Lodge #689, a thirty-second degree Mason and a Shriner of Rizpah Temple in Madisonville. Mr. Melton invented a Power-Factor Control for power systems which was patented in 1928. He owned the Melton Control Co., Inc. of Punxsutawney, PA. Mrs. Melton was a homemaker throughout her lifetime.

Children: Carrie Alla (1907-1987) was married to Robert H. Finley. They lived in Mexico, MO where Robert was owner of the Finley Bus Line, a regional bus line serving his area. He also served as mayor of Mexico for one term. The two children of this marriage were Barbara Lee and Robert H., Jr.

Andrew Elmo (1911-___). Now living in Columbus, OH, "Elmo," as he is known in Sturgis is a retired Postal Clerk of the U. S. Postal Service. His wife is Jung Hee Kim from Seoul, Korea. His children are Joan Elizabeth, James Eddie, and Nancy Lee (deceased).

Cynthia Louise (1913-1976) was married to Maurice R. Kemp of Mexico, MO, whereMaurice still lives. They had one son, John Melton Kemp now in California.

Ruth Aline (1916-___) was married to Osborne H. Sale, son of the Carl Sales of Sturgis. Ruth is a widow and lives in Chesterfield, IN where she and Osborne raised two sons, Jerry W. Sale and Sherman H. Sale. Osborne was the Supervisor of Maintenance at the Delco Remy Division of General Motors.

Eddie Jenkins an Teddie Jenkins, twins (Jan. 1922). Teddie died in July of 1922. Eddie married Juanita Barron of Crystal Springs, MS. Two children were born of this marrigae, Larry Andrew Melton of Davis, CA, and Dwight Wilson Melton, who died in 1979. Eddie is a retired Elementary Teacher.

Marian Lee (1923-1954) was married to L. Edwin Lezynski of Rosiclaire, IL (now deceased). They had one daughter, Rebecca Lee, who now lives in Brandon, FL. *Submitted by Eddie J. Melton*

MAURICE DONALD MILLS

Maurice Donald Mills (born June 24, 1934) was the only child of Cydonia and Carmie Hess Mills. He grew up in Morganfield, KY and graduated from MHS in 1952. As a young man he worked as stock boy in the 5 and 10¢ Store and for the Mason Waller Drug Store. During the summers he worked for Kentucky Utilities. In September 1952 Maurice was hired as a full time serviceman by K. U. On Sept. 1, 1989, he will have completed 37 years with K. U. Maurice has served as Sec/Treasurer and Preside nt of the Sturgis Kiwanis Club and President of the Sturgis Chamber of Commerce. Maurice received the Kiwanis of the Year award in 1983 and Citizen of the Year award in 1987. He has served as deacon of the

First Baptist Church for 28 years, where his is currently serving as Chairman of Deacons.

Bessie Collins was born June 13, 1934 in Sturgis some 500 feet from where she now resides. She was the sixth child of the 14 children (7 boys and 7 girls) born to Carroll and Brilla Markham Collins. Except for Joanne Collins all of the children are living. Bessie has lived most of her life in Sturgis and married Maurice April 22, 1956. They have three daughters. Donna Kay married Ronnie Hollis and she is attending college, working toward a degree in nursing. Nancy Ann married Ralph Berry, she is a Floral Designer for Mills Florist and studying to become an interpreter for the deaf. Connie Marie married Randy Sheffer; they reside in Henderson and Connie is working toward a degree in Elementary Education.

Maurice and Bessie purchased The Sturgis Flower Shop in 1972. They changed the name to Mills Florist and they are still in business. *Submitted by Bessie Mills*

HENRY LEWIS MOSS

Henry Lewis Moss, son of Aaron Gwinn and Viola Olivia Hodges Moss and Cora Lillian Coakley, daughter of James William and Mallie Perkins Coakley were married March 15, 1927 in their new home in Greesburg, KY.

Henry worked in his father's electrical power plant in Greensburg. In 1923 when the electrical business was sold to the Kentucky Utilities Company Henry began his long association with that firm. He served as service manager of the Springfield office and then manager at Leitchfield. Later Henry was transferred to Sturgis as the manager of offices in Sturgis and Clay.

Mallie, Cora, Jane and Henry Moss

Henry was employed by the Kentucky Utilities Company for forty-two years and was honored posthumously for his perfect safety record.

Throughout the years Henry served the community of Sturgis and Union County in many capacities. He was a member of the Union County Fair Board; the Sturgis Planning and Zoning Board; the Industrial Committee of the Chamber of Commerce; Secretary of Tradewater Area Housepower Certification Council; and held membership in Maasonic Kelsey Lodge No. 649 F. & A. M. and Union

Chapter No. 54 R. A. M. He was President of the Kiwanis Club and served as chairman of th ebuilding committee at the time the club constructed the Kiwanis Memorial Building in 1950.

Henry was pleased when the Sturgis High School Future Farmers of America bestowed upon him honorary membership.

Henry Moss was an active member of the Sturgis United Methodist Church and for many years served as conference lay leader.

Henry died Oct. 8, 1966.

Cora Lillian's teaching career began in a one room shcool in Green County, KY. At the Sturgis Elementary School, Cora Lillian taught first grade and later sixth grade.

Geography has always been of special interest to Cora Lillian. She has traveled extensively in the United States and foreign countries.

Cora Lillian remains active in the Sturgis Garden Club, Union County Retired Teachers Association, Delta Kappa Gamma Society Internation and the Henry Helm Floyd Chapter of the DAR. In addition she has served for many years as a Sunday School teacher of the Sturgis United Methodist Church were she is a member.

The World War II years were turbulent ones for all. Sturgis had a critical housing shortage. Camp Breckinridge impacted all of Union County. Sturgis was stretched almost beyond its limits to accommodate the hundreds of Army families. Many of these families spent their last days together in Sturgis before the Eighty-Third Division took part in the D-Day Invasion. Cora Lillian continues to correspond with some friends she made during these stressful years.

Henry and Cora Lillian had two daughters, Mallie Olivia and Jane Coakley. Cora Lillian and the two grils are graduates of Kentucky Wesleyan College. Mallie also holds a Masters Degree in Secondary Education from the University of Kentucky.

Mallie married Charles Franklin Lobb, son of Oscar and Mary Elizabeth Jones Lobb of Freen County, KY. Charles and Mallie live in Louisville, KY where Mallie is active in Delta Kappa Gamma Society International, the Jefferson County Retired Teachers and the John Marshall Chapter of DAR. The couple has one daughter, Lillian Mae Lobb who lives in Long Beach, CA.

Jane married David Shipley, the son of Sam and Hazel Sisk Shipley of Sturgis. David and Jane live in Sturgis. They have two children, Sandra Kay and Michael David and two grandchildren Gavin and John Michael. *Submitted by Mallie Lobb*

MUDD

Indianapolis, IN was home to George and Wanda Mudd and their three children Kym, Julie and Keith. July of 1972 the Mudds left Indianapolis for Knoxville, TN where George was to study at Johnson Bible College in preparation for the ministry.

With the schooling completed and a four year ministry at Sullivan Road Christian Church in Knoxville coming to an end, George and Wanda answered the call to minister with the First Christian Church of Sturgis, June of 1978.

George, Wanda and Keith Mudd

After the trial sermon and the official call from the congregation, the Mudd's packed their belongings and made the 325 mile move from Knoxville, TN to Sturgis, KY. It was a hot, sultry 100 degree day in the first week of August 1978 when the moving van pulled up and unloaded at the parsonage next door to the church. On that hot, unforgettable August day the Mudds took up residence at 712 Adams Street. They may hve the distinction of being the first Mudds to reside in Sturgis. Roger Latta was the first person to officially welcome the Mudds to their new ministry.

At the time of the move to Sturgis, Kym was a student at the University of Tennessee in Knoxville. She later transferred to Murray State where she met Scott Ashley. Scott had come all the way from Massachusetts to study at Murray. Kym and Scott were married and moved to Massachusetts. The Ashleys grow cranberries for a living. They have two lovely daughters, Rebekah 6, and Rachel 4.

Julie, the second daughter, was a junior in high school when the Mudds moved to Sturgis. Julie met Jim Thompson from Morganfield, also a student at the high school. Julie and Jim were married. They reside at 711 Adams Street in Sturgis with their three lovely children Heath 9, Leah 4 and Seth 2.

Keith Mudd, the youngest, was in the seventh grade at the time of the move. He entered Sturgis Middle School August of 1978. Keith graduated from U. C. H. S. at age 16 in the spring of 1983. Keith has now received his BFA degree in Commercial Art from Western Kentucky University. He is presently working on getting his teaching certification in art so he can be eligible to teach art in high school.

George and Wanda, by the time this book is published, have now completed eleven years of ministry in Sturgis. They are proud of the fact that they have been at First Christian Church, Sturgis, longer than any minister in the 150 year history of the church.

By virtue of the long ministry, Sturgis is home now for the Mudds. Indianapolis is where they are from, but Sturgis is home. George and Wanda are grateful for the love shown them form the Sturgis folks. It is the Mudd's earnest prayer that Sturgis has benefited as much as the Mudds have.

JAMES (FLUKEY) AND JOYCE NEWCOMB

Wynn Additions's First Home, 1958, built by Fred Alloway and designed by Charlie Quinn. What a difference 30 years can make. Wynn Addition now has 71 homes.

Mr. and Mrs. Newcomb moved here from Webster County. Mr. Newcomb is a veteran coal miner and Mrs. Newcomb worked for several years for Southern Bell Telephone Company as an operator until the Dial System came to Union County.

Joyce, Jimmy, and Flukey Newcomb

They have one son, Jimmy. He is a 1976 graduate of the Union County High School and a graduate of the University of Kentucky and lives in St. Petersburg, FL.

They are members of the First Christian Church and the Breckinridge Golf and Country Club.

The Newcombs think ther is no place like Wynn Addition. "Water and All." *Submitted by Joyce Newcomb*

DR. A. E. NIESE

Dr. A. E. Niese, son of Christine Nissen and William Niese. He was born July 17, 1912 in Milwaukee, WI and given the name Adolph Emil. His parents came to the United States from Germany in May 1912.

He attended Luthern Church and schools. At the age of 15 his mother died and he went to Hubbard, IA to live with an uncle. While in high school he got a broken neck in football and this injury resulted in his interest to become a chiropractor. For many years they would not let football be played at Hubbard High because of this incident. After high school his uncle sent him to Indianapolis to lincoln Chiropractic School. He graduated and then came to Sturgis in 1935. A classmate set up practice in Marion and so he came to Sturgis. He had no friends and very little money. Bill and Rogers Latta befriended him

Dr. A. E. Niese

and he found a place to live in Whitsell's home. As there were no Luthern churches inSturgis, he became a member of Sturgis First Christian.

In 1937 he married Mina Barnes and they had one daugher, Mildred Christine Sullivan. He and Mina retired to Florida and she died in1982 and is buried at Pythian Ridge.

Before retiring Doc was very active in community affiairs in Sturgis. He was a scout leader for many years and a Sunday School teacher. He was a member of Sturgis Kiwanis Club and was instrumental in getting the swimming pool. He was voted outstanding Sturgis Citizen in 1956 and in 1984 was made a Kentucky Colonel.

Doc's parents came from Ockholm, Germany in the county of Schleswig Holstein which was originally a part of Denmark. His grandfather Nissen was an officer in the Danish Army. Then, Germany and Denmark had a war and Germany took just this area. Three Nissens were born Danes and four Germans. One of the four was Doc's mother Christine.

Doc is now married to Hazel Andre (Waggener) and they live in Florida and Kentucky. They have dual membership in Cap Coral Christian Church of Florida and Sturgis First Christian. *Submitted by Hazel Niese*

ALLEN OMER

Allen Omer, son of Daniel III and Martha Stafford Omer was born in Jeffersontown, KY, 10-8-1821.

Allen's father and his grandfather Daniel Omer II came to Kentucky form York County, PA ca 1797 after Daniel II had received a land grant for service in the Revolutionary War. He was a 1st Lt. in the 4th Co., 7th Bat. York County Militia, serving under Capt. Peter Zollinger, who later became Daniel II's father-in-law.

Allen Omer

About 1846 Allen and his 4 brothers, Levi, Lewis, Benjamin and Henry Clay came to Union County. A cousin Hardin Omer came a little later. They settled on farms in areas around Sturgis and many are still operated by their descendants today. Most all of the Omers in Union County and surrounding area can trace their roots back to one of these men.

Allen settled on a farm between Sturgis and Caseyville, where he raised and trained horses. Some being thoroughbreds.

Allen was the first Omer of record to be married in Union County, when he wed Mary Cahterine Henry, daughter of Alexander McCune and Nancy Richards Henry. Nancy's mother Lucy Hunton Richards traces a genealogical path all the way back to King Edward III of England. Allen and Mary had 4 children, Marcus Henry, Allen Woodford, Sally (Narroway), and Fannie (Buckham). Marcus followed in the footsteps of his father and learned the horse training business. He was a mrashall and school trustee in Caseyville for a short time. Woodford was Town Marshall in Sturgis ca 1893.

During the Civil War troops came through Union County and confiscated all of Allen's fine horses. He received no compensation and shortly thereafter went broke, his death followed shortly thereafter. He and his wife Mary are buried in the Caseyville Ark Lodge Cemetery. *Submitted by Ronald K. Omer*

JOHN LINDLE OMER

John Lindle Omer was born 8-22-1899 in Grangertown, KY. His parents, marcus Henry and Lida Howard Omer moved to the Sturgis area about 1889 and lived around the Grangertown and Caseyville areas the rest of their lives.

John, often known as "Red" by his friends, grew up in Caseyville and attended th eold Caseyville school. He operated a restaurant in Caseyville in the early 1920s. He also worked in the mines in the DeKoven/Curlew area. It was ther he met Victoria Holland, daughter of Edward and Hattie Holland, and they were married on Memorial Day, 1927. John worked many years during and after World War II at Camp Breckinridge in the PX and warehouse.

Marcus, John L., Victoria and Ronald Omer

John and Victoria had two sons, Ronald K. and Marcus E. Ronald married Ethel Owen

and they have three children, Teresa (Holt), Brian, and Rachel (Harper). "Ron" worked several years at Robertson-Quinn Motors in Sturgis and as warehouse manager at the Peabody Coal Camp Complex. They reside at Caseyville.

Marcus married Joan Stephens and they had 4 children, Mark, Julie, Daniel and John. Marcus is now married to Michelle Larson and they have one daughter Laura and one stepdaughter Nichole. Marcus has worked most of his life at Whirlpool in Evansville.

John's grandfather Allen Omer was one of the early settlers in Union County. He came to the Sturgis area ca 1846 and raised thoroughbred horses on a farm located between Sturgis and Caseyville. *Submitted by Ronald K. Omer*

JOSEPH AND CATHERINE OMER

Joseph Omer son of John and Annie Mongel Omer was born March 7, 1910 at Grove Center, KY. He worked on farms in his early years, the last fourty years as a carpenter.

Catherine Campbell Omer was born in Crittenden County but her parents, Robertson and Mary Nash Campbell moved to Union County and settled in DeKoven where they reared their family. She graduated from DeKoven High School in 1930, and married Joseph Omer on Oct. 3, 1934.

Joseph, Catherine, Robert, David, Richard, Roger, June, Deanna, Eleanor and Brenda Omer

They are the parents of eight children, four boys and four girls. They all graduated, five from the old Sturgis High School and three form the Union County High School.

The oldest son, Richard who served 21 years in the U. S. Navy, now lives in Richmond, KY, with his wife Billie. He now works an an electrician. Eleanor the oldest daughter, is married to Gene Kesler and lives in Sidney, OH. They have three children and four grandchildren. Eleanor works as a Secretary to a Trucking Company in that city. June the next, graduated in 1961 and immediately went to Washingto D.C. where she had a job with the F. B. I. She married Ronald Flint who was serving in the U. S. Navy. this work gave them the opportunity to travel, so in the coming years, they made homes in Fairbankds, AK, Turkey and the Azores. They had four children and two grandchildren.

Brenda is married to Jerry Stevens and they live in Sturgis. Jerry is employed with Henderson-Union Rural Electric. They ahve three children. Brenka is a seamstress, working out of her home. Roger is a graduate of Murray State University, served five years in the U. S. Army, retiring as a Captain. He is now married to Cheryl Bohanan of Van Nuys, CA and they have three children. Roger is employed as a Computer Programmer for Lacheed in California.

David was employed at Breckinridge Job Corp Center before entering the service in 1969. He was trained in Cooking School at Fort Lee and Fort Myers, VA. He was later trained as a General's Aide. He was assigned as an aide to General James H. Polk in Heildburg, Germany, where he resided ithe General's home. He now lives in the Washington D. C. area where he works as a chef at the Kennedy Center. Deanna attended Freed-Hardman College in Henderson, TN for 2 years. At present she is working as a scale attendant at Pyro Company's loading dock on the Ohio River. She has four children. Robert, the youngest, was a 1969 graduate. He attended Electronic School in Evansville, IN and has been employed with the G. E. company for the past 16 years in Madisonville, KY as a Maintenance Specialist for Lasers.

Sturgis is the center of our shopping and mailing so we feel a part of the community. Teh Omers have 17 grandchildren and six great grandchildren. They celebrated their 50th wedding anniversary in October of 1984. All of their family was in attendance. *Submitted by Catherine Omer*

SHELLEY AND LONA OMER

Shelley Dorsey Omer, son of Thomas D. Omer and Mattie Hudson Omer, was born July 7, 1899. Shelley worked on his family farm, in coal mines, and for 39 years as an electrician for the Kentucky Utilities Company here in Sturgis.

Lona Riddle Omer was born on a farm near the Omers, between the little towns of Arnold Station and Cullen, KY. Her parents were Henry Fairfax Riddle and Ida Kate Hopgood. Lona graduated from Sturgis High School in 1922 and later received her B. S. degree from Murray State University. She taught one year at the "Pond Fork" school adn 26 years in the Sturgis Elementary Schools.

Fred, Shelby, Lona and Shelley Omer

They are the parents of two sons: Shelley A. and Fred W. Omer. Shelley A. is head of the Rates Department of the Kentucky Utilities Company in Lexington, KY. He and his wife, Dorothy (Holt) have one daughter, Susan. Fred Omer is a Professor of Music at Illinois State University, Normal, IL. Fred married Ordath (Boyd) and they had two sons: Boyd and David Allen.

Lona's great grandparents were among the first settlers of Union County. In 1840, her great uncle, George Riddle, met Abraham Lincoln near Shawneetown, IL in a road wagon and brought him to Morganfield where Lincoln made a speech. Lincoln spent the night at her great grandfather's inn which was located at the spring in Morganfield. Later, Mr. George Riddle was imprisoned on Johnson's Island for being sympathetic with the South during the Civil War. President Lincoln set Mr. Riddle free. The courthouse in Morganfield is located on land that was the property of Jeremiah Riddle. The first annual of the Morganfield High School was named "The Riddle" in honor of Jeremiah Riddle. *Submitted by Lona Omer*

CHARLES RHEA O'NAN

Charles Rhea O'Nan, son of Dennis Edward O'Nan and Nell Skinner O'Nan was born Nov. 20, 1927, in Sturgis, KY. Charles graduated from Sturgis High School in 1946 and has been farming full time ever since. He raises cattle, hogs, and grain. Charles serves as an elder in the First Christian Church at Sturgis, and on the board of directors at the Pythian Ridge Cemetery.

Dorothy Lillian Rowley O'Nan was born Aug. 26, 1926, on a farm between Morganfield and Uniontown, the daughter of Grover Cleveland Rowley and Lillian Reburn Rowley. She graduated from Morganfield High School and worked at the Union Bank & Trust Company until she married Charles in 1949. She helps on the farm with bookkeeping and the farm chores.

Back Row; Wesley Parker, Middle Row L-R; Charles O'Nan, Adam O'Nan, Dottie O'Nan and marsha O'Nan; Front Row L-R; Erin Parker, and Angela Parker

The residence Charles and Dottie live in on Ben Dyer Road was built in the early part of 1850. The back on the house, a log cabin, was built by Mr. and Mrs. G. C. Gaines. Their daughter Nannie B. Gaines was born in the cabin and was the First American Missionary to Japan. The front part of the house was added in 1965 by Elizah Harmon, he apparently completed the construction of his new home, but as he was finishing the structure he fell from the second story and died. His niece, Martha Ann Harmon inherited the house, she was the grandmother of Charles. The log part of the house is called the saddlebag style and the front part is a frame "I" structure. It was cut and framed in Louisville and shipped by river to Union County.

At this residence they have raised two children, Marsha Lilllian, born in 1955, and Adam Rhea, born in 1965. Marsha married Wesley Parker in 1977. He is a farmer in Christian Co. Marsha is Extension Agent for Home Economics in that County. They have two girls, Angela Rhea born in 1981 and Erin Lillian born in 1983.

Adam has been working with the Internal Revenue Service as an accountant, but has decided to come home and help his dad run the family farm. He will marry Kristi Henshaw in the fall of 1989.

DENNIS O'NAN

Dennis O'Nan was born Aug. 26, 1851 and died June 8, 1924. His mother and father died when he was young and he lived with his uncle, David O. Conn, and David's wife Melissa. Part of the time he lived with his half-sister, Sue Bean, who married W. T. Conn.

On January 9, 1875, Dennis married at Shawneetown, IL. His bride was Eliza Blue Ralph, daughter of James William and Frances (Johnson) Ralph of Union County, Kentucky. Eliza was born in Sturgis Nov. 23, 1855 and died Nov. 18, 1939. She died at her home near Sturgis. Her father formerly owned a large portion of the land on which Sturgis now stands.

James William O'Nan and Ivy Hammack O'Nan

To this union eleven children were born. Ten lived to be grown. Dennis was a successful farmer, an exemplary father and devoted husband. He was a friend and counsellor to the young. He and his wife were faithful members of the First Christian Church.

Of the ten children, five were boys and five were girls. Their sons were James William, Dennis Reeves, Walter Sturgis, Ralph Jiles and Jennings Howe. Their daughters were Fanny Sue, Martha Ann, Florence Belle, Ora Strange and Mary Eliza.

James William O'Nan married Ivy Pearl Hammack in a double wedding with Will's brother Reeves O'Nan and Ruth Henry at Princeton, KY. They went by train to Princeton.

Will and Ivy resided on the O'Nan family "homeplace" near Sturgis. They had three children: William, who died in infancy, Margaret Frances, and James Frederick, who died at age twenty-three from strep throat. Fred's death came one year before the use of penicillin.

Margaret Frances O'Nan married Ralph Coleman Hart in Akron, OH on June 24, 1934. Frances was an elementary school teacher for thirty years. They have two daughters, Barbara O'Nan and Fredericka Jean.

Barbara was born April 10, 1935. She married Henry Bernard Hina. Their children are Henry Bernard Hina, Jr., born June 15, 1963 and Ralph Ernest Hart Hina, born June 21, 1966. Unfortunately, the marriage later ended in divorce.

Jean was born on Feb. 21, 1941. She married Edwin Dale Stadelman of Chicago, IL. Ed was killed in a tragic airplane crash on May 8, 1976. They had two children: Benjamin Edwin Stadelman, born Oct. 30, 1967 and Frances Helen Stadelman, born June 16, 1970. *Submitted by Frances Hart*

THE EDD O'NAN FAMILY

Edd O'Nan was born Dennis Edward O'Nan on Dec. 17, 1873 in a house which still stands just south of what is now highway 141 between Pride and Sullivan. He was the son of John Thomas O'Nan and Martha Ann Harmon. As a young man he ran a sawmill, clearing much of the land which is near the headwaters of the Pond Fork ditch. He served as Deputy Sheriff from 1912 to 1916 and then as Sheriff until 1921. He was a silent partner in a Drug Store in Morganfield where he met Nell Skinner, the gril friend of his partner. Edd wooed and won her and they were married Juen 21, 1921. Shortly afterwards he moved to Sturgis and bought an interest in the Sturgis Implement and Hardware Store, which was operted for many years on the corner of 5th and Adam St. He served as a member of the City Council of Sturgis, a Deacon of the First Christian Church and a member of the Farm Bureau.

Nell McElroy Skinner was born Sept. 4, 1890, the daughter of Charles H. Skinner and Elizabeth Alzera Sigler of Morganfield, KY. After High School she attended business College in Evansville. She worked as a secretary for the Electric Company which was D. C. at the time and therefore had to be generated in the twon in which it was used. She worked in the County Court House in Morganfield and became the first woman Deputy Sheriff in Kentucky.

Bob, Edward, Nell and Mrs. Edd O'Nan

Nell O'Nan born Sept. 4, 1890 died May 24, 1984, was a dedicated christian woman who gave a lot of her time and eneergy to the work of the Church. She always had other people in mind and was doing for them all the time. She never got tired of helping people. Her ideas helped the Church move in the right direction and she always kept people working and involved in the work of the Church.

The women's association of the Sturgis First Presbyterian Church bestowed a distinct honor upon her on Sunday, May 9, 1982, entiling her to an honorary life membership in the Women's Program Agency of the United Presbyterian Church in the United States of America.

Mrs. O'Nan was chosen for her commitment to Jesus Christ and the mission of the church and for her years of dedicated Christian service. Mrs. O'Nan was awarded a certificate and a sterling silver pin bearing the emblem of the Agency. Mrs. O'Nan wa a member of the First Presbterian Church from 1922 until her death. She was elected it's first woman Elder and was one of the first women elders elected into the United Presbyterian Church in the United States of America.

In Sturgis, four children were born to this couple, Dennis Edward II, Charles Rhea, Robert Lee and Nell Louise. All four children attended school in Sturgis and graduated from Sturgis High School.

When the youngest child was about a year old the couple moved to a small house Edd had built on the Arnold Station Road (Now Dyer Road). The move was to be just for the summer, in order to escape the summer heat and the "1933 traffic" on Adams Street. However, the barn lot began to fill with ponies and the children with the help of some neighbor boys built a log cabin in the woods. The place was within walking distance of town so during WWII it was a good place to have end-of-school picnics. Nell finally moved back into town in 1955 after the last offspring got married

At the death of his father, Edward took over the running of the family farm. He was 17. He married Charlotte Ames Sept. 27, 1952. He continued to farm while he founded and operated a seed cleaning operation, a farm supply store, fertilizer plants, a construction firm and a lumber yard. The couple have raised 4 children.

160

Charles Rhea married Dorothy Rowley Feb. 12, 1948 and they raised two children on the family farm. They still live in the house which has been in the family since Charles' great, great, great Uncle built the major part of it.

Bobby Lee married Wanda Johnson on July 5, 1953. Wanda is the daughter of Rev. Edwin Johnson and Helen Edwards Johnson and granddaughter of Chesley and Bernie Edwards. After serving 2 years in the Air Force they moved to Albuquerque, NM where Bob works for Sandia National Laboratories and Wanda teaches preschool. They have three children.

Nelouise married Richard Blastic on Aug. 4, 1951. They had 3 children. Nell now lives in Centralia, IL and is a purchasing agent for Rockwell International. *Submitted by Bob O'Nan*

EDWARD O'NAN

Dennis Edward O'Nan II, was the son of Edd O'Nan and Nell McElory Skinner and the oldest of four children, was born Aug. 21, 1925, in Sturgis, KY. Edward was a farmer and a business man, owning and operating Land-O-Nan Warehouse and Circle-0-Farm Center for 39 years. He was a member and Elder in the First Presbyterian Church. He married Charoltte Irene Ames, the daughter of Aubry and Gertrude Ames of DeKoven, KY. Her father owned and operated a coal mine near DeKoven and was killed in that mine when Charlotte was only five years old. To this union were born four children, Dennis Edward O'Nan III, Dana Leroy O'Nan, Mary Nanette O'Nan and David Ames O'Nan. The family were members of the First Presbyterian Church and active in various organizations in the community. The family was raised on a farm on North 270, 2 miles out of Sturgis which was the old George Wallace farm.

Dennis Edward O'Nan III, born April 13, 1953, married Mary Virginia Riggs, daughter of Bill Tom and Mesia Riggs. Dennis manages and owns Circle-O-Farm Center (on the site of the old Sturgis Ice Plant) and works an an auctioneer and real estate broker with the George M. Kurtz Auction & Realty Co. Dennis graduated from the University of Kentucky with a degree in Ag Economics. The family members are Ashley Brooke O'Nan born Aug. 12, 1980 and Dennis Kyle O'Nan born Jan. 18, 1985. The family lives on highway 270, 2 1/2 miles north of Sturgis on the former Red Collins Farm.

Dana Leroy O'Nan, born June 18, 1954, married Judith Ann Duncan, daughter of Bill and Christine Duncan of near Uniontown, KY. Dana graduated from Murray State University with a degree in Animal Science and went on to receive his Master's.

He ran the farm for the family (approx. 2700 acres in Union and Crittenden Counties) until 1986. He then took a position teaching Vocational Agriculture in the Union County School

David, Dennis, Dana and Nanette O'Nan

Systems. Dana and Judy have three children, Trent Duncan, born May 30, 1982, Abby Lynn, born Dec. 23, 1984 and Kalin Christine born June 11, 1988. Dana and family live on Highway 492 near Meacham Seed House and close to the Union County School.

Mary Nanette born February 20, 1957, went to University of Kentucky two years and then spent two years with Up With People and then finished college at the Murray State University. She is married to William Charles Muno II of Chicago, IL, where he works in the Chicago Mercantile Exchange in the Pork Bellies Pit. They have two children Ali Jordan born June 5, 1986 and Bo Charles born Jan. 9, 1989. They live in Hanover Park near Chicago, IL.

David Ames O'Nan born Sept. 27, 1959 is the last and youngest member of the family. David went to the University of Kentucky and University of Southern Indiana in Evansville, IN, where he received his degrees in Electrical Engineering and Computer Science. He married Dava Katherine French daughter of Donald and Peggy French. David works for the Magnavox Corporation in Fort Wayne, IN and Dava works as a Nurse in the Hospital there. There are no children in this marriage at this time.

ELISHA O'NAN

Elisha O'Nan was the first O'Nan in the Sturgis area. He was a farmer and came here from Eastern part of Kentucky. Elisha was born in Spencer Co., KY, Sept. 27, 1816, the son of John O'Nan and Margaret Lincoln. He died in Union County, Dec. 29, 1857. He married Matilda Conn Bean of Union Co., October 20, 1845. She was born in Jefferson County, KY in 1807. Was the widow of James Bean and had a daughter Sue Bean, who married W. T. Conn.

Elisha and Matilda had 3 sons, James Thomas b. July 6, 1848 d. June 2, 1913. James Oscar, b,. June 8, 1850, d. Jan. 27, 1925 and Dennis Aug. 26, 1851 d. June 8, 1924. They are buried in Pythian Ridge Cemetery. Elisha, Matilda, Sue Bean Conn, David Conn and Melissa are buried in Old Cypress Cemetery. All are members of the Christian Church.

Dennis was 6 years old when his parents died and lived with his Uncle David Conn and Melissa and some with half-sister Sue Conn.

Dennis married Eliza Blue Ralph, Jan. 6.

Walter Sturgis O'Nan and Ariana Wyndham Callaway, 1909

1875 daughter of James William Ralph and Frances Johnson Ralph of Union County. They had 11 children, 10 lived to be grown: James William m. Ivy Hammack, Fannie Sue m. Harry Barkley, Martha Ann m. T. E. Jenkins, Dennis Reeves m. Ruth Henry, Florence Bele m. Wayne Miller, Walter Sturgis m. Ariana Callaway, Ora Strange m. Jess Collins, Ralph Jiles d. Nov. 14, 1918, Mary Eliza m. (1) Earl Bishop, (2) Walter Edwards, and (3) Morris Crane, Edna Earl, infant, Jennings Howe went to California after serving in World War I.

Sturgis was born April 11, 1888, first white male born before Sturgis was incorporated. M. April 25, 1909 Ariana Callaway, daughter of Thomas William Callaway and Maria Louisa (Lou) Long. Ariana was born April 25, 1900 d. Aug. 9, 1981. They had 4 daughters, Virginia, Eleanor, and twins Margaret and Mildred. Sturgis died March 13, 1936 with pneumonia. They lived on a farm until his health failed and then moved into town. Ariana moved to Bowling Green, KY in 1938 where Eleanor and Margaret were in school. Mildred went to Business school in Louisville, KY. Margaret m. Lee H. Newlon, Sept. 5, 1939. They went to St. Augustine, FL to live. Ariana and Eleanor moved to Louisville, so all could be together. Eleanor m. Roger Shriver Aug. 1941. He drowned in St. Augustine, FL rescuing a young girl. She married second Hugh E. Powers. Virginia m. Albert L. Thornsberry, son of Bryant Lee and Mila Caldwell Thornsberry, Aug. 28, 1929 and lived in Sturgis. Had 1 son Dr. William Thomas Thornsberry, he died July 19, 1977 with heart attack. *Submitted by Virginia Thornsberry*

CHARLES CONRAD OWEN

Charles Conrad Owen "Connie," born Dec. 5, 1917 married Dec. 1, 1936 to Anna Marion Heine born Aug. 13, 1912 at Shawneetown, IL. Children: John Aaron Owen born July 16, 1939, Charles Garland Owen born Feb. 14, 1943.

Anna Marion Owen died January 8, 1977 and is buried at Pythian Ridge Cemetery, Sturgis, KY.

John Aaron Owen, born July 16, 1939 married Oct. 6, 1957 to Betty Sue Barden born March 1, 1941. Children: Debra Gale Owen, born Sept. 18, 1958, John Aaron Owen, Jr. born Oct. 14, 1965.

Debra Gale Owen "Debbie" born Sept. 18, 1958 married Dec. 28, 1975 to Anthony Lee Collins "Tony" born Jan. 1, 1955. Children: Lee Ann Collins born September 20, 1980.

John Aaron Owen, Jr. born Oct. 14, 1965 married July 13, 1984 to Lori Leah French born March 21, 1963. Children: Steven Michael Owen, born Oct. 28, 1985.

Charles Garland Owen "Daggie" or "Chuck" born Feb. 14, 1943 married March 21, 1962 to Dorothy Elizabeth Cir "Betty" born Feb. 28, 1943 and divorced 1987. Children: No natural children, adopted: Robin Ann Owen, born Feb. 28, 1971.

Charles Conrad Owen "Connie" born Dec. 5, 1917 remarried Oct. 30, 1977 to Margaruiette H. Carter, Woodring, Stewart born February 18, 1915 at Grangertown Baptist Church by "Connie's" son Rev. John A. Owen.

JOHN WILLIAM OWEN

John William Owen "J.W." was born Feb. 18, 1916, Curlew, Union County, KY. At age 20 he married Dec. 15, 1936 to Margaret Leona Day, age 14, born May 22, 1922. They were married 52 years ago at 11:00 a.m. in Shawneetown, IL by Justice of the Peace W. S. Sanders. Connie Owen and late wife Marion Owen were their attendants.

J. W. is a retired miner, boatman, farmer and fisherman. They made and repaired their own fishing nets and passed net-making on to son, John Ernest.

Standing: John Owen, Ethel Omer, Bobby Owen, Ralph Owen, Hilda Harper, Velda Bealmear and Pam Utley, Sitting: Margaret and J. W.

They reared all seven children in Caseyville: John, Ethel, Bobby, Ralph, Hilda, Velda, and Pam. Their children John Owen, Bobby Owen, Ethel Omer and Pam Utley still live at Caseyville; Ralph Owen at Crittenden, Hilda Harper, Sturgis and Velda Bealmear at Grangertown.

They have 15 grandchildren: Ernie Owen, Jerry Owen, Jason Owen, Teresa Holt, Brian Omer, Rachel Harper, Robby Owen, Darin Owen, Casey Owen, Richard Harper, Alyssa Harper, Todd Bealmear, Chris Bealmear, Wendy Utley and Jody Utley.

They have 8 great grandchildren: Jerrod Owen, Blaine Owen, John Oliver Owen, Summer Holt, Tara Holt, Derek Omer, Brittany Harper, Heather Harper. Derek is expecting a little sister or brother July or August, 1989.

JOHN OWEN

John Owen, born Oct. 17, 1882, Bordley, Union County, KY. At age 30 he married Ollie Durbin age 19, born Oct. 30, 1894 in Caseyville, KY at the home of the bride by Rev. C. T. Baucher on Oct. 17, 1912.

John was a farmer and a fisherman. Ollie was a housewife. They made and repaired their own fishing nets. They passed net-making to son down to grandson. Their grandson John Ernest Owen still makes fishing nets, toy hangers, basketball goal nets and hammocks.

John and Ollie Owen

Their home was destroyed in the 1937 flood. They bought the home on the hill at Mulfordtown, KY. Their oldest grandson and other grandsons were born in the home. Their grandson, John Ernest now owns the homeplace on the hill. Their great grandson Ernie Owen lives at the homeplace.

John died Jan. 17, 1964 and Ollie died July 14, 1967. They are buried at Pythian Ridge Cemetery at Sturgis, KY.

They had 9 children: Glenn Owen, J. W. Owen, Connie Owen, Ada Leibenguth, J. T. Owen, Juanita Blackburn, Lidia Marshall, Cordie Parrish, Mary Cutsinger.

They had 38 grandchildren: Jim Owen, Louise Marshall, Kenny Owen, Billy L. Owen, Gary Owen, John E. Owen, Ethel Omer, Bobby Owen, Ralph Owen, Hilda Harper, Velda Bealmear, Pam Utley, John A. Owen, Charles "Daggie" Owen, Christine Pierson, Billy Don Leibenguth, Ann Garrett, Bill Owen, Karen Shirley, Debbie Piper, Kathy Powell, Eddie Owen, Sue Owen, Don Brummett, Joyce Phillips, Wally Brummett, Donna Brummett, Tim Brummett, Janice Bryant, Greg McMain, Danny Mayes, Barbara McKay, Pat Winders, John Leo Mayes, Allan Mayes, Connie Perkins, Sandie Grounds, Richard Mayes.

70 great grandchildren: Jeff Owen, Darrell Owen, Greta Snedeker, Janel Pike, Jay Marshall, Laurel Marshall, Vickie Fenwick, Lynn Owen, Steve Owen, David Owen, Scott Owen, Greg Owen, Matt Owen, Tammy Owen, Ernie Owen, Jerry Owen, Jason Owen, Teresa Holt, Brian Omer, Rachel Harper, Robby Owen, Darin Owen, Casey Owen, Rich-

ard Harper, Alyssa Harper, Todd Bealmear, Chris Bealmear, Wendy Utley, Jody Utley, Debbie Collins, John A. Owen, Jr., Robin Owen, Tina Simpson, Paula Higgs, Chris Pierson, Kim Leibenguth, Staci Proffitt, Tad Leibenguth, Kevin Garrett, Kent Garrett, Kristi Garrett, Corey Piper, April Piper, Brandi Powell, Joe Powell, Ryan Owen, Aaron Owen, Sherman Owen, Jr., Synthia Bitts, Shannon Owen, Penny Morrison, Tony Brummett, Stacey Brummett, Shirley Brummett, Kim Brown, Amanda Dyer, Michael Phillips, Becky Brummett, Jeromy Mayes, Jacob Mayes, Charles McKay, Michael McKay, Jeff Winders, Teri Winders, Nickolas Mayes, Shawn Mayes, Rachel Perkins, Jonathan Perkins, Brandon Dailey.

18 great, great grandchildren: Darick Owen, Michael W. Owen, Chris Nelson, Chase Owen, Ripley Owen, Blaine Owen, John Oliver Owen, Jerrod Owen, Summer Holt, Tara Holt, Derek Omer, Brittany Harper, Heather Harper, Lee Anna Collins, Michael S. Owen, Jessica Simpson, Brittany Leibenguth, Lauren Garrett.

JOSEPH THOMAS OWEN

Joseph Thomas Owen, born June 25, 1921, married July 16, 1942 to Bessie Irene Collins born June 4, 1922. Children: William Joseph Owen "Bill," born June 17, 1943; Karen Marie Owen born Jan. 9, 1952; Debra Kay Owen born Sept. 1, 1957; Kathy Sue Owen born Aug. 12, 1958; and Edwin Wayne Owen "Eddie" born Aug. 23, 1959.

William Joseph Owen "Bill," born June 17, 1943, married Feb. 9, 1974 to Tillaye Janet Adamson born June 28, 1955 and divorced July 13, 1978. Children: none.

Karen Marie Owen born Jan. 9, 1952, married April 14, 1989 to Frederick C. Shirley "Fred."

Debra Kay Owen born Sept. 1, 1957 married Dec. 22, 1974 to William Darrell Piper born Sept. 19, 1953. Children: Corey Andrew Piper, born May 13, 1977; and April Lynn Piper born April 12, 1980.

Kathy Sue Owen, born Aug. 12, 1958 married Aug. 12, 1983 to Dennis Richard Powell "Cotton" born Oct. 16, 1951. Children: Brandi Michelle Powell born April 13, 1987; and Joseph Richard Powell "Joe" born Feb. 24, 1974. (Joe is Cotton's from previous marriage.)

Edwin Wayne Owen "Eddie," born Aug. 23, 1959 married April 2, 1983 to Cheryl Linda Owen born June 10, 1964. Children: Ryan Edwin Owen born July 15, 1986; and Aaron Michael Owen born May 30, 1989.

JOE AND CINDY OWENS

Cynthia Lynn West Owens, daughter of Robert and Sharry West, was born March 14, 1957 in the old Our Lady of Mercy Hospital in Morganfield, KY. She is a lifetime resident of

162

Sturgis and a graduate of the Union County High School.

Cindy is married to Joe Owens son of Roscoe and Lou Vinnie Owens of Dixon, KY.

They are the parents of two children Chasity Lynn, age 14 and Bobby Joe, age 11.

Joe is presently employed at the Green River Coal Co. in Madisonville, KY. Cindy is employed with the Union Co. School of Performing Arts.

They are both active with their children in sports.

They presently make their home in Wynn Addition, Sturgis, KY. *Submitted by Cindy Owens*

OWEN-BEALMEAR

Velda Jean Owen "Jeannie" born June 16, 1951 married James Harold Bealmear born Nov. 3, 1946 Children: James Todd Bealmear born Nov. 11, 1969 and Christopher Shane Bealmear born May 25, 1974.

James is a coal miner at Peabody and a plumber. Velda is a part-time worker for Sturgis Clothing. They live at Grangertown.

OWEN-EDMONDSON

Robert Leon Owen "Bobby" born Feb. 10, 1941 married June 18, 1960 to Velma Jean Edmondson born March 18, 1943, by Rev. William Chambliss in his home. Children: Robby Dale Owen born Jan. 24, 1965. Bobby works at Morganfield School Bus Garage. Jean works at Union County School offices. They live at Caseyville.

OWEN-HARPER

Hilda Marie Owen born Nov. 10, 1948 married Aug. 14, 1965 to Ronald Louis Harper born March 30, 1947. Children: no natural children, adopted: Richard Lewis Harper born Feb. 19, 1977 and Alyssa Marie Harper born July 22, 1978. Ronnie is a coal miner, horse-trainer and horse racer. They live at Sturgis.

OWEN-OMER

Ethel Lorene Owen born May 24, 1939, married at age 18, Sept. 18, 1957 to Ronald Kent Omer "Ronnie," age 24, born Sept. 18, 1931, at

the groom's grandmother's home, Hattie Wright. Witness by Joan Stevens and Marcus Omer.

Children: Teresa Kay Omer, Brian Kent Omer, Rachel Lynn Omer. Ronnie works at Peabody Coal Company. Ethel has retired from working. They live at Caseyville.

Teresa Kay Omer born June 14, 1948, married May 20, 1978 to Henry Bruce Holt born June 2, 1954. Children: Summer Lynn Holt born Dec. 1, 1978 and Tara Suzanne Holt born March 2, 1982. Bruce works at Peabody Coal Company, Teresa works at Wal-Mart, Morganfield, KY. They live at Sturgis.

Brian Kent Omer, born Aug. 20, 1962 married Jan. 3, 1986 to Nancy Ann Robertson born Jan. 1, 1966. Children: Brian Derek Omer born Oct. 1, 1986 and expecting second child in Aug. 1989. They live at Caseyville.

Rachel Lynn Omer born Oct 14, 1968 married Feb. 14, 1987 to Charles Harper III, born June 15, 1969. Children: Brittany Lynn Harper born Oct. 10, 1986 and Heather Loren Harper born Dec. 8, 1988. Charles is in the Air Force. They live in New York.

OWEN-TRAVIS

Ralph Edward Owen born Jan. 20, 1946 married May 21, 1966 to Linda Kay Travis born Aug. 4, 1948 at Bells Mines Church. Witness by Pat Guess and John E. Owen. Children: Darin Keith Owen and Casey Lynn Owen. Ralph works at Peabody Coal Company. They live on Kiwanis Road in Crittenden County. Linda works at Sheller-Globe.

Darin Keith Owen "Duke" born De. 1, 1968 married May 21, 1988 to Mary Angela Walker "Angie" born July 28, 1969. Duke is a construction worker and a farmer. They live in Marion, KY.

OWEN-UTLEY

Pamela Suezette Owen born May 8, 1957 married May 31, 1974 to Randy Wayne Utley born Sept. 7, 1956 at Elizabeth, IL. Children: Wendy Suezette Utley born Dec. 5, 1974, adopted: Jody Chase Utley born Aug. 24, 1984. Randy is a coal miner at Peabody Coal Company. They live at Caseyville.

OWEN-VINEYARD

John Ernest Owen born Sept. 8, 1937 in Mulfordtown, Union County, KY, at age 19 married June 22, 1957 to Dorothy Louise Vineyard "Dot" at 17, born Coasa, Rome County, GA, Sept. 21, 1939 at the home of Rev. Earl Reinhart, Sturgis, KY: Witness by Ethel Owen and Ronald K. Omer. John is a Towboat Captain, Dot works for Pantry. They live at Caseyville. Children: William Ernest Owen "Ernie," Jerry Wynn Owen, and Jason Manuel Owen.

William Ernest Owen "Ernie" born June 3, 1959 at Sturgis Hospital Sturgis, KY, at age 21

Standing L-R: John, Ernie, Jerry, Liz, Jason, Jerrod and Blaine; Sitting: Dot with John Oliver

married Feb. 14, 1981 to Elizabeth Ann Brown "Liz" age 19, born June 24, 1962, Morganfield Hospital, at Grangertown Baptist Church by Rev. Donald J. Collins. Witness by Katherine M. Flahardy and Russell Greg Burnette. Ernie works at Western Rubber Company, Morganfield, KY. Liz is assistant manager for Pantry, Grangertown, KY. They live at Caseyville. Children: William Blaine Owen, born April 6, 1983, and John Oliver Owen, born Aug. 21, 1986.

Jerry Wynn Owen born March 26, 1961 at Sturgis Hospital, Sturgis, KY, at age 17 married Dec. 26, 1978 to Kathryn Maria Householder, age 17, born March 2, 1961, Morganfield, KY at the home of the bride by Rev. James Lee Reynolds. Witnesses: Susan Harris and Mark Omer. They divorced Sept. 9, 1980. They lived at Caseyville. Jerry is a laid off coal miner and a back-hoe operator. Children: Jerrod Wynn Owen born Aug. 3, 1979.

GEORGE W. PARIS

My paternal grandfather was George W. Paris, one of 10 children of William W. and Nancy (McCarsey) Paris. The William W. Paris family together withthe Hause, Funk and Reisinger families made the move from Jefferson County to Union County (KY) by boat, coming down the Ohio River between 1850-1860. They braved and survived the odds, surely feeling there was safety in numbers.

William W. Paris' second marriage was to Martha Hazel in 1876. There were 3 children from this marriage, but they died in infancy and at age 16. William's third marriage was to Eliza Clemens in 1902. My father vividly remembered how he hitched the horse to the buggy for "Billy" as he was known, to go get married for the 3rd time when he was 84! Eliza was 54. "Billy" died in 1910, age 92, buried at Hazel Bend Cemetery.

George W. Paris married my dear grandmother, Mary Elizabeth, "Lizzy," (Holman) in 1886 after his first marriage to Susan Malloy ended in a bitter divorce in 1884.

George and "Lizzy" were the parents of 5 children, Henry Clay (my father0, James, who died in his pre-teens, Fannie and Farley (twins) Farley died age age 3 from diptheria, and John Thomas.

Mary Elizabeth (Holman) Paris and husband George W. Paris taken prior to 1927

George Paris died in 1927 and as I was born in 1926, I never knew my grandfather. I understand he worked at interlock at the blockhouse near Sturgis. He controlled the switches, allowing the Illinois Central train to pass through as well as any other train coming or going in that direction. He died at age 72, just laid down for an afternoon nap and never woke up. Buried: Little Bethel Cemetery.

I stayed with my loving grandmothe a lot of the time while attending school at Grangertown especially when the road to my home in the county was knee-keep with mud. She swept the "door yards" every morning, made braided, rag rugs and we grandhcildren always had a brand new sun bonnet every summer. She was just a great person whose hands were seldom idle! When planting corn, she was most particular in dropping the grains of corn the exact distance apart. When planting potatoes, evey eye had to be facing straight up.

She passed away in 1949 at age 84 from a series of strokes. Buried at Little Bethel Cemetery. "Granny's goal in life was to be sure she had saved enough money to bury her.

My Paris ancestors from the Carolinas' to Kentucky were considered to be bold and fearless fighters during the Revolution. They were both enlistees and volunteers. Robert Pearis (that was the sur-name spelling at that time as well a Parris) volunteered his services on July 24, 1775 with an expedition to Kentucky under Daniel Boone.

Some of the Pearis Revolutionists became Loyalists, some remained Patriots. When Captain Richard Pearis, a Loyalist, was captured, he spent 9 months chained in prison. Upon returning to his home, he found it and his trading post burned, his wife and family deported. Richard was banned from the Colony and died in poverty in the Bahamas. He was an Indian trader and interpreter and he was one of the few ehite men who could speak the difficult Cherokee language. AT one time, he owned 10,000 acres of land in Greeville, SC, known as "The Great Plains" - a vast plantation.

The town of Pearisburg, VA came into existence through George Pearis III donating 53 acres of land to build the town.

From pioneer days to the present time, the owning of land seemed to be important to the Paris Clan as many generations became "Tillers of the soil."

I was touch by the Will of Robert Alexander Pearis directing that his slaves, Billy and Clary, be freed 6 months after his death. *Submitted by Mary Jo (Paris) Rouse*

JOHN THOMAS PARIS

John Thomas Paris, b. March 6, 1846, d. Jan. 9, 1924, son of William W. and Nancy Paris, followed in his father's footsteps and farmed land in the Old Bethel Church area. He married Lucinda Alice Collins, b. Oct. 2, 1848, d. July 1, 1921, the daughter of Joshua W. and Mary (Cox) Collins.

John, Lucinda, Bill, Harry and Jessie Young Paris

They were the parents of seven children: Lela Elizabeth who married George Ila Dodge, Robert Lee (Bob) who married Nora Francis, Rebecca T. died at the age of ten months, John Thomas died at the age of ten months, Trudie lived to be seventeen years of age, Wiliam Forrest (Bill) married Jessie Carl Young, Benjamin Harrison (Harry) married Bettie Sue Clements. All of their children continued farming in this area. *Submitted by Amy Paris*

MARSHALL AUBREY PARIS

Marshall Aubrey Paris, son of Benjamin Harrison (Harry) and Bettie Sue (Clements) Paris was born Jan. 13, 1921. He entered the United States Navy in 1942, serving four years as a Yoeman. He worked as a truck driver for several food companies and later as a piano tuner before he retired.

Amy (Gerth) Paris, daughrer of Albert and Nellie Gerth, was born Sept. 7, 1929 in Mt. Vernon, IN. She is a beautician and operates a beauty shop in her home. She has published a history of the Paris family.

They have four daughters and two sons.

Pam is married to George Estel Wallace. They have three sons, Wade, Joshua, and Justin.

Clayton is married to Kay (McWorthy). They have two sons, Paul and Brian.

Cinda is married to Jerry Moxley. They have a daughter, Clarissa and a son, Jerad.

Dana is married to Beverly (Cates). They have a daughter, Abigail. They reside in Henderson, KY.

Denisa (Nisa) is married to David Dilback. They have a daughter, Jennifer, and two sons, Matthew and Eric.

Benita (Nita is married to David Cates. They have two sons, Joel and Luke. They reside in Morganfield, Ky. David is a brother to Dana's wife, Beverly. *Submitted by Amy*

ROBERT CHARLES GORDON PARIS

Robert Charles Gordon Paris, born Aug. 18, 1911 and Willie Maud Voss, born April 5, 1913 were married Dec. 17, 1932 at the bride's home. Charles was the son of Robert Lee Paris and Mary Nora Frances. Willie Maud was the daughter of William Lewis Voss and Loda Mary Eleanor Collins of Union County.

Charlie and Willie Maud are the parents of four children, namely; Donald Gordon Paris born Sept. 28, 1933; Billy Lee Paris born June 14, 1938; Elinor Jane Paris born Jan. 11, 1943 and Charlie Bob Paris born Feb. 21, 1950.

Donald married Delores Oakley. They live in Washington, IL. He works for Caterpillar as Research Economist. He received his PHD from the University of Kentucky and one of the 50 leading economist in the U. S. They have two children. Sherri Lynn who is married to Gregory James Anders. They live in Abilene, TX, and have tow sons, Jason and Jeremy. Sherri is a registerd nurse. Barry Gordon is a graduate of petroleum engineering of University of Oklahoma. He lives with his wife Debbie, who is a registered nurse and two stepsons, in Houston, TX.

Billy Lee Paris born June 14, 1938 is married to Emma Kay Wright. They live on a farm in Union County. He works for the longest beltline in the world and she is a registered nurse at the Critenden County Hospital. They have three children. Felecia is married to James Bradley Johnson. They live in Madisonville, KY with their year old daughter Mallory Karla. Felecia teaches in the Madisonville community College and her husband teaches and coaches in the Madisonville School system. Karla Gay, who live with her husband Steve Clark, Route 1, Benton, Ky. She is a dietician at malle Manor, Mayfield Rest Home and Steve works at SKW Alloy in Calvert City, KY. Micael Lee lives at home. He will be a Junior in Union County High School this fall. He is active in sports. He likes baseball and weight lifting as well as other extra curriculum. He is our hope for carrying on the family name.

Our third child is Elinor Jane Paris Hall of Murray, KY. She wasmarried to the late James Oakley hall who was Vice President of Murray State University and died of a heart attack at age 41. Jane has taught accounting at the University for over 10 eyars. She lives in Murray with her two children, Jon Mark who will be a senior at MSU this fall and her daughter Bethany Jane who graduated this May from Murray High School and will be a freshman at MSU this fall. She was very pleased to have the

Honorable Senator Wendell Ford speak at her Commencement at her invitation.

Charlie Bob Paris was born in 1950. He has always been an avid sports fan. He was married to Rhonda Ann Farmer of Sturgis while he was a student at MSU. After graduation he returned to Union County High School as teacher and assistant coach in wrestling. He and Rhonda had one child Shelly Ann who now lives with her mother and stepfather Tom Skinner, Providence, KY. Her mother is a beautician. His second wife is the former Givendyln Crow Creighton of Morganfield, KY. She has one daughter Rachel from her former marriage. She will be a Senior in Union County High School this fall. Charlie Bob and Given have one daughter Jessica Jane who is 11. She will be in fifth grade at the new Middle School in the fall. This will be the second year for occupation of the New Middle School. Charlie Bob teaches health and is head football coach - also instructs in a weight lifting program at Union County High School. His wife works in the loan department of Union Bank and Trust Company, Morganfield, KY.

Charlie Paris died March 25, 1981 of emphysema and heart attack. He was a farmer, live stock producere and miner. He was deacon in Old Bethel Baptist Churhc. His grandparents were John T. Paris and Lucinda Alice Collins and Henry Frances and Grandma Frances.

Willie Maud's paternal grandparents were John Henry Voss and Addie Jane Smith of Sturgis. Her great grandparents came from Germany to this country on their honeymoon. They settled in Caseyville, KY. They came down the Ohio River and established an implement business. To advertise he placed a wagon on the ledge with his name painted on it to attract the river traffic. He was also a shoe cabbler. They were Frederick W. Voss and Ferdenandeanus Voss.

Her maternal grandparents were Philly O. Collins and Martha Elizabeth McMain Collins, of Bullett County and Louisville.

Willie Maud lives at Kelly Brook Apartments, Sturgis. She has been there six years since she uses a wheel chair and she moved from Kelsey Street.

WILLIAM W. PARIS

William W. (Billy) Paris b. March 11, 1818 in Jefferson Co., KY, wife Nancy, b. March 15, 1821, d. July 27, 1874, and four children came to Union County int he 1850's. The trip was made down the Ohio River from Jefferson County, KY. Billy, a farmer, settled in the Sturgis area.

Their children were: Sarah (Sally) who married alfred Cullen, Rebecca Ann who married Frederick Cullen, (a brother to Alfred), John Thomas who married Lucinda Alice Collins, Mary Elizabeth who married Floyd P. Mackey, Fannie who married Samuel Heavrin, George William who married Susan Malloy and later married Mary Elizabeth Holdman, James Buchanan who married

Sarah Bell Cullen (a half sister to Alfred and Frederick Cullen), Aggritpina died at an early age, Franklin (Doc) married Ida Keith, Joseph Miles married Amanda Collins and later married Eunice Ellen Williams.

William W. (Billy) Paris

After the death of wife, Nancy, Billy married Martha Hazel, widow of Fielding Hazel. Three daughters were born to them. They were: Ida Jane who married Frederick Barnaby, Jennie died at age sixteen, Willie Pearl died at age sixteen. After Martha's death Billy married Eliza Clemens.

Billy lived in the Sturgis area most of his life as did many of his children. He died Aug. 17, 1910 and is buried at Hazel Bend Cemetery. *Submitted by Amy Paris*

CLARENCE POWELL

Clarence Powell son of Ed Green Powell and Mary Virginia Cavins Powell was born March 10, 1905 in Alzy, KY a river town also born to this family were two daughters Rosie Earl Powell (Neible) and Ina Edward Powell (Waddell). In the year of 1924 after the death of their daddy they moved from Crittenden County, from the vincinity of the Enon Baptist Church where they owned a General Store for a number of years.

Clarence was nineteen years old when they came to Sturgis. He went to Tom Christian to get a job in the mines and it was told he went to Mr. Christians house 22 times befroe he got a job. His mother and sisters then wanted moved to Uniontown because she was born there. She was the daughter of Floyd and Lois Cavins. They didn't like it ther very well. But he went to work to help support his mother and sisters, after a few months they moved back to Sturgis, where he got another job from Mr. Christian. Then they made this their home.

In Nov. of 1927, he married Beulah Mae Trent from Smith Mills, KY of Henderson County. Clarence was working at No. 9 mines at this time and he received the nickname Brithes Powell from then on. Clarence and Beulah lived in and around Sturgis from then on. Born to them was Kathleen Powell, married to Richard Humphrey, Bobbie Jean Powell married to Dayne Mae Benton, Barbara Ann Powell married to Robert A. Combs, Thomas Powell married to Linda Tester, Dewayne

Powell married Peggy Brummett, Dorothy Powell married William Morgan. In 1950 they adopted a baby girl Louise and she married Claudie Caudill Jr. from Sturgis. Also Rosie Earl married a local boy named Delbert Neible and Ina married a local boy named John R. Waddell and they raised their families in and around Sturgis with children and granchildren living here now. *Submitted by Thomas Powell*

BILL PRIDE

Bill Pride was born at Pride, KY during the year 1924. His parents Wade and Mattie Pride lived in the Pride Community all their lives as did he. He was a graduate of Sturgis High School in 1942 and after high school, he went into the U. S. Army until the end of World War II in 1945. He achieved the rank of T/5 and served overseas in Italy.

At the end of the war he married his only girlfriend, Charlene Reed, who was born in Webster County in the year 1925 and was a graduate of Sturgis High School. She spent most of her lifetime in Sturgis.

It was in this union of marriage that six children were born - three boys and three girls. At the present the three boys farm with Bill in Union County in the Sturgis-Pride area. The boys are Hilliam, Doug and Joe Pride. Two daughters are deaceased and one (Dottie Davis) lives at Route 2, Morganfield, KY.

DOUGLAS FRANK PRIDE

Douglas Frank Pride, son of Bill Zane and Charlene Reed Pride of the Pride Community, was riased on the family farm along with William, Paula, Dottie, and Joe Pride. Doug attended both elementary and junior high schools in Sturgis. He graduated from Union County High School and attended college at Western Kentucky University, in Bowling Green. Before returning to Union County, Doug joined the Kentucky National Guard in Louisville, where he served for six years.

The eldest child of William Thomas and Mesia Oakley Riggs, Karla Riggs Pride, was raised in Morganfield along with Ginny, Stan, and Meg Riggs. Karla attended both elemetnary and junior high schools in Morganfield and graduated from U. C. H. S. Karla also attended Henderson Community College, where she returned in 1987, after working as a clerk for the City of Sturgis, to finish her degree in office management. Karla was the recipient of the E. L. Overfield Scholarship Award and was initiated into the Phi Theta Kappa National Honor Fraternity.

Douglas Frank Pride and Karla Lynn Riggs were married on Feb. 1, 1969. They are the proud parents of four children. Their oldest son, Douglas Jason Pride, was born in Bowling Green, on April 28, 1970. In 1972, the Pride family returned to Union County where Doug

Karla, Jason, Nathan, Kevin, Doug and Mesia Lynn Pride

became a partner of Bill Pride and Sons' farming operation.

In 1974, the young family moved to Sturgis. They purchased the Rube Daniels' home on 809 Washington Street. They also joined the Sturgis United Methodist Church at this time. Over the years, the Prides have been very active in their church, school, and community activities.

On June 19, 1975, their second son, William Nathan Pride, was born in Henderson. Two years later, on Oct. 27, 1977, their third son, Thomas Kevin Pride, was born in Henderson. And at last, Henderson was the setting for the arrival of their precious daughter, Mesia Lynn Pride, on Nov. 5, 1980, to make this family complete.

Jason Pride attended elementary and junior high schools in Sturgis, and graduated from U.C.H.S. in 1988. Jason was the recipient of the Robert C. Byrd Honors Scholarship an the U. C. Port Producers Annual Scholarship. He has just completed his first year at the University of Kentucky in Lexington, where he is a member of the Delta Epsilon Chapter of Delta Tau Delta Fraternity.

Nathan Pride attended Sturgis Elementary and just recently completed his first year at the new Union County Middle School. Nathan is very active in the 4-H program and represented his school at the state competition in 1986, in Lexington, where he was named the Champion of the 4-H Horse Public Speaking Contest.

Kevin Pride and Mesia Lynn Pride have also attended Sturgis Elementary School. Kevin will be attending U.C.M.S. this fall. In 1894, Kevin also represented Union County in state competition at the Kentucky State Fair in Louisville, where he won the state titile of Little Mr. Kentucky State Fair.

The Pride family is proud to be a part of the Sturgis Centennial History Book and to be raising their family in such a fine small town. *Submitted by Karla R. Pride*

C. W. PUGH

Sturgis was a mere "youngster" when C. W. and Mattie Pugh, coming from Barlow, Ballard County, KY in 1924 took up residence and bought the Rhodes Variety Store which they promptly renamed Pugh's Variety Store.

Upon entering Fran's Country Crafts and looking downward at the wlakway, one can see the name of their business spelled out in small marble tile declaring this fact.

Charles William, better known as C. W., was born Feb. 2, 1888 in Trigg County, Ky. Bieng a venturesome businessman, he started the Dairy Queen (later sold to Bill and Ella Wallace), The Sturgis Cafeteria (later sold to George and Hattie Roberts), a furniture store (later sold to Holt's Ladies Wear), and a fruit and vegetable market now occupied by The First Presbyterian Church. He had interests in spar and coal mines in Crittenden County, and he and Mattie donated the lot on which was built the Tabernacle Baptist Church (name changed in the 1960's to Sturgis Baptist Church) where Charlie was a deacon until his death Dec. 23, 1958.

Charlie and Mattie Pugh

Their red brick two-story home was lcoated at 4th and Monroe Street where they were living at the time of his death, and it was his request that Mattie build the new yellow brick home across the street from the Church he loved so much. It was his wish that when the two of them were gone the new home would become the church parsonage.

Mattie continued to operate Pugh's 'Variety Store until it burned April 14, 1967 about 3 o'clock in the afternoon. She had the store remodeled but did not go back into business, retiring to her home where an abundance of All-American Rose Selection Winners graced the northern edge of her well kept lawn. Although roses were her favorites, she also grew Crape Myrtle and Red and Golden Cannas. And no dandelion had the privilege of "growing" up on her lawn.

Mattie, whose proper name was Martha Christina (Jones) Pugh, born Jan. 12, 1889, died at Hopkins County Hospital in Madisonville May 18, 1976.

They had no children. Charlie's closest relatives in Sturgis were his neice, Jane (Pugh) Vancleave and her three children: Wanda, Mary Jane, and Johnny who was Uncle Charlie's cherry-coke drinking buddy. *Submitted by Jane (Pugh) VanCleave*

QUINN-FELTS

Mason Cullen Quinn, b. March 27, 1915 in Sturgis, KY, son of William Thomas and Ophie

S. Cullen Quinn, was one of ten children, all of whom received their education in the Union Co. School System. he graduated from Sturgis High School in 1935 and was captain of the Golden Bears Football team his Senior year.

Evelyn Lorrayne Felts, b. Sept. 7, 1916 at Price's Mill, KY in a log cabin, daughter of George Hamilton and Annie Belle Procter Felts, married Mason June 26, 1937 in Franklin, KY at the Presbyterian Manse.

The Quinn's left Sturgis for Peoria, IL in 1941 where Mason accepted employment with Caterpillar Tractor Company and resided in Washington, IL until his retirement in 1981. Evelyn retired from a sales clerk's position with Land's Clothing Store in Washington and they presently reside in Henderson, KY.

Children blessed to this union are: Julia Winston Quinn Hall, b. Dec. 26, 1940, Sturgis, now of Tempe, AZ - 2 children, Tracey Lorrayne Grant and Gretchen Norma Grant; Sandra Ann Quinn, b. Sept. 25, 1947, Peoria, IL, a commercial artist now of Chicago, IL; and Mason Thomas Quinn, b. March 8, 1950, Peoria, IL, now of Wheaton, IL - Amber Lorrayne Quinn, Aaron Thomas Quinn, and Stephanie Nicole Quinn (children of Mason Thomas Quinn). *Submitted by Joel Felts-Williams*

QUIREY

Many years ago, in the early 1810's, when Kentucky was known as "The Dark and Bloody Grounds," there came to what is now Union County a pioneer who fell trees, split the logs and built his home for his family. His name was Thomas P. Quirey, who with hsi wife, Nancy A., and children, settled in the areas of Union and Webster Counties. He had six sons and two daughters who were Marshall C. Thomas, Mort, Daniel, Frank, William, Sally and Kate. One son, Mort, married Molly Nunn and they had three sons and two daughters, O. C., George Hugh, Jones, May and Clore. Their son, O. C. was the first Captain of the Guard at the then new Eddyville Penitentiary and during his tour of duty, he courted and married one of the daughters of the first Warden of the Penitentiary, C. Lewis Curry. With that daughter, Sophronia Ecton, O. C. Quirey returned to Union County and they had two sons and one daughter, Louis C. (Bud), Wallace Burns (Tenny Bud), and Waller. The youngest son, Wallace Burns, courted and married the daughter of George Oliver Daniels and Emma Sue (Omer) Daniels, who was Jennie V. Daniels. The children of Wallace B. and Jennie V. are Alla Burns (Sonny), Earl Danield (Dan), and Otho Carter (Swan). Alla B. has no children. Earl Daniel has three stepchildren, Janet (Applin) Rushing, Monty Applin, and Mark Applin. Otho C. has two daughters, Jerri Nell (Quirey) Shouse and Debbie (Quirey) (Beachamp) Higgs. Alla B. is a retired office supply salesman, single, and living in Sturgis. Earl Daniel married Betty Reed, daughter of

Roy and Lucille Reed, of Sturgis in 1950. Betty died in 1983 and Earl Daniel married Ann (Lynch) Applin, daughter of Claude and Mary Lynch, in 1987. Earl Danield is a retired Federal Employee and they also live in Sturgis. Otho C. is married to Dollie Anglin, and is an ironworker and is living in Paducah, KY.

Mort Quirey enlisted in Company C 10th Cavalry of the C.S.A. on Aug 23, 1862 and was a member of Gen. John H. Morgan's "Raiders." Mort was captured and imprisoned in Camp Douglas in the Chicago, IL area. On Oct. 12, 1863, Mort and fellow Union Countian, G. H. Whitecotton, escaped and walked back to Sullivan, KY. Mort later was a farmer, tax assessor, and Sheriff in Union County.

O. C. Quirey, Mort's oldest child, was also a farmer, postmaster in Sturgis (1915-1924), and supply clerk/bookkeeper for WEst Kentucky Coal Company. Wallace Burns, O. C.'s youngest child, was a Sturgis businessman, spent over 30 eyars in the U. S. Maritime Service (Merchant Marine), and a rancher in Oklahoma.

Earl Daniel, Wallace Burn's second child, enlisted in the U. S. Navy in Oct. 1946, and was discharged 10 years later, in 1956. After receiving his Electrical Engineering Degree on the last Summer Commencement Ceremonies given by the University of Kentucky in Aug. 1958, he worked for the National Aeronautics and Space Administration for 23 years and retired. Earl Daniel is presently the Mayor of Sturgis. *Submitted by Earl Daniel Quirey*

O. C. QUIREY

It has been said that there are more names starting with Q's in the Sturgis phone book than there is in the Chicago phone book. This is accountable to the number of Quartermous's, Quinn's, and Quirey's that populate our little town.

The Quireys settled in and around Sullivan (formerly known as Quirey Station) and Wheatcroft. Our immediate family commenced in Wheatcroft with the birth of Courtney C. Quirey, Sr., in October 1905 (parents, Charles Ervin Quirey and Sharah Elizabeth Quirey) and Alma Lorene Vaughn in August 1907 (parentts, Otho C. Vaughn and Nannie Cruse Vaughn).

This marriage has produced three children: Courtney C. Quirey, Jr. (wife, Wanda Smith Quirey and two children, Charlotte Easley of Sturgis and Lina Lisman of Deerfield Beach, FL), Otho C. Quirey (wife, Kathryn Ann Kington Quirey and daughter Nancy Shelton) and Barbara Quirey (husband, Arnold Davis Sprague an dtwo children, Davis and Sarah of Henderson, KY).

Courtney Sr. spent his working years with West Kentucky Coal Comapny in Hopkins County, KY then later he worked as Superintendent of Poplar Ridge Coal Company and DeKoven Mines in Union County, KY. He

started work with Poplar Ridge Coal Company in 1942 and at DeKoven in 1955.

Courtney Jr. has now retired from working as Preservation Plant Superintendent for Peabody Coal Company in Union and Ohio Counties. He commenced work with West Kentucky Coal Company in Hopkins County and later was employed by the DeKoven Coal Mine here in Union County.

O. C. Quirey worked for 5 years at Servel, Inc. ín Evansville, IN. He came back to Union County in the mid 1950s to help in the family business which consisted primarily of an apple orchard located 3 miles north of Sturgis on Highway 60 and a family clothing store known as the Sturgis Specialty Shop. The clothing sotre was commenced by Alma (Bobbie) Quirey and Nannie (Mam) Vaughn as a small dress shop on Adams Street in Sturgis in 1949. The Store is still in operation as a family clothing store.

Barbara Quirey Sprague owns and manages one of the necer ladies clothing stores in downtown Henderson, KY known as The Fashion Tree. Her husband Dave Sprague is a Doctor of Obstetrics and Gynecology having a sizeable practice in Henderson. Dr. Sprague also farms several hudnred acres of land located in Henderson and Union Counties. *Submitted by O. C. Quirey*

LINNIE MC MURRY RASH

Linnie McMurry Rash was born July 29, 1890, the first child born in Sturgis after its incorporation and daughter of Willie Ford and Harriet Easley McMurry. She had one brother, Johnson Burns McMurry who died at age 23 in Washington, D.C. where he worked in the U.S. Patent Office. He left one son, a baby of four months old named Gene who currently lives in California and has six children.

Linnie's parents lived on Adams Street between 7th and 8th Street opposite Goads big barn at the time of her birth.

Linnie Rash

Dr. Bailey, a widower who had a son named "Lute" the only Doctor in Sturgis at that time (1890), made the delivery. Between 1890 and 1900 a Dr. Price came to Sturgis. Dr. Price had two children, Judith and Carmen ("Carmie").

Linnie left this area in 1917, but has always considered Sturgis her home.

Her home in Sturgis was built in 1889 located at 8th and Main across the alley from the First Baptist Church. The last owner was Givens Christian.

Linnie is currently residing in Madisonville, KY and is in fairly good health. She will celebrate her 100th birthday in July 1990. *Submitted by Mrs. W. E. Rash*

ROY LEE REED

Roy Lee Reed (1903-1976) was born in Webster County Jan. 21, 1903 to Lee and Myrtle Reed. He started working at an early age in the West Ky. Coal Co. Store and after that at nearly every mine in Webster and Union County that West Ky. owned. He married Tennie Bernice Clark (1906-1966) April 17, 1921, who was born in Russellville, KY. To their union were born three girls and one son they being Helen Margaret married John Hardwick McKeaig (deceased) having one daughter Judtih Helen; Dorothy Charlene married Billy Zane Pride having three sons and three daughters, William Reed who has 2 sons and 2 daughters - Parrish, Paige, Pamela and Paul; Cynthia (deceased); Douglas Frank, having three sons and one daughter - Jason, Nathan, Kevin and Mesia Lynn; Paula (deceased); Dorothy Zane having one daughter and three sons - Frances, Zane, Jack and Lee; Joseph Jeffrey having two daughters - Jody and Jennifer; Betty Jewel (deceased) married Earl D. Quirey; Lee Roy having three sons - James Lee, Thomas and Michael.

Roy Lee Reed

After the West Ky. closed all the mines in the county, the family moved to Birmingham, AL and worked for the T. C. I. Coal Co as mine foreman for a year returning to Sturgis, working at the Shipyards in Evansville for the war effort. Then moved back to Birmingham to the T.C.I. Coal Co. and the mines. Returned to Sturgis after the war and worked for the West Ky. Coal Co. and Island Creek Coal Co., helping open Atkinson Mine in Hopkins County as electrician until retirement. He and his wife were members of the First Christian Church and he was a member of Kelsey Lodge #659 and Order of Eastern Star #444. He and his wife were both hard working people and loving parents and grandparents and loved by all who knew them.

JOHN REYNOLDS, JR.

John Reynolds, Jr., was born August 1, 1879 in Russelville, KY, and died Oct. 17, 1957, the son of John and Kate Gillam Reynolds, Sr. Kate later married John M. Gilbert and she died Feb. 27, 1919. John Reynolds moved to Sturgis, KY, where he married Anna Wilhelmine Margaretha Weyer on March 16, 1904, the daughter of Henry and Mathilda Fricke Weyer of Evansville, IN. She was born Feb. 12, 1880 and died Oct. 7, 1953. Anna had one brother, William A. Weyer of Evansville.

John Reynolds was foreman of the West Kentucky Coal Company Farm and also Kentucky State Highway Department. An editorial that was written after his death wsa titled "We'll All Miss Him." He was jovial, and an ardnet admirer of sports, cheering his sons on during their football, basketball and track days. He was a lover of horses and showed them in horse shows. He was known as Mr. Republican of Union County.

John and Anna Reynolds

Anna Reynolds was a devoted mother, wife, church member and a member of the Homemakers Club. They were members of the Methodist Church in Sturgis. John and Anna were the parents of five children.

John Delmer Reynolds born Dec. 21, 1904 and died Dec. 16, 1981 at Grand Rivers, KY. He was a teacher in the Sturgis and DeKoven Schools and football coach in Providence, KY. He engaged in all sports at Sturgis High School and Western State Teachers College in Bowling Green, KY from which he graduated. He was a retired owner of a Western Auto Store in Princeton, KY. He was married to Ersley Shewmaker of Springfield, KY, who was born July 5, 1904 and died Aug. 11, 1985. They were parents of four daughters: Jean O'Neill of Alexandria, VA; Joyce Allen of Grand Rivers, KY; Joanne Ollett of Richmond, VA; and Jimmie Carolyn Leeson of Dallas, TX.

Alton Sylvester Reynolds was born March 22, 1907, and resides in Greenville, KY. He married Sylvia Page of Sturgis, KY, who was born May 15, 1915 and died Aug. 28, 1987. He engaged in all sports at Sturgis High School and attended Western State Teachers College in Bowling Green, KY. He was a football coach in Sturgis, KY and is retired from the West Kentucky Coal Co. and Peabody Coal Co after

44 years. They were parents of a daughter Linda Young of Central City, KY.

Berneda Kathryn Reynolds was born Dec. 24, 1909 and married John Earl Todd who was born October 18, 1906 and died April 10, 1976. She attended Bowling Green Business University, Bowling Green, and resides in Memphis, TN. She is a retired secretary from Pidgeon Thomas Iron Company after 43 years.

William Wayne Reynolds was born January 2, 1912, and resides in Dunedin, FL. He married Alta Lois McCann of Sturgis, KY, daughter of Earl McCann. She was born June 20, 1916, and died Aug. 30, 1980. Wayne graduated from Western State Teachers College in Bowling Green, KY, and was a teacher in the Sturgis, Caseyville and Cadiz Schools. He served in World War II. He is retired from the Veteran Administration Hospital, Omaha, NB after 25 years. They were the parents of a son John Michael of Omaha, NB and a daughter Patricia Boll of St. Louis, MO. He is now married to Patricia Schrader of Omaha, NB.

Corine Elizabeth Reynolds was born Oct. 30, 1918, and resides in Memphis, TN. She is a graduate of the Comptometer and IBM Schools in Memphis, TN. *Submitted by Corinne Reynolds.*

LOUIS ELBERT RINGO

Louis Elbert Ringo, son of John Thomas Ringo, and Martha Catherine Bean, was born November 19, 1894. His father died when he was three and his mother died when he was 17. He farmed and later bought a general store in Blackford.

Mellie Elaine Hudson, the daughter of W. H. Hudson and Sallie B. Curry, was also born in Webster County. Her father came from PeeWee valley to the 7 Gums Region of Union County before buying land in Webster County.

During the Depression Years of the thirties, Elbert and Mellie with their only daughter Kathleen moved to Bowling Green where Mellie and Kathleen received AB Degrees from Western Ky. University. Elbert sold real estate and insurance. Returning to "God's Country," Elbert bought a store in Wheatcroft which he operated until his death in 1970. He also owned and managed a farm of over 400 acres.

Mrs. Ringo taught in Blackford and was principal of the grade school when they moved to Sturgis where she taught until her retirement, a total of forty-two years.

In addition to her teaching career, Mrs. Ringo has been activ in Civic and Community affairs. While residing in Blackford, she and Elbert taught Sunday School classes, and he served as deacon. She was church clerk and pianist for 26 years. Since moving to Sturgis in 1942, she taught the Doreas Class of First Baptist Church over 36 years. While she was President of The Sturgis Senior Woman's Club, they met all required standards of the federation and through various projects raised over $2,000.00 which they contributed to many worthy causes - The Library, The Community Hospital, and the Sturgis High School Band. This record won for Mrs. Ringo in 1955 the coveted J. W. Stovall Award. Throughout her teaching career, her church and community work, Mrs. Ringo has always set and maintained high standards. During her 22 years as teacher in the Sturgis High School, certainly her influence has been felt in the lives of many graduates.

ROY WILLIAM (BUD) ROWLEY

Roy William (Bud) Rowley, son of Harry William Rowley and Cassie Faye Hort Rowley, was born Aug. 25, 1921, in Union County, KY. He served in the Armed Forces for 3 years, from Oct. 1, 1942 until the end of World War II. He was engaged in farming most of his life. He died December 14, 1976 in Henderson, KY of a massive heart attack. He was buried in the Farmons Cemetery in Henderson.

Dorothy Jean Harness Rowley, was born in Union County, March 23, 1933. Her parents were Fred Harness and Betsy Slaton Harness.

The Rowley Family

Roy (Bud) Rowley and Dorothy J. Harness were married in Morganfield in 1948. They are the parents of seven children. The oldest Donna Fay Rowley, married William (Bill) Threkeld and they have one daughter, Billy Jo. They operate Threkeld's Nursery and Greenhouse at Clay, KY.

Roy Hershel Rowley works as a Grocery Store front-end manager in Duncanville, TX.

Ray Marshel Rowley is custodian at the First Baptist Church, Sturgis. His addres is Morganfield, KY.

Robert Lewis (Bob) Rowley married Pamalea Mount, their address is Matton, KY. They have a son, Carrie Matthew. Bob also has a son by a former marriage, Billie Jack Rowley. Bob works for a furniture store in Princeton, KY.

William Edward (Bill) Rowley married Freda Jones from Benton, KY. Their address is Benton. Bill is an instructor at Paducah Tilghman Vocational High School. They have one daughter, Rachel Elizabeth.

James Allen (Jim) Rowley married Jackie Strain from Illinois. They live at Bonnie, IL.

They have two children; Jamia and Joshua. Jim works for a coal mining company in Illinois.

Patricia Ann (Pattie) Rowley married Danny McCrakin from Illinois. They operate a Cap and T-shirt Printing Shop, Mt. Vernon, IL.

The six oldest children graduated from Union County High School. Patty, the youngest graduated from Township High School, Mt. Vernon, IL.

Dorothy Harness Rowley later married John W. Murrell and they have one daughter, a half sister to the Rowley children. Her name is Paula Jean Murrell Wright. She has one daughter, Tabathia Jo. Her address is Sturgis, KY.

Harry W. Rowley was the son of Ezekel Rowley and Mildred Steward Rowley. Fay Hort Rowley was the daughter of James Russell Hort and Sallie Lea Padgett Hort. All were raised in Union County.

There is a Rowley Cemetery between Sturgis and the Shawneetown Bridge on Highway 109, where a lot of their descendants were buried.

JOSEPH BERNARD RUSSELBURG

Joseph Bernard Russelburg was the first child of Charles Richard Russelburg (1881-1964) and Mary Lillian Abell Russelburg (1885-1969). he was born Aug. 27, 1903 in Uniontown, KY. He married Francis Lucille Braddock, the first child of James Augustine Braddock (1888-1963) and Mary Ida Lefler Braddock (1888-1921). Francis Lucille Braddock was born Nov. 1, 1912 in Uniontown, KY. Bernard and Lucille were united in marriage in Uniontown, KY at St. Agnes Catholic Church by Fr. Julian Peters, on Nov. 23, 1927. Their witnesses were Stronnie Russelburg and Regina Abell.

Not long after their marriage Bernard and Lucille moved to Detroit, MI, in search of work. Their family began with a daughter born April 3, 1929 and given the name of Agnes Patricia. In November 1929 they moved back to Uniontown, KY to an area that was known as the River bottoms. Their family continued to grow with a son, James Richard born Aug. 16, 1932; a daughter Rita Evelyn born Nov. 19, 1935; a set of twin boys, Bernard Ronald and Joseph Donald born Oct. 19, 1936. Then two daughters were born, Maryily Jean born Jan. 18, 1939 and mary Yvonne born May 30, 1940; a son born June 16, 1941 that was given the name of Delphin Thomas.

In 1941, Bernard bought a farm from the Alf Johns Estate, consisting of 173 acres near Henshaw, (later known as Route 2, Sturgis, KY), where he built a home with the help of several of his friends. He farmed this land until his retirement at the age of 65.

The family grew after they moved into their new home with a son, Cletus Augustine born Jan. 30, 1943; a daughter Phyllis Ann born May 10, 1944; a son Phillip Hershel born May 9, 1945; a daughter Juanita Rose born July 18,

Bernard and Lucille Russelberg

1946; a son Glen Stephen July 7, 1947. Then two daughters, Audrey Elaine born July 6, 1948 and Diana Kay born Aug. 27, 1949; and a son, Merle Andrew was born Nov. 21, 1950.

Bernard and Lucille celebrated their 60th wedding anniversary at St. Ambrose Catholic Church in November 1987 where they repeated their marriage vows before their family and friends. Fr. Henry Cecil performed the ceremony and Mass with a reception held prior to the ceremony at St. Francis Borgia Catholic Church Hall, Sturgis, KY.

We, the family of Bernard and Lucille Russelburg continue to visit them at their home of Route 2, Sturgis, KY. The most memorable are The Christmas Day's, as most of the family arrives for dinner and gifts are opened by all. What a blessing to be a part of such a family! One that is based on faith, love, and integrity. May we continue on into the future with these teachings that were so lovingly taught to us. *Submitted by Lisa Collins Jones*

SEIBERT

Annie Willie Callender was born Sept. 30, 1905 at her grandparents J. W. and Eliza Davis house which was lcoated behind the present Valley View Methodist Hospital. Her parents, Ben and Lillian Callender were living on their farm on Ben Dyer Road. In 1919 they bought the T. K. Cissell house and farm on Old Providence Road, better known as Commercial Point. There they lived for 69 years.

After Carroll's death in 1980, Annie Willie moved to 803 Washington Street. This house had been purchased in 1959 from Shelly Bennett, by the Seiberts. It was built in 1898 by Mr. Bennett's parents.

Annie Willie (Callender) Seibert and Carroll

In 1981, the Seibert's grandson, Brian Dalton and family purchased the family home on Old Providence Road.

Carroll Leslie Seibert was born June 22, 1905 on Old Providence Roadl to Jessie and Ada Seibert.

He went to school at Sturgis and when a lad of 8 years old he had his first job, opening and closing the gate for the wagons at Mr. E. H. Long's brick kiln on Highway 109. At the age of twelve he started grinding coffee before and after school at Cusic's Grocery Store, corner of Old Providence Road and Kelsey Streets. He later drove the grocery delivery wagon drawn by a mule. In 1919, he came to live with Melton and Virginia Cusic. In 1924, on May 15, Carroll and Annie Willie were married.

They went into the grocery business on the corner of Kelsey and Highway 109 shortly after they were married. This was sold in 1929.

Carroll went to work immediately at Sturgis Furniture Co. which was operated by Forest Northern.

In 1931, on Dec. 26, Carroll and Annie Willie became parents of a daughter, Carolyn Ann.

In 1932 Mr. Will and Sue Payne and Carroll and Annie Willie purchased the Sturgis Furniture from Walter Hoe of Providence, managed by Forest Northern, Sturgis. Later in 1945, the Seiberts purchased the Payne's interest and were the sole owners of the store.

Carroll was known throughout the county and Sturgis folk have told the family of instances that he generously helped them to furnish their home or helped to provide them with some greatly needed item. He was found at Sturgis Furniture Co. for nearly 50 years, and one could say that he and Sturgis Furniture Co. were synonomous.

In 1955, Carroll was elected Chairman of the Sturgis Hospital Committee which was to raise money for the new hospital, presently the Sturgis Rest Home. In this same year, he was voted "Citizen of the Year" and honored by the Veterans of Foreign Wars.

In 1967, following a stroke, Carroll retired from the store and the reins were handed over to Thomas Dalton, Carroll's son-in-law, who had been working with him for twelve years. *Submitted by Annie Willie Seibert*

THOMAS SELDON

Pat, as most people know him was born in the Pond Fork Community on Oct. 16, 1906 to Thomas Colman and Sara Farthing. He was raised on a farm, later owning his own farm where he and Mary reside to date. Along with farming and other jobs, he took up the tradie of plumbing, pursuing it until later 1988 when health and age slowed him down.

Mary Ima Wallace Farthing was born on Sept. 29, 1910, in Clay and was raised in Lisman until 16 when on Dec. 4, 1926, she married Pat and moved to Union County, where they parented four children - Bobie Ray, Glenn

The Thomas Seldon Family

Wallace, Judy (deceased 1941) and Brownie Lee (deceased 1964).

Bobbie Ray and wife Anna Margaret Wright Farthing reside in Greenvill, KY, and Bob is a retired coal miner. Children of Bob and Anna Margaret are Anna Raye and David Wright.

Anna Raye and husband, Rev. Dale Sanders of IL, have two children, Hailey Michelle, age 11, and Heath Thomas, age 9.

David and wife, Cheryl Cornette Farthing, reside in Sturgis and are the owners of Kozy Kitchen Restaurant downtown Sturgis. They have two sons, David Wright II, age 18, and Jason Alton, age 15.

Glen resides in Florrissant, MO with his wife, Pattie Hill Farthing. Flen is employed by St. Louis County as a property evaluation officer. They have two children, Deana, married to James Ward, also of St. Louis County, and Kent, who is currently in shcool in Nashville, TN.

SHAFFER

James Alfred Shaffer, son of Walter and Mattie Johns Shaffer, born July 2, 1928 in Henshaw. He was the youngest of four children - Jane Shaffer Kurtz, Gerald and Wlater John (Dougan) Shaffer. Jim helped with the family farm, was active in 4-H and high school sports. As an agriculture student at the University of Kentucky, Jim was affiliated with Alpha Gama Rho Fraternity, an IFY to Ireland and a member of the Livestock Judging team. After serving time in the Korean War, Jim returned to U. K. Graduate school where he met and married Martha hackworth from Logan, WV.

In 1958 the ocuple moved from Lexington to Union County with daughter Brenda. Jim farmed the first land bought by Alcoa Aluminium Company in the area. James Eric was born to the couple in 1960.

Jim became involved int he oil and gas business through the purchase of Tradewater Oil Company from Jim Syers and "Pickle" Rayburn; then a service station from MY Nunn. Jim was still farming in Crittenden County at the time of his death, Feb. 1985.

Marty Shaffer was a public school librarian for 10 years, worked for J & J Jewelry then opened MB's Cards, Fabrics and Gifts which was later sold to Fran and David Woodring (1987).

Tradweater Oil and gas station was sold to Miles Farm Suply of Owensboro, KY in 1986.

Brenda Shaffer graduated from Eastern Kentucky University and Eric graduated from University of Kentucky then joined Purian Co. in 1984, In 1986, Eric married nancy Mackey; ehr parents are Barbara Jenkins and Billy Ray Mackey. *Submitted by Marty Shaffer*

CHARLES C. SHAFFER

Charles C. Shaffer, (May 6, 1863 - Feb. 11, 1909), one of nien, the son of Joseph Colbert Shaffer, born June 21, 1836, one of ten, and the son of John Frederick Shaffer, born Aug. 3, 1810.

Charles C. Shaffer married "Mollie" (Mary Lovinia) Henry Shaffer. Born in July, 1866, she was one of eleven children of Joseph Dixon and Susan Moore Henry. Other Henry girls and their husbands were Sallie - W. B. Brooks; Mattie J. - H. Bingham; Effie - John T. Slaton; Rose - Hiram Horace Smith; Lutha - James A. Dalton; Opa - Walton Dunn; Ruth - Reeves O'Nan. Brothers were Mason - Sadie Brewer; Herman - Georgia Thompson; Chester - Mary Maxwell.

Charlie C. Shaffer; Mrs. Mollie Henry Shaffer (front center). Standing; Walter Shaffer, Mrs. Mary Berry, Mrs. Naomi Benson, Mrs. Susan Cobb, Mrs. Elizabeth Stevens, Raymond Shaffer, Mrs. Pearl Woodward. Seated; Mrs. Martha Miller, Mrs. Shaffer, Mrs. Charlotte Ballou

The union of Charles Shaffer and Mollie Henry produced Raymond, Pearl, Walter, Mary, Naomi, Susan, Elizabeth, Charlotte and Martha.

Very early in life for this family Charles died and Mollie and children were confronted with making their family unit work and play together. The younger girls hardly remembered their father. The children had many jobs and Mollie had a cow, a few pigs, chickens, garden and all kinds of fruti trees. As the children got out on their own, Mollie would always have a room or two for young people wanting to live in town to work and/or go to school. This was before school bus days. Most of this time was prior to good roads.

Their children: Raymond (May 6, 1890 - March 5, 1974) married Verna Holeman of Boxville and had Raymond Henry Shaffer, bachelor; Joe (Jimmy) whose wife was Thelma; and Jean married Richard McCauley. Raymond and family lived in Louisville, KY. He was in carpentry and construction.

Pearl (Nov. 24, 1891-____) married C. W. Woodward (from Michigan) in 1919. They operated the Burlington School of Business in Burlington, IA for many years. "Chuck" was an avid fisherman; he not only enjoyed fishing - he caught them. Pearl was a great family person and was a great booster to many friends and students.

Walter (Sept. 4, 1893 - Mary 25, 1965) married Mattie Pearl Johns in 1917 and soon they were farming with her father, Alf Johns, near Henshaw. Their children, Helen Jane, Gerald Johns, Wlater Allen and James Alfred grew up farming and busy in 4-H club activities. Jane married George Kurtz (Lancaster, KY) lives near Sturgis, raised four children. (see Kurtz family). Gerald (Feb. 7, 1921) married Ann Ford, (Sturgis, KY) lives in Evansville, has three children: Thomas Johns, Lee Humphry, and Jane Russell. Walter "Dugan" (Aug. 6, 1923) married Jean Minor, (Morganfield, KY) and had one son, Walter Johns ("Johnny"). All of them live now in Norcross, GA. Jim (July 2, 1928 - Feb. 18, 1985) married Martha Hackworth of Logan, WV, lived in Sturgis, reared Brenda and Eric. Eric married Nancy Lee Mackey.

Front Row; Nancy Dean Williams, Nicholas Goetz, John Lindsey Tackett, Sydney Goetz. Back Row; Kelly Goetz, Jane Kurtz, Beth Kurtz, Bill Kurtz, Julia Tackett, Sarah Tackett, John Kurtz, George Kurtz, Martha Williams and Molly Williams Sherrell

Mary (Sept. 10, 1895 - Jan. 7, 1988) married J. Jones Berry of Sturgis who worked for West Kentucky Coal Company. Their son Tom amrried Rulene and they live in the old home place, highest point in Sturgis.

Naomi (Sept. 3, 1897 - Feb. 7, 1983) married Willis B. Benson of near Henshaw, had daughter Ann Carolyn. They farmed for some years, moved to Tell City, Indiana and were engaged in home appliance services.

Susan (Jan. 25, 1900 - April 6, 1966-) married William H. Cobb, an engineer form Connecticut. He worked for West Kentucky Coal Company, then in Missouri and then to Chicago. Their daughter Barbara Harris married James Walter Pedigo.

Elizabeth (1902-____) married John Bishop Stevens of Henshaw community. John worked in coal mining for West Kentcuky and near Logan, WV. They had three daughters,

170

May Levine, who married Ray Andre of Sturgis, Susie and Lucy.

Charlotte (Nov. 4, 1904 - 1966) upon completion of her Sturgis School education went to Burlington, IA, with sister Pearl to business college. Married Ernest Pettigrew, daughter Gwen (Mrs. Ed Minard) and family live in Burlington. Charlotte later married Charles Ballou.

Martha (Nov. 20, 1906 - ____) became a registered nurse at St. Mary's Hospital in Evansville, IN. Married Ottrell Miller of Owensboro, News Editor with Evansville Press. Their daughter Elizabeth Stevens moved to Virginia recently.

DR. JACOB L. SHAVER JR.

Dr. Jacob L. Shaver Jr. and mary Jo (Hildesheim) Shaver have lived in Sturgis since 1959, the year of their marriage. Dr. Shaver is the son of J. L. and Bonnie (Shutt) Shaver of Greenville. Mary Jo is the daughter of J. M. and Catherine (Haas) Hildesheim of Louisville. Dr. Shaver establsihed a dental practice in October, 1958 in the Humphrey Building (formerly the EMBA building) and has practiced in the community since then. In 1967 he moved his office to the corner of 11th and Main Streets where it is now located. Mary Jo, a registered nurse, worked at the Strugis Community Hospital and the Union County Hospital before accepting a position in 1973 as Health Careers Instructor at the Union County Vocational Center, which later merged with the Union County High School. She is currently teaching in the school system.

The Shavers have three children, Mary Shannon, who is married to William Cleavenger; Stephen Blaise, who is married to Lindy Bruce; and Mary Samantha. While she was in high school, Smaantha was elected state president of the Kentucky National Honor Society. Shannon and Bill Cleavenger have three children, Eddie, Jake and Cris.

Back Row L-R: Samantha Shaver, Catherine Hildesheim, Stephen Shaver, Lindy Bruce Shaver, J. L. Shaver Jr., Mary Jo Shaver, William Cleavenger, and Shannon Cleavenger. Front Row: Eddie, Jake and Cris Cleavenger

Dr. Shaver graduated from the University of Louisville School of Dentistry in 1956. In 1975 he became the first dentist in Kentucky to be named a Fellow of the Academy of General Dentistry. He has served as staff anesthetist at

the Sturgis Community Hospital, Our Lady of Mercy Hospital and Union County Hospital. He was also Dental Director of the Breckinridge Job Corps Center from 1968 to 1972. From 1972 to 1979 he was a consultant to the Department of Labor for the southeastern states.

Mrs. Shaver is a graduate of the St. Anthony Hospital School of Nursing in Louisville. She received her Bachelor and Masters degree from Murray State University, and is a rank 1 teacher in Kentucky. She has been active in civic and professional organizations and served as president of the Sturgis Younger Woman's Club, and state president of the Health and Personal Service Education Organization.

The Shavers are active members of St. Francis Borgia Catholic Church. In 1971, they moved into their present residence at 918 Main Street, which is one of the oldest houses in Sturgis. It was built around the turn of the century by J. L. Frankel, the first president of the Tradewater Coal Company. It has been enlarged and restored to preserve much of the original decor. Most of the furnishings are of the period when it was built. *Submitted by J. L. Shaver Jr., D. M. D.*

JOHN FIELDEN SHIELDS

John Fielden Shields (b. 1867) was the son of Noah William Shields (b. about 1820) and Mary Jackson. It is thought that Noah married Mary (who was a cousin of Stonewall Jackson of TN) late in his life, and that he died when John was young. They were believed to have first lived in Allen County, KY, and then moved to Union County, KY. Noah's grandfather, Jack Shields was thought to have come from Scotland as a stowaway on a ship.

John Fielden was living in Union County when he married Levonie Roberts. Her parents, Mary Frances Lewis and John William Roberts, had moved to Union County from Lebanon, TN, sometime after 1876.

L-R: L. E. Shields, Virginia Bean, Kate Hudson, Margaret Banull, W. T., Bill, Joy Hogue, Dr. Jerry Shields. Front: Beaulah and F. Harris Shields

Four of Mary Frances' sisters also came to live in Union County after the Civil War. John William Roberts had served three years in the war, probably on the side of the North.

John Fielden and Levonie Roberts had several children. They included Ernest, Ollie Lee (Rideout), Fendall Harris, Alma (who died in infancy), Lottie (Gibson), Noah William and Wallace (who died in a typhoid epidemic in Union County in the 1920s).

John died in April of 1955 and is buried in the Borderly Cemetery.

Fendell Harris, or Harris as he was called, was born in the Cullen Community in 1894. John was a farmer at the time.

Harris married Beulah Etta Williams in 1915 when she was 15 years old. She was one of the four daughters of Eugene Williams (d. 1917) and Myrtle Allen (d. 1904). They were thought to have also come from Allen County, KY, to live with relatives after their mother died.

Harris and Beulah settled near the Pride Community where he was also a farmer. They were the parents of eight children. The children were Louis Edwin (married Lenore "Pat" Richters), Mary Virginia (married James W. Bean), Mamie Katherine (married George "Josh" Hudson), Margaret Helen (married Shelby Joe "Jack" Henry and Walter J. Banull), Wilburn Troy (married Virginia Gunter), William Harris (married Lilla "Sis" Pardue), Joe Evelyn (married Paul DuPont and Earl Hogue), and Jerry Allen, M.D. (married Carol Lally, M. D.).

Harris worked very hard to provide for his family from the land in the 1920s and 1930s. They did manage to survive the hard times, but with a great deal of difficulty and by doing without.

It became impossible for Beulah and Harris to maintain their relationship, though, and they divorced in the early 1940s. Beulah moved to the Detroit, MI, area and Harris resided in Bridgeport, OH. They returned to Kentucky later in their lives and are both buried at Borderly, near Pride.

Some of the children of Harris and Beulah remained around the Union County area. Edwin presently lives in Nebo, KY. Virginia lives in Henderson and Katherine lives in Newburgh, IN. W. Troy has retired to a home near the Tradewater River in Crittenden County, KY and William runs his office equipment businesses in Henderson. Joy and Margaret both live in Florida; Joy lives in Boynton Beach and Margaret lives in Arcadia. Jerry is an opthalmologist in Philadelphia. *Submitted by Jacqueline Sue Henry Terrell*

WILLIAM ALBERT SHIPLEY

William Albert Shipley son of Francis and Mary Porter Shipley and Ellen Boettger, daughter of Frederick C. and Mary Jane Erwin Boettger were united in marriage on November 24, 1992.

Al Shipley was born Feb. 2, 1868 in Dahlgren, IL. He came as a young lad to Union County, KY with his family and they settled in DeKoven.

Ellen Boettger was born in DeKoven, KY on Aug. 24, 1873. Ellen's parents were early Union County settlers. Her father, Frederick Christian Boettger was born in Hanover, Germany and came with his family to America in 1846 and to Union County, KY in 1848.

Al Shipley and Ellen Shipley

Frederick C. Boettger was a sergeant in the Twenty-Fifth Regiment of Indiana Infantry during the Civil War. He fought at Ft. Donelson, Shiloh, Hatchee, Corinth and Atlanta. Upon his return to Union County he married Mary Jane Erwin daughter of John Erwin.

Mary Jane's father had many slaves. The family lived near the banks of the Ohio River. During the civil War raiding parties from both the North and South were frequetnly in the area. The residents and slaves were often victims. Mary Jane, a young girl at the time, did her best to detect the soldiers plans. Upon hearing of an intended raid she always warned the slaves in order for them to hide themselves as well as their food. Mary Jane often endured rough treatment by the soldiers who wanted her to reveal the whereabout of the Negroes. Because of Mary Jane's bravery the slaves were spared much abuse.

Ellen Boettger Shipley, whose nickname was Nellie, often heard the colorful Civil War stories told by her parents while she was growing up.

Shortly after 1900 Al and Ellen moved to Sturgis. From 1910-1927 Al Shipley operated a groucer store on Adams Street. The store was located on the south side of the First National Bank on a site which is now part of the present Farmers State Bank.

During the Union County epidemic of 1910-1911 Al Shi;ley had the misfortune to contract the disease. He was isolated in a tent near the Tradewater River because the available pest houses at No. 2 camp outside Sturgis were already filled to overflowing by the time he came down with the disease. Evidently Al made a full recovery because he was to live nearly twenty years after his bout with small-pox.

Al and Ellen Shipley were active in community service. Al was a member of the Sturgis Methodist Episcopal Church where he served on the Official Board at the time the church was dedicated in 1913. He was also a member of several fraternal organizations. Ellen Shipley was a member of the First Baptist Church and taught a Sunday School Class there.

Mrs. Al Shipley knew the importance of an education. According to Miss Carrie Eble, local educator, Mrs. Shipley organized the first P. T. A. in Sturgis in 1915. In addition, Mrs. Shipley served on the school board of trustees from 1922-1927.

Al and Ellen Shipley had seven children: Mary Edythe born Nov. 18, 1893; Rosetta born May 22, 1896; Russell Albert born Aug. 8, 1898; Grace Laureen born Dec. 8, 1899; Charles born March 30, 1902; Freda born Aug. 17, 1904 and Samuel born April 2, 1907.

Mary Edythe Shipley married James F. Irvine, a civil engineer form Lexington. They reared one son, James F. Irvine, Jr. in Kentucky, Wyoming, Utah, Oklahoma and Tesas. Jim is a retired Commander, U. S. Navy, having spent twenty years as a naval aviator and nineteen years as an engineer in the aerospace industry. He and his wife Colette reside in LaJolla, CA. They have five children, Janet, Lucy, James III, Richard and Barry.

Rossetta Shipley was chief operator for the local Bell Telephone Company. She died usddenly of pyelonephritis in 1936. She was unmarried.

Grace Laureen Shipley married Gilbert T. Harp. They had a duaghter named Ellen. Ellen married and had a son Kenneth. Both Ellen and Kenneth are now deceased.

Russell Albert Shipley died an infant in 1898. His mother always referred to him as little Albert.

Charles Easton Shipley died tragically at age thirteen in 1915 in a hunting accident. A gun which he was holding discharged while he was climbing a fence.

Freda Shipley married John Hammack Carney. They had one son John Helms Carney. John completed his undergraduate degree at Indiana University and his M. A. in Counseling Psychology from NOVA University, Ft. Lauderdale, FL. John lives with his wife Marybeth, in Boca Raton, FL. They have two children, Sean and Leigh.

Sam Shipley married Hazel Sisk. They had one son David who lives with his wife Jane in Sturgis. They have two children, Sandra and Michael.

Al Shipley died Feb. 20, 1930. Ellen Shipley died Nov. 10, 1942. All of their children are now deceased. *Submitted by Jane Shipley*

DAVID SHIPLEY

Daivd Shipley, son of Hazel and Sam Shipley, was born Aug. 11, 1939. He was graduated from the University of Kentucky College of Pharmacy in 1961. He married Jane Moss, daughter of Cora Lillian and Henry Moss, and returned to Sturgis to work with his father at the corner Drug Store in 1961.

David is a member of the Sturgis United Methodist Church, a member and past president of the Sturgis Kiwanis Club, served eight years as a member of the Volunteer Fire Department, a member of the Chamber of Com-

171

David, Jane "Moss" Shipley with Michael and Sandra

merce and has just been elected to a fourth term on the Sturgis City Council.

Jane attended Northwestern University, Evanston, IL, the University of Kentucky and was graduated from Kentucky Wesleyan College in 1964. Jane is organist of the Sturgis United Methodist Church where she is a member. Jane has served on the Union County Planning Commission since 1985. She is past Regent of the Henry Helm Floyd Chapter of DAR.

Jane and David are the parents of two children, Sandra and Michael, and the grandparents of John and Gavin Shipley. *Submitted by David Shipley*

SAM SHIPLEY

Sam Shipley, the son of Al and Ellen Boettger Shipley was born in Sturgis on April 2, 1907. Sam's father was a local grocer.

While attending Sturgis High School Sam played halfback on the football team. During his senior year he was captain of the track team; set a 220 yard dash indoor record in Louisville; and was high point man at the state track meet. Sam was graduated in 1925.

Sam Shipley; Hazel and David Shipley

Sam worked his way through college in six years. along the way he made the UK track team and lettered in the 1928, 1929 and 1930 seasons. One of his fellow team members was "Shipwreck Kelly."

Sam Shipley's loyalty to UK remained strong throughout his life. He was a member of Delta Tau Delta Fraternity and enjoyed the bonds of friendship created there as well as on the track team. Sam was graduated in the Class of 1931 and from that time until he died

172

he was always ready to return to Lexington to attend a basketball or football game.

After graduation Sam returned to Sturgis where he began his long career at the Corner Drug Store. Sam became manager there in 1933 under the ownership of Dr. G. B. Carr. Sam Shipley's love of people made him a natural for the job of druggist.

In 1944 Sam purchased one half interest in The Corner Drug Store from Waverly Robards who had previously purchased it from Dr. Carr in 1936. Sam bought the remaining interest in the drug store in 1947 and worked there actively until his retirement in 1978.

Sam served the community of Sturgis as a member of the City Council four terms and as a member of various boards, including the Sturgis Hospital and later the Sturgis Rest Home. Sam was also a past president of the Kiwanis Club.

Because Sam's mother was a Baptist and his father a Methodist Sam was equally at home in both churches although he was a member of the Methodist Church. Sam enjoyed his many friends in each congregation.

Hazel Shipley, the daughter of Bartie and Alpha Roberts Sisk, was born on Dec. 21, 1914. Hazel and Sam were married on Sept. 29, 1935. They had one child, David Samuel Shipley.

Hazel was a member of the Sturgis Senior Homemakers and Peace Rebekah Lodge #22. The main interests of Hazel included her extended family and many friends. A short telephone call would show of her love and concern.

For many years Hazel was a member of the Sturgis Tabernacle Church. Later, whe joined the Sturgis United Methodist Church along with Sam.

Sam Shipley died Sept. 8, 1983. Hazel Shipley died April 1, 1989. *Submitted by Jane Shipley*

SHOUSE

Jeptha Shouse, born July 3, 1855, died July 12, 1924 married Ida Ella Caldwell, born June 6, 1860, died April 13, 1921, on March 28, 1883 in Henderson County. They are buried in Little Bethel Cemetery. They were parents of 7 children; four died as infants.

Gordon Lee Shouse, born Jan. 22, 1884; died Jan. 3, 1958; Walter Oliver Shouse, born March 13, 1885; died Nov. 10, 1972; Daniel Newton Shouse, born April 17, 1889; died June 16, 1961.

Walter Oliver Shouse married Mabel Nunn, born Nov. 26, 1892, died Oct. 10, 1971 on Feb. 2, 1915. Mabel was the daughter of Eli Nunn and Maria (Phillips) Nunn of Crittenden County. They were the parents of five children:

James Oliver Shouse, born Oct. 13, 1915 drowned May 20, 1968 in a pond on his farm, married Marietta Futrell born Aug. 26, 1918 on Dec. 31, 1938. She is the daughter of Lanice and Ruth Coleman (Faulkner) Futrell of Christian County. They are the parents of four children:

L-R: James, Martha (Shouse) Baird, Richard, Walter Lee, Mary Nell (Shouse) White. Seated: Mabel (Nunn) Shouse, and Walter O.

James Coleman Shouse, born March 1, 1940; Walter Bennett Shouse, born Dec. 12, 1943; Robert Stephen Shouse, born July 19, 1945; Evelyn Shouse, born Oct. 1, 1949.

Martha Ellen Shouse, born March 17, 1917 married Dec. 31, 1939, to Carl Elmer Baird, born Dec. 3, 1910, died May 1, 1985. He was the son of John C. Baird and Frances Ellen (Williamson) Baird. They are the parents of one daughter, Mary Phyllis Baird, born March 12, 1947.

Richard Nunn Shouse, born July 12, 1919, married Grace Elizabeth Waggener, born May 1, 1919, on Dec. 31 1940. She was the daughter of Jessie R. Waggener and Clara Barton (Tucker) Waggener. They have one daughter, Barbara Nunn Shouse, born Jan. 13, 1946.

Walter Lee Shouse, born Aug. 12, 1924. After serving in World War II he obtained his B. S. Degree in Government from the University of Florida in 1949. He received his Masters Degree in Urban Planning from Harvard in 1953. In 1988 he retired from teaching in the Graduate School, University of Tennessee where he had been teaching for 24 years. He has traveled extensively throughout the world.

Mary Nelle Shouse, born Feb. 24, 1935 married John (Jack) Wynn White, born Jan. 21, 1930, on May 24, 1953. He is the son of John Robert White and Mary Katherine (Arnold) White. They have four sons: Robert (Bob) Shouse White, born April 24, 1954; Richard Wynn White, born Jan. 5, 1956; Walter Reed White, born Feb. 16, 1961; and John Ryan White, born June 27, 1974. *Submitted by Martha S. Baird*

GEORGE B. SIMPSON II AND OCTA (BARBEE) SIMPSON

George B. Simpson II and Octa (Barbee) Simpson, bore eleven children: Rebecca Simpson Reagan, Fredonia Simpson, George Brown Simpson III, Barbee Simpson, Leiter Simpson, Harry Simpson, Faust Y. Simpson, Sidney Simpson, Felix Simpson, James Bartlett Simpson, and Virginia Simpson Pope; and all are pictured along with several grandchildren and in-laws. It is impossible to list all of the offspring of these eleven children because of space limitations.

The family picture of George B. Simpson II and Octa (Barbee) Simpson - 1957; Standing L-R: Felix Simpson, Robert E. Simpson, Johnny Mac Simpson, Faust Y. Simpson, George Brown Simpson III, Sidney Simpson, Rebecca Simpson Reagan, Fredonia Simpson, George B. Simpson IV, Barbee Simpson, Leiter Simpson, Virginia Simpson Pope, Bartlett (Bean) Simpson, Harry Simpson, and Dr. E. K. Reagan. Seated L-R: Sandra Slater Simpson (George B. Simpson IV's wife), Jamie Lamond Simpson (Sid Simpson's wife), Sissy Reagan and baby, Mary Mills Simpson (Faust Y. Simpson's wife), and Jane Ellen Simpson

George B. Simpson I was born in Scotland in 1832; George B. Simpson II was born in 187? and was a merchant and grocer; George B. Simpson III was born in 1901 and was a merchant and farmer; George B. Simpson IV was born in 1929 and was admitted to the Kentucky Bar in 1954; George B. Simpson V was born on Sept. 18, 1956; and George B. Simpson VI was born on July 12, 1984. The mother of George B. Simpson I, Juliana Wood Simpson (1810-1891), was a native of Scotland and died in Union County. Her husband, James Simpson, was a native of Edinburgh, Scotland. George B. Simpson I married Sarah Evans Young, the daughter of a half blood Cherokee Indian, Phillip S. Young, who immigrated form Princeton, KY in the 1840s. Her mother was Jane Hill, whose mother was a Bone. George B. Simpson II married Octa Barbee, the daughter of Reverend James T. Barbee, a native of middle Tennessee and a Cumberland Presbyterian minister. George B. Simpson III married Nina Sue Wynns, the daughter of R. E. Wynns and Ama Withers Wynns. George B. Simpson IV married Sandra Slater of Lakewood, WA. George Simpson V married Bobetta Morgan Andrews.

ROBERT E. SIMPSON

Father: Brown Simpson d. 1982, RR #1, Sturgis, KY. Mother: Nina Sue Wynns Simpson d. 1956, RR #1, Sturgis, KY. Brothers: Jonny Mac and George B. Simpson and David Ray Simpson, Sturgis.

Birth: 1931 Madisonville, moved to Pride 1934, to near Sturgis 1937. Sturgis High School Graduate - 1949. Football and Track Scholarships, Western Kentucky University 1949-1953. A. B. Degree New York Football Giants Contract. USAF Jet Fighter Pilot - 1953-1956. Kentuckian Pilot 1957-1960. Head Football Coach - Spencer County, IN 1956-1957. Head

Football and Track Coach - Fairdale High, Jefferson County 1959-1965. Jefferson County Coach of the year 1961. Master (MA) Clinical Psychology 1963 University of Louisville. PhD Psychology 1970 the University of Alabama. Professor of Psychology, Western Kentucky University 1970 - present.

Wife: Patricia Burnette Brady Simpson. Two sons: Robert Mark - Defense Mapping - Washington, D.C. (wife, Julia). John Timothy - Lead Tenor in Opera - Bremerhauen, West German Opera.

JOHN BARTIE SISK

John Bartie Sisk, son of John Bartie Sisk, Sr. and Mary Frances O'Bryan Sisk, married on Nov. 11, 1906, Alpha Omega, the daughter of David F. and Victoria T. Woodruff Roberts of Caldwell County, KY.

Bartie and Alpha moved to Sturgis soon after they married. Bartie was employed by the West Kentucky Coal Company where he worked as a locomotive engineer.

Bartie and Alpha (Roberts) Sisk

Mr. and Mrs. Sisk were members of the Tabernacle Baptist Church. Their friends remember Bartie's quiet manner and Alpha's cheerful outspoken nature.

Bartie and Alpha were the parents of two children; Ishmael Howard, born Nov. 21, 1909 and Hazel Keith born Dec. 21, 1914.

Ishmael and Hazel along with their families hosted a Fiftieth Wedding Anniversary celebration for their parents in November of 1956. Many friends and family members were in attendance.

Ishmael Sisk married Ruth Ann (Scottie) Scott on Jan. 18, 1936. Ish and Scottie had one daughter, Barbara Ann. Ann Sisk married Robert Shelton. The Sheltons have two children, Ellen and David.

Hazel married Sam Shipley, son of Al and Ellen Boettger Shipley on Sept. 29, 1935. Their son is David Samuel. David Shipley married Jane Moss, the daughter of Henry and Cora Lillian Moss. David and Jane reside in Sturgis. They have two children, Sandra Kay and Michael David.

Alpha Sisk was in declining health when her husband Bartie, died on Sept. 14, 1961. When Ishmael Sisk died on Feb. 15, 1963 Alpha appeared to lose her will to go on alone. The family watched as Alpha Sisk faded before

them. Her cheerful nature was spent and when her fragile body could no longer sustain itself Alpha Sisk died on April 14, 1963.

Ruth Ann (Scottie) Sisk died on Oct. 30, 1978. Sam Shipley died on Sept. 8, 1983. Hazel Shipley died on April 1, 1989.

ISHMAEL HOWARD SISK

Ishmael Howard Sisk, son of Bartie and Alpha Roberts Sisk, was born Nov. 21, 1909. On Jan. 18, 1936, Ishmael married Ruth Ann Scott, the daughter of Otto and Mary Ruth Elder Scott.

Ishmael Sisk had a very friendly, outgoing manner and was a respected member of the community. Many honors were bestowed upon him. Ish was selected Outstanding Citizen of the year in 1953; commissioned a Kentucky Colonel in 1955; was President of the Sturgis Kiwanis Club in 1955; and was Lieutenant Governor, Kentucky-Tennessee Division One, Kiwanis International in 1960.

Ruth Ann (Scott) Sisk, Ishmael, and daughter Barbara Ann

Many Sturgis residents remember Ishmael Sisk as the owner of the Sanitary Cleaners. Over the years he served the community as a scoutmaster for a Boy Scout Troop. Ish would have been especially proud to know that his grandson David received the rank of Eagle Scout in 1989.

Scottie was born Jan. 14, 1914 and was a graduate of Spotsville High School, Spotsville, KY. Scottie was a registered nurse having graduated from a Louisville Hospital. For many years Scottie was the night supervisor at the Sturgis Community Hospital. Later she worked at the Breckinridge Job Corps now named Earl C. Clements Job Corps Center.

Ish and Scottie have one daughter, Barbara Ann, born April 10, 1940. Ann graduated from Bethel College in Tennessee earned an M. A. in history from Middle Tennessee State University and another M. A. in Library Science from Vanderbilt University. Ann married Robert E. Shelton. Dr. Shelton pastors a Cumberland Presbyterian Church in Dallas, TX. The Sheltons have one daughter, Ellen Ann and one son, David Sisk Shelton.

Ish died Feb. 25, 1963. Scottie died Oct. 30, 1978. *Submitted by Ann Shelton*

BEN SMALL

Joseph Benjamin Small was born in 1885 in Holland, IN, son of Charles Marion Small and Sarah Schwartz Small of Dubouis County, IN. They were of Scottish and German extraction. As a young man "Ben" worked as an electrician for his father in Evansville. In 1910 he married Margaret Etta Love from DeKoven, KY. She attended Lockyears Business College. In 1918 they moved to Sturgis where Ben was employed as an electrician for West Kentucky Coal Company. He retired from "the armature" shop in 1958.

To this union were added Velma 1912, Doris 1913, Mary Ben 1921 and Warren in 1925.

Velma graduated from high school 1930 and married William "Bill" Holt in 1931 and moved to his farm outside Sturgis. He died in 1939. Their children are Margaret Anne 1932; William J. 1935; and David 1937.

Doris developed a heart condition at eight years and was in bed for five years. She later recovered and graduated from Sturgis High School. She worked at the old Bell Telephone office where she met and married Lloyd T. Clark from Tennessee who also worked for Bell Telephone. They had no children. She died in 1970. He, in 1968. They had a home in Madisonville.

Mary Ben graduated from Sturgis High School and worked for Bell Telephone Company as an operator during war years. She married Harold Sutherland of Webster Company. He attended University of Kentucky and Evansville College. He worked for Alloway Lumber Company until they moved to Owensboro where he was estimator of construction and building at Hartz-Kirkpatrick Company. They have one son Warren, who graduated from Weyland College in Owensboro. He married Betty Jo Johnson of Owensboro. She graduated from Western.

Tragedy struck the Ben Small family in 1927 when their only son Warren, 3 1/2 years, was hit and killed by a car on Adams Street in Sturgis.

Mr. Ben was a Mason, a man of good character, a deacon for many years at First Baptist Church, a good father. They built a home on Johnson Street and resided there until 1962 when Ben passed away. Margaret died in 1974.

SMITH-HENRY

My grandfather, Jesse Harvey Smith born June 9, 1847, and died April 23, 1916, was married to Maria Ferree Dalton on Sept. 13, 1871. She was born Sept. 29, 1853, and died Aug. 5, 1911. To this union was born my father, Hiram Horace Smith, on April 5, 1877, in the Bordley area. He died Aug. 3, 1939. My mother's great grandfather, Alexander McCune Henry, born March 16, 1793, in Virginia. His wife, Ann, born in Virginia in 1795.

Both died in Caseyville. Their eldest son, William Alexander McCune Henry, married Mary Sitler. Their eldest son, Joseph Dixon Henry, married Susan Moore. To this union there were eleven children. My mother was one of them. Rose Edna Henry born March 13, 1878; she died March 9, 1943. She was born on a farm just north of Sturgis, on what is now Highway 60 and 641. She and Hiram Horace Smith were married June 1, 1897. Horace and Rose came to Sturgis in its very early days.

My father worked for West Kentucky Coal Company and became their commissary manager over several stores. He was there when the union tried to organize the company in the early 1920's. He was President of Tradewater Milling Company, and a farmer along with other business interests. They had three sons; Harvey Latta Smith married Christine Sparks, no children; Mason Venner Smith married Nancy Gene Cottingham, four children Roseanne Smith O'Daniel, Indianapolis, IN, Eugene Cottingham Smith, Louisville, KY, Elizabeth Downard Smith Land, Virginia Beach, VA, and Anna Catherine Smith Howard, Louisville, KY. Horace Henry Smith married Lois Ruth Holeman. She was born Feb. 6, 1919, and died Feb. 21, 1989. Four children Michel Henry Smith, Evansville, IN; Steven Venner Smith, deceased; David Byron Smith, San Clemente, CA; and Nancy Ruth Smith Flittner, Milburn, NJ.

God must love Sturgis! He put his very finest people there with fertile land, an abundance of water and good climate. When I grew up there in the 1920s and '30s, girls were the prettiest you could find anywhere. Morganfield boys thought they were too. Saturday nights downtown on Adams Street - how could anyone forget? American Legion 4th of July picnic - best barbeque in the world - spectacular fireworks - band, games, fellowship, everyone turned out for it.

Mrs. Fred Alloway was one of my Sunday School teachers. Oh, how she tried! Some of the school teachers that I remember so well, trying to build and improve Sturgis, were Mrs. Lillie Winston, Fred Schultz, Lillie Pearl Kuykendall, Lena Jo Calvert and Denver DeHaven to mention a few that tried to teach me. How could anyone be more dedicated? There are many others. These are just a few I knew so well. There could be a few others that knew me too well. Mr. Rehm thought the way to reach my brain was by pounding on the seat of my pants.

The American Indians must have loved the area too. Indian relics were one of my hobbies when I was young. I have picked up hundreds of flint arrowheads and Indian artifacts around the area and still have most of the collection.

Good attracts good, and fine people of Sturgis keep it that way. I am proud to be from Sturgis, KY. *Submitted by Horace Henry (June) Smith*

ARNOLD DAVIS SPRAGUE JR.

Arnold Davis Sprague Jr., son of A. D. and Clella Seaton Sprague, married Ama Katherine Wesley, daughter of Charles and Roberta Wynn Wesley, in 1938.

A. D. attended his first year of school at Mount Pleasant, then went to the Sturgis City Schools where he graduated from Sturgis High School. Kas attended the one room school at Templeton and then attended Sturgis High School where she graduated and met A. D.

A. D. and Kas Sprague

After marriage, Kas and A. D. first lived in the Sprague home place on Highway 602 across from the Sturgis Airport until their home burned. They then returned to the home place, to the house which A. D. Sr. had built, where A. D. Jr. was born and where he lived until his death in July of 1980.

They were the parents of four children, three sons and a daughter. William Robert (Billy Bob), the oldest, is married to Julia Nobles of Providence. They live in the Pond Fork Community, and have two children, George Andrew and Shelly Ann. Andy, a graduate of the University of Kentucky with a degree in engineering, is married to Tina Parsons of Lexington. They currently reside in Lexington, KY. Daughter, Shelly Ann, a Business and Finance graduate of the University of Kentucky, is now working in Washington, D. C. pending a career in law.

Joseph Wesley Sprague is married to Brenda Woodring and Stacy Jo, the oldest, is a graduate of U. K. and received her Masters Degree in Home Care from U. A. B. in Brimingham, AL. She is married to Dr. Hugh Sims M. D. and lives in Gainsville, FL. Trisha Ann is a Senior at Western University in Bowling Green.

Arnold Davis Sprague III, is married to Barbara Quirey and they live in Henderson where A. D. III is a physician and surgeon in Obstertrics and Gynecology. They have two children; A. D. IV. a Junior at U. K. majoring in Agriculture, and Sarah Elizabeth, a Senior in Henderson County High.

Clella Suzanne Sprague, the only daughter of A. D. and Kas, married Joe Woodring who was a partner with his father in the Woodring Furniture Company of downtown Sturgis until the store was sold in 1980. Joe is now engaged in farming. They have three children; Thomas Casey, a Senior at Union County High, Ashley Katherine, a Freshman at Union Co. High, and Lesley Jo, who is in the sixth grade at the Union Co. Middle School.

All four children of A. D. and Kas Sprague, and their families, are active members of the Christian Church of their community. The four children and their spouses are all college graduates and are all engaged in farming on land that has been in the family for five generations, carrying on the tradition of their ancestors. All of the families are involved in community affairs both at home and on the state level.

J. C. STANLEY

Mr. and Mrs. J. Crit Stanley were married Jan. 18, 1909 by a Justice of the Peace in the old Green Tree Hotel in Mt. Vernon, IN. Mrs. Addie Stanley was the daughter of the late Newton and Rebecca Arnold of Arnold Station and granddaughter fo Sam Holeman. Mr. Crit Stanley was the son of James W. Stanley and Margaret Jenkins of Boxville, KY and grandson of Michael Stanley of Wales, England. Mr. Crit Stanley was a rural mail carrier for 41 years in Sturgis, KY. He began his duties in 1915 and traveled 500,000 miles without an accident when all roads were dirt except two blocks of rock road in towns from I. C. Depot to the First Christian Church.

Mr. Stanley wore out two buggies twelve horses and seventeen automobiles. To this union were born five children. A. O. Stanley, Lorraine Stanley McGovern, Lois Stanley Cobb, Louise Stanley Simpson, and Jimmy Stanley. Thirteen grandchildren and 20 great grandchildren.

James Crit Stanley; Louise Stanley Simpson Family

Louise Stanley Simpson was married to Bartlett Simpson (see G. B. Simpson) on her parents 31st anniversary at the First Christian Church in Sturgis, KY, 1940. Bartlett Simpson entered the Armed Forces March 2, 1945. He served in the Cavalry Division at Fort Riley, KS and on to the South Pacific. Many a time the Japanese enemy was found in their chow line eating.

To this union four children were born; Tonja Simpson Hunter, J. B. Simpson, Jr., Virginia Addette Simpson, and Stanley Keith Simpson. Three grandchildren, three step-grandchildren, and three great grandchildren.

STEELMAN

The Steelman family moved to Southern Indiana near Hazelton from Springfield, OH in the 1870s. They purchased land to farm and built a house, a school and a Methodist Church on this property. The church was named Steelman Chapel and is still used as the meeting place for an inter-denominational congregation. Frank L. Steelman was one of the first generation that was born after the move to Indiana. He entered the Banking profession at an early age and worked in banks at Hazelton and New Harmony, IN and served as an Internal Revenue Agent in Evansville. In 1935 Frank and Edna Steelman and their daughter Betty, moved to Sturgis where he was employed at the Farmers State Bank. Mr. and Mrs. Frank Steelman were active in the Methodist Church and he and a group of interested men revitalized the Masonic Lodge in Sturgis after years of little activity. Betty was killed in a tragic auto accident during her junior year of high school.

In 1946, his son F. Leslie (Bing) Steelman and his wife Edith Grabert Steelman and their children, John, Gloria and Nancy moved to Sturgis. Bing was employed at the Farmers State Bank and later became President of that institution after the retirement of his father.

Front row; John, Edith and Patrick Zane Steelman. Second row; Patsy, Diane and Wesley Zolton Steelman. Third row; Paul and Susan Steelman

Bing Steelman was active in community development. He was a member of the Sturgis Industrial Foundation which was instrumental in the locating of the Richman Bros. factory in Sturgis. He was the Treasurer of the Union County Fair Board which was responsible for starting the Union County Fair. Bing was an avid sportsman and was a member of many sportsman associations such as the Tradewater Fish and Game Club and the Cat Alley Coon Club. He remained active in Banking and community affairs until his death.

Members of the Bing Steelman family still in this area are his wife, Edith Steelman and son, John Steelman of Sturgis and daughters, Gloria Morgan and Nancy McCulloh of Morganfield, ten grandchildren and 16 great grandchildren.

Edith Steelman is active in the Sturgis United Methodist Church and was recently inducted into the Mt. Vernon, IN High School

Sports Hall of Fame. She played on the Mt. Vernon High School Girls basketball team of 1925 which was undefeated and State Champion.

John Steelman married Patsy Barnard, daughter of Wallace and Lillian Barnard in 1950. They have two children, Paul and Susan. Paul is married to the former Diane Tinsley of Marion, KY. They have two boys, Wesley and Patrick. Paul is a Coal Miner and Diane teaches at Union County High School. Susan in a Coal Miner and self-employed.

John and Patsy have lived in the same house in Sturgis for 35 years. They are both active in their respective churches and in community improvement. John was named Citizen of The Year by the Sturgis Junior Chamber of Commerce several years ago for his efforts in the construction and lighting of the Little League field. Patsy was named Citizen of The Year in 1988 by the Sturgis Kiwanis for her efforts to improve the appearance of Sturgis by planting flowers and encouraging clean-up campaigns.

STEVENSON

The Stevenson family came to Sturgis from Christian County, KY. They migrated to Christian Co from Iredell County, NC, and were of Scottish descent, farmers, and Presbyterians. Two brothers settling in Christian Co. were James Turner Stevenson and Will Stevenson. James was the father of Adlai Stevenson (Vice President of U.S.) and Adlai E. (Governor of Illinois and UN Ambassador). Will became the great grandfather of Fred Ellis Stevenson.

Fred Ellis Stevenson was born Jan. 3, 1912, and died June 26, 1981, and was the youngest son of William Hugh Stevenson and Martha Susan (Burba) Stevenson. William Hugh was born Oct. 18, 1861, near Hopkinsville and died in 1947 one of the oldest residents of Sturgis at that time. Martha Susan Stevenson was born in 1876 near Hopkinsville and died in 1959. Her parents died when she was young and she was partially raised by relatives. She and William Hugh married Feb. 13, 1896. William H. was engaged in farming for a number of years, then he associated with the Stone Hardware in Sturgis as a tinsmith and a painter. They became parents of eight children:

Fred E. and Dorothy K. Stevenson

Marguerite S. McConnell b. 12/31/1896 d. 1981 married Clyde McConnell, resided in

175

Akron, OH and had three sons and three daughters.

Ruth S. Griffin b. 8/29/1904 married Ted Griffin is now living in Arkansas and has no children.

William Hugh Stevenson b. 2/3/1902 married Elizabeth (Libba) Bardwell O'Shea and they have one daughter Gene Griffith, and resides in Ashland, KS.

James Burba Stevenson b. 1899, d. Aug. 7, 1983, married Sadie Yontz lived in Kansas City, MO and had no children.

Dorothy S. Handle of Lancaster, KY, b. 3/23/1910 married Carl Handel and had two children George (Butch) Handel and Susan Handel Shank.

Laura S. Gaines Boner of Lancaster, Ky, b. 1/6/1907 married Claude Rice Gaines and had two children Edward Rice Gaines (deceased) and Bettye Claire Gaines Weiderhold (deceased).

Fred Ellis Stevenson b. Jan. 3, 1912, d. June 26, 1981, married Dorothy Kern and had three children Sandy S. Arnold, Martha Jane Young, and James Frederick Stevenson.

Grace Stevenson Read b. 4/27/1914 married Davis Read and resides in Arlington Heights, IL, and had four children John, Jim, Jennifer and Martha Ann.

Fred and Dorothy Stevenson remained in Sturgis and reared their three children. Fred attended the University of Kentucky and worked in the old West Kentucky Store and at Poplar Ridge Coal Mines prior to becoming Cashier at the Farmers State Bank where he worked for the next 18 years. He was a city councilman, a past president of Kiwanis, and he and Dot were active Presbyterians.

Dorothy Kern Stevenson was a graduate of Christian College for Women, Columbia, MO. She taught school in Union County for 33 years, mostly in the sixth grade, and will probably be best remembered for her culinary skills and school history tours.

Their oldest child Nancy Sandra, married Dr. John Arnold, Chiropractor in Sturgis, where they reside with their two children, Alisa Beth a senior at the University of Kentucky and John-John who will be a senior at Union County High. Also residing in Sturgis is their second daughter, Martha Jane a secretary at the Farmers State Bank. Her daughter Andrea Stevenson Biddle is a graduate of the University of Kentucky with a degree in Journalism.

Fred and Dot's son James Frederick (Freddy) is a Vietnam veteran and is employed as an A & P (airplane) mechanic in Illinois.

Fred and Dorothy both died in 1981 five months apart and are buried at Pythian Ridge Cemetery. *Submitted by Sandy S. Arnold, Jane S. Young*

WILLIAM HUGH STEVENSON

In late 1928 William Hugh Stevenson left Sturgis, KY and came to Ashland, KS to work

176

for the Stockgrowers State Bank, which was then the Stockgrowers National Bank. He had graduated from Centre College, Danville, KY where he was a member of Sigma Alpha Epsilon Fraternity, and had worked for about a year for the Bank of Sturgis with his good friend Mr. Charles Ellis. He didn't really intend to stay in Kansas but a few years, but his love of this community and its people prompted him to remain here permanently. He retired from banking (as Vice-President) in March 1974 but continued to serve as a director of the bank and the Home lumber and Supply Co., as well as trustee of several estates until his health no longer permitted.

Hugh was born in Sturgis, Feb. 3, 1902. His parents were William Hugh and Martha Burba Stevenson. He was the third of eight children.

Gene, Steve and Libba Stevenson

In about 1938 Elizabeth Bardwell O'Shea (known to her friends as "Libba") came to Ashland to visit a college friend. She was a Mississippi girl with a southern "drawl" and an eight year old daughter. After a few years of letter-writing and occasional visits Hugh and Libba were married, Oct. 17, 1945. Hugh legally adopted her daughter giving her the Stevenson name also.

Libba was born Sept. 23, 1914 in Charleston, MS. Her parents were Dr. David Guyon and Morris Neely Bardwell. Their daughter Gene is now Gene Griffith and lives in California where her three sons also reside.

The Stevensons remain active in the Presbyterian Church where Hugh has served as Elder and was Treasurer for many years. He is a Mason, served on the City Council and other community projects. Libba attended Lindenwood College, St. Charles, MO one year and was graduated from the University of Tennessee where she was a member of Tri Delta Sorority. She is a member of P. E. O. and Ashland Study Club, served on the Library board and numerous church, school and community activities and was once active in D. A. R. *Submitted by Elizabeth B. Stevenson*

VIRGIL STEWART

Virgil Stewart (1910-1941) married Addonis (Dona) Neible (1908) in 1929. Virgil's parents were Thomas H. (1888-1973) and Nora Belle Barnaby Stewart (1890-1976). Thomas H. was born in Equality, IL, the son of Frank (1864-

1935) and Harriet Baldwin Stewart (1868-1944) and Nora Belle Stewart was born in Crittenden County, KY. Virgil's great, great grandfather, Elisa Stewart was from Scotland. Frank and Harriet settled in the Commercial Point area in the late 1890s.

Dona was the daughter of John (1858-1926) and Margaret Spitzner Neible (1870-1958). John was the son of Shrylas Neible (1831-1879) and Transylvania Hoyt Neible (1831-1914). Shrylas Neible came from Hesse Castle, Germany as a young boy and settled in Crittenden County, KY about 1860, later moving to Illinois. John Neible's family settled in the Sturgis (Grangertown) area in early 1890s. Margaret Spitzner was the daughter of Fred Spitzner who came from the Netherlands as a small child.

Donna, Tommie, Jackie and Virgil Stewart c 1940

Virgil and Dona had two children, Jacqueline (Jackie) (1929) and Thomas W. (1938) both were born in Grangertown.

Jackie married Willie Davis Edens the son of Dennis and Ella Edens of Pride and they have one son, Michael Stuart (1947). Michael married Deborah Paris the daughter of Freeman and Jackie Paris. Michael and Deborah have one daughter, Kacie Leigh (1975).

Tommie married Brenda Murphey of Henderson, KY. Brenda is the daughter of Hazeal Edds Murphey. Tommie and Brenda have three children, Wallace W. (Walley) (1962) Elise M. Stewart Starkey (1964) and Addonis F. (1969). Walley married Jill Bumpus form Dixon, KY and they have two children, Ashley A. (1985) and Brent W. (1988). Elise married A. David Starkey of Sturgis and they have one daughter LaDarra (1988). We think the original spelling of the name was STUART. *Submitted by Jacqueline (Jackie) Stewart Edens*

MINA LOUISE MACKEY TERRY

My name is Mina Mackey, my mother's name is Louise, and daddy's name is Joe. I am six years old. I have been to see Grandma Mackey who lives on a farm near the Tradewater River. I get to do a lot of fun things at grandma's house, like pick beans, feed the chickens, slop the hogs, and today we are going to town in the wagon pulled by two old mules, Jon and Don. I got to ride in the back of the wagon down the dusty yellow road, dragging my feet as we clip-clopped along, stopping ever now and then to deliver milk to neighbors.

I am ten years old now, and we live in a big grey house on King Street. Perl Daily lives next door and has lots of kids to play with. Every day I walk down the railroad tracks to school. On the way home I stop at Thomas Woodring Feed and Furniture Store. Dock gives me two or three baby chicks every day. I have 100 now. I have to sweep up loose corn at the feed mill on Main Street to feed them. Today Daddy had to kill them to put in the deep freeze, I cried.

The Terry Family

I work at Springers Grocery Store at lunch hour during school. When school is out I work as a waitress at the Main Street Cafe, and the Greyhound Bus Station. I am thirteen years old now. With my first three pay checks I bought a green dress from the Sturgis Specialty Shop.

I am sixteen now, and in two weeks will marry Milton Terry. We will be wed at the Baptist Church in Uniontown, all the family will be there: my sister Sheena, Theresa, and brother Eugene, Momma and Daddy, and lots of aunts, uncles and cousins. Milton and I have had thirty-one wonderful years together and three beautiful children, Patrice, Sandy, and Mike. Mike was killed in a tragic fire at our home in Uniontown, along with my sister Sheena's two children Keith and Tabbitha. Sandy was severely burned and spent much of her life in and out of the Shriners Burn Institute for treatment. This time in my life was the worst, but I am happy to say that Sandy has given me one beautiful grandchild Brandy, and Patrice has given me two, Heather and David, and I thank God for them all. *Submitted by Mina Louise (Mackey) Terry*

BRYANT LEE THORNSBERRY

Bryant Lee Thornsberry, son of John and Virginia Ragsdale Thornsberry, born Oct. 26, 1885, died Aug. 2, 1938, married Sept. 1907 Mila Niece Calwell, born Aug. 7, 1891, died July 10, 1979. They had three children, Albert Leslie, Willis Lee and Martha Lois. He was a mine foreman at DeKoven, KY where they lived until the mine closed. They moved to Sturgis in 1924 and had a grocery store.

Albert went to Lockyears College, Evansville, IN. Worked in grocery store, Farmers State Bank, Electrician at Servel dur-

ing WWII, after war went into Insurance Agency with James L. Long Sr. After James died had Thornsberry Insurance Agency, retired, and sold Agency to brother Willis and his son Gary.

Albert and Virginia Thornsberry

Albert helped get Union County Fair started, was Administrator of Sturgis Hospital for awhile, and helped get it changed into Sturgis Community Rest Home, on Board there and First Christian Church. Received Disabled American Veterans Citation for Distinguished Service in 1954 to Disabled Veterans.

Albert married Virginia O'Nan Aug. 28, 1929 and they had one son, William Thomas O. D. M.D. He died July 19, 1977 with heart attack. S*ubmitted by Virginia Thornsberry*

WILLIS THORNSBERRY

Willis Thornsberry, the son of Bryant and Mila Thornsberry, was born on Oct. 8, 1914. Willis attended Bowling Green Business College and received an A. A. degree in accounting. After receiving his degree he worked as an accountant for about five years before returning to Sturgis. For many years he operated Thornsberry's Grocery (now South "N" Foods) and more recently Thornsberry's Insurance Agency. On Nov. 10, 1934, Willis married Jane Hall. Jane Hall is the daughter of Benjamin Franklin Hall and Lilla (Bishop) Hall. They have two sons: Willis Junior and Gary Thornsberry. Willis Junior is a research chemist for Freeport-McMoRan Inc., New Orleans, LA and Gary is a partner with Willis Senior in the Thornsberry Insurance Agency, Sturgis, KY. Willis Junior is married to Mary Gaswint, originally from Hinton, IA and they have two children, Brian and Michele. Gary is married to Jennifer Cornwell and they have two children, Derek and Lindsey.

The Thornsberry name has been in the Sturgis area since about 1924. Bryant and Mila Thornsberry moved to the DeKoven area where he worked for the Madison Coal Company until he opened Thornsberry's Grocery which he operated until his death in 1938. He was originally from the Guilford County area of North Carolina. Mila (Caldwell) Thornsberry's family came from Tennessee. Benjamin Hall operated a tailor and cleaning

shop in Sturgis during the late 1920s and 1930s and was state deputy banking commissioner.

MANSEL DAVIS THRELKELD

Mansel Davis Threlkeld was the son of Rev. Claud Threlkeld, a Baptist preacher and fruit grower, and Luna McClendon. He was born on May 14, 1913. Mansel graduated from Wheatcroft High School in 1931 and worked in his family's orchard and nursery until his marriage. After his marriage he worked in the coal mines, as a butcher in a company store for West Kentucky Coal Company, and worked for ten (10) years in the Sturgis Post Office. In 1948 he formed a partnership in association with his brother, J. H. Threlkeld, a nurseryman and owner of Clay Nursery. Mansel started Threlkeld's nursery in 1950, which he conducted successfully until his death in 1981. It was located on Highway 60, one mile north of Sturgis.

Lucy Brown Threlkeld was born on Dec. 17, 1919, in Wheatcroft, KY. She was one of eight children born to Walter Edward Brown and Margaret Drennan. She attended Wheatcroft High School until her marriage on Oct. 10, 1936. She an Mansel moved to Sturgis in 1938 and lived there the rest of their lives.

Mansel and Lucy were the parents of one son, Claude Edward. Claude has been Superintendent of Landscaping at Western Kentucky University since 1964. He and his wife Mildred (Miles) have one daughter, Laura.

The early ancestors of nearly all the Threlkelds in the United States came from Virginia and in 1792 came to Kentucky and settled in Mason County. Many different branches of the Threlkeld family spell the name differently, such as Threlkel, Thirkeld, and Thrailkill, but most of these are known to be the same family. *Submitted by Claude Threlkeld*

J. ROBERT TRUITT

J. Robert Truitt, son of Chester and Lora Truitt of Crittenden County, married Amy Elizabeth Davis, daughter of Roy B. Davis, Sr. and Glenna Hawes Davis of Sturgis, KY, on July 20, 1940. Bob and Amy are the parents of two children and four grandchildren.

Their daughter, Betty Sue Truitt, married Earl Brinkmann of Hermann, MO on July 30,

1966. Earl is the owner/operator of Sturgis Motor Parts Store in Sturgis. Betty Sue is the secretary at Sturgis Elementary School. Earl and Betty Sue are the parents of two children. Jennifer Lee Brinkmann is a student at W. K. U. and Daniel Davis Brinkmann is a student at Union County High School.

Robert and Amy Truitt

Their son, Robert Davis Truitt, married Judi Crabtree of Nashville, TN on Aug. 3, 1968. Robert and Judi are the parents of two children. Amy Elizabeth (Beth) Truitt and Bradley Davis Truitt. Both are students in Louisville Schools. Robert is pastor of the First Cumberland Presbyterian Church in Louisville, KY and Judi teaches at the University of Louisville. *Submitted by Amy Truitt*

VANCLEAVE-SYERS

Joseph Joel VanCleave was born Oct. 1, 1889 on a farm between Sturgis and Henshaw called Francis Hill. He was one of seven children born to William K. and Emma Dobbins VanCleave. He was orphaned by age 10 and was reared by various families around the Morganfield, Henshaw, Sturgis and DeKoven farm communities, where room and board were exchanged for manual labor on the farms. The first of these families was the Bascom Crowe family.

Joe, as he was known by many, married Mary Edna Syers on June 2, 1913. She was the only daughter of John and Rosina Wisenfelter Syers of DeKoven. The Syers family were of German descent.

They set up housekeeping in DeKoven and Joe worked in the coal mines, farmed and at any type of odd job to eke out a living. Joe was employed at the shipyards in Evansville, IN during the WWII and later was a janitor at the Sturgis High School, as well as for the First Baptist Church of DeKoven.

Mary Edna, for a short time, taught school but also served as bookkeeper for her father's businesses, a general store and coal mines both located in DeKoven.

Their union was blessed with one child, daughter Mary Kathryn Rosina VanCleave, b. March 10, 1919 in DeKoven (see Felts-VanCleave).

Mary Edna passed from this life on March 29, 1964 and Joe lived to the age of 96 years, passing Nov. 15, 1985. Both are interred in the

Pythian Ridge Cemetery, Sturgis. Joe spend his last few years at the Sturgis Rest Home where he shared his wisdom and inspiration with young and old alike. *Submitted by Joel Felts-Williams*

CECIL E. "PETE" VANCLEAVE

Cecil E. "Pete" VanCleave, son of John Albert and Addie Jane "Jennie" Collins VanCleave was born Sept. 9, 1920 near Sturgis. Pete worked as farmer, store clerk, and Superintendent of Gas Works for the City of Sturgis.

Jane Pugh VanCleave was born in Clear Springs, Graves County, KY, Oct. 30, 1921. Her parents were Terry A. Pugh and Gertie Lee Barnes Pugh. Jane graduated from Smith Mills High School in 1940. She was a legal secretary in Sturgis for 15 years.

Standing: Mary Jane, Johnny, and Wanda. Seated: Pete and Jane VanCleave

They are the parents of two daughters: Wanda who married James E. Owen, and Mary Jane who married Freeman L. Evans; one son John Terry (named for both his grandfathers) who married Paula Wingo of Providence, KY.

Pete's great grandfather Alfred B., was born 1829-30 and was living in Union County in the 1860's where he enlisted and served in the Civil War, Company E, 37th Ky. Volunteers. He was injured and crippled in 1863 and applied for a pension April 8, 1880. His son, William K. was the father of John Albert, father of Cecil E. "Pete."

Alfred B. was the 6th generation of VanCleaves. Jan/John VanCleef, the progenitor of the VanCleef family in America was born 1628, his ancestors being from the Rhemish Duchy of Cleve adjacent to the Netherlands. He was married to Engeltje Laurens and emigrated to America in 1653.

The second generation in line with Union Counties was Isabrant, born in 1677 in Kings County, NY. He was married to Jannetje Vander Bilt. (Margaret VanCleef Reeder, granddaughter of Isabrandt, had a daughter Catherine who married Dan Wright, Jr., ancestor of Orville and Wilbur Wright, of Dayton, OH the first to fly aeroplanes.)

With the third generation Aaron, born 1704 on Staten Island, NY, the surname VanCleef became VanCleave/Vancleve. In 1764 he and his wife, Rachael Schenck, bought a farm from

Daniel Boone and Rebecca, his wife who were moving to Kentucky. Aaron participated in the Mecklenburg Convention and its declaration of May 20, 1775, considered by some to have been the first declaration of independence in this country. (Jane VanCleave, only daughter and youngest child of Aaron Sr. and Rachael, married Squire Boone, Jr., younger brother of Daniel Boone. He erected Squire Boone's Station, where Shelbyville now stands and was elected first representative from Kentucky in the Virginia legislature.)

Fourth generation Aaron, Jr., fourth son of Aaron Sr. and Rachael, was born 1745 near New Brunswick, NJ. He was married to Rachel Brent. Aaron, Jr. served in the Revolution under General George Rogers Clark. He was also a pioneer of Kentucky. In 1787 he went west to hunt buffalo but was shot by Indians and lost a finger and part of his gun.

Fifth generation, Cary Allen, born Aug. 23, 1802, married Pauline Jane Ball. He was a wealthy farmer. *Submitted by Jane VanCleave*

BETTY JEAN VINEYARD

Betty Jean Vineyard born Sept. 18, 1934, married May 8, 1954 to Darrell Wayne Owen, born April 25, 1932. Wayne is a construction worker and a carpenter. Betty is manager for Pantry at Grangertown, KY. Children: Amanda Kay Owen born March 29, 1955; Terry Wayne Owen born April 1, 1956; Melinda Fay Owen born Dec. 30, 1957; Marla Ann Owen born July 5, 1962; Darrell Ray Owen born June 1, 1971.

Amanda Kay Owen, born March 29, 1955, married June 1, 1973 to William David Timmons, born Sept. 12, 1952, and divorced June 2, 1980. Children: Billy David Timmons III, born Jan.13, 1974. Amanda is a nurse.

Terry Wayne Owen, born April 1, 1956, married May 7, 1978 to Valerie Lou Bryant, born April 26, 1961, and divorced Dec. 22, 1981. Children: Millonda Joanna Owen born June 18, 1979. Terry Wayne Owen remarried April 4, 1989 to Ida Mae Gordon Hutchinson born July 15, 1953. Children: Patricia Jean Gordon, born Aug. 18, 1972 (Patricia is Ida's daughter). Terry is a carpenter and farmer. Ida is a nurse.

Melinda Fay Owen, born Dec. 30, 1957, married April 17, 1976 to Robert Hughes Whitfield born Feb. 24, 1952 and divorced June 16, 1986. Children: Natosha LaMae Whitfield, born Jan. 17, 1977, Stephanie Jean Whitfield, born April 13, 1980.

Melinda Fay Owen remarried June 1, 1987 to Kenneth Allan McKinney, born Nov. 23, 1965.

Marla Ann Owen, born July 5, 1962, married to Jim Dave Belt, born Oct. 22, 1951. Children: Stephanie Shawn Belt "Shawnee" born March 6, 1971, Christina Ann Belt "Christy" born April 20, 1973, Steven Daniel Belt "Steve" born July 30, 1975, and Owen Zeth Belt "Zeth" born May 5, 1986. Shawnee, Christy and Steve are

Jim's children from previous marriage. Jim is a mechanic at Providence I Island Creek Coal Mines.

DOROTHY LOUISE VINEYARD

Dorothy Louise Vineyard "Dot" born Sept. 21, 1939 married June 22, 1957 to John Ernest Owen born Sept. 8, 1937. Children: William Ernest Owen "Ernie" born June 3, 1959; Jerry Wynn Owen born March 26, 1961; and Jason Manuel Owen born February 23, 1975.

John is a towboat captain and makes hammocks and fishing nets. Dot works at Pantry.

William Ernest Owen "Ernie" born June 3, 1959 married Feb. 14, 1981 to Elizabeth Ann Brown "Liz" born June 25, 1962. Children: William Blaine Owen born April 6, 1983 and John Oliver Owen born Aug. 21, 1986. Ernie works at Western Rubber Company, Morganfield, KY. Liz is assistant manager for Pantry at Grangertown.

Jerry Wynn Owen born March 26, 1961 married Dec. 26, 1978 to Kathryn Maria Householder born March 2, 1961 and divorced September 9, 1980. Children: Jerrod Wynn Owen born Aug. 3, 1979. Jerry is a laid-off coal miner. He is a backhoe operator.

GEORGE DELBERT VINEYARD

George Delbert Vineyard "Dale" born Dec. 17, 1944 married June 5, 1965 to Marie Ann Frad born Aug. 14, 1946. Children: Pamela Marie Vineyard born Sept. 10, 1968 and Christine Louise Vineyard born March 25, 1971. Dale is an auto mechanic at Dixon's, Morganfield, KY. Marie works at Sturgis Clothing Co., Sturgis.

Pamela Marie Vineyard born Sept. 10, 1968 married April 11, 1989 to James Allen Lynn born March 24, 1968. Children: Kyla Dale Vineyard born June 22, 1985. Kyla is Pam's daughter. James is a front-end alignment adjuster at Dixon's, Morganfield. Pam is a bookkeeper at C & C Ford, Sturgis.

Christine Louise Vineyard born March 25, 1971 married June 3, 1989 to Nathan Shane Russell born Sept. 22, 1969. Nathan is in the Navy.

MANUAL VINEYARD

Manual Vineyard born June 14, 1912 Broomtown, AL married Sept. 18, 1933 to Vera Mae George born February 19, 1912, Lindale, GA.

They lived in and about Rome, GA. They both worked in cotton mills, also picked cotton. Their three older children were born in Georgia, the two younger were born in Harlan County, KY.

They followed the coal fields first to Harlan County, KY and lived in several coal mining towns. They came to Union County in 1953 and lived in Crittenden County, Caseyville, Sturgis, and settled in Sullivan, KY.

Front: Betty and Dot; Center: Vera and Manuel; Back: Clayton, Shirley and Dale

Vera retired from working. Manuel worked underground for 38 years in the coal mines. He loved to work on cars and worked at Texaco Filling Station a number of years. The station was sold to Marathon. He and his sons Clayton and Dale ran the Marathon Filling Station for a while. He is a retired coal miner and has a bad case of the Black Lung. On Monday morning April 24, 1989 he had surgery to remove a bleeding ulcer and part of his stomach. On Monday night, April 24, 1989 he suffered a massive stroke which left him speechless and bedfast. If he knows anyone, we are not sure.

They celebrated their 50th Wedding Anniversary Sept. 18, 1983 at their son Dale's home. They have 5 children: Betty Owen, Dot Owen, Clayton Vineyard, Dale Vineyard and Shirley Coker. They have 14 grandchildren: Amanda Timmons, Terry Owen, Melinda McKinney, Marla Belt, Darrell Owen, Ernie Owen, Jerry Owen, Jason Owen, Danny Vineyard, Pam Lynn, Crissy Russell, Shelia Pollard, Joey Pollard, Deana Coker; 12 great grandchildren: Billy David Timmons, Millonda Owen, Natosha Whitfield, Stephannie Whitfield, Zeth Belt, Shawnee Belt, Christy Belt, Steve Belt, Jerrod Owen, Blaine Owen, John Oliver Owen and Kyla Vineyard.

MANUEL CLAYTON DAVID VINEYARD

Manuel Clayton David Vineyard born July 17, 1942 married November 6, 1965 to Mary Ethel Rudolph born Dec. 31, 1939. Children: No natural children. Adopted: Daniel Clayton Vineyard born Sept. 15, 1969. Clayton is a deputy jailer at Union County Jail, Morganfield, KY.

SHIRLEY ANN VINEYARD

Shirley Ann Vineyard born Feb. 23, 1949 married April 27, 1968 to Sammy Joe Pollard born July 5, 1951. Divorced Aug. 28, 1980. Children: Shelia Jo Pollard born Sept. 1, 1969 and Sammy Joe Pollard born Sept. 11, 1971.

Shirley Ann Vineyard born Feb. 23, 1949 remarried Oct. 11, 1980 to Donald Ray Coker "Cottie" born March 12, 1946. Children: Deana Rae Coker born Nov. 13, 1972. Deana is Cottie's daughter form previous marriage.

Cottie is a Maintenance Foreman at Peabody and Shirley works for Ratley Oil Co.

WAGGENER

Jesse Richard Waggener and Clara Tucker Waggener lived and farmed all their lives in and around Sturgis. They were both known for their honesty, hard work, love for each other and their family. He was the son of Joshua Waggener and Arthusa Jane Thomas. They had six children, James, Hattie Hopgood, Nannie Hite, Bessie Stegar, Jesse, Lillie Brooks and Thomas. Josh and Arthusa's home was on highway 56 and was taken in 1942 to become part of Camp Breckinridge. Jesse and some of the other children were born there.

Clara Barton Tucker was named for the nurse Clara Barton. She was the daughter of Charles Clay Tucker and Rose Ghormley. She had a sister Amelia Fellows and brother Shellie Rucker, two half brother, Glenn and Roscoe Tucker. Her father was a judge in Union County at one time.

The "Home place" Clara and Jesse Waggener - 1946

Jesse and Clara were parents of Grace, Richard, Wayne and Ruth who died at the age of three. Grace married Richard Shouse and had a daughter, Barbara Hansen. Richard married Hazel Andre and had David, Rosanna Ratley, Jon and Judy who died at age 6. Wayne married Iva Woodring and they had a daughter, Brucie Hooks and a son Dwayne "Doby."

Josh's parents were James Waggener and Sarah Berry. She was from North Carolina. Arthusa's parents were Jesse Tine Hagger and James Augustus Thomas. We do not have an exact date of settling in Union County, but we do know as a boy one of Josh's memories. It was of his mother's death. They lived in a big two story house near Meachams. A boyhood memory echoed in a young mind. It was of how they turned the chairs over to make a stand to hold his mother's casket. We are sure that many such stories will surface when the Waggener family gets together the summer of 1989. It will be the first Waggener reunion. *Submitted by Hazel A. Niese*

CARROLL RAY WALLACE

Carroll Ray Wallace's parents were William Caske Wallace, and Nancy Catherine Wallace who were married on Nov. 4, 1875.

Carroll Ray Wallace was born on Nov. 30, 1884. His brothers and sisters were Daniel, Mary Ben, Frank, Bertha E., Grace, Rebecca and Sue.

Carroll Ray Wallace

Carroll Ray Wallace married Willie Truman Smith on Feb. 10, 1908 in Evansville, IN. She was born on Nov. 5, 1889. Her parents were John Will Smith and Mary Alice Chancellor. Her sister and brothers were Arthur, Bailey and Mildred Margaret.

To this union were born six children: Dora Harper, who married John M. Syers (now deceased) lives in Morganfield, KY. She was first employed as a teacher in Lorain, Ohio Business College. Later she was a Deputy County Court Clerk in Union County for forty years.

William Caske Wallace, who married Ella Brinkley. They had two children, Jimmy Carroll and Billie Diane. William Caske (better known as Bill) was employed by the Sturgis Milling Company; also he was employed by Ellis Trucking Company; in his later years he ran a restaurant and operated a grocery store with the help of his wife, Ella. Bill died on March 27, 1974. Ella died on Feb. 21, 1989.

Ray Howard Wallace, who married Mary Mildred Carney. They had three children, Richard Lee, Margie and Jerry. Ray worked for many years for Sears; also he is a Veteran of World War II, he also was employed by a firm in Nashville, TN, as a consultant, engineer and salesman in Heating and Air Conditioning and remained with this company until he retired. Ray died on Aug. 16, 1987 in Franklin, TN. His wife still resides there.

Otho Eastin Wallace, who married Mary Elizabeth Caldwell; they had twin boys, Otho Eastin (died at birth) and Thomas Ottis. Eastin was employed at the Farmers State Bank as a youngman; also he is a Veteran of World War II; he operated a garage in Sturgis with J. B. Holeman for a short time; then he bought Sturgis Implement and Hardware Company and he and his wife, Mary, operated this store until they retired. Eastin died on Sept. 21, 1980. His wife, Mary, still lives on the home place.

Harry Thomas Wallace died five days after birth.

Carroll Louis Wallace whose wife was Dorothy DeRemer. There are three children, Judy, Kathleen Marie, and Teddy. Carroll was employed as a butcher at various stores for

many years; he is a Veteran of World War II. At the time of his death he was employed as an Air Conditioning Engineer at Mountain View College in Dallas, TX. He died on May 6, 1989 in Dallas, TX and was buried there.

Carroll Ray Wallace, our beloved father, died in Mt. Vernon, IL on March 22, 1955, while moving a family to St. Louis, MO.

Willie Truman Wallace, our dear Mother, died on Jan. 16, 1965.

This family was born and raised in Sturgis, KY.

Our father was a drayman by occupation. When he started in business, he used horses and wagon. When the automobile age came about, he then used trucks. He hauled all freight from the depot to the merchants in Sturgis. He also moved many families' furniture from house to house and to other cities. He also transported cattle to the Evansville Stockyards and all types of farm products for the farmers in and around Sturgis. After we children were grown and away from home, our Mother worked part time at Pugh's Variety Store and for my brother, Bill, in his restaurant.

I, Dora, speak for my dear deceased brothers and myself, expressing how thankful and fortunate we were to have such loving and caring parents who always placed our wants and needs before their own. May God give them rest and peace in Heaven.

GEORGE ALLIE WALLACE

George Allie Wallace (1888-1958) son of George M. Wallace and Allie Stout Holt, married Omogene Frances Thomason (1900-1987) on Sept. 21, 1921. Omogene was the daughter of William A. Thomason and Virginia Bele Bowers. George served in both the army and navy and was very active in the American Legion. he operated the Sturgis Dairy for a number of years. They had two children: William McLain, born Nov. 21, 1922. William was employed by the State of Kentucky. He has two children: Octa Lee, born Feb. 23, 1946. She is employed by Drs. Troutman and Wright in Morganfield. George Estille, born Oct. 6, 1948 is employed by Peabody Coal Company. He is married to Pam Paris. They are the parents of three boys: Wade, Josh and Justin.

Omogene, William and George Allie Wallace; Joe Jack, John Bruce, Betty and Bowers Wallace

Bowers Holt Wallace was born Nov. 17, 1924. He served in the 36th Infantry during World War II and was a prisoner of war in Germany. He returned to college after the war and graduated from the University of Kentucky. He received his Masters from Murray State University and was employed as an educator in Union County until his retirement in 1983. He married Betty Lorine Cain, daughter of Ester Lee and Nannie Reams Cain of Lexington, Dec. 22, 1951. They are the parents of two sons: Joe Jack and John Bowers. Joe Jack, born July 29, 1956 is married to the former Heidi Schriber. He received his B. A. from The University of Evansville and his Masters of Mechanical Engineering from Stanford University. He is employed as an engineer in California. Joe and Heidi have two children: Daniel Cain, born March 10, 1985 and Halley Ann born Jan. 28, 1988. They reside in Newbury Park, CA. John Bowers, born March 8, 1965 received an Associate Degree in Electronics from Ivy Tech. He is employed as an Electronic Technician for Mine Safe Electronics in Sturgis.

Members of the Wallace family came to this section from Scotland via Virginia. They have lived in and around Sturgis since the early 1800's. They have both contributed and received much from the Sturgis Community. *Submitted by Bowers H. Wallace*

THOMAS OTTIS WALLACE

Thomas Ottis Wallace, son of Eastin and Mary Elizabeth (Caldwell) Wallace of Sturgis, and Zella Doris Brown, daughter of Mr. and Mrs. William Lloyd Brown of Rural Route, Morganfield, were married Aug. 26, 1962, at the Henshaw Christian Church. Both were students at Murray State College at the time.

Tommy completed a B. S. degree in Physical Education and Business in 1963 and began working on a Master's degree at that time. He began working for the Public Assistance Department in June 1963. He worked there for six years until June 1969 at which time he received a stipend to complete his Master's degree and be certified for elementary school so that he could begin teaching in the fall of 1969 at Sturgis Elementary School. Because Mr. Bowers Wallace was the principal and to avoid confusion with the children, Tommy became known as Mr. Tom. He has had the privilege of having every student of the school in his physical education classes for the past twenty years.

Zella completed a B. S. degree with an area in Business education in January 1964. She did substitute teaching during the spring semester at Sturgis and Morganfield. In September 1964 she began teaching at the newly opened Union County High School and has taught typewriting, Shorthand, Office Procedures and other business and computer classes for twenty-four years. In January 1986 she decided to start back to school by taking classes from Murray State University and complete a fifth-year program which she did finish in June 1987. She then began a 30-hour above program and completed the Rank I in June 1989.

Tommy and Zella returned to Union County from Murray in January 1964 and lived in Morganfield until December 1964 at which time they moved to their present home on Main Street in Sturgis. After being married for seven years, they were blessed with their "special adopted child" Clarisa Elizabeth who was only one week old. Clarisa attended Sturgis Elementary and had "Mr. Tom" as her teacher for six years. Tommy has been an avid St. Louis Cardinals fan all of his life and Clarisa has been just enthusiastic about the Chicago Cubs all of her life which makes life very interesting at the Wallace household during baseball season.

Clarisa graduated from Union County High School where she had her mom as a teacher for two years. She will be attending the University of Kentucky in the fall of 1989 where she will be a sophomore majoring in Journalism. She hopes of someday being a sports photographer/writer.

FRANCES WELLS

For fifteen years, since 1974, the Victorian House at 909 Main Street in Sturgis has been home to Frances Wells, son Jason Slaton Wells (1966), and Andrea Fawn Wells(1961). The house, which is the old Robert Rhem homeplace, also holds the art studio of Frances.

Frances Wells

Both Fawn and Jason, whose father is Charles Nathan Wells, graduated from Union County High School. Fawn is a graduate of Murray State University and was married to Rob McDonald, also a graduate of Murray State University, in 1986. They reside at 1553 Pulaski, Lincoln, IL 62656, where Rob is baseball coach at Lincoln College. Fawn is employed using her degree in fashion merchandising. Jason was employed at Kusan in Henderson, and now works at Rayloc in Morganfield.

J. QUENTIN WESLEY

J. Quentin Wesley, the fifth child of Charles R. Wesley, Sr. and Roberta Wynn Wesley, was born on Oct. 22, 1929, in the house where his mother and grandfather, were born in Pond Fork section of Union County.

Quentin, as he is known, attended the Sturgis Schools, Bob Jones University, Western Kentucky State College and the University of Kentucky, where he received a Law Degree in 1954. He served three years in the United States Air Force and retired as a Captain in the reserves.

After military service he returned to Sturgis and started Law practice in Morganfield in July of 1957. In 1965 he ran on the Republican ticket for County Attorney and was defeated by 149 votes. He was elected in 1968 to the Kentucky House of Representatives, the only Republican ever elected to a public office in Union County. He was appointed Commonwealth Attorney, in 1970 for the 5th Judicial District.

In 1955 he married Hildegarde Taylor, a native of Breckinridge County, KY, and to that union were born four children; Jeffrey Taylor Wesley, a graduate of the University of Kentucky, who presently works as a Guidance Counselor at the Earle C. Clements Job Corps; John Quentin Wesley, Jr. a graduate of the University of Kentucky, married to Karen McAnelly, of Liberty, KY, now an executive with Ashland Oil; Katherine Virginia (Kassie) Wesley, attended Indiana University and University of California, Los Angeles, married Richard C. Hankins, of McLean, VA, and is an actress on the Guiding Light Soap Opera filmed in New York; Sara Lincoln Wesley, graduated from the University of Georgia and is married to Charles Bradley Mills, a Pharmacists and lives in Staunton, VA.

The Quentin Wesley family moved to Morganfield in 1970, where they attend the First Baptist Church, and at this writing Quentin Wesley is a senior member of the Law Firm of Wesley, Simpson and Hooks.

ROBERT EARL WEST, JR.

Bobby, son of Robert and Sharry West was born April 11, 1955 at McClellan Air Force Base in Sacramento, CA, but was reared in Sturgis. He was well known in Sturgis as well as in Union County being noted mostly for his love of sports.

He was a pitcher in the Pee Wee League and pitched a no-hitter and was voted the most valuable player in his senior year at Union County High School. His football days began with the Pass-Punt-Kick contests where he earned several trophies. He began playing football in the first grade and became a member of the Braves football squad and played in the game with Lexington Tate's Creek for the state title in 1972.

Acquiring a scholarship, he attended Murray State University and was the only freshman to start on the Racers team. He was voted the OVC Star of the Week in his second year. He played defensive tackle.

He was tabbed by Coach Dobber Hina in his growing up years as "Bones" only to be named

Bobby West, Jr.

later by Coach Mojo Hollowell as "Wild West."

Upon entering college and after reaching 6 ft. two and half inches and 240 pounds in weight he was known to his friends as "Big Bob." Leaving school he went into partnership with his father and purchased a farm in Crittenden County.

Bob was a member of the Sturgis Church of Christ congregation and at the age of 21 years died in a house fire on Nov. 30, 1976. *Submitted in Loving Memory of my brother, by Renee Carter*

ROBERT EARL WEST SR.

Robert Earl West Sr. son of Willie and Thelma West was born April 30, 1930. He is a life time resident of Sturgis and a graduate of Sturgis High School in 1950.

After graduating he spent the next four years in the Air Force, 2 years in Germany and upon returning to the States was stationed at McClellan Air Force Base in Sacramento, CA where he met and married Sharry Dawn Clothier. Sharry was born Jan. 7, 1935 to Clevy and Frances Clothier in a small farming community of Sylvia, KS. At the age of 5, her family moved to Sacramento, CA. She graduated from Grant Union High School in 1953. Sharry worked at McClellan Air Force Base in the Civilian Personnel Department at the time of their marriage. Robert and Sharry had three children: Robert Earl Jr. (Bobby)., Dawn Renee and Cynthia Lynn.

Robert and Sharry West

Their son, Bobby, died in a house fire Nov. 30, 1976 upon returning home from college where he attended at Murray State.

Renee is married to David Carter and they have 2 children - Chad Wayne and Stacy Dawn.

Cindy is married to Joe Owens and they also have 2 children - Chasity Lynn and Bobby Lee.

Robert has been employed with Alcoa in Newburg, IN for the past 23 years until his recent early retirement.

They own "The Double RR" a 190 acre farm and enjoy fishing, horses and family outings for relaxation.

Both Robert, Sharry and their two daughters are members of the Sturgis Church of Christ Congregation. *Submitted by Sharry West.*

WILLIE WEST

Willie West and Thelma Hedgepath were married May 25, 1926. They lived all their lives in Sturgis.

Willie was born Sept. 18, 1902 to Oscar and Loucrease (Kanipe) West. Thelma was born July 6, 1912 to Arch and Nellie (Rich) Hedgepath. Willie worked in the coal mines for thirty years and was still working when Poplar Ridge Coal Mines ended its operation. They had five children and 21 grandchildren. Their first born was Willie Thomas born May 30, 1927. Their second child was Robert Earl born April 30, 1930. Their third child was James Delmar born Feb. 14, 1935. Their fourth child was Mary Lue born Sept. 23, 1938. Their last child, Harold Douglas was born Aug. 3, 1942. They lived on Monroe Street until the time of their death. Thelma died on July 12, 1974 with Leukemia. She was 62. She was a member of the First Baptist Church where she worked in the nursery.

Willie and Thelma West

Willie died Oct. 9, 1983. He was 81 years old. Both died in Deaconess Hospital in Evansville and they were buried side by side at the Pythian Ridge Cemetery in Sturgis. Beside them is their grandson, Robert Earl West Jr. (Bobby) that died in a house fire, Nov. 30, 1976, at the age of 21.

JOHN WYNN WHITE

Jack, as he is known was born, Jan. 21, 1930. He is the son of John Robert White, born June 16, 1904, died Dec. 22, 1988 and Mary Arnold White born Sept. 19, 1903. They were married March 26, 1926 in Morganfield Methodist Church Parsonage.

Jack married Mary Nelle Shouse, born Feb. 25, 1935 on May 24, 1953 at the Sturgis Methodist Church. Her parents are Walter Oliver Shouse, born March 13, 1885, died Nov. 10, 1972 and Mabel Nunn Shouse, born Nov. 26, 1892, died Oct. 10, 1971. They are the parents of four sons: Robert "Bob" Shouse White, born April 24, 1954 in the Old Sturgis Hospital. He married Marie Blake, born Dec. 14, 1953 on Jan. 5, 1974 at Sacred Heart Church.

They have three children. Robert Jeremy White, born Aug. 5, 1975; Cynthia "Cindy" Laural White, born Dec. 27, 1978; and April Marie White, born April 5, 1981.

Bob attended the University of Kentucky for two years. He is a member of the Union County Board of Education and has taken an active part in the County and State Farm Bureau. Marie is a Registered Nurse at Union County Methodist Hospital.

Richard Wynn White, born Jan. 5, 1956, Sturgis Hospital married Janet Davis of Rush, KY, born Aug. 25, 1956 on July 15, 1978 in Lexington, KY.

They have two sons: Richard Dustin, born Aug. 11, 1981 and Jonathan Drew, born Sept. 4, 1984.

Richard attended the University of Kentucky for three years where he met his wife. He and Janet won the State and National Farm Bureau Outstanding Young Farm Family Award in 1987. He has served on many civic organizations. Janet is a teacher at Union County High School.

Walter Reed White, born Feb. 16, 1961, Evansville, IN, married Andrea Drury, born Nov. 8, 1966 on Dec. 28, 1985 at Sacred Heart Church. He graduated with B. S. Degree in Agriculture in 1983 from University of Kentucky where he received the Otis A. Singletary Award. Upon graduation he returned to join the family farming operation. He is also active in civic organizations in the county. Andee is employed at York Neel & Co., C.P.A. as an accountant.

John Ryan White, born June 27, 1974, is a student at Union County High School where he participates in football and F.F.A. He is looking forward to farming with his family upon graduation from college.

Jack has been farming fulltime since attending University of Kentucky in 19??. Our family is active in the Mt. Pleasant Cumberland Presbyterian Church in Sullivan where Jack, Bob and Richard are elders. Mary Nelle has spent most of her time being a homemaker while helping out in 4-H, F.F.A. and Little League. She is presently Vice-President of the County Farm Bureau. For the last ten years she has driven a school bus. *Submitted by Mary Nelle White*

CARL C. WHITEHEAD

Carl C. Whitehead came to Sturgis in 1956. He was employed by Pittsburg Midway Coal Company of Kansas City, MO as Chief Electrician for the Construction of the mines. Mr. Whitehead was impressed by the Community to such an extent that he moved his family here in Feb. 1957.

Mr. White head was Chief Electrician of Maintenance until his death in 1964. Carl C. Whitehead married Rosa Kathleen (McGuyer) Whitehead in Central City (Muhlenburg County) KY, in 1938 and had seven children; Barbara Elaine Whitehead Shelton, Gary Wayne Whitehead, Ronald Wesley Whitehead, John Carl Whitehead, Cynthia Kaye Whitehead, David Martin Whitehead, Anita Kathleen Whitehead Jenkin, whom were all educated in Union County Schools.

The Whitehead family attended First Baptist Church, Adams Street Sturgis, KY. Son, Gary Whitehead is now active in Bethany Baptist Church and Gideons International, a member of Kelsey Lodge #659, 320 Mason, a member of Rizpah Temple at Madisonville, KY.

John C. Whitehead is an active member of Sturgis Church of Christ, Monroe Street, Sturgis, KY. Ronald Wesley Whitehead, a member of Kelsey Lodge #659, 320 Mason a member of Rizpah Shrine Temple, Madisonville, KY, a member of Church of Christ at Bordley. David Martin Whitehead, a member of Bethany Baptist Church, Pond Fork Road Sturgis, KY. All are Journeyman Wireman Electricians. Barbara Elaine Whitehead Shelton, a member of Baptist Temple in Henderson, KY, a member of Sturgis Chapter #444, Order of the Eastern Star of Sturgis, has worked for Peabody Coal Company for eleven years in the office warehouse. Cynthia Kaye Whitehead, still lives in Sturgis at the family home. Anita Kathleen Whitehead Jenkin is a Registered Nurse working at Madisonville Regional Medical Center, now resides in Shady Grove, KY.

Carl C. Whitehead was a member of Central City Masonic Lodge, 320 Mason, a member of First Baptist Church, Adams Street, Sturgis, KY, active in IBEW Apprenticeship Program, taught the class in Owensboro, KY, at night, while working at Pittsburg Midway Coal Company.

Carl C. White invented the Ground Fault Interrupter concept on Electrical Circuits to protect persons and property in the mines.

Mr. Whitehead started an Electrical Construction Company with his wife Rosa Kathleen and his sons Gary, Ronald, John C. and David. Barbara worked in the Business until starting to work for Peabody Coal Company, to do Electrical Service for the Sturgis Community, which has grown to more Industrial, Commercial Construction.

Barbara Elaine Whitehead Shelton now resides in Henderson, KY. She has two sons, John Crawford Shelton and Randall Wade Shelton, and one grandson, John Crawford Shelton, Jr.

Gary Wayne Whitehead married Joyce Gayle French, daughter of J. L. and Evelyn

Cecila Collins French. They have a daughter, Susan Kathleen, and a son, Robert Wayne Whitehead.

Ronald Wesley Whitehead now lives in Marion, IL. He has three daughters; Ronda Gay Whitehead Hancock, Jeanne Michelle Whitehead, and Carla Raebeth Whitehead, who now attends Henderson Community College, and one granddaughter, Ruby Nicole Hancock.

John Carl Whitehead married Nancy Lou Brown, daughter of Harry M. and Joline Brown of Sturgis. They have two daughters; Melissa Jo Whitehead, a junior at David Lipscomb University majoring in Bio-Chemistry, and Sarah Renee Whitehead, a Sophomore at Union County High School.

Anita Kathleen Whitehead Jenkin married Roger Lee Jenkin, son of Smith Jenkin and Geneva Ann Tily Jenkin of Webster County. They have two sons, Damon Wesley, Kyle Zachery, and a daughter, Kimberly Rachelle Jenkin.

The Whiteheads are proud of their Community and are proud to say Sturgis is their home.

WILLIAMS-FELTS

Jack Edward Williams, b. March 18, 1946 in Henderson, KY, son of James Frederick and Ethel Catherine (Loney) Williams married Joel Ann (Felts) Kramer, b. March 30, 1939 in Sturgis, KY, daughter of Arthur Procter and Mary Katheryn Rosina (VanCleave) Felts, on May 23, 1969 in Elizabethtown, IL.

Jack and Joel Ann moved to Union County in Oct. 1988 and remodeled a home in DeKoven, KY which has been in the Syers-VanCleave families since the early 1800's. They christened their abode Holly Hill and rebuilding, while preserving everything of historical significance, is their hobby and goal.

Along with Joel Ann's brother, Bill Felts and his wife, Merilyn (Gillespie) Felts, the Williamses formed a business partnership, wear care, and purchased the Modern Cleaners, a dry-cleaning operation which had been in the Jack Wicks family for the past sixty years.

Jack and Joel Ann reared four children. Scott Raymond Kramer, b. Oct. 8, 1956-Sturgis and Simone Kimberly Kramer, b. Dec. 12, 1960-Evansville, IN are the natural children of Harold Hibbs (deceased). They were adopted in 1965 by Neil R. Kramer, second husband of Joel Ann. Todd Neil Kramer was born De. 19, 1964 in Peoria, IL to this union. Jason Lee Williams, whose natural mother is Janice Rae Stallins, was born March 5, 1968 in Henderson, KY.

Scott married Nancy Marie (Hart) Kramer, March 14, 1975 in Sturgis, KY and they reside in Carbondale, IL. Simone married William Anthony Seay Feb. 17, 1979 in Bloomington, IL and she resides in DeKoven. Todd married Cynthia (Curtis) Kramer June 21, 1985 in Murfreesboro, TN and is still living there. Jason lives in Lexington, KY.

Presently, there are 5 grandchildren: Anthony Joseph Edouard Procter Seay, Ashley Kathryne Anabelle Anastasia Seay, Andrew Jonathan Scott Hamilton Seay, Krystle Christina Angelica Kramer and Todd Brandon Neil Kramer. When the Seay children were born, there were 5 living generations; hence, the long names. *Submitted by Joe Felts-Williams*

THOMAS D. WOODRING

Thomas D. Woodring came to Sturgis from the Boxville Community in the year of 1939. He is the son of Joseph Henry Woodring of Union County, and May Blackwell Woodring of Webster County.

Thomas Woodring married Alma E. Liles from DeKoven, KY in 1940. She was the daughter of Ben H. Liles and Ruby E. Morris Liles. Thomas and Alma have to children a daughter Brenda Thomas Woodring and a son Bennie Joe Woodring.

Thomas D. and Alma Woodring

Brenda Woodring married Joseph Wesley Sprague. The Sprague's have two daughter, Stacy Jo Sprague and Trisha Ann Sprague. Joseph Sprague is a Union County farmer. He also operates two Farm Supply Stores, one in Morganfield and one in Sturgis.

Bennie Joe Woodring is married to Suzanne Sprague Woodring. Bennie Joe and Suzanne have three children Thomas Casey, Ashley Catherine and Lesley Jo. Bennie Joe is also a Union County farmer.

Suzanne (Sprague) Woodring is a sister to Joseph Sprague. All of Thomas and Alma Woodring grandchildren are double cousins.

SAMMY ROBERTA WYNN

Sammy Roberta Wynn, known by her friends as "Bert", was born the first child of Robert E. Wynn and Amma Withers. Bert was raised in the Pond Fork section of Union County with her only brother, John Wynn, and four sisters.

Since her birth in 1894, she remained a Union Countian even though she and her husband, Charles R. Wesley, lived in Casey County a few years after their marriage. Bert met her husband at Bowling Green While attending Western State Normal School, where she and Charles received teaching certificates.

The Wynn Family

During their early marriage, both taught in one room schools in Casey County for a salary of $15.00 a month.

Bert's education included attendance at the Ohio Valley College in Sturgis and one year at Georgetown.

After moving back to Union County from Casey County, Charles R. Wesley started farming at the ole Wynn Place between Pride and Sullivan near the site of Pyro Mines. Seven children were born to the union, with one dying at a very early age. The first four children attended a one room school, Templeton, about a mile from the ole Wynn homeplace. All the children of Bert and Charles, except Robert E. Wesley, were born in the house which still stands on a ridge on Kentucky Highway 141 across the road from Bert's grandchild, Nancy Ruth Thomas. Bert's father was also born in the house.

The children remember the rigors of the depression of the 1930s when the whole nation suffered economic woes. All remember riding horseback to Templeton School, playing barefoot in the dirt roads and the trip to grandmothers and papa's house on Thanksgiving and Christmas. The children, Mary, Kas, Bo, Bob, Quentin, and Suzy, remember the school system that evolved into a consolidated high school in Sturgis, where they all graduated.

Eventually, all the children married: Mary, to a New Yorker, Fred Cowan; Kas, to A. D. Sprague, Jr., a young County and National Outstanding Farmer; Bo, to Lillian Martin, a school teacher from Ohio County; Bob, to Ida Lee Stanton, the daughter of and early publisher and editor of the Sturgis News and Clay Tribune; Quentin, to Hildegarde Taylor, the daughter of Alfred Taylor, a druggist from Breckinridge County, KY; and finally, Suzy, to Robert M. Davis, from a prominent farm family from near DeKoven, KY.

Bert and Charles attended the Pond Fork Baptist Church, where their children were baptized and were raised as Baptists. Charles, being born and reared in Casey County, was a Methodist and Republican, by birth. Charles gave in and joined the Baptist but never gave up his membership in the Republican Party. From the early 1920s until his death at age 90 in 1983, Charles Wesley was a staunch Republican leader in a rock-ribbed Democratic County of Union.

Bert and Charles went through the usual

ups and downs, raising their children, sacrificing for their education and giving them the values of truth and honesty to live by. The children, although average in intelligence, raised 18 outstanding grandchildren, which were the pride and joy of Bert and Charles, known to the grandchildren as Panny and Papa Charles.

Most all the grandchildren received college educations, ranging from Oxford, Harvard, Dartmouth, Michigan, Georgia, Mississippi, Indiana, UCLA, and the University of Kentucky. One became Attorney General of Kentucky, one a prominent Henderson County medical doctor, two are mining engineers, one a television actress on a day time soap, one became one of the Outstanding Young Farmers in the USA, one the curator of the Cincinnati Museum of Nation History, one a college professor at Emery University.

All were devoted to Panny and Papa Charles and loved and respected them dearly. Like many families in Union County, the family name comes and goes because the offspring leave home, marry, and return to Union County only on visits. The Wesley name, like the Wynn name, will fade, but living in the Spragues, the Cowans, and the Davis, is the Wesley and Wynn blood.

Reflecting on the lives of your ancestors makes one realize that life is fragile. Placing your parents' short memoirs in the history of Sturgis does not do justice to their real accomplishments. Their lives saw the advent of the car, airplane, radio and television, to name just a few of the drastic changes in this great county during their 90 year stay here. What they did as parents and grandparents, however, is the real test of their accomplishments. Their teaching, tenacity and encouragement to achieve and "be somebody" will live on.

ANDREW JACKSON YOUNG

Andrew Jackson Young was the son of Thomas Young and Julia Young. Thomas Young was the son of Christian Young and Nancy Ann (Hume) Young.

Thomas Young and his wife, Narcissa (David), and his father, Christian Young, came to Union County, KY about 1835 from Jefferson County, KY. He purchased a farm of 150 acres and at that time, the deed stated the farm was lying on the Water of Cypress Creek.

Christian Young (father of Thomas Young) was born in Pennsylvania in Lancaster County, March 18, 1764 and died in Caldwell Co., KY, May 1849. He married June 17, 1788 in Kentucky to Nancy A. Hume whom was born in 1768. Nancy A. Hume's ancestors were of Scottish Descent and her descendants have been traced back for more than 40 generations. Yes back to the year 1010 A.D. when one was killed by Macbeth.

Thomas Young's wife Julia Young was of no relation to Thomas. Her folks were of German Origin. Julia's grandfather whose name was

This picture was taken in November of 1911 at the residence of A. J. Young who resided near Gum Grove, KY, 6 miles from Sturgis, KY. The names of the ones in the picture, date of birth and death listed. Front Row, L-R: Julia Young-b: 1870, d. 1943; Myritie Young-b: 1875, d: 1931; Narcissa (Davis) Young-b: 1847, d.: 1929; Andrew Jackson Young-b. 837, d: 1918; Emily Young-b: 1885, d: 1969; Mary S. Young-b: 1869, d: 1935; Back Row, L-R: Clyde R. Young-b: 1890, d: 1950; Harry M. Young-b: 1887, d: 1968; Sylvanis B. Young-b: 1879, d: 1956; Hugh J. Young-b: 1877, d: 1951; Virgil L. Young-b: 1873, d: 1924; and Miles D. Young-b: 1867, d: 1943

Johann George Jung when he first came to America was later changed to John Young. He came to the Port of Philadelphia, on the ship Neptune in Sept. 1752. Later he settled in the state if North Carolina. No records have been found in North Carolina of whom he married but the records show that he fathered 9 children. On of whom was named Jacob Young, and this was Julia Young's father.

Julia Young's father (Jacob Young) married Rachael Goodnight on the 16th day of De. 1792. To this union was born 12 children. She was born Nov. 10, 1807 and on April 24, 1815 her brother Solomon Young was born.

This Solomon Young later became the grandfather of our former President Mr. Harry Truman. All of this information can be proved as I have the information to prove this.

All of the above information was not gathered by myself but with help of people from more than 8 states and by making two trips to Iowa all of the above has been located. And anyone wishing to see my records are welcome. *Submitted by Raymond O. Young*

S. B. (VAN) YOUNG

Narciss Davis (3/5/1847 - 12/11/1929) married Andrew Jackson Young (1/20/1837 - 7/17/19180 in Union County, Feb. 15, 1866. Andrew Jackson Young was a farmer all his life. At one time he was engaged in buying poultry for a market in New Orleans, making his trips to that city by boat. On one trip he decided not to return on the same vessel that had taken him down the river, but came back by a different boat. After applying for passage, he received a premonition that something was going to happen. He changed his mind and took the same boat back, fortunately, for the other boat ran upon a snag, caught fire and was destroyed. Most of the passengers drowned.

Narcissa and Andrew Jackson Young had 11 children. Sylvanus Baster Young (10/28/1879 - 12/22/1956), the seventh child, married Mollie B. Henshaw (10/25/1888 - 7/27/1977), daughter of Thomas and Alota Henshaw, in Union County in May 23, 1906. S. B. (Van) Young worked most of his life as a farmer and coal miner. He was a devoted Baptist, Democrat, and honest man, which he instilled in all of his 11 children. He took pride in six boys playing football. In World War II they had 5 boys and 2 sons-in-law in service. In this home was happiness, love, and always room for an extra plate at the table.

The eleven children of S. B. (Van) and Molly (Betty) Young are as follows:

Carl Young (4/1/07 - 12/22/88) - attended Sturgis School, later moved to Detroit, MI, married, retired, 2 daughters.

Marvin (Tub) Young (11/2/08 - 7/19/82) attended Sturgis School, attended Union College, taught school at Salem School in Union County, moved to Detroit, married, US Army, retired, no children.

Jeanette Young Cosby (8/22/11 - ____) attended Sturgis School, worked for Southern Bell Telephone, moved to Henderson, married, retired, no children.

Edna Young Bugher (7/7/15 - ____) attended Sturgis School, attended St. Mary's Nursing School, moved to Evansville, married, retired, 2 daughters.

Richard (Cotton) Young (7/16/16 - ____) attended Sturgis School, US Army, retired U. S. Postal Service, married, 3 children.

Ila (Pete) Young (2/28/18 - 11/15/87) attended Sturgis School, attended University of Kentucky, US Air Force, owned service station in Sturgis, married, one son.

Thomas (Tommy Jack) Young (5/16/19 - ____) attended Sturgis School, Merchant Marines, married, coal miner, retired, 2 children.

Cathryn (Cattie) Young Jankowski (1/22/21 - 6/1/75) attended Sturgis School, worked Southern Bell Telephone, married, moved to Henderson, retired, 3 children.

Roger (Bull) Young (4/27/22 - ____) attended Sturgis School, attended Murray State University, US Navy, Louisville University, married, coal miner, retired, 2 sons.

Elizabeth (Lizzie) Young Brown (9/15/23 - ____) attended Sturgis School, worked for Southern Bell Telephone, retired, married, 2 children.

Hilda Young Wells (2/26/30 - ____) attended Sturgis School, married, lives in Union County, housewife, 2 children.

FAMILY TREE

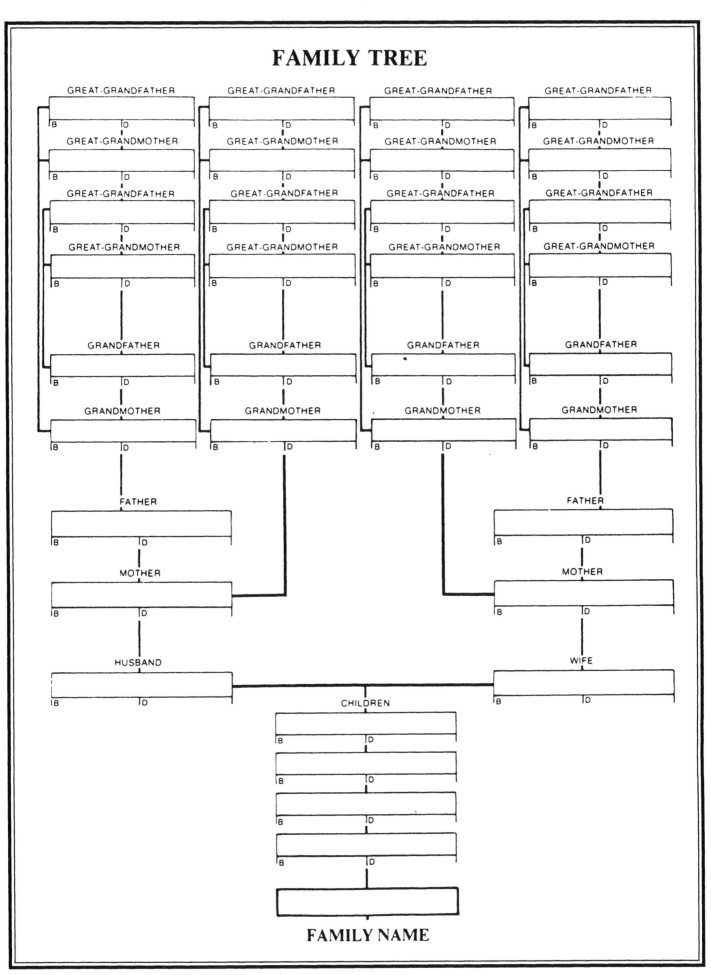

FAMILY NAME

185

Notes

Notes

Notes

Notes

The snowstorm of 1917-1918 necessitated this tunnel to the cafe.

The Walter Shouse farm, 1924. Martha Shouse in cart, Richard Shouse, standing, Walter Shouse, by tractor and James Shouse, on tractor.

PLATE III

Old Sturgis

Sturgis, J

STURGIS
HOSPITAL

FRANCES KNIGHT WELLS

F. WELLS

Hospital

entucky

Printed in the USA
CPSIA information can be obtained
at www.ICGtesting.com
JSHW060053150824
68134JS00032B/2724

9 781681 625584